John Boardman

THE GREEKS OVERSEAS

THEIR EARLY COLONIES AND TRADE

new and enlarged edition
with 319 illustrations

Thames and Hudson

This edition first published in the USA in 1980 by
Thames and Hudson Inc., New York

Library of Congress Catalog card number 79–66132

Printed and bound in Great Britain by Fakenham Press
Limited, Fakenham, Norfolk

Contents

MAPS

Preface

Rhubarb, rhubarb; Barbara buzz buzz – stage conversation which is intended to be unintelligible stresses the *bar-bar-bar* noises of ordinary conversation. Foreigners make similar incomprehensible noises, and it was not only the Greeks in antiquity who characterized those whose speech they could not follow as *bar-bar* talkers – '*barbarians*'. When Greek met Greek the result may often have been violent, but at least they could understand each other's language, and this bond of speech was one which the Greeks always acknowledged and respected. But the Greeks did not use the term 'barbaros' quite as we do 'barbarian'. For them it embraced all non-Greek-speakers, both the 'rude, wild, and uncultured' of our dictionary definition, and the kings and subjects of the great empires of the east.

This book deals with the material evidence for relations between Greeks and barbarians down to about 480 BC. It is inevitable that in this early period the material remains should prove the most rewarding, and part of our first chapter will be devoted to an assessment of the value of sources, material and otherwise. The enterprises overseas include both those which were undertaken with the avowed objective of founding colonies, and those which served trade, with or without the establishment of trading posts. So we shall look for the physical evidence for Greek presence on foreign soil – their relations with and effect upon native populations, and the effect of the natives upon them. In their travels to the east and Egypt it is the latter which is the more important, for contact with the older civilizations of Mesopotamia and the Nile Valley provided the spark which fired the new Greece, and kindled that flame which the discerning may still cherish in modern western civilization. To do as full justice as possible to these matters, it has proved necessary to devote part of the book to a study of the effect of the Near East and Egypt upon the Greeks at home, as well as on the Greeks overseas. Only in this way could the whole story be told. Even so, we deal here with material things only, and the reader must turn elsewhere for an account of the debts of Greek literature, religion, and thought to the east and Egypt.

The testimony of ancient historians will also be used. More than most 'archaeological' histories of ancient cultures, this should be read as a supplement to what is known from other sources, although our evidence may often fill gaps in the record or even correct it. But it would be otiose here to do more than allude to the ancient sources and to the many modern studies devoted to those aspects of our search on which ancient texts may shed light. There are many modern histories which offer this, but they generally give second place to the primary material evidence, and here, to redress the balance, greater emphasis is placed on the archaeology of the subject.

It must be remembered that this is only part of the story of the Greek renaissance, and can take little account of the Greeks' own genius except in so far as it led them to explore and learn from older civilizations. With so much left unsaid it might even seem that classical Greece could have been nothing without this inspiration, but we have only to look at what the Greeks made of what they had borrowed and how soon they outshone their models. Sappho wrote her poems only 200 years after the Greeks had learnt their alphabet. The Parthenon and its sculpture appear only 150 years after Greece's first steps in monumental architecture and sculpture. And all these things – alphabet, architecture, sculpture – the Greeks had in some degree learnt from the 'barbarians'.

There were material benefits too which determined the quality of life in Greece for later years. A comic poet of the late fifth century, Hermippos (fr. 63), lists some of the goods from overseas which his countrymen enjoy – silphion and hides from Cyrene, mackerel from the Hellespont, pigs and cheese from Syracuse, sails (linen) and papyrus from Egypt, frankincense from Syria, ivory from Libya, slaves from Phrygia, nuts from Paphlagonia, dates and flour from Phoenicia, carpets and cushions from Carthage. He intersperses his list with joke offerings but the rest are real enough and we shall be studying the Greeks' first experience since the Bronze Age of these foreign sources. It is interesting to see that the poet says nothing of metals, which modern scholars judge to bulk large in early trade overseas.

Then there is the other side to the story. With their colonizing and trade in the west and the north, the Greeks made contact with people who were less advanced culturally, and technologically, and we are able to observe the beginnings of the spread of Greek civilization into Italy and western Europe, with benefits to be enjoyed by Rome and by all later western cultures.

Learning in the east and south; teaching in the west and north. The story is a balanced one, and the two parts run concurrently. The late ninth and eighth centuries see the first moves to east and west; the seventh, the first moves to north and south; the sixth, consolidation in the face of powerful opponents and rivals – Persians, Phoenicians, Etruscans. In these three centuries the Greeks passed from isolation and comparative poverty to a position of power and enjoyment of the highest culture. This is the 'archaic' period in the broadest sense of the term. In these years the foundations of classical Greece were laid, and it is these formative years only that we shall be studying. They culminate in 480 BC with the Greeks' successful stand against the challenge of Carthage in the west, of Persia in the east, and in this book we shall rarely be led to consider the fortunes of the Greeks overseas after that date.

Earlier editions of this book, in paperback (Penguin Books, 1964, revised in 1973), are the basis of the present edition. The texts of all chapters have been revised thoroughly, and some substantial passages added (as in Chapter 1). The earlier editions offered only brief bibliographies to each chapter, with the apology that, fully documented, the work would have needed three volumes, not one. Here I have given notes to all subjects or objects discussed or mentioned and the only reason that there are not three volumes is that I have been selective and have often given secondary summarizing sources in preference to fuller lists of primary sources. The illustrations too have been completely reworked.

My descriptions of sites and particular objects are not often, I fear, based on first-hand experience of them. Where my dating of objects differs from that given in some publications (as it often does), this is deliberate and, I hope, in better accord with the evidence now available. Many of the monuments and objects which have to be considered are of no less documentary value for being considerable works of art. This is, after all, one of the many compensating factors in any archaeological study of ancient Greek affairs.

It is usual to give some explanation or apology for the spellings of place-names and personal names, and to excuse inconsistencies. I have preferred to accept the inconsistencies, and my spellings are those which are most familiar to me and come most readily to my pen. I doubt whether anyone will be seriously misled, and I hope few will be annoyed by the lack of system in this matter.

This edition has profited from the comments and criticism of many scholars, offered over the years. I owe them my thanks, but mention only Roger Moorey who kindly cast his eyes over part of the revised script; and, in the publishing house, Pat Mueller and Thomas Neurath, for their unfailing patience and encouragement.

1

The Nature of the Evidence

Our Sources

Since 'history' still means, for many people, ancient historians and the study of their texts, spiced where possible with archaeology, anthropology and historical intuitions, it is perhaps necessary to introduce a work which is intended to be history but which leans heavily on archaeology with a reminder about what our evidence for antiquity amounts to, what our sources are, even – in a highly personal way – to rate them in order of merit:

1. *Contemporary evidence* must surely stand at the head, and of the contemporary evidence pride of place must go to –

(a) texts, because they speak directly to us in a language we understand well, though not perfectly. In our period there are no contemporary texts written by historians and the nearest we come to them is in inscriptions dealing with contemporary events. Otherwise we have works of imagination, generally poetic, through which we may glimpse the society for which they were composed. Next come –

(b) monuments and objects, selected for us partly by merit (as were the texts), partly by the accidents of survival and excavation, partly by the durable quality of the materials of which they are made. They are mute, therefore they cannot lie, but we may misinterpret them by failing to allow for their incompleteness, or through inability or unwillingness to treat them on their own terms rather than in the terms dictated by modern typologies and models. (These are too readily thought to carry some near-divine sanction, while in fact they are no more than aids to orderly thought, some degrees more useful than a typewriter and potentially far more dangerous when abused.) It is not merely time, of course, that has selected the monuments for us. It is also the choice of excavators and, more important, the treatment by excavators (and curators) of what has been found. Excavation destroys far more than it uncovers to view. Most excavations are never fully published. As Rhys Carpenter put it, some archaeologists are slow to realize 'that they are burning the book of history page by page as they read it'. More loss of scholarly information is suffered through excavation in the cause of scholarship than through tomb-robbing for collectors and museums, yet the non-publishing excavators continue to enjoy credit for their discoveries (credit better paid to the ancient creators of what they unearthed) rather than be branded as academic felons.

(c) Other sources of insight into conditions rather than events of antiquity are provided by the natural sciences which now enable us to assess more accurately states of technology, agriculture, climate. And of course simple but accurate maps can be as much sources of historical information as illustrations of it (though we lack any wholly reliable and up-to-date atlas of the classical world).

2. *Near-contemporary evidence* must take second place in merit though it inevitably occupies a major part of conventional histories.

(a) Ancient historians who present narrative accounts of events or periods have to be judged in terms of the validity of their apparent (not always admitted) sources, their remoteness in time and place from the events described, and the motives which led them or their sources to make their records. They generally make little use of the types of evidence considered in our first section, but there are honourable exceptions, notably among the earlier historians such as Herodotus and Thucydides.

(b) Passing allusions in ancient authors, not necessarily historians, are subject to the same disadvantages as the historical narratives of (a), plus the danger they present of appearing to comment on more than their immediate concern. This is magnified by the habit of using these allusions, even when they are quotations from historians, in isolation from the context in which they were quoted; of citing modern corpora rather than the passages in which allusions or quotations were imbedded.

(c) In the study of conditions rather than events the records, literary or material, of possible survivals of practices or styles bulk large in reconstructions of ancient society, especially in works devoted to law, religion and myth. Since part of the fascination of classical antiquity is the picture it offers of change, sometimes rapid and radical change, in all these areas, it is clear that any 'survival' needs to be proved rather than assumed, and this is a most hazardous way of completing gaps in the evidence for earlier periods.

3. Modern comment and scholarship is our usual route to the ancient sources already mentioned, and their deductions supplement what is missing from those sources and may often have a validity superior to that of the non-contemporary evidence, though many deductions are often too readily honoured as facts rather than opinions. The scholarly presentation of material ranges from the invaluable work of our hewers of wood and

drawers of water and the mainly secretarial skills involved in presenting lexica, corpora, catalogues, excavation reports; through observation of categories in prosopographies, attribution of works, hands, and workshops, identification of ancient copies; to assessment based on perceptive understanding of the nature of all the evidence, textual, stylistic, excavational, iconographic. Often an apparently simple description or quotation or juxtaposition can be a notable work of scholarship. Finally come those works of interpretation and insight, based often upon several skills in several disciplines, which break through the silences of antiquity to render a truer account of man's history and achievement.

The relevant rewards and limitations of our two main classes of evidence now require a closer look.

Archaeological Evidence

It is not too difficult today to recover the archaeological history of any well-excavated Greek site. Studies in the stylistic development and chronology of pottery, bronzes, and other likely finds have been carried to a degree not matched in the scholarship devoted to any other culture of comparable antiquity. A large part of the evidence is afforded by decorated pottery – the archaeologist's bread and butter. A vase of fired clay may be broken readily enough, but its pieces are almost indestructible. As the fragments were virtually useless, they were left about ancient sites, whence they can be recovered by excavation. The pottery placed in tombs can often be recovered intact. Other objects disappear too readily – iron corrodes, bronze and precious metals are melted down for re-use, marble feeds the lime kilns – but potsherds had no value and so have survived. A Sunday-newspaper columnist has written with wit and sympathy of the 'blue-saucer folk' whose ware litters his and many other back gardens in England. A small fragment may give away what the whole shape was – a teapot, saucer, or cup. A scrap of willow pattern, a '. . . ade in Birm . . .', part of a monogram from a Coronation mug, may reveal design, provenance, and date. Antiquity has left similar clues in its rubbish dumps, and on or under floors. And in ancient Greece it was the potter who provided vessels for purposes now served by bottles, tins, glasses, cardboard boxes, plastic bags, and even barrels. But even with our mass of evidence, interpretation is a tricky matter. The willow-pattern plates still made today prove no close cultural ties with contemporary China! But there *is* an explanation for them, which *could* be worked out by some post-atom-age archaeologist. In the same way, if a town rubbish dump were to yield in its lowest (earliest) levels empty packets of Woodbines, and in its upper levels empty packets of Gauloises, or of chewing-gum, the deduced changes in habits might lead to a reasonable guess about trade, or at least changes in life style. The scraps and fragments which will form a great part of our evidence in this book may seem miserable substitutes for fine whole vases, but it need hardly be remarked that such pottery evidence is not less important because it has failed to survive intact; nor is it the less important when it is of such merit that it offers information for the art historian, iconographer or student of religion, although there is a tendency for some students of other periods to regard such studies as non-archaeological.

The importance which the Greeks attached to the vase-painter's art in the centuries with which we shall be dealing, and the characteristically Greek sensitivity to changes in decorative fashions, mean that arguments based on *stylistic* study of vases can carry much weight. Add to the stylistic sequences which can be determined for the various Greek wares some indications of *absolute* dates, and you have a system which will permit the dating of decorated pottery to within a generation, or sometimes a decade. This is already to some degree true in the mid eighth century BC, and the degree of precision increases through the seventh and sixth centuries. Not only can dates be assigned, but regional studies have made possible the attribution of most wares to particular cities, and in many instances we are able to distinguish even individual workshops, painters, and potters.

This is no place for any detailed survey of the background to the systems of dating which we shall be using throughout this book, but something must be said of the most important wares which will be mentioned and the grounds for dating them.

Furthermore, although the interpretation of finds on a homeland Greek site may be a comparatively easy matter, we have to deal largely with Greek finds on foreign shores or in newly founded Greek settlements overseas. It is necessary therefore to say something of the principles which should – but rarely do – govern the interpretation of such finds, for they often form our only evidence to support some far-reaching theories.

First, then, the pottery wares and their dating. We begin in the early Iron Age, the 'Dark Ages' of Greek history after the collapse and decay of Mycenaean civilization by about 1100 BC. The finds in Athens cemeteries show that after a very short while, probably by about 1050 BC, the new 'Protogeometric' style of vase-painting had been evolved from the debased Mycenaean forms. The decoration is simple, precise, and extremely effective, often of neat concentric circles or semicircles, and the patterns are never allowed to crowd the surface of the vase. The style is most distinctive, and although finds elsewhere in Greece show that many other towns, most of them less prosperous than Athens, evolved their own 'Protogeometric' idioms, these were always dependent – artistically – on Athens. In the ninth century, the feeling for proportion and restraint in the matter of decoration weakens, and a growing repertoire of Geometric patterns spreads like a rash over the surface of the finer vases. After 800 BC, the figure decoration – animal, then human – is admitted, with formal geometrical stylization for natural forms. Athens still leads, but other cities have their own distinctive Geometric styles, in varying degrees still dependent on Athens: especially Corinth, Argos, Boeotia, Crete, and the Eastern Greeks. How much the new Geometric figure styles may owe to the Mycenaean, preserved in the form of objects discovered or styles kept alive in other materials, is still hard to judge, but the possibility must be borne in mind before all or too much is assigned either to foreign influence or to native genius.

The influence of the Near East is seen on Greek pottery already by the end of the ninth century BC, but only becomes strong a hundred years later. We shall have more to say of the nature and source of this influence in Chapter 3. In Corinth a new, refined style, which has become known as 'Protocorinthian', is evolved, and 'orientalizing' figures and decoration are used as well as a new incising technique known as 'black-figure', which may have been inspired by eastern incised metalwork. Now, too, we have some indications of absolute dating. Ancient historians give dates for Greek colonies in Sicily, and the earliest pottery found in each of those sufficiently well explored can be plausibly attributed to the first generation of the colonists, the very earliest being probably that which they brought with them. Even in detail the sequence of dates given by historians, and the stylistic sequence of the earliest pottery found in the west agree remarkably well. We shall be considering these in Chapter 5. Some confirmation too is provided by the find of an Egyptian scarab, naming a king, with Greek vases. Since dates for Greek cities from Greek sources do not go undisputed (happy the site with only one authority for its date!) it is more of this independent dating evidence which is required. For earlier centuries stratified finds of Greek pottery in Syria and Palestine give broad hints, while the association of Greek with local vases at Al Mina and the finds in the 696 BC destruction level at Tarsus (but not the one identified by the excavators) confirm what we deduce from Greek sources. These we study in Chapter 3.

In the seventh century Corinth sets the pace, and the sequence of fine Protocorinthian vases can be followed down to beyond the middle of the seventh century. Athens, meanwhile, went her own way with the older silhouette and outline techniques of drawing, although orientalizing patterns were admitted, and by now human figure decoration and mythological scenes had become more common. The East Greeks and Cretans too were slow to follow Corinth's lead, and they developed their own highly individual styles. Fortunately the Corinthian vases were popular, and it is possible to determine reasonable chronologies for these other wares from contexts – as in graves – in which imported Corinthian vases are found beside local products. For dating now we turn to the earliest pottery from Selinus and Marseilles or the Lydian destruction level at Smyrna – none of which can be used with great confidence, but by now the inter-relation and sequence of Greek vases is clearly mapped, and the presumed absolute chronology cannot be far wrong. We rely very much on the dating of Corinth's vases in these years, but it is easy to fall into the error of saying that 'the earliest imported vases found at x are Corinthian', when all that can fairly be said is 'the earliest *datable* vases ... are Corinthian'.[1]

In the last third of the seventh century the Corinthian black-figure or full 'Corinthian' series begins.[2] The style of drawing coarsens as the output increases, but by now the Athenian potteries are again commanding attention. They have accepted the Corinthian black-figure technique, and apply it with a sense for narrative and the monumental which had always escaped the Corinthians. In Corinth fine painted styles flourished beside mass-production, but by about the mid sixth century the industry there failed, for reasons still not properly understood, and Athenian vases won most markets. The contexts of Athenian, Corinthian, and other Greek vases in tombs of these years confirm the clear stylistic sequences and allow a chronological system which has been worked out for one to be applied to the others. In the 560s can be set the earliest vases which were made in Athens to celebrate the re-inaugurated Panathenaic Games; around 545 and 525 comparisons with sculptured reliefs on independently dated buildings at Ephesus and Delphi (the Siphnian Treasury) give further 'pegs'; and, again in 525, the Persian dismantling of a Greek-manned frontier fort in Egypt (Daphnae) gives another terminus.

By about 530, the Athenian painter had developed a new vase-painting technique – the red-figured – in which the figures are reserved in the clay ground of the vase, the background filled in, and the details painted, where before, in black-figure, they had been incised in the black silhouette. The new style appears beside the old into the fifth century, when it becomes paramount, and now the Athenian red-figure vases virtually command all markets. Dating points become more frequent – the Persian sack of Athens in 480; funeral monuments with vases in them at Marathon (490), Thespiae (424), and Athens (the grave of the Spartans: 403); the dumping of the contents of graves from Delos on Rheneia during the purification of the island in 425; and, a less sure criterion, the appearance on vases of complimentary remarks about handsome youths. The last depends on the identification of the youth in his later career, military or political, an estimate of his age then, and a general estimate of the span of years in which a Greek youth might be called beautiful (*kalos*). Women were seldom thus celebrated, and at any rate in this period we could hardly expect to find any independent historical evidence for their ages.[3]

Allowing, then, some degree of confidence in assigning vases to one Greek city rather than another and in dating them within fairly narrow limits, we have still to determine their possible historical significance when they appear on foreign sites. It is easy to attach undue significance to stray finds of Greek vases or other objects. The archaeologist may overestimate the importance of the evidence or be unrealistic in his explanations for its appearance. The historian may not be able to judge well enough the circumstances and archaeological background to the finds. In the study of Greek history in the eighth, seventh, and sixth centuries BC there is still much need for intelligent liaison between the two professional disciplines, one which works primarily from recorded evidence, the other which works from first-hand evidence of objects.[4]

For our immediate problem it may help to discuss the various reasons why Greek painted pottery may have travelled overseas in antiquity.

1. The first and most obvious occasion would be for the supply or use of Greeks overseas who had not their own kilns or could not be satisfied with local non-Greek products. Emigrating families would take with them their best dinner service, and probably domestic utensils, and in their new homes they would be likely to create a demand for replacements of the same type of pottery from home. Until local kilns were built – probably to produce imitations of the wares most familiar to them – the pottery used by, say, Corinthian families in Sicily was likely to be much the same as that they were used to at home. The identification of our emigrant Greeks will then depend on what we know of tastes at home. When we deal with well-known pottery-producing centres like Corinth, the matter may seem easy – too easy; for other Greeks may have been used to Corinthian vases and have had no distinctive local wares of their own. I think of Aegina, where there was no production of decorated pottery and where Corinthian vases were in general use. Ancient historians tell us much of Aegina's overseas trade, but if Aeginetans settled or carried pottery overseas they could not be recognized archaeologically or, from the pottery, distinguished from Corinthians. Again, many colonial Greek sites have been better explored than their mother cities in Greece – than Chalcis and Megara, for example.

What is important for us is the probability that minor vases which would never have travelled as containers or *objets d'art* may be taken as proof of the residence or at least regular visits of Greeks. In quantity they should imply some kind of settlement, but the presence of even a few such vases may be an indication of regular trade in other commodities which they accompanied casually, or perhaps of temporary quarters for Greek traders or their agents.

2. Vases which travelled by way of trade may have had commer-

cial value (a) from what they contained, or (b) for their own sakes as *objets d'art*.

(a) Oil and wine were generally exported in large, plain vases, but only in the seventh century can we begin readily to distinguish the containers of the various producing centres, like the Chian wine jars (*Fig. 1*), and the SOS oil or wine jars (*Fig. 2*) long thought to be Athenian, but now shown to be also of Euboean manufacture.[5] Then, it becomes possible to make useful observations about the distribution of these commodities. Stout, plain vases may of course be re-used, perhaps even re-exported. Thus, a sixth-century Chian wine jar was re-sealed in Egypt with cartouches of King Amasis (*Fig. 152*). Perfume, or perfumed oil, may have been carried in bulk, but was certainly also carried in elegant small flasks – *aryballoi* or *alabastra*. To help sell their contents, these regularly carried elaborate decoration or were moulded into unusual or striking shapes. A very large proportion of the finest paintings by Corinthian artists in the 'Protocorinthian' period is to be found on these flasks. Corinth, it seems, was a major exporter of perfume in the flask. At least, it is difficult to see why she should have specialized for so long making these flasks if she did not also fill them. Crete may have shared in the trade in the later eighth and early seventh centuries, and after the late seventh century Rhodes came to rival Corinth. There was probably a lot of opportunist trading by Greek and non-Greek skippers, but where a considerable quantity of, say, Chian wine jars or Rhodian perfume flasks have been found, it seems not unreasonable to think that the carriers were Chians and Rhodians. But it is, of course, not necessary. The Aeginetans were exclusively carriers, not producers, and any captain would probably have been happy enough to carry a load of fine Corinthian perfume flasks.

1 Chian wine jar from Smyrna, used for a child burial; late 7th c. (Izmir Mus.)

(b) The elaborate decoration of the small perfume flasks would certainly have encouraged a taste for finely decorated pottery, and it may well be that already in the mid seventh century other Corinthian vases were being carried for their own sakes, as *objets d'art*, or at least best plate, particularly to the west. Later, the Corinthians exploited the uncritical welcome given to their painted wares by increasing production and coarsening finish. Athens was already beginning to challenge in both the eastern and western markets, in the first quarter of the sixth century, with her fine black-figure vases which must certainly have been carried for their intrinsic value. In the second quarter of the century the Corinthians rallied with a line in mixing bowls (craters) decorated with colourful mythological scenes. These found some favour in Etruria, but their success was short-lived. In the same years an Athenian pottery was making vases (we call them 'Tyrrhenian') for the Etruscan market, and these, together with the finer products, won the day. The 'Tyrrhe-

2 Athenian 'SOS' amphora for wine or oil (the type was made in both Athens and Euboea); about 600 BC. (London 1848.6–19.9; H. 68 cm)

nian' vases (*Fig. 237*) are cheap, gaudy things, often carrying mock inscriptions to impress the Etruscans who could probably not read Greek at any rate. Even after their success, the Athenians had to face the competition of new shops set up in Italy itself, many of them staffed by emigrant or refugee Ionian artists. One Athenian potter, Nikosthenes, went so far as to copy purely Etruscan vase shapes (*Fig. 238*) and decorate them in the current Athenian style in place of the plain grey ware (*bucchero*) in which they were familiar in Etruria. This enterprise we shall study further in Chapter 5. There are copies too of some Cypriot and western 'Chalcidian' shapes, and of patterning on Spartan vases (on the 'Droop cups'). From this time on Athenians were the only Greeks to make money from the export of painted pottery. From the prices which merchants scratched on some of the vases, the profit could not have been great and certainly could never have formed an important part of the state revenue, even through taxes.[6] Other works of art – in bronze or ivory – would have commanded higher prices, and we can see some evidence of Corinthian and Spartan success in the export of bronze vases in the sixth century, but finds in these materials are naturally far more rare than those of pottery. Much the same problems about carriers apply here as they do with the commodity containers. It was certainly not Athenian traders only who carried the fine red-figure vases which have been found from Spain to Persia, from South Russia to the Sudan.[7]

3. Casual finds of Greek vases may mean many things. I have already mentioned the possible significance of the plainer small vases which had no commercial value. Otherwise stray pieces could wander far from any colony or trading post, and probably not in the hands of Greeks or necessarily because there was a specific demand for them. Such would be travellers' or native traders' curios, and can tell us nothing of importance. An example of different material may be the little Spartan bronze warrior which was picked up in the South Arabian desert,[8] but even this has been cited to support the theory that there was a Greek post on the Red Sea in the sixth century BC.

Other material exports and imports will concern us little, mainly because the evidence for them is lacking, and not because they were not important. The survival of bronzes is haphazard but in some areas they can be almost as informative as the painted vases. Trade in the raw metals or ores was presumably important, and in recent literature it is taken, probably rightly, to be decisive in promoting a number of overseas enterprises which we shall be considering especially in Chapters 3 and 5. But once we begin to have text evidence about trade in the Classical period, when the supply of metal must have been just as important, virtually no comment is made about it, while evidence about trade in foodstuffs – corn, wine, oil – is comparatively plentiful. Possibly, like the pottery trade, it did not call for comment, any more than did the traffic in slaves which might have been a vital element for a country with little yet in consumer goods or raw materials to offer.[9]

Coinage and weight-standards will also seldom be mentioned. Coins are not common until the mid sixth century and in early years weight-standards are imprecise and only of local significance. So too were the coins themselves, and they did not even serve inter-state trade until towards the end of our period when the precious metals could pass as bullion and comparability of weight-standards became therefore of some importance. It is not until the end of the sixth century that enough coins were in circulation to contribute much to the archaeological and historical record.[10] Thus, it has been argued that the number of North Greek coins in Egypt shows whence the East Greeks trading there acquired the bullion to pay for their corn, and in part explains East Greek interest and colonizing in the silver-producing areas to the north of Greece (Thrace). We shall have something to say about the eastern inspiration for the use of coinage in Greece in Chapter 3.

Literary Evidence

The poet of the *Iliad* was creating his original narrative from older recited lays by the end of the eighth century or at least in the first half of the seventh. In both the *Iliad* and the *Odyssey* much of the background derives from contemporary behaviour and experience and there are some asides on easterners which are relevant to us although colonization is, surprisingly, ignored. Hesiod, writing about 700, found the crossing from Boeotia to Chalcis (now bridged) enough but is aware of sea-trade.[11]

The lyric poets offer a little: notably Alcaeus' remarks about his brother, a mercenary in the pay of the Babylonians. Sappho's remarks about *her* brother, a wine exporter to Egypt who had become infatuated with a lady of easy virtue there, are unfortunately not all repeated verbatim by the later writers who mention the affair. Snatches of Callinus and Mimnermus sing of Ionian struggles against the Cimmerians and Lydians in Asia Minor. Some of the poets were also men of affairs[12] – Alcaeus meddled with his island's politics and Lydian gold. And some men of affairs were also poets – Solon transformed Archaic Athens in his legislation: his poems relate mainly to local affairs but he was a traveller and could recognize the good fortune of a man who could boast sons, sound horses, hunting dogs and a foreign guest-friend.[13]

In the later part of the sixth century BC Hecataeus of Miletus wrote his *Periodos* – a *Journey round the World*. 'This is the story told by Hecataeus of Miletus. I write here what I consider to be true, for the tales of the Greeks are manifold and, in my judgement, ridiculous.' Unfortunately we have his work only in fragments quoted by later writers. They show that he had an acute interest in geography and assembled the available information about the ends of the earth from the reports of Ionian captains, and perhaps in part from his own travels. He liked legend too, and may not have satisfied modern standards in his tempering of fantasy to fact, but there can be no doubt that he would have had much of importance to tell us of early travels by the Greeks. Even in his day a Carian traveller, called Scylax, had been sent by the Persian King Darius to explore India as far as the Indus (?) and to circumnavigate Arabia; while, yet earlier, Phoenicians had sailed round Africa for an Egyptian king.[14]

Some information of value can be gleaned from early non-Greek sources. Assyrian historical inscriptions, dealing with the *res gestae* of the Kings, have occasion to mention the Yaman (Ionians) whom the Assyrians met in eastern waters and on eastern shores; Yawan, an 'Ionia' which vaguely embraced all Greek territory; and Iadnana, Cyprus. The major campaigns which led to the overthrow of the empires of Assyria, Babylon, and Lydia are also recorded in inscriptions. There are few direct references to Greeks here, but at Babylon and Susa there is epigraphical evidence for the presence of 'Ionians', some certainly craftsmen.

Our first detailed account of early Greek history from a Greek pen is in the *Histories* of Herodotus (*Fig. 3*), the very Father of History. He was born in East Greece, at Halicarnassus, at a time when his countrymen were being pressed into the Persian service against the cities of mainland Greece. He was writing about the middle of the fifth century. The aim of his work was simple: 'To preserve the memory of the past by putting on record the astounding achievements both of our own and of the Asiatic peoples; and, more particularly, to show how the two races came into conflict.' Fortunately, then, for our purpose, he was led to discuss at length the dealings of the Greeks with the countries of the east. He digresses readily, to tell of the earlier fortunes of the peoples who play the major parts in his story. The Persians, of course, receive his full attention, and the story of the first Greek intercourse with the east leads him to an account of Lydia. The growth of the Persian Empire and expeditions of its Kings give us long accounts of Egypt, Babylonia, Libya, and Scythia; and it seems there was also a long section on Assyria, which is missing in our texts. Much of his information he picked up on his own travels from the Black Sea to Syria and Egypt. He asked questions and recorded the answers, generally registering how much he believed to be true. 'My business is to record what people say, but I am by no means bound to believe it.' His descriptions of the offerings of foreign kings to Greek sanctuaries may sometimes tax the archaeologist, but they can generally be explained in terms of excavated finds.

Of later historians Thucydides helps us very little. The fourth-

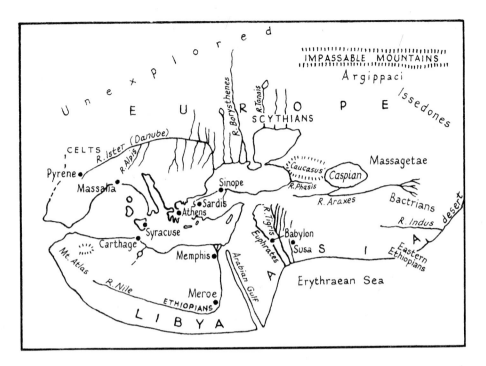

Unexplored

EUROPE

IMPASSABLE MOUNTAINS
Argippaci
Issedones

R. Borysthenes
R. Tanais

SCYTHIANS

CELTS R. Ister (Danube)
R. Alpis
Pyrene
Massalia

Caucasus
R. Phasis
Caspian
Massagetae

Sinope

Sardis
Athens
Syracuse
Carthage
Mt. Atlas
Memphis
R. Nile
Meroe
ETHIOPIANS
LIBYA

Arabian Gulf

R. Tigris
Euphrates
Babylon
Susa S
Erythraean Sea

R. Araxes
Bactrians
R. Indus
desert
A
S
I
A
Eastern Ethiopians

century historians, notably Ephorus, may have commanded more 'documentary' evidence in the form of king lists, priest lists, foundation stories, or local chronicles, but by their day a great part of this evidence may have been artificial, the invention of local savants, and at any rate the historians' works are lost to us except in so far as they were used or quoted by later writers. Herodotus remains our single literary source of any real importance. We may be grateful that so much of his work survives, grateful too for his curiosity and interest in the affairs of countries outside Greece. Plutarch criticized him for being over-fond of the barbarian – 'philobarbaros'. We are perhaps better able to appreciate such quality in a man and a historian.

3 Map of the world, following Herodotus' description (after Thomson, *History of Ancient Geography*)

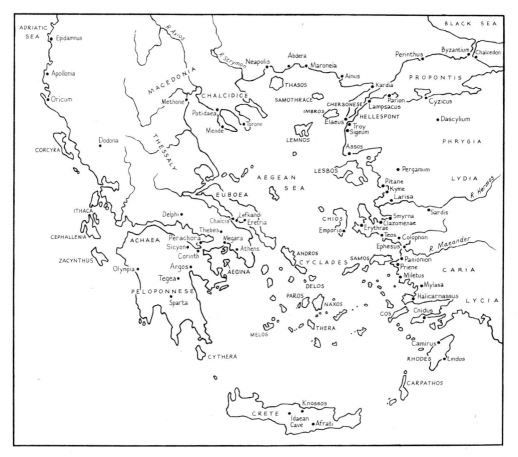

Greece and the Aegean Coasts

2

The Background

In the days of her flourishing Bronze Age civilization, of the Minoan palaces and Mycenaean citadels, Greece had been in close contact with those other early civilizations which bordered the Eastern Mediterranean. It is not my purpose here to tell of this age, but much the same ground was to be covered again by the Greeks, and it is as well to bear in mind that the seventh century BC was not the first 'orientalizing' period in Greece, and that the Greek language must have been heard in Egypt more than 500 years before the Greeks built their trading town on the Nile Delta. So a few words on these early contacts will not be wasted.

Many of the earliest stimuli to the growth of the Minoan civilization of Crete can be traced to both Egypt and the Near East. The connections remained strong, and when the Mycenaean Greeks succeeded to the to-them-foreign supremacy of Crete the contacts were maintained. This we can tell from the finds of Mycenaean pottery in Egypt and the apparent influence of Minoan–Mycenaean art forms on the Egypt of Akhenaten and his successors – the Amarna period. Some would have it too that relations might have been closer even earlier, and that Mycenaeans fought for Egypt against the Hyksos invaders.

With the east too there were close ties. The original population of Crete – perhaps even that of Greece – may have come from Asia Minor (Anatolia), although the parallels to be drawn between the cults and architecture of Asia Minor and Crete in the second millennium BC are not wholly convincing. The coasts of Syria and Palestine gave access to the riches and technical skills of Mesopotamia. Nor was the only contact a matter of trade in necessities or luxuries because the Minoans, and then the Mycenaeans, seem to have planted trading posts or colonies at various points on the coasts of Asia Minor and Syria.[1]

These overseas ventures by Mycenaean Greeks are another story of which I shall tell part in the introductions to later chapters. Here I want to set the scene, introduce the protagonists, and carry their story down from the collapse of Bronze Age Greece to about the eighth century BC when the Greeks again set out in earnest to buy, learn, fight, or settle on foreign soil.

The course of the twelfth century B C saw the destruction and abandonment of almost all the important Mycenaean citadels and towns. The archaeological record is clear. The literary record tells of an invasion, or succession of invasions, of other Greek-speakers – the Dorians – from the north, and when we are again able to distinguish the Greek races, by their dialect or customs, we find that the Dorians are in possession of much of southern Greece (the Peloponnese) and the southern islands, including Crete and Rhodes. The story of the overthrow of the Mycenaean palaces may not, of course, have been such a simple matter. Other, non-Greek tribes may have passed through Greece, internal dissensions probably contributed to the break up, and the arrival of the Dorians need not have been the most destructive of these visitations, indeed it may have been peaceful and it had the most lasting effect.

Across the Aegean the story is much the same. The Hittites in Asia Minor succumbed to northern invaders. The countries of the Near East were torn into small states and kingdoms by tribes moving down from the north, joined, it may be, by Mycenaean Greeks from the west – the Akaiwasha (Achaeans) and Daniuna (Danaans) of the Egyptian records.[2]

The islands were restless, disturbed among themselves; they poured out their people all together. No land stood before them. ... The countries which came from their isles in the midst of the sea, they advanced upon Egypt, their hearts relying on their arms.

Egypt withstood the invasions with difficulty, but the upheaval left her too exhausted, and happy enough to let well alone those new cultures of Greece and the Near East who knew iron but had, it seems, no heart for their predecessors' arts and achievements.

The succeeding 'Dark Ages' in Greek history present a real challenge to the archaeologist, and perhaps a too ready field for the ingenuity of scholars attempting – with some justification, it is true – to rescue the history of the illiterate centuries from the myths and poems remembered and recorded by later generations.

To the archaeologist the picture is deceptively simple. On most homeland Greek sites there seems to have been the sort of cultural break which betokens either complete abandonment or considerable depopulation. To this there are few, but notable exceptions, where folk lived still in a sort of Mycenaean twilight, as in Athens and Crete. The literary record tells us that Athens did not fall to the Dorians or any northern invaders, and the archaeological evidence from the city suggests that this was certainly true, although she may have been hard-pressed and her people confined to within the stout walls of her Acropolis. The finds in her cemeteries, and from nearby Salamis, show that Mycenaean forms and decoration were still remembered, though often much debased. In Crete the Mycenaean tradition, heavily tinged by the native Minoan, survived in two different ways. First, in the refugee settlements – like Karphi, on a nearly inaccessible hill-top where the people sought to avoid the disasters of the preceding generations by removing themselves from contact with possible enemies. Secondly, in the open city of Knossos, which seemed still able to maintain some cultural contact with mainland Greece. Knossos was Dorian by this time, yet it is the cultural influence of non-Dorian Athens which is most strongly felt.

In Athens, before the end of the eleventh century, the first new Iron Age culture of Greece was born. We know it as the 'Protogeometric' because the patterns on its pottery foreshadow the 'Geometric' styles of the ninth and eighth centuries, and it is from its pottery that its character can best be judged. From the finds made with the pottery in tombs, we can see that iron was coming to be used more and more both for ornaments – the big dress-pins – and for weapons. Cremation too was adopted in Athens, although many other parts of Greece were slow to make the change from ordinary inhumation of the dead, and, except in Thera and parts of Crete, it was never the exclusive method of burial.[3] It was as though Athens was sloughing off the worn-out idioms of Greece's Bronze Age, and replacing them by the new discipline and precision which were to remain hallmarks of Greece's later achievements in the arts. In the tenth and ninth centuries the archaeological evidence for the awakening and growing populations of other once-rich Greek centres shows that in their arts and crafts they were in varying degrees dependent on Athens' lead. This was true even of Crete, although Knossos and other cities of the lowlands were still highly conscious of their past, and the old chamber tombs were still used, although for ash urns and not for bodies. The mountain refuges were at last being abandoned. This Protogeometric spirit is wholly and simply Greek, not Dorian or Ionian or Aeolian. The cultural 'koine' cuts across the otherwise clearly defined boundaries of speech or politics. And to the historian a common way of life may be of greater significance than a common dialect.

These centuries saw not only the regeneration of prosperity in Greece, but also the beginnings of renewed interest in lands overseas and of migrations to new homes. I write of these events here rather than in later chapters because, for the greater part, they involve a return to towns and islands on the eastern shores of the Aegean which had already once been visited by Mycenaean Greeks. In some respects these Eastern Greek states may never have lost their Hellenic character after the débâcle of the end of the Bronze Age. The interruption in their archaeological record may be interpreted in much the same terms as it is for the many homeland Greek sites which seem dead in the eleventh and tenth centuries. And although the Dark Age migrations may have had to displace non-Greek peoples, the political aspect of what we call 'East Greece' cannot from now on be divorced from that of the rest of Greece, and many East Greek states are to play leading roles in the later enterprises overseas which are our main interest.

The tradition, which is perhaps only in part the fabrication of patriot-historians, assigned Athens a position of considerable importance as the departure or marshalling point for the migration of the Ionians to their ultimate homes on the eastern shores of the Aegean. Athens' survival of the disaster which attended other Mycenaean cities, and her record through the Dark Ages, show that there is likely to be more than a grain of truth in this. The tradition also speaks of yet earlier migrations by the Aeolians, who settled the islands and cities on the northern half of the coastline of Asia Minor while the Ionians were busy in the south. Ancient historians tried to rationalize these two migrations into two separate and organized movements, while it seems far more likely that the dispossessed or homeless peoples of Greece were crossing the Aegean on many different occasions from the eleventh to the ninth centuries, following the routes explored by their predecessors, or still remembered from the days of Mycenaean trade and settlement.[4]

The later importance of many of the cities, and the fact that the migrations led directly to more immediate contact with 'the barbarian' and set a pattern for later colonial development, justify a brief survey of the archaeology of these early East Greek sites. The equating of this archaeological record with the quasi-historical indications in ancient authors is again a matter of some difficulty which need not be dwelt upon. In general the literary evidence gives higher dates for the migrations than the archaeological evidence so far available, and it is still not possible to say whether this is due more to the incomplete nature of the latter than to the mythical or contrived sources of the former.

The questions we should like to be able to answer about each of the new towns in the east are the following:

1. What sort of site has it; and why was it chosen?
2. Had it been occupied by Greeks (i.e. Mycenaeans) before?
3. Was Greek occupation continuous through the Dark Ages?
4. If not, are there signs of non-Greek occupation?
5. When and whence did the new settlers come?

Of the native Anatolian peoples with whom the Greeks might have had dealings, or whom they may even have had to displace, we know best the Phrygians. They were the heirs to the empire of the Hittites on the plateaux of north-central Anatolia, but, like the Hittites, only intermittently interested in the fortunes of the western seaboard. We shall have more to say of their relations with the Greeks in Chapter 3. The people who occupied the coastal areas of Asia Minor in the Early Iron Age are still little known archaeologically. Their plain pottery is related to the grey Phrygian wares, but there is no quantity of painted pottery until the seventh century, when we see other influences at work. The literary record, on the other hand, offers a plethora of names of peoples whom the Greeks met. Some may refer rather to the state of affairs which the Mycenaean Greeks had found in Asia Minor, but others, like the Carians, survive as recognizable units into later periods. Archaeologically they are not so easy to recognize in the years which interest us, but 'Submycenaean' people in East Greece may have been Carians, and it was perhaps they who were responsible for the survival of some Mycenaean motifs in East Greek art. Where we meet archaeological evidence for a native population we will try to explain it, but otherwise our concern is with the character of the new Greek towns and what has been found in them. The character of the material evidence from them is such that we unfortunately cannot yet make useful deductions about the exact provenance of the new settlers.

We begin in the south, with those places where there is either some possibility of continuous Greek occupation or at least only a short break in the Dark Ages.[5]

The island of RHODES, with Cos, Calymnus, and no doubt others of the Dodecanese (still little explored), was a flourishing Late Mycenaean centre with several important settlements. These were all abandoned at the end of the Bronze Age, but Cos, and to a lesser degree Rhodes, have yielded evidence of reoccupation by Greeks using Protogeometric pottery, possibly from the Argolid and perhaps before the end of the tenth century, so the break was not a long one. There is no sign of any other inhabitants in the interim. From this time on there is a steady and rapid increase in population and multiplication of settlements. The history of the cities of Rhodes is tied so closely to that of the Greek mainland that despite the island's geographical position, its reoccupation in the tenth century can barely be considered an adventure on foreign soil.[6]

On the mainland opposite we still have much to learn of the earliest Greek cities HALICARNASSUS and CNIDUS, and their archaeological relationship with non-Greek peoples. Cnidus lay near the tip of the long peninsula at the extreme south-west point of Asia Minor; Halicarnassus was in a similar position on the next peninsula to the north. A considerable Carian element in the population of Halicarnassus in classical times is shown by personal names, and the town must always have been much involved with its Anatolian neighbours. Muskebi, near Halicarnassus, may have received Mycenaean refugees,[7] and two or three sites in this area, notably Asarlik and Dirmil, have tombs with Protogeometric pottery of Attic type which might indicate short-lived Greek communities which came over from Athens early in the Iron Age. At both the sites named later finds are no earlier than the eighth century, so we do not know whether occupation was continuous, but it is likely.[8] It may be remarked that one theory would explain the cemetery at Asarlik, and most of the Mycenaean finds in this quarter of Asia Minor, as evidence of Carians living within the Mycenaean cultural ambit and not of Greeks themselves.[9]

MILETUS may tell a somewhat different story from Rhodes, for all that it lies actually on the mainland. Cretans had settled there in the Middle Bronze Age, and Mycenaeans had followed them in the Late Bronze Age. The story of the Greeks taking Carian wives from the native population they found there[10] might belong to the transition between Minoan and Mycenaean settlements, but at the time of Homer's Trojan War Miletus was, it appears, Carian and not Greek.[11] The German excavators allege continuity of Greek occupation, through the Submycenaean and Protogeometric periods, to Classical and Roman times, and what they have published seems to bear this out.[12] The main site lay, at all periods, on the peninsula which projected north into the bay (now silted up) at the mouth of the River Maeander. It commanded good farm land, but the inland route along the Maeander valley may not have been of great importance at first. Details of the early town are obscured by Hellenistic and Roman building, but recent excavations may teach us more. There may too have been other communities near by. On Kalabaktepe, a hill barely half a mile away, there was a settlement from the eighth century on, with its own circuit wall and temple. This was perhaps at first a place of refuge in the years when Cimmerians and Lydians were threatening the city. All the pottery found at Miletus is Minoan, Mycenaean, or Greek, so any Carian occupation did not interrupt the at least superficially Greek character of the site. Miletus will play an important part in our story, and it is a pity that excavations there have so far denied us any very clear idea of the specifically Milesian products – especially pottery.

Of the other sites near by, both MYUS and PRIENE may have occupied peninsula sites in the same bay, but the earliest settlement at the first has barely been explored, and that of the second has yet to be found. MAGNESIA lay inland, on the Maeander, commanding a route to the north and Ephesus; it did not become Greek until the seventh century, but an ancient tradition implies some Bronze Age Greek or Cretan settlement there.

At the other side of the Mycale headland, Protogeometric pottery has been found at PYGELA, and Mycenaean and Protogeometric at Tsangli, near the later site of the headquarters of the Ionian League (PANIONION). The town of MELIE here was destroyed by the Ionians.[13] An eighth-century cemetery has been found, but there is later occupation too and the date of the destruction is still not wholly clear. This whole area, according to ancient writers, had to be wrested from the Carians.

EPHESUS lay at the mouth of the River Cayster. It commanded good farmland and was readily accessible from the north and inland. The earliest Greek settlement has yet to be found, but the sixth-century Temple of Artemis (the 'Diana of the Ephesians') probably occupied the site of its earliest sanctuary and Mycenaean pottery has been found near by. Protogeometric pottery has been reported some way to the south.

North of Ephesus lies the great Erythraean peninsula bounded to the north by the Gulf of Smyrna. On its south flank are the cities of TEOS and LEBEDOS, neither of them excavated. The former figures in Bronze Age myth-history. A little inland is COLOPHON, which has been described as strikingly like the sites of the major Mycenaean cities of Old Greece, on a steep acropolis commanding a rich plain.[14] Excavations have been unlucky in that the finds were lost, but it seems there was a Mycenaean walled town here. Geometric pottery is reported, but we cannot say whether occupation could have been continuous. The full literary record suggests that Cretans preceded the Mycenaean Greeks and that the later Greeks came straight from Pylos and established themselves by force of arms.

ERYTHRAE lies on a bay at the extremity of the peninsula to which it gives its name. The earliest town may lie on a small peninsula site some way from the later Classical town. Later tradition implies a Bronze Age Greek settlement here. On the northern arm of the peninsula, within what was later the territory of Erythrae, is a small peninsula site (Mordogan) with Protogeometric and later pottery, and we should perhaps assume that the larger sites on the peninsula were occupied just as early.[15] On the north coast of the main peninsula, looking on to the Gulf of Smyrna, stood CLAZOMENAE. Parts of the archaic cemetery have been excavated, but not the town, which stood at the end of a low spur near the shore, and was later removed to an offshore island when the Persians threatened. The literary record of the Greek foundation seems to refer to the Iron Age settlement, but some quantity of Mycenaean pottery has been found, and since there is no mention of evidence for a native town, this too may have been twice settled by the Greeks.[16]

SMYRNA, or Old Smyrna – to distinguish it from the Hellenistic and modern city (Izmir) – lay on a small promontory, well served by harbours on either side of the causeway leading to the mainland. It has been excavated in recent years by British and Turkish archaeologists, so that much of its early history is now clear, although the publication of the finds has barely commenced.[17] Here there are clear signs of a flourishing native – or Anatolian – Bronze Age settlement, and the few Mycenaean sherds suggest an awareness of the Greeks but not settlement by them. Some painted Protogeometric vases show that the Greeks had arrived there, perhaps by about 1000 BC, but the mass of plainer grey pottery which accompanied them proves that these were Greeks who shared the culture of Aeolis, not Ionia, and in this the archaeological and historical records are at one. By the eighth century, the pottery which we associate rather with the Ionians is predominant, and we read of the city's capture by them.[18] Old Smyrna affords the most complete picture we have so far of an early Greek settlement in Asia Minor, and its colossal walls, laid out in the ninth century and remodelled in the eighth,

4 Reconstruction of the
city of Smyrna in about 600
BC. (by R. V. Nicholls)

are witness both to the strength of the city and the very real threat presented by its barbarian neighbours, notably the Lydians.[19] A view of the town as it may have appeared at the end of the seventh century is shown in *Fig. 4.*[20]

PHOCAEA lay on the north side of the mouth of the Gulf of Smyrna. It is another promontory site with a good sheltered harbour. There has been a false report of Mycenaean pottery from the site, and recent Turkish excavations have found nothing earlier than the eighth century.[21]

Of the islands of Ionia, SAMOS has yielded enough Mycenaean pottery, both from its main town – on a small promontory by a good harbour – and from the later sanctuary site of the Heraeum, to suggest Greek settlement in the Bronze Age. There are no non-Greek 'native' finds of the period which interests us. At the Heraeum, where the great temple later stood, the Mycenaean levels are immediately overlaid by heavy Greek Geometric deposits of the eighth century, although there are reports of Late Protogeometric, and some Early Geometric (ninth century) from a tomb, and the excavators thought that the earliest of the temples there could be of the ninth century. It is possible that new finds will prove uninterrupted or barely interrupted occupation by Greeks, but there is clearly a significant growth in prosperity and probably immigration in the Geometric period.[22]

CHIOS tells much the same story. At Emporio, a good harbour site near the south point of the island, recent British excavations have shown that there was a Late Mycenaean settlement beside and probably on the rocky promontory by the harbour. This may have been a short-lived refugee settlement of the twelfth century. In the eighth century there was a new Greek settlement, not exactly on the site of the Mycenaean, although the harbourside may have been occupied, and there was an important sanctuary there, but on a less readily accessible hill a little inland (*Fig. 5*). This had an acropolis wall, temple, and 'palace' ('Megaron hall') within, and the town houses on the steep hill slope outside the walls. It was abandoned for the comfort of valley dwelling before the end of the seventh century.[23] Again there is no clear indication of native or 'Carian' occupation, unless the later Mycenaean or Submycenaean finds are such. Another important sanctuary and harbour site in the south of the island, at Phanai, is less well explored but has yielded Mycenaean and Greek pottery from perhaps the late ninth century on.[24] The main town of ancient

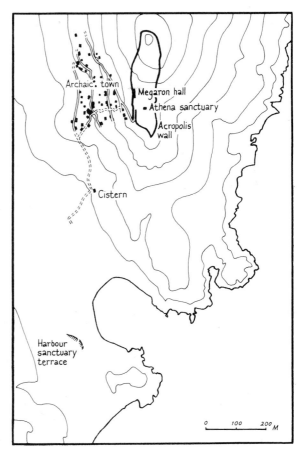

5 Plan of the site and sanctuaries of Emporio in Chios; 7th c.

Chios is covered by the modern city, but here too Mycenaean and Geometric have been found.[25] At Volissos in the north-west, reputed home of the poet Homer, and on the island Psara there is also Mycenaean and archaic pottery. As on Samos, there seems to have been a real break in Greek occupation but no recognizable native interregnum. The literary record also tells of two periods of settlement but admits Carians between them.

We have now looked at the settlements of Dorian Greeks on and off the south-west corner of Asia Minor, and of their Ionian neighbours to the north. Here and there are suggestions of continuous Greek occupation from the Late Bronze Age into historical times – in the Dodecanese and at Miletus. The sites chosen, especially in Ionia, are often promontories or peninsulas which afforded protection on the landward side. This in itself implies a fear of hostility, yet each site clearly relied also on its command of good farmland, and only at Smyrna have we seen clear indication of a native settlement being gradually taken over by Greeks. The literary record is full of references to Anatolian peoples met by the Greeks and displaced by them, notably the Carians, but their archaeological presence can only be sought in the Late Mycenaean or Submycenaean culture which they may have absorbed. For it must be remembered that the majority of the sites which have been adequately explored seem to have already been chosen by Mycenaean Greeks for settlement or at least visits.

The main Ionian cities had been organized into a League perhaps by the end of the ninth century.[26] These were Miletus, Myus, Priene, Ephesus, Colophon, Lebedos, Teos, Clazomenae, Phocaea, Samos, Chios, and Erythrae; the last five named may not have been 'founder-members', being, it seems, partly Aeolian settlements at first. Smyrna was never admitted, although it became Ionian after capture by refugees from Colophon. The original function and purpose of the League are not clear, but if there was a military aspect to it there is little reason to think that it was primarily directed against possible barbarian enemies in Anatolia. Ephesus seems to have stood at the head of the League, and there are mentions of her championing Ionians against the native Carians. On the other hand there is evidence for intermarriage between the Ionians and Carians, and Herodotus remarks that some of the Greeks set up Lycian kings, or accepted the joint rule of Greek and native royal houses.[27]

The story of Greek settlement in Asia Minor north of Ionia is not so easily told. This is the area of the Aeolians, although it is not possible to define any clear borderline, physical or cultural, between them and the Ionians. The Aeolian sites are fewer and less well explored, but as we have seen already at Smyrna, there are clearer indications of relations with native Anatolian peoples. We are here closer to the heart of the Phrygian kingdom, and the archaeology of the coastal areas is akin to that of western Phrygia, distinguished by the use of monochrome grey pottery, like what is known as *bucchero*, long popular in this part of Anatolia. This was the ware which the Greeks found in use when they first came to Smyrna.

On the island of LESBOS, the great prehistoric site of Thermi yielded Mycenaean pottery in its last phase, and there is some from three other sites in the island. Thermi was violently destroyed, and the story of Achilles' raid on the island at the time of the Trojan War is often cited in this connection.[28] Trifling finds of Protogeometric, including an alleged Athenian import, lend a little support for the early date of the new Aeolian settlements suggested by the literary evidence, but otherwise there is hardly anything which need be earlier than the eighth century, from the few archaic sites which have been explored.[29] Characteristic of the earliest finds is the occurrence of fine *bucchero* pottery, unpainted and generally of a silvery grey appearance, in shapes which are not wholly derived from the contemporary Greek repertoire.[30] The technique and perhaps some shapes may reflect Anatolian fashions, and the great popularity of this ware in Lesbos may be taken as evidence for close relationship with the mainlanders, or with the non-Greek peoples still resident in the island.

We still know very little about the Aeolian cities on the mainland of Asia Minor. MYRINA has yielded a little Mycenaean, but otherwise nothing earlier than the seventh century. PITANE is another peninsula site. A Mycenaean vase is alleged to have been found there. The cemetery recently excavated on the isthmus is said to have produced an Attic Protogeometric vase but the published finds are no earlier than about 700.[31] KYME has been tested but the finds not published. It must have been an early Aeolian foundation, sought out for the farmland to which it gave access. The father of the Greek poet Hesiod had lived there in the eighth century before moving his family back to Boeotia, and we also hear of a royal marriage with Phrygia at this time. We shall have something to say of later Aeolian foundations in Asia Minor in Chapter 3. As in Ionia, most of the places chosen for the early towns seem likely to have been known to Mycenaean Greeks, although probably not settled by them.

This is as far as we need pursue the story of the resettlement of Greeks on the coasts of Asia Minor and the islands. Their history now is at one with that of the homeland Greeks, although necessity or convenience at times led them into unholy alliances with Greece's enemies. By the eighth century, the main East Greek states are established and rapidly growing. Indeed they were outgrowing their territories. With that enterprise and ambition which characterizes people who have established themselves successfully far from home and at the gates of powerful neighbours, they were ready to join the states of mainland Greece in those ventures overseas which were to help fashion Greece's new 'Classical' civilization, and at the same time to begin the spread of that new civilization to all corners of the western world.

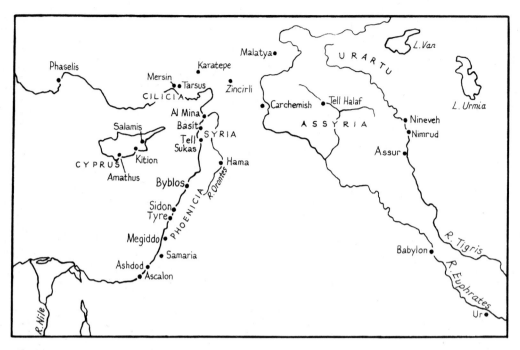

The Near East

3

The Eastern Adventure

The Near Eastern peoples with whom the Greeks resumed contact in the ninth century BC were heirs to the great civilizations which had flourished in the rich plains of Mesopotamia. Early in the Bronze Age the Aegean world had felt the impact of the sudden growth of these new cultures, and had come to learn from them their new metallurgical techniques. Indeed the very people of Minoan Crete may have owed their stock to immigrants from the east, despite the independent and brilliant culture which we see they evolved in their island. Relations between the mature Minoan civilization and the east are not easy to make out, but at least in North Syria there is some archaeological evidence for intimate connections, even in the Middle Bronze Age, before 1550 BC. At the end of the Late Bronze Age, when Mycenaean Greeks had won ascendancy over the Aegean and succeeded to the Minoan 'empire', there are more clear indications of what can almost be called colonizing by Mycenaean Greeks in the Near East, although the establishments may have been no more than trading posts admitted under treaty with local kingdoms. The most notable example is at Ugarit (Ras Shamra), but there was also a fair quantity of Late Mycenaean pottery imported into Palestine, perhaps from the Mycenaean kingdom of Rhodes rather than from the Greek mainland.[1]

The break-up of the Aegean Bronze Age cultures, and the period – in the myth-historical record – following the Trojan War, saw the migrations of many peoples, from west and north, through the countries of the Near East.[2] Some were carriers of Mycenaean pottery, themselves surely Mycenaean Greeks, and to these years may be assigned new Greek settlements in the east, many of them acquired and no doubt held by force of arms, although none are long-lived. The archaeological record shows this most clearly at Tarsus, but the literary record also tells of other new settlements at this time.

The travels of the Greek heroes after the Trojan war were given as the occasion for a number of these foundation stories, though they must be explained either by dispersal after events in Greece rather than at Troy, or by attempts to provide a heroic pedigree

6 Phoenician inscribed bronze bowl from Knossos; 10th c. (Heraklion Mus.)

7 Cypriot bronze tripod stand from the Pnyx, Athens; 12th c., said to be from an 8th-c. grave (Athens NM 7940; H. 45 cm)

for later foundations. Some, at least, can be taken more seriously. In Cilicia the Theban seer Mopsus was said to have founded Mopsuhestia and Mallus.[3] A dramatic illustration of this story is given by the inscription found at Karatepe in 1947, set up in the eighth century by a ruler who refers to the 'Danunim', apparently a memory of the Greek Danaans. With other towns, he mentions Beit Mopsu – the Phoenician form of Mopsuhestia, 'hearth' or 'home' of Mopsus.[4]

The memory of Greek occupation had survived clearly enough here in Cilicia. Much farther west, in Pamphylia, there were also reports of post-Trojan war settling by Greeks and this has been thought an early Greek enclave in the otherwise native kingdoms along this coast, but legend and the apparent evidence of dialect have yet to be supported by material evidence.[5]

On eastern shores, as on the western coastline of Asia Minor, it was to the same areas and cities that the Greeks returned after the Dark Ages, to found new settlements or open new markets, but here there was clearly a complete break in the continuity of Greek occupation, despite the survival or memory of names like Mopsus or the Danaans. During this break, Greek awareness of the countries of the Near East is shown archaeologically by occasional eastern products which found their way to Greece and sometimes had a limited effect on local crafts. These may briefly be reviewed, for they suggest a pattern of casual trade with one part of the Greek world in particular, Crete. But it was not, it seems, the Cretans who were later to sail east and establish themselves in the eastern markets.

Cyprus provided the intermediary between Crete and the east, and all the 'orientalizing' objects or ideas which Crete accepted during the Dark Ages are either derived directly from Cyprus, or involve the type of object which was as much at home in Cyprus as on the eastern mainland.[6] Even in the depressed period following the end of the Bronze Age, when bronze was scarce, iron was still a novelty (its use perhaps introduced from Cyprus) and

Cretan artists were still working in a Minoan–Mycenaean tradition, there are signs of continued relations between these two islands, which had been among the most important centres of the Late Mycenaean world. The evidence lies mainly in the choice of decoration on pottery and in the shapes of some vases (e.g. duck-vases[7]). Iron spits of a Cypriot type appear with a tenth-century burial at Knossos.[8] In bronze a recent find is a Phoenician inscribed bowl, which may have come from or via Cyprus[9] (Fig. 6), but the most important objects which travelled west were openwork vase-stands, largely composed of rods bent into volute patterns. Examples of the simplest forms[10] – tripod stands (Fig. 7) – have been found in Crete in tenth- and ninth-century contexts. The more elaborate form, square in plan with a hoop on top and sometimes wheeled, like that from Larnaka in Cyprus (Fig. 8), was apparently also known in Crete, to judge from the clay imitation of one found at Karphi (Fig. 9). This is a remote mountain village in Crete, sheltered by its position from hostile interference, and so cut off from the cultural progress of other Cretan centres that even when a foreign form is admitted and copied – as with the stand – the decoration on it remains Minoan in its style. This type of stand was later, in the eighth century, copied in Crete in bronze; there are fragmentary examples from the Idaean Cave, Kato Syme (Fig. 10) and Knossos, and another, found at Delphi, may have been made in Crete.[11] The import and limited influence of Cypriot pottery is also admitted in Crete in the eighth century, and we might have expected that the Cretans would be the first Greeks to take the initiative in the east, but it seems that the Cretan Dorian temperament lacked the spirit of enterprise which had characterized the Minoans. There is important evidence, however, for the arrival of easterners in Crete from the ninth century on, as we shall see.

In other parts of Greece the evidence is very slight for even minor and casual imports from the east before the eighth century; but ninth-century Euboea is receiving various minor objects of jewellery[12] and pottery from the east and Cyprus – not surprisingly, as we shall discover – and there are a Syrian bronze bowl and possibly Cypriot gold earring pendants in mid-ninth-century Athenian tombs.[13]

It is none too easy to fit the Phoenicians into this picture of relations in the Aegean in the Early Iron Age – or at least to justify the reputation which the Phoenicians had acquired as mariners and traders, which is how they appear to Homer, especially in the *Odyssey*.[14] It is likely that Greeks at home, and their poets, would not have been too nice in distinguishing the sources and races in the east of whose life and products they were beginning to become aware, through imported objects or traders' visits. Their sailors would come to know them better, perhaps, but travel- and guide-books were not written until the sixth century, and by then the political pattern of the eastern kingdoms had considerably

8 Cypriot bronze wheeled stand from Larnaka; 12th c. (Berlin 8947; H. 34 cm)

9 Clay stand from Karphi, Crete; 10th c. (Heraklion Mus.; H. 32 cm)

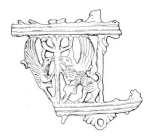

10 Part of a bronze openwork stand with a Phoenician subject of griffins and floral, from Kato Syme, Crete; 8th c. (Heraklion Mus.)

altered. We shall see that it is only after Greeks establish themselves on the Syrian coast that Greece begins to receive and
appreciate eastern products; and there is no clear evidence for
Phoenician trading colonies overseas earlier than the Greek ones.
For all that, they may have been the carriers of what little did
travel into the Greek world from the east before the eighth century. The nature of this trade did not require the establishment of
regular trading posts or colonies until Greek example and competition led them to similar undertakings.

With the eighth century, the picture begins to change completely. We may distinguish four main areas in the Near East
which were either penetrated by the Greeks, or whose cultures
had a profound influence on them. They are:

1. *North Syria*, both in its role as the home of neo-Hittite and
Aramaean cultures and as the gateway to the Urartian, Assyrian,
Babylonian, and Persian Empires, which successively engaged or
occupied it.

2. *Phoenicia and Palestine*, whose cultures and their influence on the
Greeks are not always readily distinguishable from those of North
Syria, especially after the Assyrian conquest.

3. *Cyprus* plays a somewhat equivocal part as intermediary for
both North Syria and the countries to its south. It is as an intermediary rather than as an independent centre that it is best considered here. It was peopled largely by Greek-speakers, having
been 'colonized' by refugees at the end of the Bronze Age and it is
still in touch with Crete, as we have seen. The great Phoenician
settlement at Kition was established over an older Mycenaean site
in the ninth century and from this time on it becomes difficult to
assess the influence of Cypro–Phoenician art on Greece and
Greeks separately from the influence of the Phoenician homeland.
In the eighth century far stronger links with Geometric Greece
develop, typified by the heroic style and some of the contents of
the royal tombs at Salamis.[15] By 709 Cypriot kings were paying
tribute to Assyria.

4. *Anatolia*, and the kingdoms of *Phrygia* and *Lydia*. We have
already seen how the Greeks established themselves again on the
sea-board of Asia Minor. It will be their relations with these
kingdoms of the hinterland which will concern us here. This, to
early Greek writers, is 'Asia',[16] though some confined the term to
Lydia, and later it was applied to the whole Persian empire, whose
effect on Greeks and Greece will occupy us at the end of this
chapter.

North Syria and the Empires beyond

Al Mina, at the mouth of the Orontes in North Syria (now within
the Turkish border province of Hatay) is the site of what was

probably the most important and earliest of the new Greek trading posts in the Eastern Mediterranean, and it is our best and earliest source of information about the Greeks overseas.

We know little of the Bronze Age history of this area but it had been visited by Greeks and Mycenaean pottery has been found near by (at Sabouni), so the new town may not have been in exactly the same place as the old.

Al Mina was excavated by Sir Leonard Woolley before the last war.[17] He was exploring in Syria, which he recognized as the key area, for sites which would throw light on the relationship between the countries of the Aegean and Mesopotamia. He was soon rewarded, with the fine Bronze Age site of Atchana, and the no less significant Iron Age port at Al Mina. The site had been in part washed away by a change in the course of the river. Woolley thought that part of its early history had been washed away as well, but there can be little doubt that we have some at least of the earliest Greek material there.

Woolley distinguished ten different levels at Al Mina, numbered from the latest, I, to the earliest, X, but we are concerned with two main periods only, which can be readily picked out from the architectural history of the site and the finds. The first (Levels X–VII) covers the earliest history of the town, down to about 700 BC. The second (Levels VI–V) carries us to about 600 BC, when there seems to be a break in the Greek occupation, or at least a serious recession. The excavation was in the town and warehouses, and we unfortunately know nothing of the cemeteries or any sanctuaries, Greek or native.

AL MINA: THE FIRST PERIOD, TO 700 BC.

The configuration of the Delta of the Orontes and the coastline in antiquity is not quite clear, but it seems that the town of Al Mina served through much of its history as a port and depot for sea-going vessels. Its architectural remains of our first period are not particularly impressive. The walls of the buildings were of mud-brick upon a low stone foundation or socle – a type of construction which remained the rule at Al Mina and was common on both Greek and Near Eastern sites at this time. No complete house plans can be made out, but it seems that many of the earliest walls (Levels X–IX) were re-used in buildings of Level VIII, and that Level VII was no more than a re-shaping or restoration of existing structures. What is important for us is the fact that Greek pottery is present in some quantity from the earliest levels on.

Before the second main period – the seventh century, Levels VI–V – there seems to be a real break in the history of the site. Not perhaps a long one, but certainly an important one. There is a complete change in the character and origins of the Greek finds, as we shall see, and the new buildings are laid out on quite different lines. Some rooms are more spacious, like storerooms, and the excavator observed that 'it already becomes possible to recognize – without undue exercise of the imagination – early examples of the type of office and magazine building which was to become the standard for future times'. Level v was a re-modelling of Level vi, and we are not for the moment concerned with the replanning of the town in Level iv and its subsequent history down to its eclipse by the foundation of Seleucia in 301 bc, although it is in this later period that the form and character of the Greek warehouses are best appreciated, because the latest buildings are better preserved.

Who then were the Greeks who established this trading station? What did they buy and sell, and what were their relations with the local population? The finds at Al Mina answer the first question for us; for the others we must appeal both to literary record and to the cumulative evidence of other sites, and we must also for the most part simply guess.

The finds of our first period are largely pottery. The Greek vases fall into a number of clearly defined groups, and by taking first what are stylistically the latest – because they are more readily identified – we can win some idea of the source of the pottery and of the Greeks who carried it.[18] The groups are as follows:

1. The smallest, but most distinctive, is of small straight-sided cups painted with Geometric patterns which are sometimes filled in with a white or cream slip. Such vases have otherwise been found only in Euboea, and belong to the last quarter of the eighth century (*Fig. 11*).

2. There are imitations of the elegant cups (*kotylai*) which were made in Corinth in the later part of the eighth century. Their clay, which is pinkish, and the occasional use of white paint for stripes within, show that they are not true Protocorinthian. Imitations which carry all the features of this group have so far been found only in Euboea and in the western colony of the Euboeans, on Ischia (Pithekoussai). See *Fig. 202*.

3. Cups (*skyphoi*) with simple Geometric patterns in panels (the 'metope' pattern). The class is well known in the islands of the Cyclades and Euboea, but the general absence of mica in the clay points especially to Euboea, and so does the particularly common pattern of concentric circles on the lip, which excavations at

11 Euboean bichrome cup from Lefkandi; late 8th c. (Eretria Mus.; H. 6·5 cm)

12 Euboean cup from Lefkandi; late 8th c.
(Eretria Mus.; H. 7·5 cm)

13 Euboean cup from Lefkandi; 9th c.
(Eretria Mus.; H. 7 cm)

Lefkandi (see below) have now shown to be peculiarly Euboean (*Fig. 12*).

4. Stylistically the earliest are cups decorated with compass-drawn semicircles. Since the first edition of this book was written excavations at Lefkandi, a site between Eretria and Chalcis in Euboea, have dramatically confirmed the suggestion that Euboea was a prime source for these cups (*Fig. 13*),[19] which were also current in Thessaly and the islands down to about the middle of the eighth century.

5. A group of cups (*skyphoi*) of the late eighth century had been identified by the writer as possible local products by Greek potters at Al Mina (*Fig. 14*).[20] The exterior decoration, with metope patterns and use of the multiple-brush freehand, and the fine potting, are Greek, but their interiors are striped in the Cypriot

14 Cypriot or local, Greek-made cup from Al Mina; late
8th c. (Oxford 1937.409; H. 8 cm)

manner and some are bichrome, another Cypriot trait. More have been found in Cyprus itself now,[21] and one or two reached Tarsus and Byblos.[22] It may be safer to regard them still as the produce of emigrant Geometric Greek potters, but living in Cyprus rather than Syria, with much of their ware naturally being taken up by nearby fellow expatriates.

Of the other pottery which from its level or style belongs here, there are scraps only of vases of a type made in East Greece, especially in Rhodes, and one piece only of true Protocorinthian; nothing Cretan. We shall return to consider the non-Greek pottery in a moment.

It seems likely then that it was the Euboeans who led the Greeks to Al Mina, together perhaps with islanders of the Cyclades, over some of whom Eretria (in Euboea) apparently enjoyed control, probably in this period.[23] The evidence for the Euboeans' role in the east is wholly archaeological. The literary record does not contradict it; indeed it says nothing at all of this truly epoch-making enterprise.

What the Euboeans brought with them to sell we do not know. At this period it could hardly have been pottery, although this no doubt accompanied other goods and was certainly as fine as or finer than anything made in the Near East at this time. It is difficult to see what eighth-century Greece had to offer, except perhaps slaves, but certainly a flow of trade ensued; and this could hardly have been one way, however highly we rate the Greek flair for business, for here they were meeting their equals in this matter. Many Greeks may have travelled east to serve as mercenaries, but they would not have won the commodities which the merchants and rulers at home wanted. From the east came works of art whose profound influence we shall discuss later. Of more immediate importance would have been the supply of metal: iron and copper, which were in particular demand in Greece, where the city states or kingdoms saw the need for increasing their force of arms in step with their increasing prosperity and population, and the growing jealousy of any less fortunate neighbours. The Euboeans, whose merchants had first sought out these new sources of metals for the Greek worlds, were also the first to precipitate conflict on a national scale in the late-eighth-century 'Lelantine War' which provoked other local rivalries in homeland Greece and between the Euboean cities' trading partners in East Greece. The war was conducted mainly still in a pre-hoplite manner, but the new bronze panoplies for the citizen armies may have been in general demand by about 700. Euboea was one of the first areas to take up the new iron metallurgy of the east and had some local resources.[24] There is evidence for bronze casting at Lefkandi (*Fig. 15*) already by about 900.[25] Chalcis in particular held a reputation in antiquity for being the home of various innovations in bronze armour. Her name, the 'brazen town', suggests an earlier association with metal working, but growing demands may have necessitated a search for new sources of material. We cannot say that metals were the main commodities sought by the Euboeans, but they surely played an important part in trade with the east. The initial voyages were probably casual private ventures which opened a new world to Greek eyes, a world which was rich enough and sufficiently disturbed to give promise of quick and profitable business. In effect the new trade route provided something of an escape or outlet to the easterners as well as a source of wealth and inspiration to the Greeks.

When the Euboeans first came to Al Mina the town must have lain under the suzerainty of one of the minor Aramaean kingdoms whose peoples had pushed into this area earlier in the first millennium BC. Beyond lay the neo-Hittite kingdoms, by this time culturally similar to the Aramaean, so this was an area affected by both Anatolian and Semitic traditions, from north and south. The northern carried knowledge of metals and their sources; the southern, with the Phoenician of the coast, an amalgam of Egyptianizing arts and crafts. Farther off to the north-east lay the kingdom of Urartu (Armenia, up to the Caspian), a land rich in metals and in its period of greatest power, in the first half of the eighth century, thrusting towards the Mediterranean coast; and the homeland of Assyria, whose empire later in the eighth century was to embrace the whole coastal region and Cyprus. It has not always proved easy to disentangle the varied artistic traditions in metalwork – Aramaean and neo-Hittite (broadly 'north Syrian'), Urartian and Assyrian – in identifying the sources of objects and techniques which reached the Greek world. But it is clear that from the start the Greeks had access to rich supplies of metalwork, and the passages of arms inland rarely if at all inhibited the flow of goods, and certainly did not prevent the establishment of what was to be a long-lived trading post.

The town at Al Mina was not, of course, wholly Greek. It is likely that there was already a settlement there of some kind, which only assumed real importance as an emporium when the Greeks began to visit the port and established a small community there. The non-Greek pottery from Al Mina may give us some idea both of the antiquity of the settlement and of the culture of the people who admitted the Greeks. The latter is more easily judged, for the pottery is plain or very simply decorated, and there is nothing like the rapid stylistic and decorative development to be observed that there is in the Greek wares. Also, for all their careful excavation, the chronology of various comparative sites in the east is still the subject of considerable discussion.

A recent study of the non-Greek pottery at Al Mina[26] shows that none of it need be earlier than the mid ninth century. The Greek pottery which was found beside it in the lowest levels can plausibly be dated around 800 or before, so that occupation here

15 Clay mould for the leg of a bronze tripod from Lefkandi; 10th c. (Eretria Mus.)

before the arrival of the Greeks may have been but slight. Through the eighth century the volume of non-Greek pottery seems to match that of the Greek. All must have been for daily use, since there was no organized trade in Greek pottery at this time, but the majority of the minor objects found are not Greek. The Greek community may therefore have been a minority, although it seems to have been the direct cause of the port's prosperity, if not of its existence. Most of the non-Greek pottery in our first period has a marked Cypriot appearance, but other wares which were current in Phoenicia and North Palestine are well represented. The Cypriots were trading freely with this coast, and part of the population of Al Mina is likely to have been Cypriot, making its own vases there, or near by, in a Cypriot style.

The Greek pottery found in Cyprus itself – mainly in the coastal towns – is of much the same sources and in much the same proportions as that at Al Mina in these years. The main difference lies in the number of Athenian vases which arrived in Cyprus already before about 750 and which testify to a brief but active period of direct Athenian interest in the east.[27] There is no question yet of new Greek settlement there, but the Phoenicians had become well established on the island, and the fact that they were settling in Kition in the ninth century, at about the time the Greeks were reaching the eastern mainland of Syria, may not be merely coincidental.

In 743 the Assyrian king, Tiglath-pileser III, broke Urartian power in the west, and by the end of the century Assyrian rule had spread over Syria and Cilicia, to Cyprus in the west, to Palestine in the south. Cyprus logically formed part of any empire embracing North Syria and Cilicia. At Al Mina Woolley declared that his Level VIII bore almost exclusively Cypriot pottery, but there are many Greek sherds from the site labelled Level VIII, and, although the Cypriot element at Al Mina may have been considerable in the eighth century, Level VIII certainly ends earlier than 709, the year of the first record of Cypriot submission to Assyria. The transition from Level VIII to Level VII is marked by extensive repairs, which may relate to Assyrian action against rebels in Syria about 720, which could have disturbed relations with Cyprus. It might be suspected that it was the Cypriots who led the Greeks to Al Mina, and the quantity of eighth-century Greek pottery found in the island shows the extent of Greek interest there. They must certainly have travelled via Cyprus. Assyrian domination had no adverse effect on Greek trade. The Greek pottery can be dated by external evidence and clearly continues in quantity at Al Mina to the end of the eighth century.

Before we consider more closely the end of our first period at Al Mina, marked by the abandonment – though brief – of the houses of Level VII, and followed by the new planning of Level VI, we may review what other evidence there is for the Greeks in the Near East in these years.[28] Clearly Al Mina was not the only port

which attracted Greeks. Two smaller coastal sites just to the south
were also being visited by Greeks in the second half of the eighth
century. One is the Greek Posideion (another post-Trojan war
foundation to later writers), whose name lingers in the modern
Ras el Basit, and the other is Tell Sukas, which lies on a low
promontory between two good anchorages.[29]

Through Al Mina and these other ports some Greek pottery
passed to the hinterland and to the south, in the hands either of
Greeks or of local traders. Scraps are reported from various sites in
the Amq plain behind Al Mina. The distinctive cups with pendent
semicircles (our group 4, above) have been found at some six
other sites in Syria, and two in Palestine.[30] Other Geometric vases,
or fragments of them, have been found in Syria at Hama and Catal
Hüyük; in Assyria at Nineveh (reported, not published); near
Sidon; in Palestine at Megiddo, Samaria, and Tell abu Hawam.
These include Athenian vases of the first half of the eighth century
(as in Cyprus) and Euboean or Cycladic. There is no archaeological evidence for any profound influence on the local arts which
might be attributed to these casual contacts with Greek things.
Only in pottery had the Greeks anything to teach, and the Near
Easterner (outside Cyprus, where there were both imports and
local Greek production in a Greek Geometric manner) was not
much interested in elaborately decorated vases.[31]

Assyrian records of dealings with the Greeks are sparse but
intriguing. In the 730s one of their agents on the Phoenician coast
reports raids by 'Ionians' (see below), which suggest that some of
the newcomers to eastern seas were not beyond practising the
piratic ways of the Aegean. Farther south, at Ashdod, Assyrian
records tell of a Yamani who was put up as king by rebels. Sargon
crushed the revolt in 712, and Yamani fled to Egypt and Nubia,
where he was handed over to Sargon by King Shabako. Yaman
was the Assyrian spelling for the familiar Yawan – the Ionians of
the Bible. Though they used a separate name for Cyprus – Iadnana
– it seems probable that the easterners were none too careful in
their use of the term Yamani, and there is evidence that it could be
applied also to a Cypriot or to Anatolian peoples whom they met
beside the Greeks.[32]

To the north, in Cilicia, the evidence is yet stronger, and Greek
Geometric pottery has been found in several places, notably Mersin[33] and, even more important, Tarsus, at both of which sites the
pendent-semicircle cups appear.[34] Local sources of iron may have
been one of the attractions of the area.[35] Tarsus is another of these
sites which had been settled by the Greeks for a short while in the
Late Mycenaean period and then returned to in the Geometric
period some 400 years later. The Greek pottery from Tarsus
suggests that there may have been some Greeks admitted there as
early as they were at Al Mina. The types of Greek and other
pottery found seem to be much as at Al Mina, with more local
Cilician wares. The East Greek, probably Rhodian, element,

which appears slight and late in the first period at Al Mina, may have been somewhat stronger at Tarsus.

Cilicia, with Syria, had fallen to the Assyrian king Sargon after his accession in 720. Twenty-four years later the Assyrian governor in Cilicia revolted, the Greeks at Tarsus rose in arms with him, and beside them, perhaps, the Greeks of Injira (if this is Greek Anchiale). Sennacherib, who had come to the Assyrian throne in 705, crushed the revolt and destroyed the city of Tarsus. This we know from Assyrian records, and a destruction level at Tarsus was readily distinguished by the excavators. Later records speak of a sea battle between Assyrians and Ionians,[36] and this may have happened in the course of the campaign. Even if the revolt did not spread as far as Al Mina, it seems likely that the Assyrians would hardly look with favour on Greek or Cypriot under-takings; and as the pottery evidence at Al Mina suggests that the abandonment of the Level vii houses fell at about this date, I am inclined to associate this break in the site's history with the events which led to the destruction of Tarsus in 696.[37] Two years later Sennacherib had 'Ionian' and Phoenician sailors working for him at Nineveh.[38]

AL MINA: THE SECOND PERIOD, TO 600 BC

The second phase of our story of the Greeks in the east is again best represented archaeologically at Al Mina, in the excavated Levels vi and v. The architectural history of the period has already been discussed. The continuity in the style of the Greek pottery found before and after this break at the start of the seventh century shows that the break was not of long duration. But it was virtually a new town which arose over the ruins of the old, barely acknowledging the lines of the earlier roadways and the limits of individual properties. Levels vi and v at Al Mina bring us through the period of Assyrian domination to its collapse and the spread of the new Babylonian empire to the shores of the Mediterranean.

The Greek pottery seems now to form a more significant proportion of all the pottery found, and is perhaps the major part of it. This would suggest that the Greeks were beginning to command the trade which passed through the port rather than share it with the Cypriots, and Woolley notes that although there is still a certain amount of Cypriot pottery in Level vi, it fails in Level v. The Greek vase fragments will again help us to identify the homes of the Greeks mainly concerned in the eastern trade, for although some fine Greek wares (such as Corinthian) might have been carried by any Greek traders, it is still too early to speak of a serious or deliberate trade in decorated pottery as such. Woolley writes that 'Lesbian *bucchero* was favoured by one or two dealers, and one at least kept . . . Chiote pottery'. These finds, if significant at all, may rather suggest the nationality of the warehouse keep-ers, for the distribution of decorated Greek pottery in the Near

16 East Greek 'bird bowl';
7th c. (Oxford 1928.313;
W. 14 cm)

East in the seventh century presents if anything a poorer picture than it does in the eighth.

The main classes of pottery from Al Mina in the seventh century are:[39]

1. *Euboean* imitations of Protocorinthian cups – our group 2 above. Sufficient fragments are labelled 'Levels VI–VII' or 'Level VI' to suggest that this ware may still have been arriving.

2. *Corinthian.* Fine Protocorinthian *aryballoi* and cups appear now in some quantity. The earliest may be as early as the first quarter of the seventh century, and the flow continues uninterrupted to near the end of the century.

3. *Athenian or Euboean.* Scraps of storage jars, called 'SOS amphorae' from the patterns on their necks (as *Fig. 2*).[40]

4. *Argive* (?). Some unusual polychrome fragments[41] are similar to fragments from the sanctuary of Hera near Argos, but also to pottery found in the *Euboean* colony of Cumae in Italy, and even to styles current in Megara's Sicilian colony.

5. *East Greek.* There are several important types:
   (a) 'Bird bowls': shallow cups of fine fabric, decorated with

17 East Greek 'bird oinochoe' from Crete;
7th c. (Munich 455; H. 22 cm)

simple Geometric patterns. Rhodes must have been an important centre of production, but there were factories elsewhere for
this long-popular ware (*Fig. 16*).[42]

(b) 'Bird *oenochoai*': jugs related to the last for their decoration,
but they do not long survive the middle of the seventh century
on other sites. Again, Rhodes is an important centre, but they
were made also in Samos, Chios, and perhaps elsewhere (*Fig.
17*). The Al Mina jugs have round mouths, without the trefoil
lip for pouring like many Chian and a few Rhodian.[43]

(c) 'Wild Goat' vases: various shapes decorated with animal
friezes – often of goats – in the style which is adopted in East
Greece by about the middle of the seventh century (*Fig. 18*).
Some of these, particularly the shallow dishes, are clearly Rhodian. Others must be from elsewhere in East Greece – Chios,
Samos, or Miletus. There are no examples with the incised
'black figure' technique which begins to appear on such vases
about 600 BC.

(d)[44] Cups: plain painted cups with reserved stripes at the level
of the handles and the lip: the so-called 'Ionian cups', perhaps
Rhodian.

(e) Polychrome striped vases, mainly fine cups painted black
with thin red and white stripes; certainly Rhodian.

(f) Chian chalices and fragments of other vases with the distinctive Chian white slip.

(g) 'Lesbian' *bucchero* is mentioned by Woolley, but none has
been published; and Lesbos may not have been the only place in
Aeolis where grey *bucchero* was made in the seventh century.

It is clear from this survey that most of the Greek pottery arriving
at Al Mina in the seventh century is coming from parts of Greece
other than those which served the Greeks living there in the eighth
century. The Euboean interest has virtually disappeared. The
years around 700 may have seen the last or most decisive of the
struggles between the two main Euboean cities, Eretria and Chalcis (the so-called Lelantine War). The balance of trade and colonization interest in the two cities probably changed, and it is at
Eretria, not (so far) Chalcis, that we find the type of vase still
carried to Al Mina; but this may mean nothing. Both cities retire
from the arena for many years. The islanders of the Cyclades who
came with the Euboeans are also seen no more, although there are
scraps of one of the distinctive island wares of the earliest seventh
century at Al Mina.[45]

In their place we find Corinthian and East Greek vases. The
evidence of the Corinthian pottery must be treated with caution.
It was of the highest quality, worth possessing and carrying for its
own sake by any Greek, and need not mean the active participation of Corinthian traders in the east. The vases have been found
all over the Greek world – and beyond it – and do not present any
very clear pattern of specifically Corinthian trade and interest.

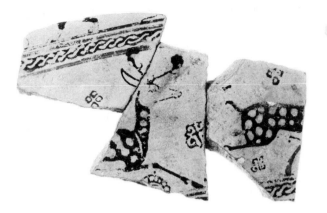

18 East Greek Wild Goat fragments from Al Mina; late 7th c. (Oxford 1954.290, 294)

The East Greeks, themselves active producers of decorated pottery, were glad enough at times to use this most elegant of all seventh-century Greek wares. But this alone can hardly explain the quantity of Corinthian pottery at Al Mina, especially early in the century; and if not necessarily for Corinthians, we should look for Greeks closely connected with Corinth. I suspect the Aeginetans, who at home nearly always used Corinthian vases, having no local potteries for fine vases. I say 'nearly always', for excavations on Aegina show that Athenian and Argive vases were also imported for use. Athenian, and perhaps Argive too, are the only other recognizable scraps of mainland Greek pottery at Al Mina (3 and 4 above). Finds on Aegina itself indicate an interest in eastern matters throughout the seventh century.[46]

The leading part was now clearly played by East Greeks. They had already been seen in Al Mina in the later eighth century, and it was on these eastern routes that the Samians and Milesians met the Euboeans and became involved in their rivalries. We can certainly identify Rhodian pottery, and Chios, Samos, and perhaps Lesbos are also represented. Miletus clearly should be also, from what we know of her other enterprises in the seventh century, but we still know too little about Milesian pottery. When we know more, it seems likely that the Milesian share will be recognized at the expense of the Rhodian. This is historically the more likely, and it is interesting that the earliest East Greek pottery at Naucratis in Egypt (see Chapter 4) is very like the latest at Al Mina, and at Naucratis there is every reason to look for the Milesians. Rhodian pottery may have been used and carried by East Greek states much as Corinthian was by mainland Greeks. The island's role in the expansion of Greek interests in the seventh century has perhaps been exaggerated. It is remarkable how very few of the finest 'Wild Goat' vases have been found in the otherwise prolific cemeteries of Rhodes.

The latest datable pottery from this second main period at Al Mina is of about 600 BC, and thereafter the evidence for occupation becomes very slight. There are fragments of pottery, East

Greek and Athenian, from Al Mina, and especially from Sabouni,
the hill town associated with the port, of the middle decades of the
century; but it is not until the last quarter of the century that Greek
vases appear again in quantity. What is the reason for this break?
At the end of the seventh century the Assyrian empire fell to
Babylon, and in the early years of the sixth Nebuchadrezzar II
extended this empire to the coast of the Mediterranean. If the
break in Al Mina's archaeological record is not wholly illusory, it
may be connected in some way with this shift of power. And for
the continuance of trade with Greeks through the Phoenician port
of Tyre in the early sixth century we have the record of Ezekiel
(27,13), which also reflects on the character of the commerce –
slaves and bronzes – 'Jawan ("Ionians"), Tubal (north Cilicia) and
Meshech (Phrygia), they were thy merchants: they traded the
persons of men and vessels of brass in thy market.'

Of the other eastern sites occupied by Greeks, Tarsus revived as
quickly after 696 BC as did Al Mina, and except for a relative lack
of Corinthian pottery, its record through the seventh century
seems much as that of the North Syrian town.[47] Slighter evidence
of Greek interest, though not settlement,[48] is found elsewhere in
Cilicia (Mersin, Sakjegözü, and minor sites), Syria (Catal Hüyük,
Zinjirli),at Babylon, and in Palestine (Tell abu Hawam). The
pottery, as at Al Mina, is nearly all East Greek and Corinthian, as
are the imports in Cyprus in the seventh century. The foundations
from Rhodes of Phaselis and Soloi, on the south coast of Asia
Minor, may date to the earlier seventh century, but there is no
archaeological evidence for this, unless it is seen for the latter in
the quantity of Rhodian pottery reaching nearby Tarsus.[49]

There is a little evidence too for Greek mercenaries in the east in
the seventh century. Soldiers dressed like Greek hoplites appear in
the siege scene on a silver bowl found in Cyprus (Amathus) but
probably of seventh-century Phoenician workmanship (*Fig. 19*).[50]
Unfortunately the 'Ionian warriors' which some have detected on

20 Bronze shield from
Carchemish; 7th c.
(London WA; Diam. 70 cm)

Assyrian reliefs are certainly easterners, and the scrap of what
might be a Greek helmet shown on a painting from Til Barsip[51] is
inadequate evidence for any Assyrian representations of Greek
soldiers. From the ruins of Carchemish, overthrown by the
Babylonians in 605, came one Greek greave and a shield (*Fig. 20*)
with decoration of concentric friezes of animals and a central
gorgon's head.[52] This is likely to be Greek work of the mid
seventh century or a little later, and a similar, rather finer example
has been found at Olympia. It is probable, however, that the
shield was carried by a Greek serving not the Assyrian or Babylonian king, but the Egyptian king Necho who had occupied Carchemish.

A site near Ashdod and just south of Tel Aviv (Mezad
Hashavyahu) is thought by its recent excavators[53] to have included a settlement of Greek mercenaries, paid off by the Egyptian Psammetichos I. It is fortified, and the East Greek pottery
there is all of the end of the seventh century. It is suggested that it
was abandoned in the face of Necho's invasion in 609; but might
not these be Necho's Greeks, ousted by Babylonians (see p. 115)?

THE SIXTH CENTURY

Greek trading on the Syrian and Phoenician coast south of Al
Mina in the first half of the sixth century must have been tolerated,

or even sponsored by the Babylonians, possibly to spite the more southerly Phoenicians whose capital city Tyre never fell to them. At Tell Sukas, for instance, the main period of prosperity begins by about 600 and the excavators detect Greek influence in the architecture of a small sanctuary there, identified by the Greeks as of Helios. Much of the pottery is East Greek, with some Athenian, but Cypriot is also well in evidence. The site suffered more than one destruction in the sixth century but real decline and interruption in the arrival of Greek pottery happen only in the early fifth century.[54]

There is a profound discrepancy between the history of these sites and that of Al Mina, which declined on the approach of the Babylonians and only revived under the Persians. It may be that the new overlords found it expedient that the Greeks should continue their trading activities at Tell Sukas rather than Al Mina, but that the Greeks returned to the more favourable port as soon as they were able. Or it might mean that in this period there was more interest in direct trade with central Syria, and less with the remoter centres also served by Al Mina. The relatively greater prosperity of the Phoenician cities on this coast in all periods is no reflection upon the importance of Al Mina as the one entrepot manned and favoured by Greeks for trade with sources beyond the coastal strip.

There are very few other finds of Greek pottery in the Near East for some fifty years after the beginning of the sixth century – the Babylonian 'interregnum' between the Assyrians and the Persians, and the gap in the Greek record at Al Mina seems matched in Palestine.[55]

The Babylonians themselves employed Greek mercenaries. The Lesbian poet Alcaeus sings for his brother Antimenidas 'fighting beside the Babylonians you accomplished a great feat and delivered them from distress, for you slew a warrior who lacked only one span from five royal cubits in height' (i.e. eight feet four inches tall).[56] There is a hint that he served in the Palestine campaign, at Askalon (taken in 604). At Babylon there is inscriptional evidence for the presence of 'Ionian' craftsmen, but perhaps only from Lycia or Cilicia, to judge from their names,[57] and some mid-sixth-century Athenian pottery which reminds us of the finds at Tell Sukas and scraps at Al Mina (Sabouni).[58]

Babylonian supremacy was shortlived, and a new power from the east takes the stage. The Persian king Cyrus entered Babylon in 539 and succeeded to the dominion over Syria, Phoenicia, and Palestine. He had already subdued the Ionians in East Greece after his defeat of Croesus and the Lydians. Under Persian rule, Greek trade seems to have prospered again in the Near East, after its setback under the Babylonians. In Phoenicia and Palestine there is a little East Greek and Athenian pottery,[59] mainly of the second half of the century, but in the north the Greek port of Al Mina was rebuilt and in operation again before the end of the century. By

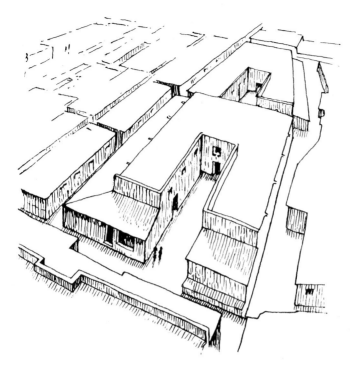

21 Reconstruction of the warehouses at Al Mina

now it seems to be a wholly Greek establishment, and its regeneration can only be understood in the light of positive encouragement of the Greek traders by the Persians. The new town at Al Mina (Level IV) was laid out in a quite new plan and style. The buildings or warehouses are grouped in large rectangular blocks, and some approach the form, around a courtyard open on one side, which appears in a later stage of the town's history (Fig. 21).[60] Al Mina was to suffer two more changes in its plan, after fires, but despite these setbacks its prosperity was uninterrupted until its importance was eclipsed by the foundation of Seleucia, four miles to the north, in 301 BC.

For the identity of the Greeks now dealing with Al Mina we can no longer rely on the sort of archaeological evidence which has served us before. Athenian pottery had won all markets now, and finds of decorated Athenian vases anywhere in the Greek world or outside it do not imply the active interest there of Athenians rather than other Greeks. In view of East Greek and especially Ionian relations with Persia, and the analogous record of Naucratis in Egypt, we may reasonably suppose that the East Greeks still ran most of the trade. From the end of the sixth century, the Greek decorated pottery at Al Mina is all Athenian, most of it of poor quality, for an uncritical market, it would seem. There are still, of course, Cypriot objects, and some minor trinkets from Phoenicia. Local or native wares are still in evidence and are profoundly influenced, usually for the better, by the quality of the Greek

22 Marble sphinx from Al Mina; about 470 BC. (Oxford 1938.323; L. 17·5 cm)

imports. In general it may be said that the greater part of the fine pottery was Greek, but that the minor objects were more typical of the finds in any other Near Eastern port or city with extensive overseas connections. By now, of course, the Athenian pottery was being imported for its own sake, and it appears with growing frequency on many Near Eastern sites. To confine our attention only to the years after the resumption of trade through Al Mina and before the end of the Persian Wars in 479 BC, we find Athenian pottery at some half-dozen sites in North Syria, the remotest being at Carchemish, some at Babylon, and in somewhat greater quantity in Palestine, from Tell abu Hawam in the north (near Haifa) to Tell Jemmeh in the south. It is invariably bad and late black-figure, the poorest, almost mass-produced Athenian products. Standards improve a little in the fifth century. I illustrate here one Greek *objet d'art*, rather later in date, which had passed to Al Mina, because it has not hitherto been published and is of some intrinsic interest. It is the fragmentary statuette of a seated sphinx (now in Oxford), carved in fine white marble (*Fig. 22*). The work and finish are exquisite. Comparisons with similar statuary in Greece, such as the sphinx from Aegina or the sphinx vase by the potter Sotades suggest a date about 470. It may have been in Al Mina only to delight a Greek resident agent, but the Persians had already acquired a taste for Greek works of art, for all the poverty of much of the Athenian pottery which was brought to Al Mina.

Few Greek coins have so far been found on Near Eastern sites before 480 BC.[61] Most are Athenian or Aeginetan issues of the late sixth or early fifth century, but an important hoard from Ras Shamra has a preponderance of Thracian issues, and Thracian coins are otherwise more common than one might expect. The same phenomenon is true of finds in Egypt of this date (see p. 130). There are also a few Ionian and Cypriot coins. At Persepolis a number of coins were found in association with the foundation deposits for the Hall, or 'Apadana', of Darius (511 BC); there are eight Lydian staters (of Croesus), and in silver one Aeginetan, one Thracian, and three Cypriot pieces.[62]

We shall have no more to say of the fortunes of the Greeks in Syria and Palestine in the fifth century, except in so far as Greek relations with the Persians affect this area. It was the Greeks of Ionia who first had to deal with the Persians and it is to them and to their experience of the native kingdoms in Anatolia that we shall return later in this chapter.

Eastern Influence in Greece

To complete the picture, something must be said of the effects in Greece of this lively intercourse and trade with the Near East, at least as they are seen by the archaeologist. The part the east played in inspiring new ideas in religious, literary, or scientific matters cannot be discussed here.[63] Nor, in summarizing the often superficial influence of oriental motifs in Greek art, can we pay adequate attention to the native Greek contribution, and to the way the Greeks translated and adapted what they borrowed into an art unparalleled in any Near Eastern land. The account is thus bound to be unbalanced, and the reader must bear in mind the steady evolution of the Greeks, their institutions, and their art, which the east may have accelerated or conditioned. The superior attitude of the Greeks to the barbarian and their consciousness of their debt to him and of the alchemy of their own skills, died hard. 'Whenever Greeks borrow anything from non-Greeks, they finally carry it to a higher perfection' – Plato.[64]

This, then, can be no more than a survey of the likely media and motifs in which the archaeologist can observe the influence of the east in Greece – an influence stimulated in the first place by the Greeks themselves in their visits to the east, and not vice versa. There are three aspects of the problem: the actual imported objects; the apparent influence of eastern artists who came to Greece, worked and taught there – the foreign *demioergoi* mentioned by Homer,[65] and the Greek copying and adaptation of eastern objects and decoration. Somewhere, at some time in the long history of the Near East, a parallel can be found for any artistic motif under the sun, be it naturalistic or abstract. Comparisons can only profitably be drawn if a plausible relationship in time and a means of transmission can be demonstrated. Sometimes vital links are missing, although the debt seems direct and certain. At all times it must be remembered that this was not Greece's first contact with the east, and that some motifs or forms may well have survived from the Bronze Age or have been rediscovered.

The different sources of the oriental influences upon Greece are more complicated than the geography of the area might suggest. The following may be distinguished:

1. *North Syrian.* Several sites in North Syria and Cilicia bear witness to an art which seems to owe more to earlier Hittite styles than to those of the east or south (Aramaean). It is best known from its relief sculptures, and the most important sites are Carchemish, Zinjirli, Sakjegözü, and Malatya. Most of the relevant works were executed before or in the eighth century BC but were still visible in the seventh.[66]

2. *Urartian.* Armenia was an important centre of metal-working, and the rich finds from sites near Lake Van often have close kin in Greece.[67] Urartu invaded the north Syrian states several times in the first half of the eighth century but may never have enjoyed direct rule over any part of the Mediterranean coast.

3. *Assyrian.* The art of Assyria is better known from works of sculpture, especially reliefs, than bronzes or other minor objects.[68] An important source of Assyrian decorative motifs for the Greeks

may have been textiles, which have of course perished. Assyrian influence cannot be earlier than the seventh century; indeed, most is of the mid or late seventh century.

4. *Phoenician.* The ivories from Phoenician sites, and those carried off as loot to Assyria, reveal an amalgam of Near Eastern and Egyptian forms. The ivories[69] and some bronzes are the most important products for us, but the other minor objects reflect the same often ill-welded mixture of motifs.

5. *Cypriot* art offers much that was more at home on the mainland to the east, and little of notable originality, except for a remarkable series of figure-decorated vases[70] in a style apparently unacceptable to the Greeks, and certainly ignored by them. The island was in continuous contact with Greeks in the Early Iron Age. This is reflected by minor imports and unimportant borrowings. Its main function may have been as purveyor of Phoenician motifs and objects to the west, and there were important Phoenician cities established on the island by the ninth century.[71]

The Phrygian, Lydian, and later Persian contributions will find their places later in this chapter.

The distribution of oriental ideas and goods in the Greek world will become apparent in the following pages. Our best sources are sanctuaries, with their richness of dedications, and the occasional well-furnished tomb. There is no evidence that particular cities or sites had any special relationship with a particular area in the near east, except where propinquity counted – with east Greece and the Anatolian states. The principal route of entry must have been from the Syro–Phoenician coast, past Cyprus and Rhodes. Overland routes in Anatolia are important for our understanding of the development of some aspects of Phrygian and Lydian cultures, but only at second hand for Greek orientalizing. And the Black Sea route does not demonstrably carry goods from the Mesopotamia–Persia area. Within Greece the disparity of the record in orientalia between different sites – ivories here, bronzes there – must be accounted for in part by the accidents of excavation, in part by the character of the presiding deity in sanctuaries since this determines the style of dedication – for a warrior god or a fertility goddess, to take extreme examples.

IMMIGRANTS

Technical innovations which suggest instruction by immigrant craftsmen will be mentioned in later sections, but there are a few clear instances of immigrant artists and others whose work was distinctive although their influence was limited.[72] They are worth discussing on their own: most are in Crete.

1. The late ninth century saw the arrival in Knossos of metalsmiths skilled in working gold filigree and granulation, and

23 Gold pendant from Teke, Knossos; 9th c. (Heraklion Mus.; W. 5·5 cm)

24 Design on a bronze quiver from Fortetsa, Knossos; 8th c. (Heraklion Mus.)

in cutting hard stones – techniques forgotten in Greece since the Bronze Age. They seem to have adopted a cleared Minoan tholos tomb as their family vault and consecrated it in the eastern manner by burying two crocks of gold just inside the door. These contained working material in the form of dumps and bars, fine gold jewellery involving crescent motifs (*Fig. 23*), human figures and crystal inlays, and an impressed gold band. The style of work is met in later jewellery from Knossos and the Idaean Cave and on decorated bronzes – a belt (*Fig. 61*) and quiver (*Fig. 24*). From their own 'vault', at the end of the eighth century, comes more figure work in gold which we may relate to hammered bronze statuettes of deities found in a small temple at Dreros. These seem to mark the end of their career and their techniques were not learnt by other Cretan studios.[73] Much of their early work is related to gold from Tell Halaf in Mesopotamia, a site overwhelmed by the Assyrians in 808, but the general style may prove Phoenician and even Cyprus could prove to be the immediate source for Crete. However, the well-excavated island of Cyprus has yet to yield much of relevant style and date to demonstrate this.

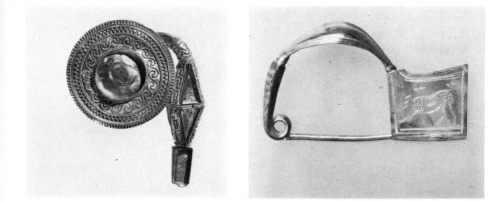

25 Gold pendant and fibula from Attica (London 1960.11-1.18 and 46; Diam. 2·9 cm; L. 6 cm)

2. Gold jewellery, broadly similar in style but by no means identical, was being made in Attica in the first half of the eighth century, and seems to represent the work of a similar immigrant group which enjoyed a shorter career than that at Knossos (*Fig. 25*).[74] It was probably also responsible for the impressed gold bands with animal decoration (see below, and *Fig. 65*).[75]

3. North Syrian metalworkers reached Crete perhaps as early as the Knossos goldsmiths and established a strong tradition for beaten metalwork, which in its beginnings is quite oriental but becomes progressively more hellenized.[76] One of the earliest works, surely by an eastern hand, but, it seems, made to serve or illustrate a Cretan cult, is a bronze tympanum (like a tambourine) from the Idaean Cave in Crete (*Fig. 26*).[77] The scene on it shows a god striding over a bull and swinging a lion above his head. At either side winged men clash cymbals. The style is eastern, so are the god on a bull and winged figures, but the latter clash their cymbals in a Greek manner and the god wears non-oriental (though perhaps Cypriot) bloomers. The piece was dedicated in a cave where the infant Zeus was said to have been hidden from his father, and where his attendants clashed shields and – no doubt – cymbals (his mother Rhea's instruments) to drown his cries. In the same style are bronzes from Olympia and Dodona in Greece, and two fine cauldron stands and a bowl found in Etruscan graves.[78] We cannot say whether these last were brought there from Crete, or whether eastern craftsmen travelled farther still. The former is the more probable, and some motifs are matched on Cretan vases, for example, the bee-like blossoms. Although the style of these objects is wholly eastern, no work from the same school has yet been found outside Greece and Etruria.

In a related style are the great conical shields with animal-head bosses which were also made for the Idaean Cave (as *Fig. 27*), but have been found elsewhere in Crete, and travelled even to Delphi, Dodona, and Miletus.[79] These span the eighth century and the first half of the seventh, and they show well the progressive

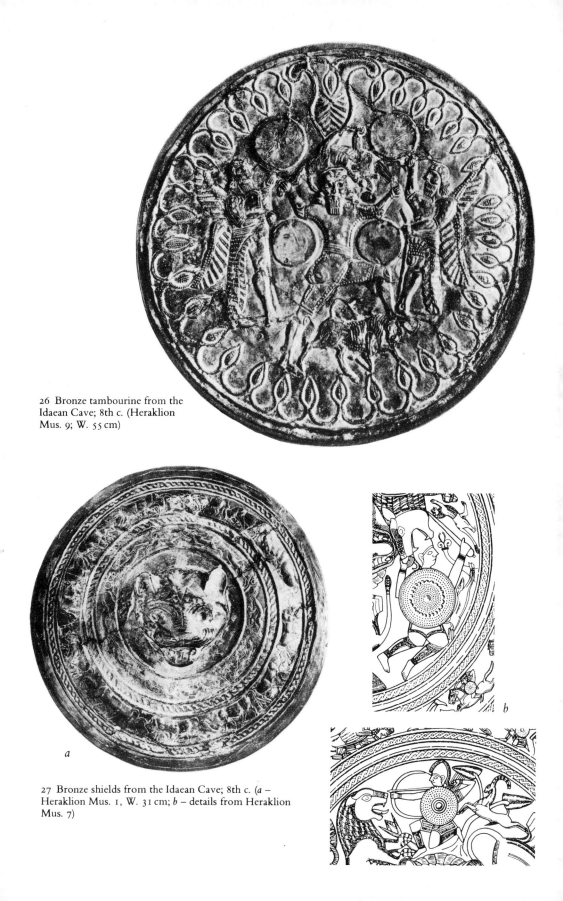

26 Bronze tambourine from the Idaean Cave; 8th c. (Heraklion Mus. 9; W. 55 cm)

a

b

27 Bronze shields from the Idaean Cave; 8th c. (*a* – Heraklion Mus. 1, W. 31 cm; *b* – details from Heraklion Mus. 7)

28 Restoration of a bronze head vase
from the Idaean Cave; 7th c. (Oxford
and Heraklion Mus.; H. about 18 cm)

hellenization of the style and motifs – generally animal friezes or groups with monsters. This type of shield was known in Assyria and in Urartu, for we see it in a Urartian temple at Musasir, which was shown on an Assyrian relief depicting the sack of the town.[80] In the same Cretan workshop and in the same technique was made the bronze head-vase shown in *Fig. 28* (in Oxford; the lip and handle restored in the drawing). The conception is Greek, the execution and details eastern.[81]

4. During the first half of the seventh century sites in south central Crete (notably Afrati) yield several objects in clay which imitate North Syrian objects in other materials – stone oil bowls fed by lion-head spouts (a clay copy, *Fig. 29*),[82] bronze cauldrons with ring handles or with griffin head attachments (*Fig. 30*) of the type by then current and being imitated in bronze in other parts of Greece but not Crete[83] (see below) – and there are some figure motifs on vases which may own the same inspiration. Not a matter of immigrant craftsmen, then, or imitation of common imports (not found), but perhaps of the arrival of foreigners who were to some degree able to impose their taste on local studios. A further indication of this may be the fact that many cremation burials at Afrati from now on are of a distinctive type, with urns set on dishes and covered by inverted pots, matched closely only in the Iron Age cemetery of Carchemish on the Euphrates (*Fig. 31*). It is perhaps right to associate with this immigration the evidence of authors and epigraphy which places the first codification of laws in Greece in Crete and in this period, since written laws were regular in the east and there is much in Greek law which recalls the east.[84]

It should be possible in time to isolate the works and influence of other immigrant craftsmen in Greece, and there will be hints of

29 Cretan clay bowl; 7th c. (Heidelberg 59/1; W. 15·7 cm)

30 Clay bowl from Arkades; 7th c. (Heraklion Mus.; H. 21 cm)

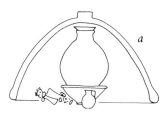

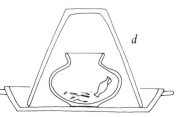

31 Drawings of 7th-c graves at Carchemish (a, b) and Arkades (c, d)

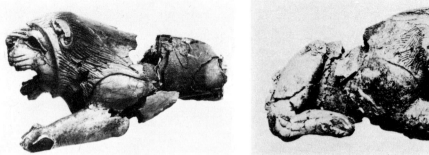

32 Ivory lion from Thasos; 7th c. (Thasos Mus. 1512; L. 10 cm)

33 Ivory lion from Zinjirli; 7th c. (L. 12·5 cm)

this in the following paragraphs, where the different crafts and subjects are taken in turn.

IVORY WORK

Eastern ivories have been found in Greece in Samos, Smyrna, Erythrae, Ephesus, Thasos (*Fig. 32*, cf. *33*), Crete, Rhodes, and Athens.[85] Many may have arrived before 700 BC. Syria was still an important source of elephant ivory at this time, and the tusks found at Al Mina may reflect the trade in the raw material which served the many Greek schools of ivory-workers of the seventh century.[86]

In a grave at Athens, which can be dated by the pottery found in it to the third quarter of the eighth century, was a group of five nude female figures[87] (the largest, *Fig. 34*) which clearly imitate the eastern 'Astarte' type of the nude fertility goddess (*Fig. 35*, from Nimrud). They are imbued with a strength and sense of form which reveals a Greek hand, working still within the confines of Geometric convention but in a technique learned from

34 Ivory girl from Athens; about 750–725 BC. (Athens NM 776; H. 24 cm)

35 Ivory girl from Nimrud; 8th c. (London WA 118102; H. 13·2 cm)

36 Ivory seal from Ephesus; 7th c. (Istanbul Mus.; H. 3·3 cm)

37 Ivory head from Perachora; about 700 B C. (Athens N M 16520; H. 4 cm)

38 Ivory head from Corfu; 7th c. (Corfu Mus. M R 710)

39 Ivory man with lion from Delphi; 7th c. (Delphi Mus.; H. 24 cm)

an eastern craftsman working in Athens, as likely as not. This will be the earliest of these new schools. In the Peloponnese others supplied votives in ivory and bone for the temple of Artemis Orthia at Sparta[88] and the temple of Hera at Perachora[89] (near Corinth). The figurines are more hellenized adaptations now, and some new forms appear. Ivory seals, with their backs carved as recumbent animals, resemble eastern ivory groups, most of which did not serve as seals although one of apparently Syrian origin, with two lions, reached Samos.[90] Disc seals were worn as pendants or perhaps on bracelets. These are to be found in other parts of Greece too, from Ithaca to the Aegean islands.[91] Among the minor objects in bone and ivory we may pick out plaque inlays and the 'spectacle'-shaped brooches which imitate a metal form. These are decorated with simple compass-cut circles or more elaborate cable patterns of exactly the types which we met on eastern ivories and plaques.[92]

In East Greece there were other ivory workers who had learned from the east. Among the minor finds from Rhodes and Ephesus we find again the small couchant animals, and there is a ring seal from Ephesus, of Hittite shape (*Fig. 36*), which is almost certainly of Phrygian make.[93] The finest work appears in statuettes of the seventh or earliest sixth centuries (as *Fig. 99*).[94] These match their eastern counterparts in technique and perhaps excel them in artistic quality. There are several from Ephesus, a few on Samos, Chios,[95] and at Smyrna.[96] With them may be associated the schools of ivory workers in Lydia, and perhaps some stray finds in mainland Greece, like a fine head from Perachora[97] near Corinth (*Fig. 37*), one in Corfu (*Fig. 38*)[98] and the god with a lion from Delphi (*Fig. 39*).[99] The last is very like some Assyrian Gilgamesh groups in composition, although in nothing else, and its base carries a pattern met in Lydian, and later East Greek, art.

40 Bronze rider from Samos; 7th c. (Samos Mus. B 452; H. 9·2 cm)

BRONZE WORK

Here the material is bewildering in its variety, but some sources or connections are clear.[100]

We have already noted the bronzes of Cypriot type which reached Crete early in the Iron Age, the immigrant schools in the island, and other early eastern finds in Crete and Attica.

For the eighth century on, the problem of identifying the sources of eastern bronzes and eastern influence in bronze work becomes acute. While a few years ago the kingdom of Urartu was claiming much of the credit, scholars now tend to favour North Syria although evidence for styles of metalwork there in the relevant period is mainly circumstantial.[101] Influence and imports from even farther afield, in Persia, can also now plausibly be argued. Objects may have moved very freely in the Near East, through trade or conquest, and from those that reached or influenced the Greeks it is not necessary to read direct relations between Greece and their assumed place of origin. Already in the Geometric period of the eighth century we find some strange echoes of Caucasian metalwork in Greece, especially in openwork

41 Bronze siren attachments from Olympia; about 700 (Olympia Mus. B27, B28; H. of busts 7·5, 6 cm)

42 Bronze cauldron from
Cumae; 7th c.
(Copenhagen HM 4952;
H. 28 cm)

bronze pendants and some bird figurines on openwork stands.[102]
Their date in the east is not assured, nor is the means of transmission to Greece clear. One of the most striking examples is the
bronze rider with a child, from Samos (*Fig. 40*). It is possible that
the Cimmerians are responsible, but not through their incursions
into Asia Minor so much as round the north shores of the Black
Sea, and there are equally obscure connections with bronzes from
Central Europe. But these are a special case and we have to do
primarily with later bronzes from other areas.

Bronze cauldron attachments, and no doubt the cauldrons
themselves, reached Greece from the east in the first half of the
seventh century, and perhaps a little earlier. Some of these were
copied and adapted to Greek standards and taste. The best known
types are the 'siren' attachments, with a human forepart rising
from a bird's tail and wings which clasp the cauldron beneath the
rim while the heads peer within. They, and their Greek deriva-
tives have been found in Olympia, Delphi, Athens, Boeotia
(Ptoon), Argos, Delos, Rhodes, Cyprus and Etruria.[103] With such
attachments can also be associated the bronze lion's paw feet for
tripods which are found on many of the same sites. These cauldrons reached Phrygia also, as we have seen, but it is unlikely that
the motif or object first became known to the Greeks from that
quarter. There are Urartian and Assyrian versions but it is likely
that the type which most influenced Greece came from North
Syria. *Fig. 41* shows an eastern siren head beside a Greek imitation
which has rejected, or 'geometricized', the soft oriental features.

Another variety has bulls' heads, rising from the wings and tail
or attached on their own. These are found in Olympia, Delphi,
Athens, Amyclae, Argos, Rhodes, Samos, Macedonia, Cumae (in

43 Bronze griffin-bird attachment from Olympia; 7th c. (Athens NM 6147; W. 12·5 cm)

Italy, *Fig. 42*) and Cyprus. It is not the Urartian but the probably North Syrian type which is imported and copied.[104] Less well represented are attachments of similar construction with the fore-parts of griffins (*Fig. 43*) or 'real' bird bodies, from Olympia and Athens.[105]

One other type of cast attachment, all examples of which seem imported, has a whole animal body (bulls, stags, goats, lions and some winged monsters) on stand-plates which are fastened to the shoulder of the vase (*Fig. 44*). These are found in Olympia, Delphi, Athens, Crete, Rhodes, Samos, Argos, Amyclae, Ithaca and Macedonia.[106]

The best known of the cauldron attachments are the griffin heads and necks which are found on many sites in Greece (but not Crete), in Etruria and Cyprus, in the seventh and sixth centuries. The earliest are hammered and only the later series cast (*Fig. 45*; cf. *Fig. 262*) like the attachments already discussed. Early examples of lion heads attached to cauldrons are certainly imported.[107] Some-times the hammered griffin and lion heads are found on the same cauldrons with the sirens (Olympia, *Fig. 46*),[108] but on an example

44 Bronze bull attachment; 7th c. (Providence 36.190; L. 10·5 cm)

from Salamis in Cyprus the sirens are unusual in being hammered
(and janiform, which can be matched in cast specimens) while the
griffins are cast (*Fig. 47*). Not all the elements decorating the
cauldrons found in Greece need to have been put on at one time, or
made in one place, and since none of the griffins have been found
farther east than Cyprus (except for an obviously late arrival in
Persia) it could be argued that the type was developed in Greece,
possibly inspired by attachments like *Fig. 43*. The motif with the
neck tendril or crest and incipient forehead knob is certainly
eastern even though its use there as a cauldron attachment has yet
to be convincingly demonstrated. There were Greek workshops
producing the griffin protomes for Olympia and on Samos,[109] and
already the Greek artist is exercising choice and originality in
handling these new ideas and techniques.

It is interesting to note that the 'orientalizing' workshops in
Greece preferred at first to beat out the metal and trace (hammer)
details on to it, while the imported eastern attachments are usually
cast and have their details incised. It may simply be that the metal
was scarcer in Greece, but the difference in technique is a real one,
and might prove significant in determining the source of eastern
craftsmen in Greece and the degree to which they had to adapt
eastern models and techniques.

45 Bronze griffin head
from a cauldron from
Olympia (Olympia Mus.)

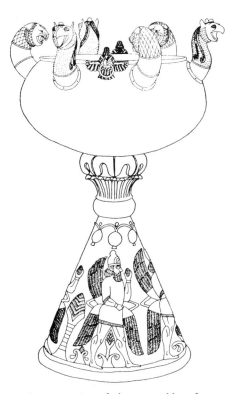

46 Reconstruction of a bronze cauldron from
Olympia; early 7th c. (lip diam. about 65 cm)

47 Bronze cauldron from Salamis, Cyprus; late 8th
c. (Nicosia Mus.; H. 55 + 70 cm)

48 Bronze bowl from Olympia; 7th c. (Oxford G 401; W. 27 cm)

Of other bronze vases we should mention *phialai* or bowls, some with a central boss or navel (mesomphalic). The type is eastern, met in Phrygia, Assyria, and Phoenicia. Decorated examples, generally of Phoenician type and probably of the eighth century, reached Athens, Delphi, Olympia (*Fig. 48*), Delos, and Crete.[110] Those with ribbed floral patterns were often copied in Greece, in bronze and clay.[111] The Persians still used them, and a peculiarly Persian type (*Fig. 49*) is figured on an Athenian vase fragment of the late sixth century (*Fig. 50*).[112] In Greece the shape was generally used for ritual libations, and at Perachora some two hundred thrown into a small pool had probably served some rite of divination and gave omens by sinking or swimming.[113] Animal-head cups are seen on Assyrian reliefs.[114] Bronze examples reached Phrygia[115] (*Fig. 51*) and Samos, but the motif was not copied until the fifth century, then in imitation of Persian models.[116] Arched handles with a floral knob appear on Assyrian bronzes and were copied all over the Greek world. I illustrate a Chian variant on the theme (*Fig. 52*), in which the central bud is replaced by a bearded head peering between the petals, as over a

49 Bronze phiale, perhaps from Deve Huyuk; 5th c. (London WA 108764; W. 18·3 cm)

50 Athenian red figure vase fragment by Euphronios from the Acropolis; late 6th c. (Athens NM, Acr. 176)

51 Bronze lion-head vase from Gordion; late 8th c. (Ankara Mus.)

52 Bronze floral-head handle from Emporio, Chios; 7th c. (Chios Mus.; W. 13·6 cm)

wing collar.[117] The ring handles on metal vases (as *Figs. 97, 98*) may be derived from Urartu, Assyria, or Phrygia. These, and swing handles, were imitated in clay in Greece, and of the latter an original in bronze was found at Al Mina, indicating the route of transmission.[118]

Some other imports or borrowings can be noted. There are North Syrian bronze plaques with elaborate figure decoration in relief (*Fig. 53*),[119] bowls,[120] and on Samos mace heads (*Fig. 54*) and figurines of Syrian and Assyrian origin.[121] Cypriot candelabra arrive in Samos, Athens and Olympia.[122] In Crete North Syrian bronze figurines were imported and inspired a small group of local bronzes at the end of the eighth century.[123] On Samos (*Fig. 55*) and Rhodes, and at Miletus and Eretria (in Euboea), are pieces of relief-decorated harness which seem peculiarly Syrian,[124] and it was an Assyrian type of bit which was adopted in Greece in the seventh century.[125] A bronze camel-rider found in Rhodes (*Fig. 56*) is of eastern origin.[126] From farther east, from Persia and especially Luristan, come pieces of harness, which are copied in Greece, vases in Samos, and a pendant in Crete.[127] None are securely dated, but most are likely to be of the seventh century, some of the eighth. The 'tremolo' technique of decorating metal with a notched line made by rocking a chisel across the surface may have been introduced from the east where, however, the usage of comparable date is on ivory, not bronze.[128]

Other Greek bronze work may reflect eastern types. Some cutout plaques in Crete are reminiscent of plaques from Assyria in their technique.[129] A helmet type with a crest fitted close to the crown seems anticipated in Urartu, but the resemblance may be superficial, and the Greek helmets of this type are not like the Urartian 'caps', but cover the ears and cheeks.[130] Finally we should remark that the incised technique for figures on bronzes –

53 Syrian bronze plaque from Olympia; 7th c. (Olympia Mus. B 1950; H. 15·7 cm)

54 Bronze mace head from Samos; 7th c.
(Samos Mus. B 1076; H. 6·2 cm)

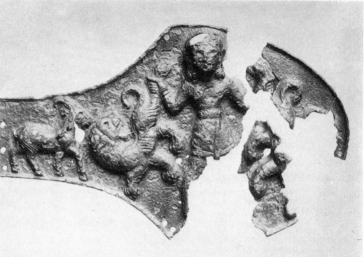

55 Syrian bronze horse
cheek piece from Samos;
7th c. (Samos Mus. B 149;
L. 20 cm)

56 Bronze camel rider
from Rhodes; 7th c.
(London WA 135845,
Bronzes Cat. 222; H.
8 cm)

as on the imported bowl, *Fig. 48*, or the Cretan shields, *Fig. 27* – probably inspired the incised black-figure technique on Greek vases, which lent a new range of detail after the simple Geometric silhouette styles.

MINOR ARTS AND OBJECTS

Here we are led into a great pot-pourri of subjects and materials.

The earliest Greek Iron Age seals are ivory, of the mid ninth century.[131] The stone seals of the eighth and seventh century may be inspired by eastern, mainly Syrian, stamp forms, but one important class, the Island Gems, copies Greek Bronze Age shapes with orientalizing figures.[132] Seventh-century ivory seals have already been mentioned. There was a considerable import of faience scarabs and amulets from the east.[133] A special class of stone scaraboid made in Cilicia in the second half of the eighth century (the Lyre Player group) was well distributed – by the Euboeans, it seems – to Ischia and Etruria, but also to many homeland Greek cities and a little in the Near East (*Fig. 57*).[134] Simpler glass gems of Phoenician type reach Rhodes and other parts of Greece in the first half of the seventh century.[135] Assyrian cylinder seals reached Olympia and Samos, and what may be a North Syrian one Delos.[136] A fresh source of influence appears in the second quarter of the sixth century, probably through the Phoenicians of Cyprus, when Greek studios start cutting scarab seals in harder, semi-precious stones, having learnt the necessary techniques again from the easterners.[137] The eastern cartouche-shaped finger rings are also copied in gold and silver in the seventh and sixth centuries.[138]

Great tridacna shells from the Red Sea were incised with elaborate floral and animal designs, like gorgeous ashtrays or scoops (*Fig. 58*).[139] The distribution of these in the Near East and their style seem to point to Syro–Phoenicia as their source. They may be no earlier than the second half of the seventh century. In Greece they reached Aegina, Smyrna, Samos, Rhodes, Cos, Paros, the Greek site at Naucratis, as well as other Egyptian towns with Greek connections, Cyrene, and sites in Etruria. They provoked no imitations, and resemble nothing more than the gaudy gew-gaws sold to tourists in Levantine bazaars. Ostrich eggs,[140] invariably shattered, have been found on several archaic Greek sites, and were brought from the east or Africa, and there is coral,[141] perhaps from the Red Sea.

There will be more to say of objects in faience in the next chapter, but the material was familiar in Phoenicia, Syria and Cyprus even though it has not always proved easy to determine origins closely. One class of pointed flasks in glazed clay (*Fig. 59*), however, is clearly made in north Syria and is found, mainly in seventh-century contexts, on several East Greek sites, as well as Aegina, Delos, Perachora and in Etruria and Sicily.[142]

57 Lyre-Player group seals of serpentine from Ischia; a Bes-demon – bird with winged disc – lion and bird; second half of 8th c. (Ischia; L. 1·9, 1·9, 1·55 cm)

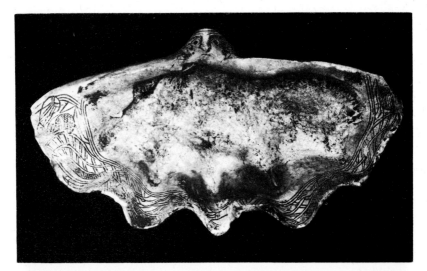

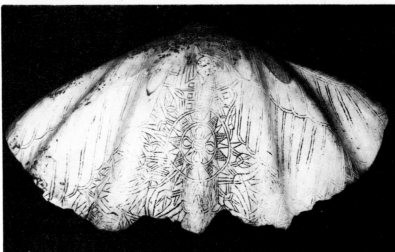

58 Incised tridacna shell from Rhodes; 7th c. (Karlsruhe, Badisches Landesmuseum 63/38a; W. 21·5 cm)

59 Glazed clay flask from Camirus, Rhodes; later 7th c. (London 65.12–14.50; H. 21 cm)

60 Limestone relief from Chania, Crete; a shrine with goddess protected by archers against chariots; 8th c. (Chania Mus. 92; H. 39 cm)

61 Bronze belt from Fortetsa, Knossos; centre piece of warrior and women flanked by defending archers, and chariots; 8th c. (Heraklion Mus.; H. of frieze 6·4 cm; Fanourakis drawing)

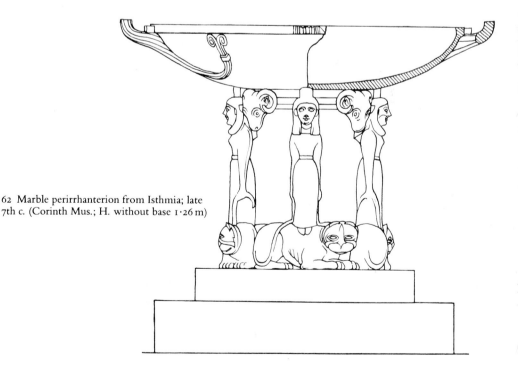

62 Marble perirrhanterion from Isthmia; late 7th c. (Corinth Mus.; H. without base 1·26 m)

63 Limestone statuette from Camirus, Rhodes; early 6th c. (London B 330; H. 25·4 cm)

In stone there is in Samos a censer with a lion–head duct of north Syrian origin[143] (the type imitated in clay in Crete, *Fig. 29*). The east's main achievements in major sculpture are in relief work, usually disposed in friezes and used architecturally. Crete follows this practice, and one of the earliest examples (*Fig. 60*), still of the eighth century, has many affinities with Assyrian work:[144] notably the disposition of archers one above another, a motif met on a Cretan bronze of the same period (a belt, *Fig. 61*). These are works of the group discussed above, p. 57. The placing of the relief sculpture on Cretan temples of the seventh century seems partly at least to have been determined by eastern practice – dado slabs and half-round figures in doorways.[145]

Similarly inspired are a number of late seventh-century marble perirrhanteria (lavers, rather like large bird-baths) whose supports take the form of women standing on or beside lions. The type derives from Syria or Cyprus and in Greece a centre of production may have been Sparta but examples are found also at Olympia, Isthmia (near Corinth: *Fig. 62*), Delphi, Rhodes, Samos, Selinus (Sicily) and the Ptoon in Boeotia.[146]

Cyprus produced many undistinguished statuettes in soft stone which were carried to East Greek sites and to Delos. In Rhodes and Naucratis they seem to have encouraged local imitations, sometimes in a better style (*Fig. 63*). Some might be the work of immigrant Cypriots.[147] Most are of the later seventh century but the style lingers through the sixth century, becoming more thoroughly hellenized – as indeed were the native Cypriot products.[148] On Samos a dedication of about 540 is a limestone statue of a man in Cypriot dress (*Fig. 64*),[149] which suggests some intimate relationship between the islands of a commercial or personal nature. Although the main inspiration for monumental stone sculpture came from Egypt, the characteristic spherical East Greek heads (Samos, Miletus, Rhodes) are clearly influenced by Babylonian models which other Greek studios ignored.[150]

We have discussed already the immigrant goldsmiths and their work.[151] The only important orientalizing Greek jewellery of the eighth century is the series of impressed gold bands from Attica,

64 Limestone statue of a figure in Cypriot dress from Samos; about 530 BC. (Samos, Tigani Mus. 364; H. 39 cm)

65, 66 Impressed gold bands from the Kerameikos cemetery, Athens; 8th c. (Copenhagen NM 740, 741; H. 3·1, 2·4 cm)

67 Gold earring from Lefkandi; 9th c. (Eretria Mus.; H. 1·6 cm)

68 Lead figurines from the sanctuary of Artemis Orthia, Sparta; 7th c. (Oxford 1923.248, 247, 247; H. 4·8, 4·5, 1·3 cm)

69 Lead figure from Boğazköy; mid-2nd mill. (Ankara Mus.; H. 7·5 cm)

70 Lead disc from Ephesus; 7th c. (Vienna Br. 3245; W. 5·25 cm)

71 Silver disc from Zinjirli; 7th c. (W. 3·2 cm)

72 Syrian clay relief plaque showing Astarte from Corinth; 7th c. (Corinth Mus. MF 4039; H. 10 cm)

73 Clay mould (cast) made from an eastern model, from Corinth; 7th c. (Corinth Mus. KH I; H. 6 cm)

at first with eastern animal figures (*Fig. 65*), ánd possibly the work of immigrant craftsmen since the technique was one practised by the eastern goldsmiths in Knossos (see above), and only towards the end of the eighth century with Greek Geometric figures (*Fig. 66*).[152] Hera's triple-bossed, berry-shaped earrings in the *Iliad* are an Assyrian type, imported (ninth-century examples in gold at Lefkandi, *Fig. 67*)[153] and then copied in Greece.[154] In the mid seventh century Greek artists re-learnt the techniques of granulation and filigree, applying them to pendants and earrings in the 'Dedalic' style.[155] Techniques of glass production may have been introduced to Rhodes in the sixth century.[156]

Some small *lead* discs from Sparta and Chios[157] closely resemble Assyrian pendants – and indeed gold-work at Ephesus and, long before, at Mycenae. The cast lead figurines like toy soldiers found in such numbers on Peloponnesian sites, especially in Laconia (*Fig. 68*), are similar in technique and subject to a number of eastern lead figures and groups, though generally of a somewhat earlier date (*Fig. 69*).[158] Rather later, in the sixth century, there are some lead medallions from Samos, Ephesus, and Chios showing a goddess standing on a lion's back (*Fig. 70*), such as appears often in the east, notably on a very similar medallion in silver from Zinjirli (*Fig. 71*).[159]

In clay the eastern Astarte plaques, showing the naked goddess frontal, with hands to her breasts and loins, had a profound influence on Greek art.[160] An imported example may be recognized at Corinth (*Fig. 72*), and the type was copied for Aphrodite figures, although the Greeks soon preferred to clothe their goddess, while retaining the suggestive position of her arms. More important was the use of the mould (*Fig. 73*), which revolutionized the production of clay figurines and relief plaques (*Fig. 74*).[161] The mould is used also for decorating coarser vases (the so-called relief-pithoi).[162] For this purpose too stamps were used from about 700 BC, and this usage finds both eastern (Nimrud) and Bronze Age Greek parallels.[163] Whole-figure moulds for plaques became common on mainland Greece and in Crete.[164] It was probably this usage that introduced to Greece the 'Dedalic' style in sculpture, which dominated the seventh century. It is expressed most commonly in frontal relief figures with angular faces and wig-like hair, and the idiom could be employed in decorative sculpture (as on Cretan temples) or on clay relief vases or even jewellery.[165] In Crete it could aspire to monumentality, but this was to be achieved in Greece under the inspiration of a different source – Egypt.

In East Greece a different use of the mould – for the heads alone – was inspired by the many Cypriot figurines which were imported from the beginning of the seventh century. These have been found on many East Greek sites, and on Aegina and Delos.[166] The rounded, puffy, oriental features were translated (as with the bronzes, *Fig. 41*) to the more angular alert forms which Greece

74 Clay relief plaque from Crete; 7th c. (Oxford AE.403; H. 14 cm)

75 Clay mask from the sanctuary of
Artemis Orthia, Sparta; 7th c. (Sparta
Mus.; H. 27·5 cm)

had developed through her Geometric art. For all that the early
Greek attempts at relief and other minor statuary may owe to the
east in technique or composition, the proportions and line of the
figures remain profoundly non-oriental. This can be seen as early
as the ivory girls from Athens (*Fig. 34*).

A more bizarre example of copying appears in the grotesque
clay masks found on Samos, Thera and in considerable numbers
at Sparta (as *Fig. 75*), some of which are closely modelled on
eastern masks of the demon Humbaba (as *Fig. 76*) while most have
their closest parallels in clay masks from Phoenician and Punic
sites.[167] The only eastern clay vases to reach Greece are Cypriot
and Syro–Phoenician. In Cos they are already being imitated in
the ninth century.[168] In Crete they had some superficial effect on
shapes and decoration, especially the globular flasks adorned with
concentric circles.[169] In East Greece they reached Rhodes (where
some were closely copied, perhaps to compete in the perfumed-
oil market)[170] and Cnidus, and (in the islands) Thera, Delos, and
Aegina. There are trivial reflections of Cypriot in some Athenian
Geometric vases, and the rows of concentric circles on the lips of
Euboean cups (as *Fig. 12*) may have been picked up from Cypriots
(? at Al Mina), while Cypriot vases reached Eretria.[171] Various
Greek clay vases copy eastern metal shapes, and the loop feet for
storage jars may have been inspired in the same quarter.[172]

76 Clay mask of Humbaba
from Ur (London W A)

DECORATION

From the surviving bronzes and ivories of the sort the Greeks
brought back from the east we can get some idea of the impression
that eastern decoration made on Greek artists, but we should
remember too the patterning there may have been on textiles or
embroidery, which have perished. There is certainly great similarity between Assyrian and archaic representations of dress
patterns.[173] In Greek work the medium which tells us most about
the way the artist used oriental motifs is not the one in which they

77 Lions attacking a man on a vase from Knossos, Teke Tomb E; 9th c. (Heraklion Mus. 21147)

78 Lion types. *a* – Athenian vase, late 8th c.; *b* – neo-Hittite relief (see *Fig. 80*) from Carchemish, 8th c.; *c* – Corinthian vase, mid-7th c.; *d* – Assyrian relief from Nineveh, 7th c.; *e* – Corinthian vase, about 600 BC

were ever much employed in the east, but vase painting. The richly decorated vases of Corinth, Crete, Athens, and East Greece will tell us much about those eastern patterns which caught the Greek eye. But it may be wrong to discount altogether the possibility that the example of eastern works had already stimulated Greek figure styles in the Geometric period. On Athenian Geometric vases the total translation to the Greek idiom suggests that the influence was generalized rather than a matter of model and copy, which is more characteristic of the later, full orientalizing period. But even the impetus to develop any form of figurative art may derive from observation of eastern models. Where individual Geometric motifs are thought to derive from eastern arts, such as the fighting groups, it becomes virtually impossible to demonstrate the transmission, and since such groups were to be found in the Greek Bronze Age too other sources are possible,[174] if indeed any outside inspiration at all is to be looked for. The Greeks' debt to their Bronze Age past can be easily exaggerated but it cannot be ignored.

Animal figures become particularly common. Few Greeks could ever have seen a lion. A scene showing two devouring a man appears on late Geometric vases and gold bands (*Fig. 65*) and seems likely to be copied from an eastern group, though this is hard to place and a ninth-century vase found recently at Knossos takes the motif even earlier in Greece (*Fig. 77*) and makes its origin even more puzzling (possibly even Bronze Age Greek, like the sphinxes on the other side of the vase).[175] When the creature is shown on Greek vases at the end of the eighth century it is distorted to suit Geometric canons (*Fig. 78a*), but soon the square-headed neo-Hittite lion with its lolling tongue (*Fig. 78b*) is copied, especially on the vases of Corinth (*Fig. 78c*). After the mid seventh century it is superseded by the Assyrian type of lion, with pointed nose, folded ear, and heavy mane (*Fig. 78d*: Assyrian; *Fig. 78e*: Corinthian). On lions and many other animals in seventh-century Greek art we see also the odd 'boxed-in' way of drawing the shoulder which appears on many neo-Hittite and some Assyrian creatures.[176] In the later eighth century, cocks and hens found their way into Greek art – and into Greek farmyards – for the first time, and they came from the east. To the Greeks a cock remained a 'Persian bird'. Sphinxes and griffins had already lived in the Greek art of the Bronze Age, but they reappear in their new

79 From a Corinthian vase (aryballos); mid-7th c. (Boston 95.11)

80 Relief from Carchemish; 8th c. (London W A)

Near Eastern form, the sphinx[177] sometimes with misunderstood Egyptian 'apron' and crown (turned into a helmet), the griffin[178] with long ears, forehead knobs, and a tendril crest – not the mane of the Bronze Age griffins. Of other *monsters* there is the lion with an extra human head (*Fig. 79*), which may owe something in its general construction to the creature seen on neo-Hittite reliefs (*Fig. 80*) and other objects. Similar surgery produced the Greek chimaera:[179] a lion with a goat's head growing from the small of its back and a serpent tail (as on *Fig. 270*). The goat head and neck may have been evolved from a simple wing and the tuft on the tail was often shown as a bird's head in the east. Eastern lion-headed demons, like Pazuzu (*Fig. 81*), may have helped the Greeks determine on the lion mask for their own bogy, the Gorgon (*Fig. 82*).[180] Another Assyrian and neo-Hittite demon or deity, half man and half fish, suggested the Greek Tritons.[181] Of other mixed creatures, the goat-fish Capricorn may also derive from Assyria, and winged horses (like Pegasus) and lions are eastern; but many owe their forms to the artist's native wit and invention.

81 Bronze head of Pazuzu from Nimrud; 7th c. (Oxford 1951.33; H. 4·3 cm)

Compositions with animals in friezes were already common in Geometric Greek art, but from the late eighth century heraldic groups become just as common, and these derive from eastern art,[182] although they were well known also in the Greek Bronze Age. An important early example is the group of two goats browsing at a tree – an old eastern motif – which appears on several Greek island vases of the later eighth century (*Fig. 83*) and of which imported examples can be shown on an ivory found on Thasos (*Fig. 84*) and a gold band from Aegina.[183]

82 Gorgon head from a Corinthian figure vase from Syracuse; notice the horns, as on *Fig. 81*; mid-7th c. (Syracuse Mus.)

In human-figure decoration the stimulus of eastern narrative art came at the same time as the spread of the Homeric poems, and led the Greeks to develop an individual idiom of narrative art which was still acceptable in Rome and at the Renaissance, and to a lesser degree is still acceptable today. The east may have provided the

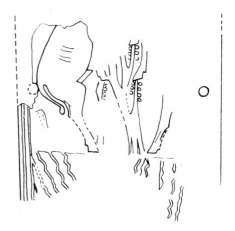

83 Late Geometric hydria from Chalcis; late 8th c. (Chalcis Mus.; H. 18·5 cm)

84 Incised ivory from Thasos; the animals must be restored as goats at a tree; 7th c. (Thasos Mus.; H. 8·5 cm)

stimulus for this practice but it seldom provided the subject matter, which we have seen to have been mainly of individual figures and motifs translated to Greek taste. The more detailed styles of drawing introduced by incised eastern metalwork or ivories certainly enabled the Greek artist to display more explicit figures, with attributes and eventually even expression, but the grammar of Greek narrative art is peculiar to Greece alone.[184]

We may pick out a few figure scenes or groups in Greek art which seem to owe something to eastern inspiration. In the Late Geometric period there are ritual scenes on Attic vases of seated figures on either side of a table or altar (*Fig. 85*) which bear a superficial resemblance to some eastern reliefs of a divine feast.[185] A lion-fighter on an Attic Late Geometric stand adopts the pose of an eastern hero with his quarry, and might have been taken as a Herakles by the artist or his customer.[186] The goddess standing on a bull appears on a Late Geometric bronze disc from Tegea (Peloponnese) and must be explained in terms of similar eastern scenes (*Fig. 86*).[187] The horses with fish or scorpions beneath them on some late eighth-century vases and seals resemble groups in Syrian glyptic and sculpture.[188] Even the eastern winged sun-disc over a palm tree attended by demons seems to have been copied, and misunderstood, on a Cretan bronze of the mid seventh century, and winged disc and tree appear on a Melian gem of about 600 (*Fig. 87*).[189] The symbolic eastern group of a lion fighting another animal is later in its impact on Greece, but it becomes very important and also apparently symbolic in significance, from the second quarter of the sixth century on, as in the pediments of

85 Ritual group from an Athenian vase; late 8th c.
(Liverpool)

86 Bronze disc from Tegea; about
700 BC. (Tegea Mus.; W. 7·1 cm)

Athenian Acropolis temples.[190] The resemblances – including some cited here – may be superficial or even illusory, they are comparatively rare, and even the certain borrowings are more adaptations than copies.

Eastern *floral* decoration played a most decisive part in determining the character of the subsidiary ornament in Greek art. Nothing floral had been admitted in the Geometric period. The eastern 'tree of life', with volute-coiled branches and often a palmette at the top, is a favourite motif, especially for the centrepiece of a heraldic group. In *Fig. 88a* I show the device from a North Syrian silver cup, and in *Fig. 88b* the free Greek adaptation of the motif on a Protocorinthian vase of about 700 BC.[191] It becomes easy to find eastern 'trees of life' everywhere; the least happy attempt would derive both the form and significance of the floral finials on archaic Greek gravestones from the eastern motif.[192] Floral friezes were yet more commonly copied. The lotus, once an Egyptian motif, is the most important single element, and may alternate with buds, palmettes, or rarely pine cones. The fan-shaped Assyrian lotus retains its shape on the earlier Greek vases of the seventh century, and far longer in East Greece, but in the later seventh century in mainland Greece it is squared off to make a better-packed frieze, and a palmette is induced to grow from the centre.[193] The structure of the lotus and bud was also changed by the Greeks, who omitted the invariable

87 Serpentine 'Island Gem'
from Aegina; about 600 BC.
(Aegina Mus.; W. 1·6 cm)

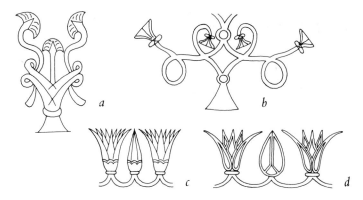

88 Floral patterns. *a* –
Syrian silver bowl from
Tell Qatiné, 8th-7th c.; *b* –
Corinthian vase, about 700
BC; *c* – Assyrian relief from
Nimrud, 8th c.; *d* – East
Greek vase, about 600 BC

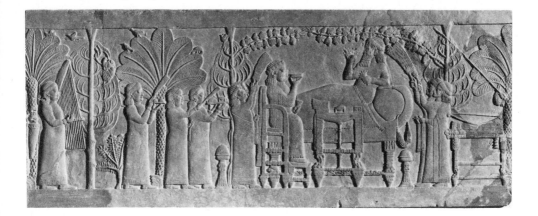

89 Alabaster relief of
Ashurbanipal from
Nineveh; 7th c. (London
WA; L. 1·39 m)

eastern calyx for each (compare *Fig. 88c* and *d*; Assyrian and
Greek). Less common are pomegranate friezes, also Assyrian.[194]
The filling ornament in the background of figure scenes on vases
derives in part from Greek Geometric patterns, in part from the
east, particularly tapestry patterns like rosettes.

Some features of eastern *furniture* were copied directly by the
Greeks, like animal feet – especially lions' paws – and figures
supporting the seats and arms of thrones.[195] Other details – the
finials of supports or balusters in the form of volutes or a girdle of
pendent leaves – were copied in a different way. When the East
Greeks were led by the example of Egypt to develop an order of
monumental stone architecture, such as was never known in
eastern lands, they enlarged these eastern motifs and adapted them
to make the stone capitals of their Aeolic and Ionic columns.[196]
They wedded the Egyptian conception to oriental patterns, and
bred a new architectural form. The last of the progeny of this
union are the marble lions' paws used as anta-bases by Chian
architects. Perhaps the only direct architectural borrowings are

90 Symposium, with
Herakles and Iole, from a
Corinthian vase; early 6th
c. (Paris, Louvre E 635)

more simply constructional: drafted masonry, the use of clamps, and 'Palladian' stairways on to a terrace, which appear in a sanctuary on Chios and were long popular in the east.[197]

A loan from the east which affected behaviour more than furniture was the practice of reclining on couches (*klinai*) at a feast. Reclining to eat was and is a nomadic habit, but seen once in Assyria in a ritual context for a banquet of Ashurbanipal (*Fig. 89*), and adopted by the Greeks about 600 to become the normal feature of their symposia (*Fig. 90*) and to determine later the design of dining rooms.[198]

It would be wrong not to mention here also another borrowing, which although not of material form or object is attested by archaeological evidence in the beginning: this is the *alphabet*.[199] The Mycenaean Greeks had written their palace accounts in the clumsy syllabary adapted for them by the Minoans from their own script. When the palaces fell, the need for writing disappeared and the script was forgotten. Greece remained illiterate until, on the Syrian coast, her traders met a people using, not a syllabary, but an alphabet. This they borrowed, adapting it a little to suit their tongue, and at home admitting some regional preferences for certain letter forms which only became standardized as writing was used more and more for inter-state business. From Semitic inscriptions it seems that it was the letter forms current in the late ninth or early eighth century which the Greeks copied, and this is exactly what our knowledge of the Greeks in North Syria would lead us to expect. The Greeks called their letters 'Phoenician' and in late Archaic Crete a scribe is a *p(h)oinikastas*.[200] The earliest examples of the Greek use of the alphabet appear scratched on vases and painted on a clay plaque, the earliest of the extant inscriptions being perhaps of the third quarter of the eighth century (*Fig. 91*). Some of them are in verse,

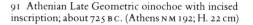

91 Athenian Late Geometric oinochoe with incised inscription; about 725 BC. (Athens NM 192; H. 22 cm)

83

and it may even have been this new alphabet which enabled Homer to compose and set down his great poem(s), drawing on the rich oral tradition of poetry which had survived the Dark Ages.

The occasion for the carriage of these imports and ideas into the Greek world was the Greek initiative in reopening relations overseas, in the east, and we may suppose that the carriage was largely in Greek hands, although in early days the Phoenicians may have been welcomed at Greek ports. We have suspected immigrant craftsmen too, from the ninth century on. By the sixth century there was little that the east had still to teach Greece – except power-politics; but in the Athenian potters' quarter we find a painter who signs himself 'Scythian', another 'the Lydian', a Phintias (an eastern name), and in the early fifth century a potter Brygos (? a Thracian or Phrygian). No few of the artists in Athens may always have been 'metics' (resident foreigners) whose work would enrich the strong tradition, itself once quickened by just such support and inspiration from overseas.[201] By the end of the sixth century, when part of the Greek world already lay within an eastern empire which we have yet to describe, easterners must have become frequent and familiar visitors to Greek cities and ports. Perhaps honoured residents too, to judge from the statue-base in Athens which at the end of the sixth century was inscribed for a Carian in both his native script and in Greek.[202]

Phrygia and Lydia

In the eighth and seventh centuries, the Greek hold on the coast-line of Asia Minor became stronger. The older cities of Aeolis and Ionia outgrew their walls and local resources of land, and new settlements were made, often at the expense of the native population. We have first to say something of this expansion.

In the north, several new settlements are of this period and owe their origins to the Aeolians of Lesbos or other long-established Greek communities. TROY, after the disaster which it seems natural to equate with its famous siege and sack by the Greeks under Agamemnon, revived briefly in the settlement known archaeologically as Troy VIIb1, and was then occupied for perhaps a century by intruders from Thrace or the upper Balkans (Troy VIIb2). In the eleventh century the site was completely abandoned, and the next signs of occupation are finds of Greek pottery of what may broadly be termed 'Aeolian' character. These show that the town was resettled by Aeolians in the second half of the eighth century.[203]

Much farther south, in the valley of the River Hermos which leads into the heart of Lydia, there is a good acropolis site which has been identified (perhaps wrongly) as the Greek Larisa. There is one scrap of pottery from it which seems Mycenaean, but in the early Iron Age it was occupied by Anatolians using grey unpainted pottery. Some Greek sherds show contacts with the Greeks in the eighth century, but at about 700 it seems that the natives were ejected and their place taken by Aeolians who fortified the site and from it were able to overlook if not command the important route inland as well as the overland route between Smyrna and the coastal cities of Aeolis. In the sixth century the town was graced by semi-palatial buildings and some interesting stone buildings of the 'Aeolic' order.[204]

Of the islands, TENEDOS may have been occupied about this time.[205] In SAMOTHRACE there was a native Thracian population in possession when the Aeolian Greeks arrived about 700 B C. The survival of pre-Greek pottery forms, language, and religious practices shows that the natives were peaceably absorbed by the Greek invaders, who were themselves profoundly affected by the indigenous culture. The earliest Greek vases made on the island show an appreciation of the shapes and the plain wares which preceded them, and which, indeed, were probably still being made there.[206]

Offshore islands seek new land by settlement on the mainland opposite them, in districts then known from their positions opposite their mother-islands as *peraiai* (*pera* = opposite). Thus Methymna in Lesbos founded Assos, probably by the end of the eighth century, although nothing Greek has been found there earlier than the sixth century[207] (see p. 266). There are other foundations from Lesbos on the coastline south of Troy with surface pottery which suggests that they were established by about 700.[208]

The story of LEMNOS is somewhat different. It was an important island, which could command access to the Hellespont, had good harbours and two main towns – Myrina and Hephaistia. In the Bronze Age it had close connections with Troy and in the *Iliad* we hear that the Lemnians provided wine for the Greeks besieging Troy. It is doubtful whether there was ever a true Greek settlement on the island in the Late Bronze Age or Early Iron Age. The archaeological evidence amounts to a Mycenaean gem found in a later tomb and what may be a Protogeometric vase, once in Smyrna, alleged to be from the island.[209] Early in the Iron Age the 'Tyrsenoi' from the mainland were said to have occupied Lemnos. It was peoples of the same stock and origin who were thought to have sailed to the west, where they became known as the Etruscans. In 513 B C the Persians occupied the island, which was still peopled by the 'Pelasgians' (our Tyrsenoi); but it may have won its independence again, for it was Pelasgians who were in possession when the Athenian statesman and general Miltiades, who was established on the Hellespont, took the island in about 500.[210] Of the Tyrsenian occupation we have evidence of a cemetery at Hephaistia and some other finds in the island. Nothing seems obviously earlier than the eighth century, and at all times the painted decoration of the pottery is strongly influenced by Greek Aeolian fashions, although shapes may be closer to native

92 Stele from Kaminia,
Lemnos; 6th c. (Athens NM
13664; H. 95 cm)

models. East Greek fibulae (bronze safety-pins) are already imported in the eighth century, and Corinthian pottery appears from the mid-seventh. In fact the culture seems to have been fairly thoroughly hellenized in all but speech. The Tyrsenoi–Etruscan story is complicated by stories about 'Tyrrhenian' pirates in the Aegean, who should be Etruscans; some architectural features of Archaic Lemnos which recall Etruria of the Villanovan period; and the presence on Lemnos in the sixth century of some graffiti on pottery and an inscribed stone stele (from Kaminia) with letters related to the Phrygian and in a language which may be related to the Etruscan (*Fig. 92*).[211]

In Ionia a similar expansion continues through the eighth and seventh centuries. The islands develop *peraiai* on the mainland opposite them – Chios on the Erythraean peninsula,[212] Samos on Mycale and perhaps at the expense of other Ionians (of Priene).[213] Inland, Ephesus occupies Magnesia in the seventh century,[214] an important station on the routes along the Maeander valley and to the north. But most of our evidence for these is literary so far. Farther south, Dorian Cnidus occupies coastal areas which are later to form part of Rhodes' *peraia*. The penetration of LYCIA begins about 700 to judge from recent finds of Greek pottery at Xanthus.[215]

In all these operations the Greeks are immediately concerned with the people occupying the coastal areas, and not the major power of the hinterland – Phrygia – which was more occupied with its southern and eastern frontiers. The natives met by the Aeolians shared generally in the west Phrygian 'grey-ware' culture. Those of the south are not archaeologically distinguishable, until their pottery, of which some has been recovered in recent years from various sites in south-west Asia Minor, shows the clear influence of Greek painted vases. At Iasos this seems to have happened already by the eighth century,[216] and at Sinuri, a native Carian temple site near Mylasa, a quaint local style of figure-decorated pottery has been identified.[217] On other Carian sites (as Kaunos) East Greek bowls of Late Geometric type are quite skilfully imitated (*Fig. 93*),[218] and later these areas are permeated by provincial variants of the East Greek 'Wild Goat' style of orientalizing pottery.

But the Greeks, especially the Ionians, were fully aware of the Phrygians and the archaeological evidence for their relations is full and varied. From the literary record, we may note in passing the marriage of a Phrygian king, Midas, to the daughter of a king of Aeolian Kyme, Agamemnon – probably in the eighth century; and that a Midas, perhaps the same man, was the first eastern monarch to send a dedication – a throne – to the Greek sanctuary at Delphi.[219]

We are lucky to be able to study the Phrygians from such varied, although not always very full or explicit, sources. Herodotus tells much of their early dealings with the Greeks. In

93 Carian cups imitating the East Greek 'bird bowl' type; early and late 7th c. (once London Market; Diam. 14·6, 11·1 cm)

Assyrian records we recognize our Midas in that Mita of the Muski whose territorial ambitions carried him to the borders of Syria and who offered peace and tribute to Sargon of Assyria in 709.[220] And American excavations at Gordion in recent years have yielded a mass of precious data to add to earlier, generally less helpful because less precise, excavations of other Phrygian sites and ground surveys.[221]

The probable origins of the Phrygians, and their appearance in Asia Minor, are likely to have been connected in some way with the movement into Greece in the Early Iron Age of Greek-speaking tribes from the north. Approaching the historical period the evidence for the penetration of Greek goods or ideas is still sparse, though one early ('pre-Cimmerian') ivory relief in local style from Gordion has a cavalier equipped like a Greek[222] and a very little Greek pottery is arriving in the late eighth century. There are, however, two archaeological matters in which correspondences between Greek and Phrygian products have been thought to require an explanation going beyond the simple matter

94 Phrygian vase from Gordion, Tumulus III; early 7th c. (Ankara Mus.)

of Ionian–Phrygian relations in the eighth century or later. They are:

1. Pottery. The fine Phrygian painted pottery is distinguished by some distinctly oriental metalliform shapes and a rather banal repertoire of Geometric ornament[223] (*Fig. 94*). Many of the decorative motifs recall Greek Geometric patterns so closely that is seems unlikely that the resemblances are fortuitous, or even perhaps explicable by reference to a common model. There is very little Greek pottery in Phrygia in the late eighth century,[224] and not much more from the mid seventh century on. But there seems no question of Phrygian influence in Greek Geometric styles, for the points of resemblance come late in the Greek Geometric series, and are largely confined to the Eastern Greeks. (For the relationship with Macedonian wares see further below, p. 235.)

2. Bronze fibulae. The distinctive fibula (safety-pin) type in Phrygia has a semicircular bow, with heavy symmetrical mouldings on it, and often an elaborate form of 'safety catch' (*Fig. 95*).[225] It is closely related to East Greek forms, but in many ways more involved than they are. Yet it seems hard to believe that the type came to Phrygia otherwise than from the Aegean world. The elaboration of the Greek form may be due to Phrygia's more profound experience in metal working. The only excavated mould for a fibula of Phrygian type has been found at Greek Smyrna.[226] The appearance of the type on an early Greek electrum coin (*Fig. 96*) suggests that metal fibulae might even have served as an informal currency.[227]

In about the middle of the eighth century, the Phrygians copied and adapted the Greek alphabet (itself only recently 'invented' – see above) for their own language,[228] but at this time it seems to be the Greek cities of Ionia who are more often in receipt of Phrygian ideas. In metal-work we find the most profound influence of Phrygian crafts. The Phrygians themselves imported and used Assyrian decorative metal-work (*Fig. 51*),[229] but it was probably not through the Phrygians that the Greeks came to learn of such things, as we have seen. It is only those objects which seem peculiar to the Phrygian workshops that the Greeks of Ionia thought to copy or adapt.

1. Cauldrons or *dinoi* with ring handles set in spool-like attachments at the rim (*Fig. 97*). These are found in the royal Phrygian tombs from the eighth century on. An iron ring handle in a bronze mount found in Chios seems to be a Phrygian import. Otherwise this type of vessel is not represented in early Ionia although the form reached other parts of the Greek world and is copied in clay in some East Greek and Cretan vases, and in Aeolian *bucchero* from Troy and Larisa. The ring handle and spool attachment appear again on another Phrygian vase (see below, 2) and on various

95 Phrygian fibula from Gordion; late 8th c. (Gordion B 901; W. 7·5 cm)

96 Electrum coin from East Greece; early 6th c. (Oxford)

97 Bronze cauldron from Gordion; late 8th c. (Ankara Mus.; H. 15 cm)

98 Bronze bowl from Gordion, Tumulus MM; the Phrygian inscription is incised on wax, below the rim; about 700 BC. (Gordion B 818)

Greek bronze vessels, but Phrygia may not have been the only source of inspiration for this sort of handle in Greece, and a related type is found at Al Mina.[230]

2. *Shallow dishes* with ring handles set in spool-like attachments at the rim, and with horizontal strengthening bands having spool-shaped members. The Phrygian examples are from tombs at Gordion (*Fig. 98*, inscribed) and Ankara, and there are two from Magnesia (on the Hermos), the earliest of them being of the late eighth century. Exactly this type of dish is held by the little ivory statuette of a priestess found at Ephesus (*Fig. 99*) and dating to the second quarter of the sixth century, and there is another example,

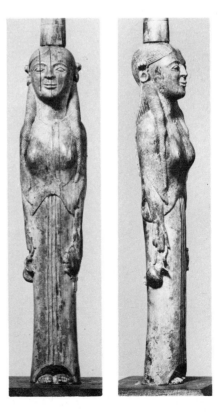

99 Ivory statuette (handle to a wand) of a girl holding a jug and bowl, from Ephesus; about 560 BC. (Istanbul Mus.; H. 10·7 cm)

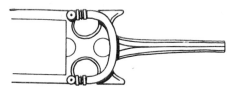

100 Bronze belt from
Gordion; late 8th c.

in bronze, from Cyprus. Fragments of similar bowls have been
found in Greece at the Argive Heraeum and Olympia. Dishes
with the ring handles, but without the strengthening band which
is the more distinctive feature, were imitated in clay in Phrygia,
and there are intimations of the same form in seventh-century clay
vases from Larisa, Samos, and Chios (where they are on high
conical feet). But it must be repeated that there are other possible
sources in the east for ring handles.[231]

3. *Bronze belts*. In the Princess's Tumulus at Gordion, which was
opened by American excavators in 1956, were found two bronze
belts. They were formed of a continuous strip of metal with a long
hook at one end which engaged in one of three loops cut in a
separate sheet of bronze fastened to the other end. Behind the
hook there was a fibula-like attachment fastened rigidly on to the
belt, making a sort of handle which would have helped in taking it
in a notch. There was incised decoration on the belt-strip, not
shown in *Fig. 100*. Fragments of a more elaborate openwork belt
strip had been found at Ankara, but with no 'handle'. In the year
before the Gordion discovery, British excavators on Chios found
a series of belts of this type, which had been dedicated in a
sanctuary there from the later eighth century to about 600 B C.
From these more complete examples it was possible to recognize
parts of similar belts which had been found elsewhere in Chios (at
Phanai), in Samos, at Ephesus, Erythrae, Didyma, and Smyrna.
The Ionian belts (*Fig. 101*) are in some ways more elaborate than
the Phrygian. There is greater variety in the form of the 'handles',
which may have animal-head terminals (*Fig. 102*), and it is possible to discern independent centres for their production in Ionia.
The hooks are made separately and riveted to the belt, and they

101 Bronze belt from
Emporio, Chios; 7th c.
(Chios Mus.; W. 6·3 cm)

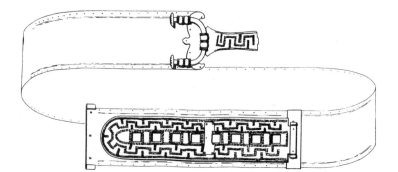

102 Anatolian bronze belt handle with lion-head terminals; 6th c. (London WA 132961; W. 6·8 cm)

engage in one of many holes in a long tongue which is actually hinged to the other end of the belt. The strip was probably backed by linen or leather, rolled over the edges and stitched through the holes at the edge of the bronze. The earliest are perhaps as early as the Phrygian examples, but there can be little doubt that the latter are the inspiration for the Ionian versions. In Ionia it seems that they may have been worn by women, and dedicated at adolescence or on marriage. That they were still being worn in the sixth century is shown by the representation of one worn by a winged Artemis on an East Greek bronze relief which was found at Olympia. The belts are unknown outside Ionia (but see p. 218, below, for possible imitations in the west).[232]

These belts are a clear example of a Phrygian form adopted by the Greeks. It seems not to have been introduced to the Greeks by imported models, but immigrant craftsmen could have set the fashion in the eighth century.

The Phrygians had been driven from their southern Anatolian provinces by the Assyrians in the late eighth century,[233] and in the early seventh they were overwhelmed at home by the Cimmerian invaders from the north and east. The same Cimmerians, displaced from their homes by the Scythians, swept on and past the Greek cities, which they raided. Ephesus was attacked, and there are records of Thracian 'Treres', who seem to have participated in these raids in the seventh century, occupying Antandros in the Troad, and sacking Magnesia.[234] The Cimmerians – and the Scythians – are identified by a form of bronze arrowhead with socket and barbs, found on various sites but later used also by the Greeks.[235]

Phrygia lost her position of power in Asia Minor, but her cities revived after the Cimmerian raids and became part of the great Lydian empire. We can now detect a change in relationships with the Greeks. From the mid seventh century a little East Greek and Corinthian pottery appears on Phrygian sites, and the bronze

103 Clay relief revetment from
Pazarli, Phrygia; late 6th c. (Ankara
Mus. 45 × 45 cm)

dishes with ring handles are being made and copied by Greeks.[236] But now, more and more, it is Greek ideas and motifs which are penetrating Phrygia. The painted pottery admits motifs copied directly from archaic East Greek vases.[237] In various parts of Phrygia we find clay relief plaques, which served to decorate the façades of buildings. The style and inspiration of these revetments seems purely Greek, as are many of the motifs, although they are often much distorted (*Fig. 103*).[238] We are also meeting here for the first time the phenomenon of 'orientalizing' Greek motifs being returned, translated, to the east. The revetments are of the sixth century. In these years too more Greek pottery is imported – Athenian and Corinthian for the most part – and other more exotic articles, Egyptian alabaster and northern amber, may have been carried there by the Greeks.[239] Of more monumental work

104 Marble basis from Ankara
(Ankara Mus.; H. 53 cm)

105 Fresco fragments from Gordion; 6th c. (drawing P. de Jong)

there is a stone basis (*Fig. 104*), oriental or Anatolian in shape, decorated with relief motifs which, though orientalizing, are wholly Greek in their form.[240] Thus the lotus and bud appear in the Greek manner, without the calyxes at their bases which always appear in Assyrian and other eastern examples of the motif. Another pattern on the basis is clearly derived from the Greek Ionic capital. The piece is in Ankara and has no certain provenance, but is likely to be from one of the Phrygian towns and to be of the end of the sixth century. At Midas City were found the lower parts of two limestone statues which appear to be Ionian of the mid sixth century, and the figure on a rock relief not far away owes much to Greek models.[241]

At this time too there is even clearer evidence for the work of Greek artists in Phrygia. Fresco wall paintings have been excavated in Gordion which are wholly Greek in their style[242] – and specifically north Ionian (*Fig. 105*). It is interesting to note that one motif which appears in them, a crown or circlet of small griffin protomes worn by a woman, has its counterpart in Chios, where at Emporio some small lead griffin protomes are thought to have decorated the helmet peak of a cult statue of Athena in the mid sixth century.[243]

It was perhaps from Phrygia that the Greeks adopted the worship of Cybele, the Anatolian Mother of the Gods. Most of the evidence for her worship in Greek lands is of later date, but one of the earliest Cybele monuments, perhaps even of the sixth century, is a rock-cut model of the goddess's shrine – again on Chios.[244] The setting and technique are strongly reminiscent of sixth-century Phrygian rock-cut thrones, which served as cult-places. But the grandest sixth-century Phrygian statue of the goddess (*Fig. 106*), from Boğazköy, is herself influenced by East Greek sculptural fashions in the rendering of her dress (*Fig. 107*).[245]

106 Limestone statue of
Cybele with attendants
from Boğazköy; 6th c.
(Ankara Mus.; H. 1·26 m)

107 Marble statue
dedicated by Cheramyes to
Hera on Samos; about 560
BC. (Paris, Louvre 686; H.
1·92 m)

108 Gold plaque showing a
bee-goddess, from
Camirus, Rhodes; 7th c.
(London *BMC* Jewellery
no. 1118; H. 3 cm)

Cybele was a popular goddess in East Greece,[246] but normally shown seated in her shrine, as in the Chios model. There too the many goddess-cults associated by the Greeks with a Hera or an Artemis may owe their origin in part at least to Anatolian cults, perhaps even pre-Phrygian. The Artemis at Ephesus is a particularly good example, and representations of her or her attendants as bees may well reflect a Hittite cult.[247] The bee-goddess is shown on gold plaques from Rhodes, as *Fig. 108.*

In the sixth century Phrygia was no longer a great power, and we have to retrace our steps a little to pick up the story of the Greeks and their neighbours, to the mid seventh century and the rise of the kingdom of Lydia. Lydia may have been a province of Phrygia, but its heart lay nearer the sea, in the valley of the Hermos, with its capital at Sardis. The site is dominated by the massive acropolis, but the Lydian town was probably at its foot, near the later temple of Cybele. Here we have one of the very earliest of the Cybele monuments of the general type just discussed, where the goddess is standing in the door of her marble shrine, its walls decorated in shallow relief, all executed in a purely East Greek style of the mid sixth century (*Fig. 109*).[248] The recent excavations are telling us more of Sardis' early history.[249]

Mycenaean pottery has been found and later local wares. The identification of Greek Protogeometric imports is somewhat less certain and the first pottery certainly influenced by Greek fashions looks no earlier than the eighth century (if so early), and Greek vases only begin to appear regularly in the seventh. Out in the plain stood the massive tumuli of the cemetery, dominated by the Tomb of Alyattes, some 70 m. high and 1,000 m. in circumference.[250]

109 Marble Cybele shrine from Sardis; mid-6th c. (Sardis Mus.; H. 60 cm)

Lydia came into her own after Phrygia had fallen to the Cimmerians and with the new dynasty established by King Gyges. Gyges himself fell in battle with the Cimmerians (in 652), but he and his successors generally dealt successfully with the raiders and kept them at bay, perhaps with the help of the Assyrians. He took a more active interest in the coastal cities than did the Phrygians. He may have controlled much of the south coastline of the Hellespont, and we hear of him allowing Miletus to send settlers to Abydos there.[251] Miletus, however, was attacked by him, as was Smyrna, and he took Colophon. His son, Ardys, continued the attacks on the Ionians, took Priene and again attacked Miletus, which the Lydians seemed to regard as a particular menace. He did not go entirely unscathed, however, and in his reign the Cimmerians attacked again, and even sacked the lower town at Sardis. Sadyattes and Alyattes continued the attacks on Miletus without success, although Alyattes sacked a temple at Assessos in Milesian territory, stormed and sacked Smyrna soon after 600, and even moved against Clazomenae. Only the islands escaped the fury of the Lydians, but of these Chios at least is recorded as going to the assistance of the Milesians. Alyattes eventually came to terms with Miletus.[252]

Croesus succeeded Alyattes, and continued hostilities against Ionia with an attack on Ephesus, followed by others in which he seems to have forced the acquiescence of all the mainlanders of Ionia.[253] The islanders too fell under his sway, although Herodotus says that he was dissuaded from naval action against them. Under Croesus the Lydian kingdom seems to have embraced most of the western coastline of Asia Minor and the offshore islands, although the Greeks were clearly left a considerable measure of independence and on Chios an inscription shows that some form of democratic institutions was being practised.[254] For the first time the East Greeks found themselves owing allegiance to a native kingdom – a barbarian one, for all the hellenization and enlightenment of Croesus' court. 'Before Croesus' rule all Greeks were free,' comments Herodotus, and at another point he speaks of the enslavement of Ionia by the Lydians in the same terms as their position under the Persians later. It seems a tribute to Greek and especially Ionian resilience and opportunism that despite this their general prosperity and trade flourished as never before.

The archaeological record of this period is rich and varied. For the Lydian attacks on Ionia, the recent Anglo-Turkish excavations at Smyrna have given vivid evidence of their method and effect.[255] By the end of the seventh century the city was enjoying its greatest prosperity (see *Fig. 4*). Its walls had been newly built and stood in mudbrick on a stone base, at places some eighteen metres thick. Within the walls the houses were laid out on a regular rectangular plan, but it is clear that by now a large part of the city's population was living outside them, on the hill-slopes and shore facing the compact peninsula site of the city. A new sanctuary for the city goddess, Athena, had been laid out, with an entrance court and ramp up to the temple platform. A new temple too had been planned, one of the earliest monumental stone temples in the Greek world, but as yet only its platform had been laid and some of its members carved. The votives in the sanctuary reflected the city's wealth and importance overseas – pottery from the other Ionian states and from Corinth, clay figurines and stone statuettes from Cyprus, the finest orientalizing ivories and bronze work. This was the splendid city which faced the army of Lydian Alyattes.

The excavations have shown how thoroughly the Lydians sacked Smyrna, but they have also shown exactly how the city

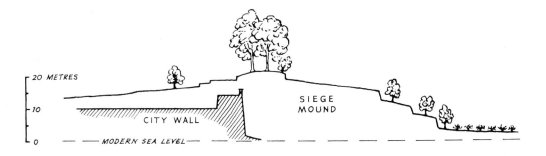

110 Section through the
highest part of the city
mound at Smyrna

fell. The highest point of the low hill which now represents the
site is formed today not by its natural summit but by the mass of a
great siege-mound which had been thrown up against its north-
west wall (*Fig. 110*). This technique of attacking a walled town is
an eastern one, and this was probably the first time that the Greeks
had to face it. The mound was composed of earth and building
materials from the houses outside the walls, and was strengthened
with timbers. Some light is thrown on armaments too by the finds
of bronze arrowheads respectively within and outside the walls.
The Lydians used triangular heads with three flanges and a socket
– a type associated with the Scythians. The Greeks used leaf-
shaped, socketed heads, some squat ones with four flanges, and
even some of iron. The thoroughness of the Lydian sack is shown
by the utter overthrow of all the seventh-century buildings and
the fact that the town seems to have been left desolate for some
twenty years.

Of Greeks in Lydia itself we know little. The kingdom was
fabulously rich, according to ancient authors, and 'golden
Croesus' passed into legend. The Lydian culture is still barely
known, although we hope for much from the excavations at
Sardis.[256] Its art seems partly dependent on the later Phrygian
styles, but it is soon thoroughly permeated by the influence of
East Greek art; and for all that Lydian influence was blamed for
degenerate or effeminate habits learned by the Greeks, the 'ener-
vating' luxury must have been very Greek in appearance if not in
character. The poetess Sappho comments, complains rather,
about her girls who have gone to grace high society in golden
Sardis – a 'Hollywood' of opportunity and wealth; and elsewhere
in her poems she acknowledges Lydia as the home of luxury and
comfort – and formidable armies.[257] Both Lydia and Phrygia were
said to have introduced to the Greeks various musical novelties
and indoor games. The seven-string lyre, one of the Lydian
innovations, is shown on a seventh-century Greek sherd found at
Smyrna (*Fig. 111*), and on a vase from Pitane.[258] Lydian dress and
music came to have a profound effect on the party-giving habits
of Athenians at the end of the sixth century, through the example
of the Ionian guest poet Anacreon, who contributed a word for
those affecting these habits – *Lydopatheis*. Their dress must have

111 East Greek vase fragment from Smyrna; first half of 7th c. (Izmir Mus.)

112 Athenian red figure lekythos by a Mannerist painter, from Gela; about 470 BC. (Boston 10.185; H. 39·2 cm)

seemed almost transvestite to Athenians – the Lydian turban (*mitra*), soft leather boots (*kothornoi*), a new deep lyre (*barbiton*)[259] – (*Fig. 112*) – sometimes a parasol. The Lydian alphabet, like the Phrygian, was adapted from the Greek, probably about the middle of the seventh century.[260] The more elaborate Lydian pottery is distinguished by the use of a heavy white slip and figure decoration in low relief. The content of the decoration seems derived from East Greece, while the technique may owe something to Anatolian styles of long before. The plainer vases resemble East Greek, and some, with multiple circles and hooks, are akin to the sort of pottery made and met by East Greeks at

113 Vase from Aphrodisias; about 600 BC

home and in Cilicia and North Syria. The fine Wild Goat style of vase painting, as practised in Rhodes and Ionia, also appears in a very provincial manner, rather like that of some Aeolian cities,[261] and it is transmitted to other native towns of the interior, such as Aphrodisias (*Fig. 113*).[262] A distinctively Lydian style of vase decoration is the marbled ware, with massed wavy strokes in thinned paint. This has been thought to be in imitation of glass, but it is perhaps more like beaten copper work. It appears especially on perfume pots (*Fig. 114*), which may have held the famous Lydian perfume *bakkaris*, and were themselves known as *lydia*. They were carried to Greece, even to Etruria and were imitated – the shape at least (Egyptian originally) – in East Greece (*Fig. 115*), Sparta, Athens (*Fig. 116*), and Etruria.[263] But this is a rare instance of Lydian ceramic influence in the Greek world. Some fine ivories from Sardis[264] are close to Greek orientalizing work, and, again at Sardis, gravestones with palmette finials,[265] like those made in East Greece, were set up before some tombs. Of the other arts we still have much to learn, also of the extent of Greek influence on the local craftsmen, or perhaps the presence of Greek craftsmen in Lydia. We shall see that the finest dedications sent by Lydian kings to Greek sanctuaries were made for them by Greek artists. One independent find may be noticed – some gold jewellery from Aidin (Tralles) on the southern periphery of the Lydian empire (*Fig. 117*).[266] There is much in its technique and something in the motifs to remind one of archaic Greek work, especially the Cretan (*Fig. 23*).

The kings of Lydia seem to have cultivated relations with the Greeks, however harsh their treatment of the Ionians. Gyges was the first barbarian king, after Phrygian Midas, to send offerings to Delphi, notably six golden bowls weighing thirty talents. Alyattes sent a golden bowl and a remarkable iron stand, which was the work of an Ionian artist, Glaukos of Chios.[267] The Lydians could offer bullion more easily than works of art, from their native resources. To Alcaeus they offered the colossal sum of 2,000 gold pieces to help his party overthrow the government of Lesbos.[268] Croesus was particularly generous to Delphi, and won from the oracle the ambiguous answer that he would 'destroy a great empire' by marching against Persia, without admitting that the empire might be his own. He sent the sanctuary a gold lion set on ingots of gold and electrum, and among other things two great bowls of gold and silver, which were again the work of an Ionian Greek, Theodorus of Samos.[269] Even the Ionian cities enjoyed something of his beneficence. At Didyma, near Miletus, we hear of gold offerings matching those at Delphi. At Ephesus a new great temple for Artemis was being built, in emulation of the temple of Hera which had just been built on Samos, but larger – indeed one of the largest ever to be attempted by a Greek architect. Croesus paid for many of its columns, and scraps of columns bearing the record of his gift – 'King Croesus dedicated . . .' – were

114 Lydian clay 'lydion' flask; 6th c. (Hamburg Mus. für Kunst und Gewerbe 1962.40; H. 13·7 cm)

115 East Greek clay 'lydion'; 6th c. (Munich 532; H. 11·3 cm)

116 Athenian clay 'lydion'; mid-6th c. (Paris, private; H. 9·8 cm)

117 Gold pendant from Aidin; 6th c. (Paris, Louvre; H. 6·8 cm)

excavated there in the last century and are now in the British Museum.[270] Herodotus says too that several Greek sages visited his court, notably the Athenian lawgiver Solon; and that Ionians fought for him on his campaign against the Persians, Thales of Miletus serving as a military engineer.[271] The Lydians probably employed many Greek mercenaries, and it has been thought that it was Gyges who sent Ionians and Carians to help the Egyptian king Psammetichos I (see Chapter 4). In Croesus' army against the Persians were 'Egyptians' – perhaps Greek mercenaries sent by the Egyptian king – who acquitted themselves well and were settled in Lydia (at Larisa and Kyllene near Kyme) by Cyrus after the defeat of the Lydians.[272] On a more domestic-political level, we hear of a marriage between Alyattes' daughter and an Ephesian ruler, Melas.[273] An Athenian father paid Croesus the compliment of naming his son after him.[274]

The Greeks were profoundly impressed by the wealth of Lydia, especially in gold. The dedications made in Greece by the Lydian kings were spectacular, showy, and golden. Alcmaeon of Athens was supposed to have made his family's fortune by making the most of Croesus' offer to give him all the gold he could carry on his person:

He crammed it into his boots, all up his legs, as much as they would hold, filled the baggy front of his tunic full, sprinkled the dust all over his hair, stuffed some more into his mouth, and then staggered out, scarcely able to drag one foot after another (Herodotus).[275]

The Spartans sent to buy gold from Croesus for a cult statue, and were given it. They had been courted by the Lydian king, who was trying to make the Greeks like him. In return for the present, the Spartans sent a bronze cauldron (of the same type as our *Fig. 261*), which was intercepted by Samian pirates. The Samians had already intercepted another gift to Lydia, 300 Corcyrean boys sent by Periander of Corinth to Alyattes to serve as eunuchs.[276]

A more profound and salutary effect of Lydian gold, however, was the beginning of coinage in Greek lands.[277] Our most important sources of information for this are the foundation deposit and other finds in the temple of Artemis at Ephesus. The associated finds show that the coins were deposited about 600 BC.[278] All are of electrum – a mixture of gold and silver, 'white gold' – but there are also some more primitive pieces, simple dumps of metal, mainly of electrum but some of silver. Some dumps have striated surfaces and have been punched, so that the striations are clear and can indicate the degree of wear. When the dump is punched over an engraved or cut die we have something we can recognize as a coin. Lydia was clearly the source of the electrum, which could, for instance, easily be panned from the River Pactolus which runs through Sardis, and excavations at Sardis have recently yielded early evidence for gold working.[279] The primitive dumps are presumably Lydian, then, and were made to guarantee weight; or, it has been suggested, to provide a ready means of paying mercenary soldiers. The coins from the Ephesus deposits are all on roughly the same standard. Some with lion's head or paw devices must be Lydian. One is inscribed in Lydian, and this, with similarly inscribed coins, has been associated with Alyattes. But now more fully inscribed coins of this series are known and the attribution called into question.[280] None were necessarily struck before Alyattes' reign. Others have other devices – animal heads, etc. – and must be Greek. A seal's head may suggest Phocaea (it was later the canting device on her coins), but we cannot certainly attribute any of them to individual Ionian states. Two other electrum coin types of about this date, or soon afterwards, are inscribed 'I am the device of Phanes' (*Fig. 118*) and (a smaller coin) 'of Phanes', which suggest a private merchant's mint. Herodotus implies that the Lydians were the first to mint coins,[281] and the material of the early dumps makes this seem most probable. Whether it is the Lydian lion heads or the Greek animal heads which are the earliest *devices* on coins is a different question. In

118 East Greek (probably Ephesian) electrum stater from Halicarnassus, inscribed 'I am the seal of Phanes'; early 6th c. (London)

later seventh-century Greece the cognate art of seal engraving – in ivory or stone – was at least as well developed in Greece as it was in Asia Minor. The idea of a figure device for a coin might well have been Greek. We cannot say whether it was applied first in a Lydian or a Greek mint.

The Persians

King Croesus of Lydia challenged the empire of the Persians and Medes, with whom his father Alyattes had already once joined battle. Croesus was defeated and Sardis was taken. Herodotus tells of the immediate effect on the Greeks who had paid allegiance to the Lydian king. They sought from the Persian Cyrus the same terms that they had enjoyed under Croesus, but only Miletus was thus favoured. The other cities looked to their defences, as the Persian general Harpagus moved against them. He took all the mainland cities, although the populations of Phocaea and Teos escaped to settle elsewhere.[282] The islands too submitted, and may even have suffered invasion, for on Samos the great temple of Hera is burned down and a cemetery by the town pillaged at about this time.[283] When Harpagus turned his attention to the south, against the Carians, Caunians, and Lycians, he marched with Ionian and Aeolian Greeks in his army.[284] And when Cyrus returned home he took with him Croesus and various Ionians, the first of many Greeks to take the road to Persia in the Great King's service.

Under Persian rule, Ionia formed a department of a province or satrapy whose administrative centre lay at the old Lydian capital of Sardis. The Persians were generally tolerant rulers, although they sometimes interfered in the affairs of the Greek states, establishing 'tyrants'. Samos prospered under Polycrates, whose ships ranged freely, sometimes piratically, in the waters of the eastern Mediterranean. He supplied manned ships to serve the Persians. But before the end of the century the Persians had to visit the island with fire and the sword for a second time.[285]

In general, however, the Greek cities seem to have flourished. Much of their trade lay in places which were already, or were soon to be, within the Persian empire – Al Mina, and Naucratis in Egypt. Only when they had taken Lydia did the Persians become aware of the attractions of 'civilized' life, and the Greeks were to serve and instruct the Persians in these matters as they had the Lydians before them; although it was sometimes the 'effeminate' eastern powers who were held responsible for the over-fondness for good living shown by the Ionians. Herodotus, at least, says that it was *from* the Greeks that the Persians first learned the vice of paederasty.[286]

There are many stories about the Greeks who visited or were entertained in the Persian court. Darius, for instance, had a Greek physician whom he especially favoured.[287] We are here concerned

more with the artists who worked in Persia and the archaeological evidence for the influence of Greeks there. Documentary evidence is afforded by an inscription of King Darius, who came to the throne in 522, at Susa. In it he says: 'The ornamentation with which the wall was adorned, that from Ionia was brought.... The stonecutters who wrought the stone, those were Ionians and Sardians' (i.e. of Sardis); and it was Carians and Ionians who carried the timber from Babylon to Susa.[288] Again, Pliny mentions an Ionian sculptor, Telephanes of Phocaea, who worked for both Darius and Xerxes.[289]

Tangible evidence of Greek taste and artistry is afforded mainly in stone-carving, both architectural and sculptural. The Ionic order of monumental stone architecture, with volute capitals, disc bases, and elaborate mouldings, had already been developed in the islands and East Greece by the mid sixth century. We have had occasion to remark how much the appearance of the new architectural decoration relied on eastern patterns, and how little the conception did so. Now we find the new idea of monumental stone orders of architecture being planted in eastern countries by the Greeks, and with it the return to their homeland of certain eastern patterns which the Greeks had made their own and had sometimes adapted out of recognition.

King Cyrus' palace lay at Pasargadae, in Persia. When he died, in 529, he was buried in a small temple-like mausoleum raised on a stepped base (*Fig. 119*). The gabled monument is not readily explained in terms of the traditional forms of burial in Persia, but we are concerned with details rather than its general resemblance to Greek buildings. There is the *cyma* moulding which runs round the top of its walls and is wholly Greek in type, incipient Ionic 'dentils', and a large rosette carved at the gable top which recalls

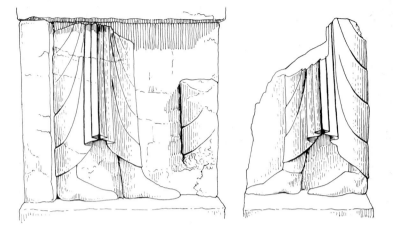

120 Relief sculpture from Pasargadae; about 510 BC

the clay disc acroteria on Archaic temples in East Greece and the Peloponnese.[290] Also at Pasargadae are cylindrical stone columns – themselves innovations in the east – standing on cushion bases with horizontal flutes of exactly the Ionic type, and many very close parallels with East Greek work in the dressing of masonry and execution of architectural detail like rosettes.[291] The Greek mason's new invention, the claw chisel, is in use here, and the masons' and sculptors' marks on blocks of stone[292] closely match the personal blazons on Lydian pyramidal seals (see below) of the Persian period. This is graphic confirmation of Darius' inscription naming Ionian and Sardian stone cutters. Any masons in Lydian Sardis of this period are likely to be Greeks, perhaps employed once by Croesus for a temple rivalling those of the Ionian cities.[293]

It is at Pasargadae too that we first see a sculptural innovation which can also be assigned to Greek influence. This is the semi-naturalistic representation of folds in drapery: a sort of surface patterning which eastern sculptors had never much cared for, but with which the Greeks had been experimenting since early in the sixth century. This is the sort of novelty which Greek artists working for Persians could well have inspired, or even executed (*Fig. 120*).[294]

Darius (522–486) built the palace at Susa of which we have the inscription mentioning Ionian craftsmen. He also began work on the great complex of buildings at Persepolis which marks the culmination of Achaemenid (the Persian royal house) architecture, and is the fullest expression of the influence of Greek craftsmen both in Darius' reign and under his successors who continued his work there. We need not dwell on the details which betray Greek inspiration – the bead-and-reel mouldings, the orientalizing (not oriental) Greek patterns, the fluted columns. The capitals, like Greek Ionic, are no more than furniture writ large, but the motif of double opposed volutes is less well suited to monumental architecture.[295] What is more important is the now complete acceptance of what had already been foreshadowed at Pasargadae – the significance of the column as a decorative as well as (and sometimes rather than) a structural unit. Egyptian architecture had already discovered this, and the Greeks had learned from them. There are several Egyptian motifs in the architecture of Persepolis, but the Persians who had earlier built at Pasargadae in the same manner had at that time no very intimate dealings with Egypt itself.

Some minor objects at Persepolis also attest the interest there in Greek works of art, and the presence of Greek artists. On the foot of a colossal stone figure an artist lightly incised drawings of heads and animals, in such a purely Greek style that he must himself have been a Greek and trained in Greece. Comparisons with Greek vase paintings of the end of the sixth century make this quite clear. The sketches themselves would finally have been covered with paint. A fragmentary stone panel was prepared in a similar way for painting with a purely Greek, late Archaic scene, of Heracles' struggle with Apollo for the tripod, with Artemis watching (*Fig. 121*).[296] The Greek coins in a foundation deposit at Persepolis have already been mentioned.[297] In his great inscription, Darius said that the Ionians also made the ornamentation for the walls of Susa; not, it seems, the famous glazed reliefs, but perhaps other decorative work. Certainly the lotus patterns which appear on fragments from Susa are of the Ionian rather than the Assyrian eastern type.[298]

Back at home, the East Greeks who now found themselves in the Persian empire had at times to serve in their masters' army. Quite soon after their submission to Cyrus, the Persian general Harpagus led Greeks against native tribes in the south, and Lesbian ships were used to take the islands of Lemnos and Imbros in the north.[299]

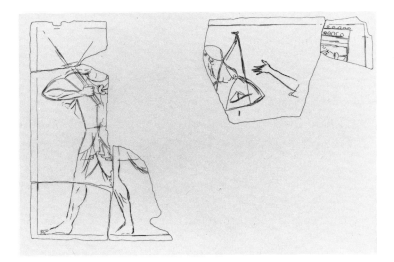

121 Stone panel incised in preparation for painting – Heracles, Apollo, Artemis – probably the struggle for the tripod; about 500 BC (H. 18 cm)

122 Tomb paintings from Elmali; early 5th c.

In other parts of the Persian empire, but nearer the Greeks themselves and in areas already permeated by their influence, the presence of Greek artists is even more obvious. The built tombs of Lycia, some of which belong to this period, are decorated with reliefs in a purely Greek although somewhat provincial manner, with only few eastern motifs, like the piles of dead bodies.[300] Also in Lycia there are recent discoveries of tomb interiors painted in a Greek Anatolian style and some with purely Greek subjects, though the funerary scenes, especially a feast, are decidedly Anatolian in inspiration (*Fig. 122*).[301] But these are so much part of the history of Greek art that they warrant no more than a mention here. From the middle of the sixth century too both Athenian and East Greek vases appear with growing frequency in Caria and Lycia.[302] In Cyprus both the influence of East Greek art and the import of Greek pottery grow apace, and now for the first time we may seriously believe in new Greek settlements in the island. Athenian potters copy a Cypriot vase shape for this market ('Cypro-jugs', *Fig. 123*).[303]

123 Athenian 'Cypro-jug' from Amathus, Cyprus; about 530 BC. (London 94.11–1.476)

Although trade, particularly with other parts of the Persian empire, prospered at first, the East Greeks felt some setback to their business in Egypt when that country too fell to the Persian Cambyses in 525. But it was probably not only commercial considerations that led the Greeks to look for an escape from the Persian yoke, and already in 511 some Greek states on the north-west fringe of the empire attempted to revolt. The Persians too were beginning to covet mainland Greece where Sparta was championing the cause of her enemies. They had already met the Athenians at Sigeum, near the Hellespont (Dardanelles), and given refuge to an exiled Athenian tyrant, Hippias. In 499 the Greek tyrant of Miletus and the Persian satrap attempted to take the island of Naxos; but in the same year the East Greeks revolted, burned the capital of the Persian satrapy, Sardis, and enjoyed an uneasy freedom for some five years.[304] The Persian counter-attack in 498 on the Greek cities in Cyprus is well illustrated by the excavations at Paphos, which have shown that the city fell to a siege mound of the sort the Lydians had thrown up against Smyrna (*Fig. 110*) a century earlier.[305] In 490 Darius's generals sailed against Greece to punish those who had supported the rebels, and in their fleet were Ionian and Aeolian Greeks. Eretria in Euboea was sacked, and her folk deported to Arderikka, near Susa in Persia, where they were still living as a community in Herodotus' day.[306] On the plain of Marathon the Persians were thwarted of their next and prime objective, Athens, and sailed away. Ten years later, their last hopes of adding a satrapy of Greece to their empire were dashed in the waters around Salamis and on the battlefield of Plataea. Even then, many eastern Greeks and many mainlanders served in Xerxes' army and fleet, and the exiled king of Sparta, Demaratus, was among Xerxes' advisers. The Eretrians were not the first to be deported. Darius had already

.{·ΛΛΑΘΕΝΑΙΟΙΜΕΔΟΝΛΑΒΟΝΤΕ΄

124 Bronze helmet, Persian spoil
dedicated by the Athenians at
Olympia; early 5th c. (Olympia Mus.
B 5100; H. 23·1 cm)

125 Bronze knucklebone from
Susa, once in the temple of
Apollo at Didyma; 550–525
BC. (Paris, Louvre; H. 23 cm)

taken back with him the men of Branchidae (Didyma, near Miletus), who had surrendered their temple to the Persians and feared the consequences from their fellow Greeks. He settled them in Sogdiana, but their descendants suffered for this treachery at the hands of Alexander.[307] Other Milesians were deported and settled at Ampe on the Persian Gulf, near the mouth of the River Tigris.[308] Many Greeks travelled or were taken to the east in these years. Darius had threatened to carry off the Ionian maidens to Bactria, but in the event sent them to his own court.[309]

There are many archaeological reflections of these events, mainly of course in Greece herself, and notably on the Acropolis of Athens, which was despoiled by the Persians. Loot from the victory over the Persians was to become a feature of the state treasuries there; and we may mention briefly a memorial of the ultimate Persian defeat – a Persian bronze helmet from Olympia inscribed simply 'The Athenians, to Zeus, having seized [it] from the Medes' (*Fig. 124*).[310] In Persia itself there is loot from the Ionian cities[311] – like the inscribed bronze knucklebone which had stood as a dedication in a sanctuary near Miletus (Didyma) and was found at Susa (*Fig. 125*);[312] the griffin protome from a cauldron of the Samian type, also found at Susa;[313] part of the relief decoration from a Spartan bronze mixing bowl of the later sixth century, from Persepolis;[314] and the scrap of bronze relief decoration from a shield of the earlier sixth century, found at the same site.[315] A golden crater, the work of Theodorus of Samos, was said to stand in the royal palace, and may have been either a present to the Persian king or loot from Ionia or Lydia.[316]

Whether or not Persian architectural forms also had their effect in Greece it is hard to decide, but some have seen them in the round 'tholos' building in the Athenian market place – like a

126 Pyramidal stamp seal (impression) inscribed in Lydian 'of Manes' and with a personal device before the bull; about 500 BC. (Geneva 20564; L. 1·8 cm)

127 Stele with representation of an ekphora (procession to the grave) from Dascylium; about 500 BC. (Istanbul Mus. 5764; H. 3·08 m)

monumental eastern parasol; in the forest of columns of the Periclean Music Hall (Odeion) at Athens; even in the replanning of the Acropolis itself.[317] Certainly Greek artists still worked for Persians in the fifth and fourth centuries, and contributed a very great deal to what we know as Achaemenid art. In Persian Sardis officials used stamp seals of eastern shape (pyramidal; *Fig. 126*) but some were decorated with Greek motifs or made by Greeks.[318] A comparable phenomenon is the appearance of funeral stelai in Anatolia with Persian subjects but Greek palmette finials (*Fig. 127*).[319] It has been suspected that some are Greek gravestones re-used. In the Classical period Greek studios in south Anatolia cut gems for local Persian officials or appointees,[320] and made coins for them. In Sardis the Persians maintained the old Lydian mint but in time a Persian figure appears on the gold 'Daric' coins (*Fig. 128*).[321] In return, types of oriental animal-head cups already met in Assyria, and most popular with the Persians, were copied by Greeks in clay and metal.[322]

The details of the history and the archaeology of the Persian Wars and their aftermath cannot concern us here, but they mark an important stage in Greece's relations with the 'barbarians'. Greek ventures overseas had at last brought them face to face with a major power which was stimulated or goaded by their presence within its territory to march against the mother country.[323] That power was repulsed, and the Greeks pursued with even more vigour and freedom their trade with eastern countries and interest in eastern affairs. Exactly a century and a half later Alexander the Great was to compass the fall of that very empire and march beyond it; his soldiers burned Persepolis and liberated 800 Greeks there, and the lands of the Hittites, the Assyrians, the Babylonians, and the Persians were embraced in a new and Greek empire.

128 Gold 'Daric' coin with incuse reverse; late 6th c. (Oxford)

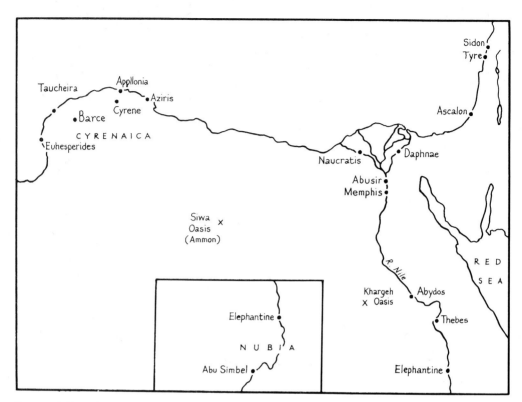

Egypt and Cyrenaica

4

The Greeks in Egypt

In many accounts, especially archaeological ones, of Greeks over-seas, Egypt is grouped with the states of the Near East in a single oriental 'bloc' whose effect on and relations with the civilizations of the Aegean are treated as part of a single story. This leads only to confusion and complication. Whatever the relationship of the two great valley civilizations – of Mesopotamia and the Nile – in their earliest days, their subsequent development and history are quite distinct, and the records and fortunes of the Greeks who travelled east to Syria or south to Egypt are quite different. So too is the nature of the reciprocal influences of the east and Egypt upon the Greeks themselves. Here only one source of confusion and error is found, for one of the main routes from Egypt to Greece followed the coast of Palestine, Phoenicia, and Asia Minor, and Egyptian objects which reached Greece thus were probably passed by eastern traders for much of the way. Egyptian influence was also strong in Phoenicia, whose art is deeply tainted by Egyptian fashions, while even in the North Syrian neo-Hittite monuments which we mentioned in the last chapter, Egyptian motifs can often be found. It is certain, then, that much of what seems Egyptian in Greece may have been derived at second hand through the countries of the Near East, especially Phoenicia; but it is equally certain that much was brought direct from Egypt by the Greeks, and it is often possible to distinguish this 'pure' material. But our primary concern is with the Greeks in Egypt itself.

The only part of the complicated story of Egyptian–Greek relations in the Bronze Age which is of relevance here is its end. In the Near East we have seen how the spread of Mycenaean culture or peoples set a pattern for later Greek settlement. In Egypt the character of the Mycenaean Greek contacts was quite different, and has no bearing on the course of Greek interest in Egypt in later centuries. Late Mycenaean pottery has indeed been found in some quantity on over a dozen different Egyptian sites as far up the Nile as Thebes, and isolated finds are reported as far south as Aswan and Nubia. The vases are generally stirrup jars of a type made in the Peloponnese. They attest no more than a brisk trade in oil, and can nowhere be taken to represent any regular Greek community, although many Greek traders were no doubt temporarily resident in the country.[1]

The 'Peoples of the Sea' who so disrupted the countries of the eastern Mediterranean in the late thirteenth century, and who may have included Greeks, were with difficulty, but with complete success, kept from Egyptian territory.[2] But, despite her success in keeping at bay the troubles which heralded the beginnings of the Iron Age in the Aegean and Near East, Egypt also suffered a long period of comparative decline after the brilliance of her New Kingdom dynasties. A brief rally in the later tenth century brought an Egyptian army again into Palestine, but in Egypt itself these are barren years archaeologically.

It is not until the later eighth century that the course of Egyptian history begins to be of much more than local interest. In the far south, in Nubia (Sudan), was a flourishing kingdom, worshipping Amun, as did the great cities of Egypt, and with kings related to the Egyuptian royal line. The Nubian king Piankhy invaded Egypt in 730, and fifteen years later the 'Ethiopian Dynasty' (Dyn. x x v) was established. The Nubian kings ruled Egypt until 664, often threatened by the growing power of the Assyrian kings, whose invasion fleets were partly manned by Cypriots. It was the Nubian King Shabako who surrendered the Greek 'Yamani', who had stirred up revolt in Ashdod against the Assyrians in 712. In 671 Lower Egypt fell to the Assyrians, and the Nubian kings' hold on the Nile delta was never fully regained. We hear of a free Egypt again under Psammetichos (Psamtik) I (664–610), the first king of the new dynasty (x x v i), and now too, for the first time, we hear of numbers of Greeks in Egypt.

Up to this time Greek awareness of Egypt seems to have been slight, but some Egyptian objects were reaching Greece, and these indicate the possibility that at times there was some more direct contact. We may briefly review these imports before coming to the question of Greeks in Egypt, but unfortunately for most we can say no more than that it is likely that they antedate the mid seventh century. The earliest objects – beads, figurines, vases, scarab seals of faience, and some stone seals – appear occasionally on Greek sites throughout the early Iron Age, and represent no more than casual imports, perhaps via the Near East. They are found in Crete, at Sparta, Argos, Sunium, Athens, Aegina, Thera; at Eleusis (some in Geometric tombs); in an eighth-century tomb at Corinth; in a Geometric context at Perachora near by; and in East Greece on Rhodes and Chios.[3] It is possible, however, that already in the earlier seventh century there was a workshop producing very similar faience trinkets on Greek Rhodes, as there was certainly later in the century.[4] Some minor objects were even carried west, and in the Euboean colony of Pithekoussai (Ischia) and in Etruria a seal and a faience vase bearing the name of the Egyptian king Bocchoris (720–715 BC) have been found.[5] Of isolated finds of Egyptian bronzes, we may mention a bronze

129 Egyptian bronze mirror from Perachora;
late 8th c. (Athens NM; H. 14, W. 15·8 cm)

mirror from Perachora certainly earlier than 650 (*Fig. 129*),[6] a
Horus figure in Argos (the Heraeum);[7] two bronze women and an
ornament in Rhodes;[8] and an ibis statuette at Miletus (*Fig. 130*).[9]
Small bronze flower pendants have been found on various East
Greek sites, and may well be from Egyptian earrings or diadems,
in their turn inspiring the floral or fruit pendants on East Greek
jewellery.[10]

There are, however, two places in the Greek world which
attracted a different class of Egyptian objects – fine bronzes –
certainly straight from Egypt itself with no eastern inter-
mediaries. These are Crete and Samos. Understandably so, for
Crete was the first stop on the direct sea route to Greece, and there
is good evidence for Cretan interest in North Africa, in Cyrenaica;
and it is a Samian captain whom we will first hear of trading with
Egypt just after the middle of the seventh century. In Crete, as
well as the minor faience objects, we find a bronze bowl and fine
bronze jugs with openwork handles in the form of an Egyptian
lotus. Five of these have been found in the Idaean Cave, two in
tombs near Knossos, and one at Amnisos.[11] The finds at Knossos
suggest that they are likely to be of the years before the middle of
the seventh century. Indeed, another example found recently at
Lefkandi in Euboea (*Fig. 131*)[12] indicates that the type could have
reached Greece as early as the ninth century. There are also
Egyptian ivory plaques from the Idaean Cave and Knossos.[13]
Crouching lions holding a bowl between their forelegs are found
– in faience in the Idaean Cave, and Cretan clay versions at various
places. One from Afrati is of the mid seventh century (*Fig. 132*),

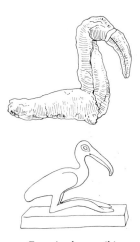

130 Egyptian bronze ibis
from Miletus (the fragment
compared with a complete
statuette in Berlin); 7th c.
(H. 6 cm)

131 Bronze jug from Lefkandi; 8th c.
(Eretria Mus.; H. 8·6 cm)

132 Clay lion vase from Arkades, Crete;
mid-7th c. (Heraklion Mus.; L. 32·6 cm)

and the type is Egyptian, although it was copied also in Palestine.[14] On Samos many of the rich series of Egyptian bronzes (*Fig.
133*) and ivories are of this early period, although not earlier than
700.[15]

Our first literary evidence for Greeks in Egypt is in
Herodotus.[16] First there is the mention of the Samian merchant
captain Kolaios who was on his way to Egypt when he was
carried off course to the west. The story implies that the Egypt
run was nothing out of the ordinary for him, and it seems that his
spectacular voyage (see below, p. 213) happened in about 638. So
we have here the suggestion of at least casual trade visits by East
Greeks about the middle of the seventh century.

Another incident concerns not Greek traders but Greek soldiers
– mercenaries. Psammetichos I – to give him the name by which
the Greeks called him (as I will the other Egyptian kings) – had
been encouraged by an oracle to enlist the aid of 'brazen men' to
regain his throne. At that time Ionian and Carian pirates were
forced on to the Egyptian coast by bad weather. They had bronze
armour – either the Greek 'hoplite' corselet of sheet bronze, or
perhaps 'scale armour', made up of many scale-shaped pieces of
iron or bronze sewn on to leather in the eastern fashion. With their
help Psammetichos prevailed; he rewarded them with two pieces
of land – known as the Stratopeda, or Camps – on either side of the
Pelusian branch of the Nile (the sites have not been certainly
identified). Herodotus says that they were well treated and
respected by the king, who even founded a school of interpreters.
'They were the first foreigners to live in Egypt, and after their
original settlement there, the Greeks began regular intercourse
with the Egyptians, so that we have accurate knowledge of Egyp-

tian history from the time of Psammetichos onwards.'[17] The historian Diodorus adds that Psammetichos also encouraged the Greeks in trade with Egypt.[18] In Herodotus' story the Carians and Ionians arrive by accident, but it is possible that they were sent by the Lydian king Gyges.[19]

In Necho's reign (610–595) we have no direct evidence for the use of Greek mercenaries, but the king was moved to dedicate the armour in which he fought in his Syrian campaign in 608 to Apollo at Branchidae (near Miletus),[20] and this may imply the welcome participation by Greek soldiers. Later, in 605, he suffered defeat at the hands of the Babylonians at Carchemish. In ruined Carchemish, in a house well furnished with Egyptian objects[21] including sealings naming King Necho, was found a Greek bronze shield (*Fig. 20*). Its find-place suggests it might well have been carried by a Greek soldier in the pay of the Egyptian king. Necho also made 'trireme' warships for service in the Mediterranean and the Red Sea,[22] and it may be that here, as under Psammetichos II (see below), we have evidence of Greek nautical experience – never a strong point of the Egyptians – being exploited.

For some later activities by Greek mercenaries in Egypt, we can enlarge considerably on Herodotus' bald statement that Psammetichos II (595–589) made an expedition to Nubia.[23] The Egyptian monuments show that this was a considerable expedition, made in 591 BC, against the Nubian kingdom which was again threatening Lower Egypt.[24] Eloquent testimony to the part played by foreign mercenaries is paid by the inscriptions cut on the legs of the colossal rock-cut statues at Abu Simbel (*Fig. 134*), some 700 miles up the Nile. The inscriptions are by Greek and

133 Egyptian bronze statuette from Samos; 7th c. (Samos Mus. B 1216; H. 17.3 cm)

134 The colossi at Abu Simbel (before removal)

Carian soldiers who accompanied the king and, it seems, held important commissions in his army.[25] The longest Greek inscription (*Fig. 135*) says:

> When King Psammetichos had come to Elephantine, this was written by those who sailed with Psammetichos, son of Theokles, who went as far upstream as they could – above Kerkis. Potasimto led the foreigners and Amasis the Egyptians. This was written by Archon son of Amoibichos and Pelekos son of Eudamos.

We do not know the status of the Greek Psammetichos but there were Egyptian generals in charge of the Foreign Legion and the Egyptians. Potasimto is styled 'General of the Greeks' on Egyptian monuments.[26] The other inscriptions are hardly more than the idle exhibitionist scratchings with which soldiers and others can always be relied upon to deface any convenient wall or monument; but some are important, for they reveal the home city

135 Graffito at Abu Simbel (see text for translation); about 591 BC

of the men. We have Elesibios of Teos, and Pabis of Colophon, both Ionians, and a Dorian, Telephos from Ialysos in Rhodes. It is not certain whether we can argue from the Egyptian forms of some of the names that the men were born in Egypt, perhaps children of the mercenaries who had served Psammetichos I. In this same period we read in Egyptian inscriptions of an Egyptian Admiral Hor, 'commander of the foreigners and Greeks' (perhaps Cypriots), and there were Greeks at the southern fortress of Elephantine which had been established by Psammetichos I and housed a Jewish garrison also.[27]

Returning to Herodotus' account we find little more that concerns the Greek mercenaries. King Apries (Wahibre; 589–570) led the mercenary army of 30,000 Carians and Ionians against Amasis (Ahmose) in 570. They acquitted themselves well, but were defeated, and Amasis became king (570–526). A version of the episode is preserved on a stele in Cairo.[28] Despite his encounter with the Greek mercenaries of Apries, Amasis too came to favour the Greeks, and seems to have used them early in his reign against an attack by the Babylonian king Nebuchadrezzar.[29] He married a Greek princess from Cyrene. He is said to have moved the mercenary camps from Stratopeda to Memphis to 'protect him from his own people',[30] but there is archaeological evidence too (see below) for a fort at Daphnae, in the area of Stratopeda, partly manned by Greeks throughout his reign. But the most important of the privileges which he accorded the Greeks is reported by Herodotus[31] and concerns Naucratis:

He gave them Naucratis as a commercial headquarters for any who wished to settle in the country. He also made grants of land upon which Greek traders, who did not want to live permanently in Egypt, might erect altars and sanctuaries. Of the latter the best known and most used – and also the largest – is the Hellenion; it was built by the joint efforts of the Ionians of Chios, Teos, Phocaea, and Clazomenae, of the Dorians of Rhodes, Cnidus, Halicarnassus, and Phaselis, and of the Aeolians of Mytilene. It is to these states that the sanctuary belongs, and it is they who have the right of appointing the officers in charge of the port (*prostatai*). Other cities claim a share in the Hellenion, but without any justification; the Aeginetans, however, did build a temple of Zeus on their own initiative, the Samians one in honour of Hera, and the Milesians another in honour of Apollo. In old days Naucratis was the only port in Egypt, and any one who brought a ship into any of the other mouths of the Nile was bound to state on oath that he did so of necessity, and then proceed to the Canopic mouth; should contrary winds prevent him from doing so, he had to carry his freight to Naucratis in barges all round the Delta, which shows the exclusive privilege the port enjoyed.

We should perhaps here mention too the account by Strabo of a raid by Milesians, and a fort built by them in the Delta before they founded Naucratis, and the Egyptian post at Rhakotis (the later Alexandria) which was stationed to ward off Greek pirates.[32]

The archaeological evidence shows clearly enough that Naucratis was founded long before Amasis' reign, but we may understand Herodotus' words as an indication of some reform or regularizing of its status. But it is time to consider in more detail what is known of this great Greek trading town in the Nile Delta.

Naucratis

THE SITE

The town of Naucratis lay on the east bank of the Canopic branch of the Nile, some fifty miles from the open sea and the later Hellenistic capital, Alexandria, and only ten miles from Sais, the capital of the xxvi Dynasty kings. Petrie discovered the site at the mounds of Kôm Gi'eif, some two miles from the village el-Niqrâsh, which preserves the ancient name. He dug there in 1884–5, and his work was followed by that of Gardner, Griffith, and finally Hogarth, in 1899 and 1903.[33] The excavations were not conducted under the happiest conditions (*Fig. 136*). To a great extent the excavators were digging around or through the work of their predecessors, and Petrie's technique of publication, if not of digging, left much to be desired when quantities of decorated pottery and minor objects, whose dates could be controlled by finds elsewhere in the Greek world, were involved. Recent

136 Excavations by Hogarth at Naucratis, 1899

137 Sketch plan of Naucratis

attempts to resurrect the stratigraphy of parts of the site have proved inconclusive.[34]

Much in the principal buildings of the town was dug piecemeal in this way, but hardly any of the houses, while the cemeteries of the earlier period were not located. Nor is the student today helped by the way the finds have been scattered through museums and private collections throughout the world, although an attempt is now being made at a comprehensive study of the material.

There were two centres of archaeological interest in the town as excavated, in the northern and southern quarters. The history of their main buildings has been made much clearer by the late Baron W. von Bissing, but there are some problems of identification and date which may for ever remain obscure (*Fig. 137*).

In the southern part of the town, one of the dominant buildings was a stout structure which Petrie took for a fort and von Bissing has understood as a treasury or storehouse of Egyptian type which may have been built before the end of the seventh century. Just to the north of this lay the Greek temple of Aphrodite, a simple two-roomed building with a stepped altar before its door, standing within a small walled enclosure. The temple itself was rebuilt at least twice, but always to about the same size (about 14 m. × 8 m.) and plan, and of the same material – mudbrick.[35] The offerings excavated in the temple clearly belong to its earliest period. Among them we should pick out particularly the mass of Chian vases, some certainly as early as 600 BC. Otherwise there is a fair proportion of East Greek and Athenian pottery from the earlier sixth century on, and some objects of Cypriot type. The dedications painted (as *Fig. 141*) or incised (as *Fig. 139*) on the vases give us the name of the goddess. Herodotus does not mention a temple of Aphrodite, but a later reference attributed to a local writer implies that the cult may have been of some antiquity there, and alleges that the cult statue was brought from Cyprus. The finds might suggest that the Chians had something to do with the foundation.[36] The stepped altar is an interesting and important construction, if it does indeed date to the earliest years of the sanctuary. It consists of a flight of four steps, about three yards wide, leading to a flat platform for the sacrifices. The type bears some resemblance to Egyptian stepped altars, which are generally higher and with narrower steps, and it has been suggested that Ionian architects adopted it from Egypt.[37]

East of the temple of Aphrodite was a small factory for faience scarab seals, which was active mainly in the earlier sixth century, and to which we shall have occasion to refer later.

The temples in the northern part of the town are hardly better known than those in the south. A temple to Hera, which must be the Samian one, is attested by inscriptions on scraps of sixth-century pottery, and the outlines of a sanctuary and perhaps of the temple itself. Next to it lay the Milesian temple of Apollo, also in a defined sanctuary enclosure. The pottery dedications here show that the cult goes back to the early days of the settlement. Of the temple buildings we have only architectural fragments, some preserved, some merely described. For instance, the only fragment of a stone capital which Petrie saw was smashed before he could fetch his camera to it. There seem to be several pieces from a fine limestone temple with Ionic columns, built about the middle of the sixth century, if not earlier. One feature of the columns was a necking carved with a floral pattern, such as has been found on Samos. The temple was replaced by a marble one, with similarly elaborate mouldings, perhaps early in the fifth century.[38]

The sanctuaries of Hera and Apollo lay side by side. Near them – to the north, but in a separate enclosure – was a smaller shrine, to the Dioscuri, which is identified by the inscribed pottery dedications, some of them earlier than the mid sixth century; but the building is not mentioned by any ancient author.

To the east of these three sanctuaries, Hogarth digging in 1899 found another and larger sanctuary which could certainly be identified as the Hellenion mentioned by Herodotus, the joint foundation of several East Greek states. Again the site is architecturally disappointing, but the inscriptions on vases name several deities, the most significant being simply 'the gods of the Greeks'. None of the votive pottery found here need have arrived earlier than the reign of Amasis, so it may well be that the Hellenion was founded as the result of his reorganization of the status of Naucratis, while the independent sanctuaries – of Milesian Apollo, Samian Hera, Chian Aphrodite (if rightly identified by the Chian finds) and Aeginetan Zeus (mentioned by Herodotus) are of the

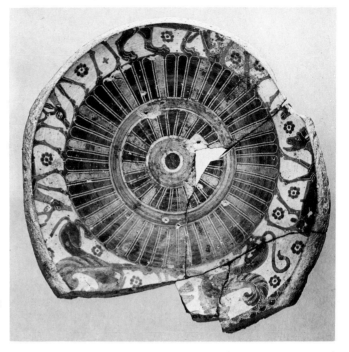

138 Corinthian vase fragment from Naucratis (?); about 630 BC. (Boston 09.210; Diam. 16 cm)

earlier years of the town, and indicate the identity of the major interests there. Unfortunately the Aeginetan sanctuary has not been found. If we could read 'Dioskouron' instead of 'Dios' in Herodotus, the sanctuary of the Dioscuri might be given to Aegina, but the twin gods have no home in the island, where there is, however, an important shrine to Zeus Hellenios, also met at Naucratis (in the Hellenion).

THE FINDS

It is the finds at Naucratis which betray to us the date of the first Greek settlement, and give the lie to what might otherwise be deduced from Herodotus, that it was founded in Amasis' reign. The earliest pottery from the site which is datable is, as usual, Corinthian: one scrap of 'Transitional', made about 630–620 (*Fig. 138*),[39] and rather more 'Early Corinthian' of the later years of the seventh century and earliest sixth. As it was largely an East Greek venture, we might expect the earliest pottery to be East Greek, and indeed there is much which certainly still belongs to the end of the seventh century. But in the present state of our knowledge of vase chronology, we cannot tell how early the earliest pieces might be, and we are left with the Corinthian as our only sure evidence. This suggests that there were Greeks at Naucratis by 620, but is equally compatible with the view that they were there some twenty years before. It should, however, be remarked that von Bissing argues a later date for the foundation – to the reign of Psammetichos II (595–589) – because of the absence at Naucratis of scarabs bearing the name of any earlier Egyptian king.[40] The

139 Chian bowl with incised dedication by Sostratos to Aphrodite, from Naucratis; about 600 B C. (London 88.6–1.456; Diam. 38 cm)

positive evidence of the pottery, which indicates a substantial Greek settlement before 600, seems to outweigh this argument *ex silentio*, but there may still be room for some adjustment.

It would be satisfactory if we could assign the classes of pottery found at Naucratis to the various states known to have had dealings there. This can be done to a limited extent. Herodotus says that of the Ionians, Chios, Teos, Phocaea, and Clazomenae were represented; of the Dorians, Rhodes, Cnidus, Halicarnassus, and Phaselis; and of the Aeolians, Mytilene (Lesbos). These shared the Hellenion, but besides there were the sanctuaries built by the Aeginetans, the Samians, and the Milesians. He is speaking of the period of Amasis, but it is likely that most or all of these states were active in Naucratis from the early days of its Greek history.

Most of the vases and fragments which were kept by the excavators are finely decorated votives from the sanctuaries.[41] The East Greek pottery may be considered first:

1. Much of it, including pieces datable to the late seventh century, is *Rhodian* in origin, or of Rhodian type. It seems to have been in general use in all the Dorian states of East Greece, and it is likely too that Miletus used and produced pottery of the same type: the problem of Milesian pottery in this period we have already met at Al Mina. 'Rhodian' vases were also used in the more northerly East Greek towns, but many of these were producing their own vases either in a style which is still hard for us to distinguish from Rhodian, or in a peculiarly local style which we can fortunately pick out among the finds at Naucratis. Such are the vases of Chios, Samos, Clazomenae, and Lesbos.

140 Chian vase fragments
in polychrome style from
Naucratis; about 560 BC.
(London)

2. *Chian* pottery is readily distinguishable by its most popular
shapes (especially the chalice and kantharos), the fine white slip on
the vases, and a distinctive style of drawing. So much Chian
pottery was found at Naucratis, before it had been recognized in
the island of Chios, that the ware was for long called Naucratite.
This gives a quite false indication of the home of the vases and
their style, but the name may not be wholly misleading, as we
shall see. The earliest Chian vases at Naucratis are still of the
seventh century; this we know from the early shapes of some
chalices and the decoration. Some of the most spectacular vases at
Naucratis are of this ware (*Fig. 139*), which although it never
seriously competed in the pottery markets of the Greek world was
still prized far from home – as in Etruria. Among the Chian vases
at Naucratis, there are some classes which have not so far been
recognized in excavations in Chios itself,[42] and it is legitimate to
ask whether they might not have been made in Naucratis by
Chian potters. Only votives are involved, which could have been
turned out fairly easily for the rich local market, even with
imported potters' clay brought as ballast in the corn ships. The
most distinctive are fine chalices with decoration in a polychrome style (*Fig. 140*) which reminds one more of Egyptian
murals than of any contemporary (second quarter of the sixth
century) Greek vase decoration.[43] Somewhat earlier are some
other fine chalices with animal scenes, also executed with a lively
sense of colour. Somewhat later, of the middle of the century, is a
host of small fine cups (mostly *kantharoi*) which are completely
plain except for a painted dedication, which must have been
bespoken by the customer *before* the vase was made (*Fig. 141*).[44]
The only places outside Naucratis where vases of these classes
have been found are Cyrene,[45] Aegina (where there was a dedication of a man who made similar offerings at Naucratis), and
Athens (one piece). We should recall that Cyrene, in North Africa,
may have been in close touch with Naucratis, and that Aegina was
the only non-East-Greek power with a stake in Naucratis. The
possible existence of a Greek pottery in Naucratis recalls the work

141 Chian votive
kantharos (restored)
painted with a dedication
by Zoilos to Aphrodite,
from Naucratis; mid-6th c.

by Greeks, over a century before, in similar circumstances in Cyprus and perhaps Syria. Of the second half of the sixth century are some other fragments which can be recognized as Chian, but the decoration of these is much influenced by Athenian fashions.[46] Before we leave Chios, we may also note the presence at Naucratis of examples of Chian wine jars, the earliest being of the earlier sixth century.

3. *Samian* pottery of the early years of Naucratis cannot yet be identified with certainty. Of the mid sixth century is a small class of exceptionally fine black-figure cups which were probably made in Samos.[47] Some plain one-handled cups with inscribed dedications to Hera (her temple was a Samian foundation) may be from the island; some were painted before the vases were fired, and so were bespoken.[48] It is possible that these, like the Chian-Naucratite, were made in Egypt, but they name only the goddess, not the dedicator, and could as well have come from a Samian shop serving the Heraeum at home. Samian oil jars have also been identified.[49]

4. Various sources – Rhodes, Samos, Miletus – have been proposed for the *Fikellura* vases.[50] These are generally large vases, amphorae, and hydriae, decorated in a style which owes much to Rhodes and a little to the Samian black-figure school. Their floruit was the middle and third quarter of the sixth century, and although the style probably lingered to the end of the century, the last phase is not represented at Naucratis. The vases are named after a cemetery in Rhodes.[51]

5. An important school of black-figure vase painters has been attributed to the North Ionian town of *Clazomenae*.[52] The vases are well represented at Naucratis, and date to the third quarter of the sixth century. The style seems to be at home on the mainland sites of North Ionia, and some of the Clazomenian vases at Naucratis, or at least those – and there are several – which seem related to 'Clazomenian' in various ways, might well be from towns like Phocaea and Teos, said by Herodotus to have traded at Naucratis.

6. The most typical vases of Aeolis, particularly *Lesbos*, are in the plain pale grey *bucchero*. There are several pieces at Naucratis, none closely datable, although most are certainly not later than the sixth century in date.

We are left with three other main classes of Greek pottery found at Naucratis which were not made in any of the states named by Herodotus. These are:

7. *Spartan* vases. Fine black-figure vases, generally cups, of the style now certainly attributed to Sparta, are found in some quantity. All are of the first half of the sixth century, the earliest are of its beginning. They are intrinsically fine, and in the Etruscan market, for example, could compete with Corinthian and Athe-

142 Athenian vase fragment from Naucratis; about 600 BC. (Toronto 962.211.20; W. 6 cm)

nian. Their numbers at Naucratis are noteworthy, but the fact that the other major foreign market for them was in Samos may in part explain their popularity. They may, on the other hand, reflect Spartan interest in another part of North Africa where they are found – Cyrenaica (where some once thought they had been made).[53]

8. *Corinthian* vases. The earliest, of the later seventh century, have already been mentioned. They continue to arrive until the middle of the sixth century, although not in quantity.

9. *Athenian* vases. The earliest at Naucratis is of about 620–600 BC (*Fig. 142*). In the sixth century they appear in fair numbers, and the quality is of the best.[54] Both quantity and quality are maintained until about 525, when there is a sharp falling off. The imports pick up again in the early fifth century. Also of the sixth century are some plainer Athenian storage jars ('SOS'; cf. *Fig. 2*).

The Corinthian and Athenian vases remain to be explained. Both were fine wares which in this period were being carried for their intrinsic worth as decorative pottery; and the Corinthian and Athenian coins found in Naucratis may suggest a strong if indirect interest in the trade there by the issuing cities. But there remains one state in Herodotus' list whose archaeological presence at Naucratis has yet to be tested. This is Aegina. We have already had cause to remark that Aegina had no painted vases of her own, but used Corinthian throughout the seventh and in the earlier sixth century. Now add that already in the seventh century she was beginning to use the best Athenian vases, and we have perhaps the explanation for the appearance of Athenian vases in quantity at Naucratis some time before they appear in comparable numbers on any other overseas market.

There are other classes of finds to be mentioned which may throw some light on trade at Naucratis and the identity of the merchants living in or visiting the town. There are a number of stone statuettes – of limestone, and a few of alabaster or marble – which

143 Alabaster statuette from Naucratis; mid-6th c. (London B 443; H. 10·2 cm)

144, 145 Limestone statuettes of a horseman and of a woman on a couch, from Naucratis; 6th c. (London EA 68835, 68821)

are clearly of Cypriot type. The earliest and best of them are equally clearly not of Cypriot origin, but produced by East Greek artists inspired by the generally dull but numerous products of the Cypriot workshops. The material of some – alabaster (*Fig. 143*) – suggests that they may have been working in Naucratis itself.[55] But beside them there are many stone and clay statuettes of certain Cypriot origin.[56] These are not, generally, so early, and need not imply any very important Cypriot element in the merchant classes at Naucratis. All may in fact date to the years in which the island was held by the Egyptians, in the second and third quarters of the sixth century. Some other stone statuettes, of horsemen and of women reclining on couches, are executed in a crude Egyptianizing style and seem to be largely of some local cult significance (*Figs. 144, 145*).[57]

Petrie found in the southern part of the town a factory for faience scarab seals which was active for part of the sixth century. This introduces us to an important class of objects – distinguished by their material rather than their form – which presents a number of important questions about Greco-Egyptian relations in the world of art (if they merit the term) in the seventh and sixth centuries, and which is best considered here. It should first be made clear that what the archaeologist calls faience bears no relation to the celebrated products of Renaissance Faenza. Ancient 'faience' is of a sandy composition and covered with a heavy glaze. It had long been used in Egypt for beads and various decorative trifles, and in the period which concerns us it is most often employed for scarab seals, small figure pendants, beads, and miniature vases. Such minor objects travelled far in the ancient world, and some time before the middle of the seventh century a factory for them was set up in Rhodes, possibly by Egyptians, but certainly intended to serve Greek markets.[58] Some of the products have a strongly Egyptian appearance – small vases in the shape of a figure or a monkey holding a pot (*Fig. 146*), flat circular flasks and bowls with figure patterns.[59] By the end of the century this series is supplemented by the produce of Naucratis, the most distinctive

objects being little figure pendants with whitish glaze and slight
added colour (*Fig. 147*). Some subjects are Egyptian – the cats,
naked girls, deities; some are Greek – pipers and lyre-players.[60]
They flood the East Greek world, especially Rhodes (where they
were probably also produced) and Samos, but they also reach
south Italy.

The Rhodes–Naucratis factories flourished still in the sixth
century producing flasks and elaborate figure vases in forms
already familiar in the Greek world (Corinth and East Greece) in
clay.[61] One exceptional example, a flask in the shape of the head of
the river-god Achelous (*Fig. 148*), found its way deep into Egypt,
to Nubia.[62] Something Egyptian or negroid in its features poses a
problem about origin, but other such flasks are purely Greek in
appearance. There are some faience flasks which bear the names of
Egyptian kings, and might also be Rhodian, although they were
probably also made in Naucratis. One in Paris, said to be from
Corinth, is more likely to be East Greek in origin: it is in the
purely Greek form of a helmeted head and carries the name of a
king, probably Apries (*Fig. 149*).[63] The others are *aryballoi* which
compromise between the Greek shape for perfume flasks and the
Egyptian kohl or mascara pots:[64] these are likely to be from
Naucratis and they have an interesting distribution, two in Egypt,
two from Rhodes, one each from Cyprus, Ibiza, the Lipari islands

146 Faience vase in the
form of a man kneeling,
holding a pot with a frog
on it, from Camirus,
Rhodes; mid-7th c.
(London 60.4–4.75; H.
9.5 cm)

147 Faience statuettes of a pipes-
and lyre-player from Emporio,
Chios; about 600 BC. (Chios Mus.;
H. 5·9 and 4·7 cm)

148 Faience flask in the
form of the head of
Achelous from Kawa; late
6th c. (Oxford 1931.482;
H. 6·1 cm)

149 Faience flask in the form of a helmeted head, marked with a cartouche on the side of the helmet, from Corinth (?); early 6th c. (Paris, Louvre MNB 1143; H. 6·5 cm)

150 Faience aryballos with cartouche of Apries (585–570 BC) from Lipara. (Oxford 1944.35; H. 5·8 cm)

(*Fig. 150*), and the Milesian colony of Panticapaeum in South Russia. The cartouches on them, not all clearly legible, name Apries and Amasis.

Production on Greek soil of Egyptianizing faience was being challenged by the end of the seventh century by the mass-production factories at Naucratis, themselves stimulated by the opportunities offered by Greek traders. Scarab seals were popular – the old Egyptian form of seal with the back carved as the sacred scarab beetle – but there were others in the form of a human or a ram's head,[65] and hundreds of small clay moulds for these good-luck charms – they were hardly more – were found in the scarab-factory. Moulds for the backs of these seals are shown in *Fig. 151*.[66] The devices are generally rough hieroglyphic mottoes or names. Other Naucratite products in the sixth century are hedge-hog vases and minor statuettes.[67] They are more poorly executed than the Rhodian faience, mass-produced, and travelled far in the Greek world. They are also, of course, well represented among the finds in Naucratis, and were probably being made through most of the sixth century. They do not command respect for any artistic qualities, and their distribution was too wide to tell us much specific about trade, but they are thickest where we would expect them, in East Greece, Aegina, the western markets (including Etruria) visited by the East Greeks, and even the East Greek colonies in the Black Sea. They afford an interesting commentary on commercial opportunism in a town whose primary function was to serve as an entrepôt, not a manufacturing town.

Among the other objects there are some stone scarab seals which have been thought the products of a local workshop, again supplying Greek markets, and there is evidence for a shop producing alabaster vases.[68] Five fragments of carved tridacna shell were found, as well as some plain pieces. We have already (*Fig. 58*) met these oriental products of the seventh century and early sixth, which were especially popular in East Greece. In Egypt they appear only at sites frequented by the Greeks – Naucratis, and one fragment each from Daphnae and Memphis.[69] Another eastern object is a worn Assyrian cylinder seal,[70] which – centuries old already – was carried to Naucratis, no doubt as a lucky charm; and Petrie also describes an ivory cylinder (? seal) with a man, goats, and a tree.[71]

TRADE AND LIFE

Consideration of Greek trade through Naucratis involves consideration of Greek trade with the rest of Egypt, and the evidence of finds outside Naucratis. For actual settlement in Egypt by Greeks we have first to think of the communities of mercenaries, but the story of Kolaios and the finds of Egyptian bronzes in some parts of Greece (notably Crete and Samos) show the beginnings of commercial interest as well, which actual settlement was able to safeguard and develop. There can only have been one commodity of importance which the Greeks sought – corn; although papyrus and linen may also have been carried.[72] The East Greek states were growing fast in the seventh century, but their expansion at home was being contained both by their Greek neighbours and by the pressure of Phrygia and then Lydia. The two obvious expedients were tried. New colonies – generally founded with a shrewd eye to their value as trading posts – dispersed part of their surplus population. For those left behind who could not readily support themselves on their local resources, or whose economy was becoming specialized – as in Chios, where wine and oil were being produced rather than corn – foreign sources of grain were sought: some in the Black Sea (see Chapter 6), some in Egypt. Aegina enters the field here as the home of merchant carriers supplying central Greece, where similar economic conditions prevailed.

Payment for the corn seems to have been made in various ways. Olive oil was no doubt bartered – some Athenian and Samian storage jars can be identified. Wine was certainly carried in quantity. There is some variety of sixth-century jars to be found in Naucratis and Daphnae, of which the most readily recognized are the Chian. One Chian jar was re-used in Daphnae and sealed with cartouches of King Amasis (*Fig. 152*).[73] The East Greek poet

151 Clay moulds for faience seal backs in the form of a Negro's head and of a scarab beetle, from Naucratis; 6th c. (Oxford)

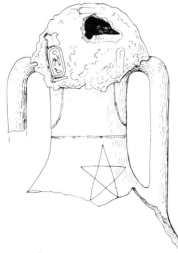

152 Neck of a Chian wine jar sealed with cartouches of King Amasis, from Daphnae; 6th c.

Hipponax uses the Egyptian word for wine, but this does not mean there was any return traffic.[74]

The most valuable commodity which the Greeks brought to Egypt was silver. The country had no coined money of its own, and the interest was in the precious metal as such, but it was naturally carried by the Greeks in the form of coinage. Even in the early period which is our main concern – before about 480 – a notable number of hoards of silver have been found in Egypt including both coins (some disfigured to test their purity) and the plain unminted metal. The sources of the coins can indicate which states carried the silver, or at least the source of the silver carried by the merchants. They correspond well with what we already expect of the pattern of trade at Naucratis. Aegina is prominent, with Athens (which by the end of the century was coining silver in some quantity as an export commodity) and Corinth. Of the East Greek states, we find Miletus and Chios, while Samos, Phocaea, and Teos are also represented – all of them states whose interest in Naucratis is recorded by Herodotus. A remarkable feature, however, is the very high proportion of silver coins minted in North Greece, in Thrace and Macedonia. This was an important silver-producing area, and the coins minted there could readily be carried, more or less as bullion, by other states trading in North Greece which had need of the metal for payment in places like Egypt or the east (see p. 54 above) rather than for circulation at home. Corinth had interests in North Greece, but there were Ionian and Aeolian towns there too, and it has been argued that some of the East Greeks, who had no ready source of silver at home, relied on their contacts in Thrace for supply of the metal for their coins.[75]

It is far more difficult to see just how trade was organized through Naucratis. The archaeological evidence tells us about the sanctuaries, not the warehouses, and it has been assumed by some that each interested state had not only its own temple but its own trading quarter. The big independent sanctuaries founded by the Samians, Milesians, and it seems the Chians and Aeginetans, may date to the early years of the town, but the variety in the sources of the dedications and dedicators in them shows clearly that they were not separate 'nationalist' centres of worship, but in general use by the whole Greek community. The Hellenion, which may have been built in Amasis' reign, afforded a larger sanctuary area for other shrines, some no doubt founded by states trading there, others by the established Greek community. Still, Naucratis was not yet quite an ordinary Greek town with its own 'citizens'. It was nothing like the colonies in Italy and Sicily. It owed its existence to the continued favour (and interest) of the Egyptian king, and the Greek states trading there – the same, it appears, who had already long been working side by side at Al Mina in Syria – no doubt saw to it that their monopoly of the Egyptian trade was not usurped. This in turn implies a measure of agreement between them, but not necessarily between the home states; rather between the interested merchant classes resident in Naucratis itself. From these were surely appointed the *prostatai* Herodotus mentions, the officers in charge of the port, for all that the historian seems to imply that they were posted there by the mother cities. Clearly too it was not only the founders of the Hellenion, but the sponsors of the other and independent sanctuaries, who had a share in the ordering of the life of the town, commercial and otherwise. The *prostatai* may have acted both as magistrates for the town and as 'consuls' for their kinsmen and for merchants from their mother cities.

The life of this large and rich Greek community, admitted to a country which had long mistrusted foreigners, and indeed still preferred strictly limiting their activities and settlement, must have been a very strange and varied one. It was quite unlike anything the Greeks had experienced elsewhere. It was not like a colony – an independent self-supporting town which had come to terms with the local population; nor a simple trading post, like Al Mina, where in the early period there may have been no properly organized Greek civic life, with pretentious sanctuaries and the like. Naucratis attracted the get-rich-quick merchants of East Greece, and their Aeginetan colleagues who ran the business with central Greece. It attracted poets, artists, statesmen, and historians, and in times of danger it may have become a place of refuge for professional men of East Greece who could there ply their trade again. Above all, it opened Greek eyes to the works of a great civilization, more impressive even then in its 'antiquities' than in its contemporary arts and crafts. Even the Egyptian products of these years are strongly 'archaizing'. Later in this chapter we shall see something of how the Greeks were influenced by what they saw. For the present, at Naucratis itself, we can glean from historians and archaeology a little of the life of the town.

It seems likely that there was already an Egyptian town or village on the site when the Greeks first arrived.[76] This, at any rate, we should expect. Its old name may have been forgotten, for the Egyptians knew the town as Piemro, which is what has been called a 'learned translation' of the Greek, although the reverse might, I suppose, be true. Certainly Egyptians always lived there beside the Greeks. There was probably a native quarter, and the labouring population would have been Egyptian, but the wretched foundations of the mudbrick houses which were excavated in the waterlogged site can tell us nothing of value about the homes of either Greeks or Egyptians there.

The dedications inscribed on vases found in the sanctuaries tell a little about the worshippers. There was Aristophanes, for instance, who about the middle of the sixth century bespoke several cups of the Chian pottery for dedication to Aphrodite, and who carried others on a business trip to Aegina, to dedicate in the temple of Aphaea there.[77] One Rhoikos dedicated an elaborate

153 Multiple eye cup dedicated by Rhoikos to Aphrodite at Naucratis; about 575–550 BC. (London 88.6–1.392)

cup to Aphrodite some time in the second quarter of the century (*Fig. 153*), and he may be the Samian architect who in these years was designing what in its day was the largest of all the Greek temples, the temple of Hera on Samos.[78] We have already had occasion to remark on some Samian architectural features at Naucratis. The Phanes who gave a cup might be the Halicarnassian mercenary of King Amasis who deserted to the Persians, in Herodotus' story.[79] Much later, but not lightly ignored except by the wholly sceptical, is the Athenian cup given by a Herodotus[80] at about the time when the great historian may have been visiting Egypt. Many of the other dedications give us names only, sometimes revealing too the home of the dedicator. Several are given by women. A Doris offered a love charm to Aphrodite.[81] Naucratis had something of a reputation for the looks and easy virtue of its women. The famous Rhodopis was brought there by a Samian procurer, Charaxos, a wine merchant dealing with Naucratis and brother of the great Lesbian poetess Sappho, and bought her freedom. She stayed in Egypt and made a small fortune, one tenth of which she dedicated to Apollo at Delphi, in the form of iron spits – an early form of money. Part of the inscribed base which carried her dedication has been found there in recent years.[82] 'For some reason or other, Naucratis must be a good place for beautiful prostitutes,' says Herodotus, and goes on to mention the famous Archedike,[83] whose name we read on another vase-dedication found in the town. A more sober and distinguished visitor in the sixth century was the Athenian law-giver Solon,[84] who came on a business-cum-sightseeing tour; others were the poet Alcaeus and the philosopher Thales.[85]

These years before the Persian invasion (525) must have been Naucratis' heyday. She regained prosperity later, but an Egypt under the Persians, the vagaries of Greek politics, and a growing civic conscience, combined to dull the brilliance of her cosmopolitan life – almost the difference between the Shanghai of before and after the Second World War. When Alexander the Great took

Egypt, the town was eclipsed by his new capital, Alexandria; but there were flourishing factories still there in the Roman period, and it was the birthplace of Athenaeus, the famous man of letters.

Other Greeks in Egypt

We have yet to consider other places in Egypt where Greeks lived, or to which Greek objects penetrated. Of these the most important in our period is DAPHNAE, Tell Defenneh.[86] The site lies between the eastern edge of the cultivated area of the Delta and the present Suez Canal, on the main route to the east, to Palestine and Syria. It was excavated by Petrie in 1886. The largest structure, roughly square in plan, had been built by Psammetichos I. Petrie reasonably took it for a fort. It is very like the large building in the southern quarter of Naucratis, which is of about the same date (*Fig. 156*). It has been argued that these are rather treasuries or store-houses than military constructions, and on the whole the finds bear this out. There can hardly, however, be any doubt that the primary importance of the town was as a fortress and frontier post, and Herodotus says that in the reign of Psammetichos guards were stationed in Pelusian Daphnae against the Arabians and Syrians.[87] Under King Apries the town afforded asylum to Jews, among them the prophet Jeremiah, driven from Judah by the Babylonians – 'and they came into the land of Egypt; for they obeyed not the voice of the Lord: and they came even to Tahpanhes' (i.e. Daphnae): Jeremiah, 43:7. The ruins of the fort are indeed still called 'Kasr el Bint el Yehudi' – Palace of the Jew's Daughter.

The earliest evidence for Greeks at Daphnae is afforded by scraps of East Greek pottery, some at least of which are of the latest seventh century. This is hardly enough to prove the presence of any substantial, or indeed any Greek force there. The mass of Greek pottery from the site belongs to the years of Amasis' reign (570–526), and this alone speaks against the identification of the site with the Stratopeda 'Camps' given to the Greeks by Psammetichos I and evacuated by Amasis. The pottery was found in various parts of the site, but there was a particular concentration in two rooms south-east of the 'fort', which have been called 'a sort of cellar or butler's pantry' – presumably for the officers' mess. The quantity of pottery is of course much less than that from Naucratis, but there are some significant differences in the classes represented:[88]

1. *'Rhodian'*. The earliest scraps only, since the distinctive Rhodian Wild Goat style vases were no longer being made after the first years of Amasis' reign. But note:

2. *Fikellura* vases. As at Naucratis (see p. 124).

3. *Situlae*. Daphnae is the principal source of these distinctive vases. Their baggy shape (*Fig. 154*) has been thought to derive

154 Clay 'situla' showing Typhon, from Daphnae; about 530 BC. (London 88.2–8.1 (B 104); H. 53·6 cm)

155 Fragment of a situla from Daphnae; about 530 BC. (London 88.2–8.3; H. 7 cm)

from Egyptian bronze vases, and some of the motifs in their decoration – such as a hawk seated on the Neb-basket on one fragment (*Fig. 155*) – are purely Egyptian. The hawk and basket hieroglyphs are part of a royal title. Some half dozen vases of this general type have been found in Rhodes, but it seems possible that most of those at Daphnae were made by Greek potters, probably Rhodians, working in Egypt. And it seems likely that they were working at or near Daphnae, for not one was found at Naucratis.

4. *Samian* and *Lesbian* jars for oil and wine respectively.[89]

The next two groups are by far the largest:

5. *Clazomenian* black-figure vases, as at Naucratis. Here again there is a possibility that some of the vases are the work of a Greek vase painter working in Egypt, for nearly all the vases of one of the Clazomenian artists, the so-called Petrie Painter, have been found at Daphnae; the rest are from Naucratis.

6. *Athenian* black-figure vases and storage jars. About as common as the Clazomenian.

Comparison with the finds at Naucratis shows a notable lack of Chian-Naucratite (one fragment is reported from near by, but there are Chian wine jars from the fort) and of Spartan, and a less notable lack of Corinthian, while at Naucratis there are no situlae. The differences are more likely to reflect the opportunities of the markets than any significant difference in the origins or tastes of the Greek customers.

Of the minor finds we may pick out iron weapons and iron scale-armour. One piece of carved tridacna shell was found, like the pieces at Naucratis – an eastern object brought by a Greek to Egypt, even to Daphnae, perhaps before 600. Crude stone figurines like those at Naucratis were found, but only two or three scarabs from the Naucratis factory.

The Greek finds on the site fail at about 525 BC, and there can be little doubt that this was the direct result of the Persian invasion under Cambyses.

This was not, however, the only Egyptian fort in the eastern Delta to have Greeks. Israeli scholars exploring Sinai have recently located a massive fort, occupying some ten acres, about 20 km. from Daphnae and a little south of Pelusium (*Fig. 156*). Here there are no fine wares, but plenty of sixth-century Greek amphorae and, remarkably, the first Greek Archaic cremation burials to be found in Egypt. The site's history is likely to be similar to that of Daphnae, and the fortunes of the Greeks there the same. It has been tentatively identified as Migdol.[90]

Elsewhere in the Delta there are scattered finds of sixth-century Greek pottery. Passing south we reach MEMPHIS, to which Amasis moved the Greek mercenary camps, according to Herodotus.[91] But here there are pieces of Greek pottery – Corinthian (*Fig. 157*) and East Greek – as well as the tridacna shell

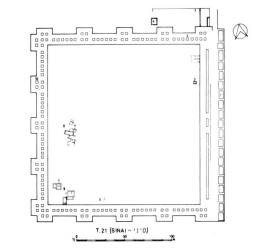

156 The fort at 'Migdol' from the air, and, in plan, compared with the forts at Daphnae and Naucratis (courtesy of Dr E. Oren)

DAPHNAE–תל דפנה   NAUKRATIS–נאוקרטיס   T.21 (SINAI – סיני)

fragments we have already mentioned, as early as any of the finds at Naucratis. Throughout the sixth century, Greek pottery is arriving at Memphis, mainly East Greek wares like those at Naucratis – Rhodian, Fikellura, Clazomenian – and there must certainly have been a mercenary camp there through Amasis' reign. There were Carian mercenaries here too, and there are sixth-century stelae for Carians at Memphis (Saqqara) with Greek-style reliefs (*Fig. 158*).[92] From about 500, the Athenian black-figure vases replace the East Greek, which are no longer being made. The finds have been made at Memphis itself – in the Palace of Apries and the Temple of Ptah – and in the outlying cemeteries at Abusir and Saqqara. A stray find is an Egyptian bronze statuette dedicated by a Greek in the sixth century and inscribed in both Greek and Egyptian, and there are other bronzes from Egypt carrying Greek dedications.[93] A uniquely early Greek find at Saqqara is a mid-seventh-century bronze griffin protome. A number of minor Greek Archaic statuettes in Egyptian alabaster attest Greek craftsmen in the Egyptian towns,[94] and an East Greek bronze statuette of a man wearing an Egyptian kilt may have travelled from Egypt to its find place in Acarnania (west Greece).[95]

157 Corinthian vase fragment from Memphis; about 630 BC. (Philadelphia 29.71. 190)

From Abusir comes a unique monument, found in the mortuary temple of Sahure, which may belong to our period. It is a limestone slab (*Fig. 159*), apparently a tombstone, bearing in low relief the scene of *prothesis* – the laying out of a dead body. The

159 Limestone grave stele with a prothesis scene inscribed in Carian, from Abusir; about 500 BC. (East Berlin 19553; H. 27 cm)

158 Limestone grave stele with an incised, lightly modelled farewell scene, inscribed in Carian, from Saqqara; about 550–500 BC. (Cambridge E 1.1971; H. 91·2 cm)

160 Faience ushabti from Saqqara; about 500 BC. (Cairo Mus. J.E. 35268; H. 9·5 cm)

161 Limestone statue (*kore*) from Memphis; late 6th c. (Cairo Mus. 27431; H. 72 cm)

scene, gestures, and furniture are wholly Greek, although there is
much in the execution of the figures which is Egyptian; and the
Egyptian winged sun-disc and *uraei* carved above, though commonly found at the top of the Egyptian stelae, have no particular
relevance here. To one side of the scene, a poorly preserved
inscription in Carian names the dead (it was formerly read as
Greek, for a Milesian).[96] Much more has been learnt in recent
years about the Carians who lived beside the Greeks in these
Egyptian garrison towns.[97] This monument, for its style and
subject, must be the work of a local, Greek-trained artist who had
already been much affected by Egyptian forms and techniques.
From Saqqara is a faience ushabti figure (*Fig. 160*) of the sort
regularly put in Egyptian tombs to serve as labourers for the dead
in the other world. But this has a Greek late-archaic head, perhaps
made especially for the burial of a Greek who had accepted some
Egyptian views about the after-life.[98] From Memphis again, we
should mention a limestone statue of a woman, superficially just
like any East Greek maiden of the later sixth century, but with
some undoubtedly Egyptian features (*Fig. 161*)[99]; an interesting
clay sealing which carries both cartouches of King Amasis and the
impression of an archaic Greek seal with the representation of a
merman or Triton;[100] and the bronze mounting for a statuette,
inscribed both in Egyptian and Greek, the latter with the dedication to 'Theban Zeus', the Egyptian Amun.[101] At ABYDOS
Greeks scratched their names on what they took to be the temple
of the hero Memnon (really the funerary temple of Seti I).[102]

South again at Egyptian THEBES, and the great sanctuaries of
Luxor and Karnak, we find more Greek pottery – Corinthian and
East Greek – of the first two-thirds of the sixth century. A Karnak
vase, fragments of which are in Oxford, is of especial interest.[103] It
shows the sacred ship of the Greek god Dionysus being carried
and accompanied by men, some dressed as satyrs, the god's
attendants (*Fig. 162*). They wear loin-cloths to keep their tails on,
brandish phalli, and play pipes. Processions like this were known
in Athens, where the ship went on wheels, and in East Greece, at
Smyrna, where the ship was carried. But they were well known in
Egypt too, and particularly at Karnak and Luxor, where there was
the great Opet festival each year in which the ship of the god
Amun was carried (*Fig. 163*). Similar processions were held at
Siwa Oasis in the Libyan desert, where there was a shrine of
Amun much respected by the Greeks, and often visited by them,
as of 'Zeus Ammon'. Here the image of the god gave oracles by
guiding the ship.[104] That the only Greek representation of this
scene should be found at Karnak seems more than coincidence,
and it may well be that it was deliberately dedicated there because
it was appropriate. It may even have been painted in Egypt, for it
is related to some other vases we have mentioned in like case. The
other side of the vase shows a vineyard scene with dogs, like the
painting in a slightly later tomb at Siwa Oasis.[105] The success of

162 Reconstruction of the
scene on an East Greek vase
from Karnak; about
540–530 B.C. (Oxford
1924.264)

these Greek potteries in Egypt is a noteworthy comment on the
flourishing Greek communities in the country, for it is doubtful
whether the Egyptians were interested in the vases in the sixth
century, and most of the Greek pottery arriving in Egypt seems to
have been destined for Greek tables. At Naucratis we have seen
potteries turning out votives for the Greek temples there; and in
the Daphnae situlae, the Karnak vase, and some others of doubtful
parentage, evidence perhaps of the work of refugee Greek artists
driven from their homes in Ionia by the Persian attacks of the
540s. A remarkable addition to these is a fragmentary East Greek
vase from Egypt bearing an ordinary figure scene on the body
but, on the neck, painted cartouches naming the Egyptian king
Apries (*Fig. 164*).[106]

Beyond Thebes there have been finds of Greek pottery at Edfu
(Rhodian of about 600),[107] and from much farther south, in Nubia,
the Rhodian faience flask of *Fig. 148*. This is all that can so far be
said of sixth-century Greek finds in Egypt. After 500, the import

163 Relief at Luxor

of Greek vases, now all of them Athenian, picked up again; but these begin to carry us outside our chosen period. Two finds only, of later date, I mention for their excellence and interest – the rhyton figure vase in the shape of a mounted Amazon which was found at distant Meroe in Nubia (*Fig. 165*); and another, from Memphis, in the shape of a camel led by a Persian and a negro (*Fig. 166*).[108] Both were made in Athens little before the middle of the fifth century by the potter Sotades.

164 Fragmentary vase of East Greek type with painted cartouches on the neck, from Egypt; about 525–500 BC. (Basel, Cahn Coll. HC 1175)

And what of the Carians who served beside the Greeks, and indeed the Greek Cypriots in Egypt? The Carians reveal themselves by their inscriptions – notably those on the funeral stelae already discussed, but there are many also scratched on rock and pottery. The most significant are those beside the Greek inscriptions on the rock-cut figures at Abu Simbel, cut by mercenaries in the Nubian expedition of 591. And there are Carian inscriptions too in Nubia itself, where there may have been a garrison.[109] For the Cypriots, we have had occasion to note their presence at Naucratis. Cypriot poetry of sixth-century type has been found at Daphnae and Memphis, and in Nubia at Sanam; and their inscriptions at Giza, Abydos, Karnak, and Buhen in Nubia; to name only the more important.[110]

The Egyptians were never well-disposed to foreigners, and it says much for Greek persistence, and for their fighting qualities which were appreciated by the kings, that they settled for so long and so successfully in the country. The Egyptians, Herodotus tells us, were careful to avoid Greek customs, and seemed rather to despise them:

No Egyptian, man or woman, will kiss a Greek, or use a Greek knife, spit, or cauldron, or even eat the flesh of a bull known to be clean, if it has been cut with a Greek knife.

And the head of a sacrificed animal would be cut off, cursed, and 'if there happen to be Greek traders in the market, it is sold to them; if not, it is thrown into the river'.[111] 'A grotesque fact,' it has been called, 'that the Greeks were quite indispensable to the

165 Athenian clay vase – a
mounted Amazon, from
Meroe, Nubia; about 460
BC. (Boston 21.2286; H.
34 cm)

166 Restoration of an Athenian clay vase – a camel led
by a Persian and a Negro (whose placing in the group
is not certain) from Memphis; about 460 BC. (Paris,
Louvre CA 3825; H. about 50 cm)

Egyptian kings, and at the same time the best-hated people in Egypt.' When Herodotus wrote, he described the attitude of a country at her nadir, under Persian domination, while Greece was at the zenith of her classical period. Egypt was to be prosperous again, but only as a member of the Greek empire founded by Alexander the Great.

The Persians in Egypt

Cambyses, king of Persia, marched against Egypt in 525 BC. In his army were Ionian and Aeolian Greeks and Cypriots, subjects of the empire which had now spread even to the Greek islands off Asia Minor. In Egypt they faced the Ionian and Carian mercenaries of the Egyptian king, one of whose number, Phanes of Halicarnassus, had already deserted to the Persians – for which his fellows took horrible revenge on his sons. The Egyptian army was defeated, and at Memphis it was from a Greek boat, of Lesbos, that the Persian herald called for surrender. The Greeks in the Persian army then had to join in abortive expeditions to Siwa Oasis (the sanctuary of Zeus Ammon) and into Nubia, before they were dismissed home.[112]

The archaeological evidence makes clear the effects on the Greeks in Egypt of the Persian invasion. The fort at Daphnae was abandoned. The import of Greek pottery to Naucratis and the rest of Egypt practically ceased. However, the setback did not last long, and by about 500, at Naucratis and elsewhere, Athenian pottery is beginning to arrive in some quantity, as well as Athenian silver coins. This does not necessarily mean that the East Greeks were no longer the merchants dealing with Egypt, for it could not have been until after the Persian Wars that Athens could have taken a serious and direct interest in Egypt as a source of corn.

Of the Persians themselves, we see sealings at Memphis from fine Achaemenid gems, for instance, and on many sites iron and bronze scale armour, some of which, however, might be attributed to the Ionian and Carian mercenaries. And from Memphis is a grave-stele with another prothesis scene, like *Fig. 159*, but less Egyptian in execution and clearly commemorating a Persian burial.[113] But the archaeology of Persian Egypt, even of the Greeks in it, is not our concern here.

Egyptian Objects and Influence in Greece

The Greeks got to know Egypt again nearly two centuries after they had reopened relations with the countries of the Near East. The impression made by the civilization of the Nile valley was no less forceful than that made by the east, but by that time the Greeks had matured in the 'orientalizing' phase of their culture and art, and were yet more discriminate in the foreign motifs or

167 Basalt Egyptian statuette of a
seated figure dedicated by a Greek,
from Camirus, Rhodes; about 550 B.C.
(Rhodes Mus. 14341; H. 14 cm)

ideas which they admitted or adopted. Even so the example of
Egypt prompted them to experiment in two new fields hitherto
ignored by the Aegean peoples and yet to produce the most
characteristic work of Classical Greece – monumental sculpture
and architecture in stone.

For all the part played by Greek mercenaries in Egypt from the
later seventh century on, it is not until the reign of Amasis that we
find the Egyptian king taking a serious interest in the Greeks at
home. Before his day Necho had dedicated armour at a Milesian
temple, probably acknowledging the services of his Greeks, and
the brother of a tyrant of Corinth, Periander, named one of his
sons Psammetichos after the Egyptian king. The name may
appear even earlier, scratched on a mid-seventh-century cup in
Athens.[114] Amasis was yet more generous to the Greek cities, and
we read of his dedications in Cyrene, Rhodes (Lindos), and
Samos, and a gift to Sparta of a figure-decorated linen corselet or
belt, which the Samians intercepted as usual. The Samian tyrant
Polycrates seems to have enjoyed an alliance with Amasis for a
time, while the Egyptian king's benevolence to Cyrene was
expressed by an alliance and his marriage with a Cyrenaean princess. Perhaps more remarkable was his contribution to the building of a new temple of Apollo at Delphi.[115]

For the actual import of Egyptian objects to Greece after the
foundation of Naucratis – earlier imports we have already mentioned – we have a mass of minor objects which were probably
manufactured in Naucratis, and so are at least half-Greek rather
than purely Egyptian works. The Naucratis faience scarabs and
seals are found in plenty on many East Greek sites.[116] They are
hardly less common in central Greece, especially at Aegina,
Sunium (en route to Athens), and Perachora (near Corinth), and
were carried to the western colonies and Etruria. In general the
distribution follows the pattern set by the states with a serious
trading interest in Naucratis. To the small objects in faience we
should perhaps add the glass flasks and alabaster vases which were
becoming popular in Greece and for which we know there was a
factory at Naucratis. Of more individual interest is the little basalt

168 East Greek clay
alabastron; about 550–500
B.C. (Oxford 1885.566; H.
18 cm)

Egyptian figure brought to Rhodes by a Greek in the mid sixth century and dedicated by him after he had written his name on it in Greek (*Fig. 167*).[117] The typical alabastron shape in stone was soon copied in clay by East Greek (*Fig. 168*) and Athenian potters (*Figs. 194, 195*).[118]

When we come to speak of Egyptian *influence* rather than objects, the material evidence is no less decisive. In non-material affairs the influence of Egypt was slight, or at any rate difficult to assess. Influence in religion was negligible, for all Herodotus' claims, although in myth and representations of myth there were certainly borrowings, as we shall see, and the Dionysiac processions with ships carried or wheeled are certainly most like Egyptian processions (see p. 137, above). Animal parodies of religious heroic action – like the Greek 'epic' of the Battle of the Mice and Frogs – had also long been at home in Egypt.[119] In geometry and medicine too the Greeks may have found something new. But in architecture and sculpture they certainly found much to impress them and lead them to new things, and these are matters which the archaeologist can investigate.

It was not until they visited Egypt that the Greeks saw colossal buildings constructed entirely of stone and featuring stone mouldings and columns with elaborately carved capitals and bases. At home they were used to mudbrick and wood, and less pretentious styles of masonry. In the Near East too brick was the main medium, columns were never of stone and were of comparatively little importance, and stone mouldings and capitals were virtually unknown. By the end of the seventh century Greek architects were moved to emulate the Egyptian manner, although not to imitate it in detail but to adapt it to local traditional architectural forms. In mainland Greece the result was the Doric order of architecture.[120] Here the column capitals are like round cushions and their form seems to owe at least as much to the old Mycenaean Greek capitals as to Egyptian ones. Details of the upper works were more a translation of wood into stone, but one moulding, the cavetto, was borrowed straight from Egypt, and was also put at the top of the gravestones in Athens.[121] In East Greece, the same interest in building all-stone temples was awakened, but here the decorative forms chosen for the parts – the capitals, bases, finials – were derived from the artist's repertoire of orientalizing forms, not Egyptian, many of them seemingly once employed in the East, on a smaller scale and in different material, for furniture. After some experiment, the Ionic order was evolved in the second quarter of the sixth century, with nothing Egyptian in it beyond the guiding principle or idea which inspired its early stages.[122] Indeed, the only architectural form which may have been borrowed from Egypt, the palm capital (*Fig. 169*), was little used. There is a seventh-century example from Crete (*Fig. 170*),[123] then others, East Greek, of the sixth century and later.[124] For the possible Egyptian origin of the Ionic stepped altar see p. 120.

169 Egyptian palm capital at Luxor

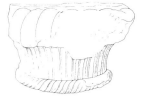

170 Limestone palm capital from Arkades, Crete; mid-7th c. (Heraklion Mus.; Diam. below, 24·7 cm)

171 Granite statue of a man from Karnak; early 7th c. (Cairo Mus. 42236; H. 1·35 m)

172 Marble statue of a youth (kouros) – Kroisos, from his grave at Anavysos in Attica; about 530 BC. (Athens NM 3851; H. 1·94 m)

At about the same time as, or a little earlier than their first experiments in monumental stone architecture, the Greeks began to make monumental stone sculpture. The inspiration was again Egypt, where colossal stone statuary was commonplace.[125] Hitherto the Greeks had made only small figures, in soft stone and in the orientalizing style ('Dedalic') and only in Crete did some seated figures in stone approach life size in the years around and after the mid seventh century. The Egyptian example of colossal statuary in hard stone encouraged them to exploit their resources of fine white marble and to create lifesize or larger figures. This, inevitably, happened in the islands, where the marble was readily accessible, not in Crete where there was none. Some figures, like the Nicandre dedication on Delos, were still in the old form, but in the new material and to the new scale. Others, the great statues of nude youths or *kouroi*, were much closer to the Egyptian models. But again the Greek artist, in accepting a new idea, a new technique, declined to copy blindly. The Egyptian figures like the *kouroi* stand back on their heels, back leg and spine straight and often supported by a pillar; and they are clothed (*Fig. 171*). The *kouroi* stand squarely on their two feet and convey a feeling of immanent life; and they are naked (*Fig. 172*). They clench their fists, like the Egyptians. From the beginning they are artistically finer and more sensitive (though less accurate) studies of the human form than any Egyptian work, although some observe even in detail the new canon of proportions worked out by the Egyptian artists.[126] The Greeks soon broke with this canon, but there are memories of its use in Greece in Diodorus' story of the two sons of Rhoikos of Samos (see p. 132) who made the two halves of an Apollo statue in different places, but effected a perfect join by observing canons of proportion like the Egyptian.[127] There are a number of other sculptural forms, some of them in the minor arts of sixth-century Greece, which seem to owe something to Egypt. The great avenue of marble lions on the sacred island of Delos (*Fig. 173*)[128] must surely have been inspired by Egyptian avenues of lions, sphinxes, or rams (*Fig. 174*); and near Miletus a processional way flanked by massive seated figures and lions seems to have been conceived in much the same spirit.[129] Herodotus himself compared the round sacred lake before the lions on Delos with Egyptian sacred lakes.[130] In smaller objects some favourite Egyptian forms seem to have been copied: the naked swimming girl as a handle to a flat dish (*Fig. 175*) copied in clay in sixth-century Rhodes (*Fig. 176*).[131] A girl, again, as handle to a bronze mirror (*Fig. 177*), becomes a most common motif in Greek art (*Fig. 178*) from the mid sixth century on, appearing first at Sparta.[132] Some of these motifs may perhaps have been transmitted via the Near East, but hardly all, and certainly not those picked up in the sixth century. The ultimate origin of all is quite clearly Egyptian. Representations of lions in Greek art have already occupied our attention for their relationship to eastern

173 Row of marble lions, approaching the sanctuary of Leto on Delos; about 575–550 BC. (Delos; H. complete about 1·72 m)

174 The alley of the ram-headed sphinxes at Karnak

175 Faience toilet dish from Sanam, Nubia; 7th c. (Oxford 1921.735; L. 11 cm)

176 Clay toilet dish from Rhodes; 6th c. (Copenhagen NM 7652; L. 11·5 cm)

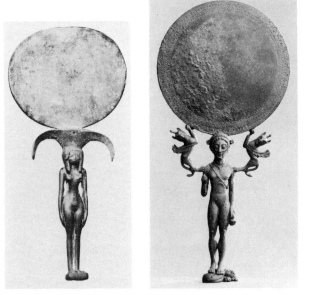

177 Egyptian bronze mirror from Saqqara (Cairo Mus. 44044; H. 35 cm)

178 Spartan bronze mirror; about 550–525 BC. (New York, Met. Mus. 38.11.3; H. 35·5 cm)

179 Marble lion from Miletus; mid-6th c. (Berlin 1790; L. 1·76 m)

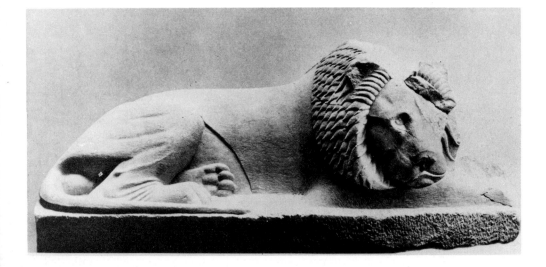

types, but in the sixth century a peculiarly Egyptian lion is adopted by Spartan bronze-workers and appears on the handles of bronze vases.[133] Other Egyptian leonine characteristics, not derived from the Near East, are displayed by East Greek stone statues (*Fig. 179*)[134] and statuettes and some mainland Greek works of the latest seventh and sixth centuries.

The number of Egyptian traits in sixth-century Spartan art which we have already remarked – and there will be more – may be due to her close relations with Cyrene in North Africa, but we must also remember Amasis' present, her vases at Naucratis, and the fact that for a time at least Sparta seems to have been on good terms with pro-Egyptian Samos.

The small faience artefacts – vases and statuettes – made in Rhodes and probably elsewhere, naturally reflect many motifs from the country in which the technique was learnt.[135] The grotesque figures of the god Bes, a distant cousin of the Greek satyr but certainly not more closely related, are perhaps the most typical.[136] Clay figures of plump dwarfs (*Fig. 180*) resemble the Egyptian Ptah.[137] In Rhodes too, some limestone statuettes are found rather like those at Naucratis, but of seated figures with rams' heads (*Fig. 181*)[138] – the Egyptian Amun.

Some new forms of wooden furniture which first become popular in sixth-century Greece seem to copy Egyptian models very closely, and no doubt the original pieces were imported as well. The best examples are the thrones with animal legs (not just feet) such as are seen on Spartan votive reliefs (*Fig. 182*) and vases, and elsewhere.[139] There is much too in the subject of these Spartan reliefs – hero and consort receiving offerings[140] – to remind one of Egyptian reliefs.

Strangely enough it seems that Egyptian wall painting made almost as profound an effect on Greek artists and visitors as did the sculpture and architecture. Here was decoration of a sort virtually unknown to them at home, and certainly uncommon in the Near East. The finest examples of Egyptian painting which

180 Clay dwarf from Tocra; mid-6th c. (Tocra 48; H. 7·4 cm)

181 Limestone statuette of a ram-headed deity from Lindos, Rhodes; 6th c. (Rhodes; H. 6·6 cm)

182 Spartan stone relief showing a hero and consort on a throne of Egyptian type, from Chrysapha (Sparta); about 550–540 BC. (Berlin 731; H. 87 cm)

147

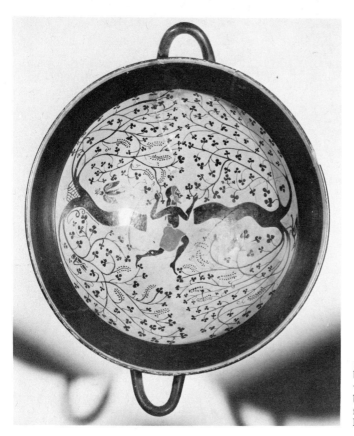

183 East Greek cup – a man between two trees, on one of which is a snake, a locust and a bird with its nest of fledglings, from Etruria; about 550 BC. (Paris, Louvre F 68; Diam. 23 cm)

we possess belong to the New Kingdom, some 500 years earlier than the foundation of Naucratis, but such was the conservatism in technique and subject in Egyptian art that it is not unreasonable to look to them for an idea of what our Greeks saw, since extant examples of painting of the seventh and sixth centuries in Egypt are so few. These major paintings had their effect in three ways: by their colour, their style, and their subject matter. It is just possible, too, that the effect was felt as early as the middle of the seventh century, as soon as we have any evidence at all for regular visits by Greeks to Egypt. Already on some Corinthian, and particularly on Athenian and island vases, we find attempts at polychromy and the laying on of broad masses of colour within painted outlines in the Egyptian manner. Earlier still there may be some intimation of an Egyptian motif in the little palmettes which grow from the foreheads of figures on Athenian and island vases, like the Egyptian lotus headbands.[141]

In the matter of style the effect was more subtle. The Greek artist was interested only in representations of men, gods, and animals, and not in the natural settings for his scenes or in landscape. When a tree or a vine is admitted it makes its way as best it may in the background or around the figures. In Egypt the natural proportions are more often observed, and on some sixth-century

184 Athenian vase (of Group E) showing Heracles shooting with a sling at the Stymphalian birds, from Vulci; about 540 BC. (London B 163)

Greek vases the same principle is to be seen in striking contrast with the normal Greek treatment. We may mention the East Greek cup with a man dancing between two trees (*Fig. 183*);[142] the vineyard scene on the Karnak vase[143] whose Egyptian provenance and subjects we have already discussed; vintages;[144] an olive harvest;[145] and a flock of birds which fly before Heracles as they might before an Egyptian noble on one of his Nile fowling parties (*Fig. 184*).[146]

Some individual scenes too are copied or adapted. On a Spartan cup (*Fig. 185*) the Greek king of Cyrene supervises the weighing and packing of wool in a scene which is very close to Egyptian representations of an overseer and the weighing and stacking of goods.[147] On a vase made by an East Greek in Etruria (a 'Caeretan'

185 Spartan cup by the Arkesilas Painter showing King Arkesilas, from Vulci; about 560 BC. (Paris, Cab. Méd. 189; Diam. 29 cm)

186 A 'Caeretan' hydria
showing Heracles routing
Busiris and his followers,
from Caere: for the reverse
see *Fig. 244*; about 530–520
BC. (Vienna 4593)

187 Athenian vase (Leagros Group) showing
Heracles on the pole of Zeus' chariot, with
Athena on foot beside them, fighting the giants,
from Vulci; late 6th c. (Vatican Mus. 422)

188 Detail from an Athenian vase by
Lydos showing a satyr holding a
bearded snake; about 550 BC. (New
York, Met. Mus. 31.11.11)

189 Detail from the
François Vase by Kleitias,
showing pygmies fighting
cranes, from Chiusi; about
570 BC. (Florence, Mus.
Arch. 4209)

190 Athenian lekythos (Cock Group) showing obeisance before a mummy or herm; about 500 BC. (Munich 1871)

hydria; *Fig. 186*) the Greek hero Heracles copes with a flock of cowering Egyptians, servants of King Busiris who had hoped to maintain his record of sacrificing all foreigners who came his way. Heracles grasps and tramples his foes like the Pharaohs whose personal successes against hordes of adversaries were celebrated on many paintings and reliefs.[148] The North African settings of both these scenes – on the cup and the hydria – add point to the Egyptianizing attitudes. A more trivial borrowing is the way Heracles, and occasionally others, are shown fighting from a chariot by advancing a foot along the chariot pole (*Fig. 187*) – a common Egyptian motif but impossible in a Greek chariot (by this time, at any rate, no longer used in battle).[149] And finally, a minor but persistent feature in Greek art from the seventh century on is the way snakes are shown with goatee beards (*Fig. 188*), which can only derive from representations of divine serpents in Egyptian art.[150] It is not easy to see why the Greeks adopted such an unrealistic convention (in Egypt it is a 'beard-box' as worn by deities) but in Greek art most snakes have some other-worldly connotation.

Other scenes or figures are inspired by contact with Egypt rather than copied. Such are those of the battle of the pygmies and cranes, which was also known to Homer. One famous version, on the François Vase painted about 570, shows the pygmies grappling the cranes with walking sticks and riding against them on goats (*Fig. 189*).[151] A strange scene on an Athenian vase shows three men doing obeisance before what appears to be a mummy (*Fig. 190*).[152] Their attitude is not one which we meet again on Greek work, but is purely Egyptian and appropriate for such a scene of mourning. The 'mummy' looks rather like a Greek herm (a pillar with a head of Hermes), but not quite: it has no arm stumps or phallus (like a herm), but a criss-cross pattern which resembles the bandaging of a mummy. Although there is literary testimony about bowing to herms, it is perhaps easier to see here a Greek copy of a common Egyptian scene than to take it as a unique version of a Greek one. These isolated Egyptian scenes of course reflect no deeper awareness or influence of Egyptian practices or beliefs.

191 Athenian Negro-head vase; about 500 BC. (Boston 00.332)

Negroes appear more often now in Greek art[153] (*Fig. 191*; no doubt many Greeks took them for Egyptians) and monkeys;[154] even camels (*Fig. 192*).[155] Memnon's Ethiopian followers at Troy are shown on vases as Negroes. The great Athenian vase painter Exekias names two such, Amasis (*Fig. 193*) and Amasos: after the Egyptian king, we might think – but there was an Amasis in Athens too, a colleague and rival potter-painter to Exekias himself. Perhaps he was dusky-skinned and had been born in Egypt, to pick up his foreign (though Graecized) name.[156] In a city like Naucratis he could have seen the finest work of eastern and mainland Greek potters and painters and might there have informed his style with those almost exotic characteristics which make his vases so attractive. We should note too that it was he

192 Detail from an East Greek vase showing a hairy man leading a camel, from Smyrna; about 540–530 BC. (Izmir Mus.)

193 Detail from an Athenian vase by Exekias; about 540 BC. (London B 209)

who, with one of the earliest of his vases to have survived (*Fig. 194*), introduced the clay version of the Egyptian stone alabastron to Athens.[157] There are some rather later clay alabastra made in Athens which advertise the history of their shape by the figures of Negroes painted on them (*Fig. 195*).[158]

The other borrowed scenes which have been mentioned must also have been inspired by artists who had themselves visited Egypt, for they could not have been readily transmitted on any portable Egyptian objects. Greeks, and artists, are inveterate travellers. The more so, then, Greek artists; and no less in antiquity than today.

194 Athenian clay alabastron by Amasis from the Agora, Athens; about 560 BC. (Agora P 12628; H. 9·2 cm)

195 Athenian clay alabastron from Tanagra; early 5th c. (London B 674; H. 16 cm)

Greeks in Libya and Cyrenaica

Greeks settled in Cyrenaica as soon as they did in Egypt; but while the Greeks of Naucratis were merchants, the Greeks at Cyrene were farmers. A severe drought at home had driven them to seek new homes overseas. The way was made easier by traders who had visited North Africa before them, and the establishment of colonies there had a considerable commercial value. But the prime attraction was the fertile land of the Cyrenaican plateau and seaboard, an area whose climate and geographical position made it a logical extension for any Aegean civilization. Crete is no farther from Cyrene than it is from Athens.

Herodotus' story of the colonization of Cyrene[159] presents an interesting account of the way these communities were dis-

196 The site at Aziris, looking
west from the town

patched, not always willingly (one adult male per family chosen
by lot, in this case), but the constitutional background to the
sending of a colony concerns us less than the physical reasons and
results of it.

The colonists came from Thera, a relatively barren small island
formed by the lip of a crater of a great volcano. It was occupied by
Dorian Greeks, and lay to the south of the main group of the
Cyclades, towards Crete. The island had seen some prosperity in
the later eighth and seventh centuries, shown by the excavations
there, but it could never support a large population. Soon after the
middle of the seventh century the Theran party sailed for North
Africa, and were guided by a Cretan to the offshore island of
Platea – which may already have served for some time as a trading
point with the mainland tribes, and is still a favourite resort of
Greek sponge fishers. A temporary settlement was established

197 The site at Cyrene, looking across the sanctuary of Apollo

there – we are told that the Samian skipper Kolaios put in on his famous voyage. Herodotus says that after two years the Therans moved to a site on the mainland opposite Platea, to Aziris, 'a charming place with a river on one side and lovely valleys on both'. The site, desolate and windswept now (*Fig. 196*),[160] has been located and pottery of the brief occupation recovered. After six years there, that is about 630 BC, the native Libyans persuaded them to move to a better site inland, and showed them Cyrene, a well-watered and easily defensible hill in good country on the high plateau (*Fig. 197*).[161] The men took native wives, and in Herodotus' day the womenfolk still observed native restrictions about the eating of certain meats.

The community prospered, and in the sixth century invited new colonists from the Peloponnese and from the Dorian islands. In the years before the middle of the century, dissentients founded

Barce, to the west on the plateau. For the foundation dates of the colonies on the coast, from Apollonia, the port of Cyrene, to Euhesperides (Benghazi) in the west, we have to turn to archaeological evidence (see below). The access of prosperity enjoyed by the newcomers alarmed the native Libyans, who invited the Egyptians to help them against the Greeks. Apries sent an army in 570; but it was heavily defeated. His successor Amasis was kindlier: he married a Cyrenaean princess, and sent dedications to the city. Later dynastic troubles in the royal family at Cyrene provoked other engagements with the native Libyans in which the Greeks did not fare so well. When the Persians took Egypt in 525, the people of Cyrene and Barce submitted and sent presents. Further dissents led to the intervention of the Persian governor of Egypt. He took Barce, and marched as far as Euhesperides before retiring, harried by the Libyans. Men of Barce were taken as slaves to Bactria (the present Afghanistan-Russian border) and settled in a town given the name of their old home, where they still lived in Herodotus' time.[162] From about 515, Cyrene formed part of the Persian empire; but the archaeological evidence shows that if anything it enjoyed increased prosperity, for to these years can be attributed the finest sculpture and tombs, the greatest of the temples, and probably its first coinage.

The material evidence about the early Greek cities in Cyrenaica is rather scrappy, but Italian excavations in Cyrene and recent British ones in Euhesperides and Taucheira can tell us something.

At Cyrene the early town lay on the heights overlooking the sacred spring which the Greeks called Apollo's fountain.[163] In front of this, and so outside any walled circuit there may have been, a sanctuary area was laid out. The earliest building we can recognize, perhaps of the early sixth century, is a simple shrine about 8·5 m. square, with two interior columns. The sixth-century votives found in it included some fine jewellery and bronzes as well as decorated pottery. Beside it, nearer the fountain, was the temple of Apollo. The earliest form of it is a fine Doric building of the mid sixth century or earlier, measuring some 16 m. by 30 m. It was rebuilt on the same foundations in the fourth century. The first temple on the heights, though still outside the old town, is that of Zeus – Zeus Ammon, as a compliment to the respected oracle in the Libyan desert, which the Greeks seem almost to have adopted. This was an immense Doric building, some 69 m. by 30 m., built before the end of the sixth century. In later times it held a marble copy of the famous Zeus made by Phidias at Olympia. On the outskirts of the city lay one of its earliest sanctuaries, to Demeter, where the earliest levels have only recently been explored.[164] In fact by 500 Cyrene was as well equipped with major temples as any of the more important cities in Greece, and it could clearly vie with them in wealth.

Of the early tombs, the most important – apart from the probable tomb of the founder, which became a cult-place – are rock-cut, with architectural façades of two or more columns. The earliest of them may belong to the last quarter of the sixth century.[165] The type is non-Greek, but such tomb façades are well known in the east, and it may be that they were introduced to the Greeks at Cyrene after their submission to the Persians, although it seems that the Persian governors of Egypt took little direct interest in the city's affairs.

The sculpture from the sanctuaries and town matches the excellence of the architecture. There are several figures of the mid sixth century or just before which betray a strong island Greek style, some clearly Samian, a fine sphinx dedication on a column, and other figures, *kouroi* and *korai*, of the late sixth and early fifth century which are closer in style to the work of the Dorian Peloponnese.[166]

The little pottery from Cyrene reflects the city's history and overseas relations. The earliest piece alleged to be from Cyrene is an eighth-century cup in Berlin, made in Athens or perhaps Sparta; but it is difficult to believe in its provenance,[167] and nothing else so early has been found in controlled excavations. Other and better authenticated finds show that the Peloponnese is well represented and East Greece rather less well. The earliest, of the end of the seventh century, is from Corinth and Rhodes, and in the sixth century there is pottery from Athens, from Sparta, which seems to have taken a close interest in Cyrenaica, and various scraps of Chian, including a piece of the fine ware which we have suspected of being made in Naucratis.[168] There are several 'Island Gems',[169] probably from Melos, and incised tridacna shells.[170]

198 Silver tetradrachm of Cyrene showing the head of Zeus Ammon, and on the other side a silphion plant and horse; about 480–470 BC. (London)

Cyrene started minting her own coins in the last quarter of the sixth century,[171] on the standard used by Athens, Corinth, and Samos. One device on them was the silphion plant (*Fig. 198*). This was a wild vegetable which resisted attempts at transplanting and flourished only in Cyrenaica. It completely disappeared, probably through bad husbandry, early in the Roman period. Its leaf could be eaten like cabbage and its root pickled, but its main value lay in the sap, which was prized as a medicine or a flavouring.[172] It must have been an important export, and contributed no little to the prosperity of the Greeks in Cyrenaica; but it was certainly not the only export of a land rich in corn, fruit, and horses.

Recent work has taught us much more about the other Greek cities in Cyrenaica. At Barce, the circumstances of whose foundation in the sixth century are attested by Herodotus, nothing before the mid fifth century has been excavated, though in the territory of the city (at Aslaia) a slightly earlier grave has yielded Attic vases, a Persian glass bowl and a large stone alabastron.[173] But it is now clear that the coastal cities were occupied very soon after Cyrene itself, certainly well before 600, with the possible exception of Euhesperides, where the earliest pottery is of the early sixth century. At Apollonia and the city later renamed Ptolemais,

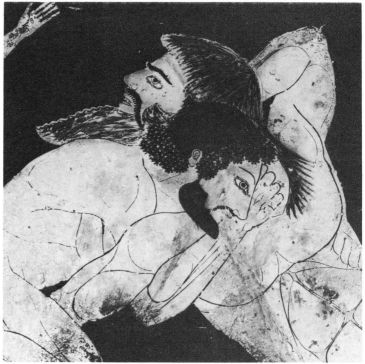

199 Detail from an
Athenian vase by
Euphronios, from Caere;
about 510 BC. (Paris,
Louvre G 103)

the evidence is from pottery scraps. At Taucheira, modern Tocra,
recent British excavations[174] have explored the rich votive deposit
of a sanctuary of Demeter and Kore which must go back to the
foundation of the town in the 620s.[175] The range of pottery is
informative. From the earliest days Rhodian and Corinthian are
dominant. In the sixth century the sources reflect either special
Dorian interests in the town – Corinth, Sparta, Crete and Melos;
or the popularity of 'international' wares like Athenian and Chian.
A piece of jewellery is matched only on Thera, whence the colonists of Cyrene had sailed, but there is also a piece of European
horse harness. Local production was confined to plain terracottas
and votives. The numbers of simple imported vases of few
specific shapes and the absence of other expected shapes may
reflect on the conduct of the bulk pottery trade and its effect on a
market likely to be at the end of a trading run.[176]

The Libyan natives, nomad tribesmen, are archaeologically
unknown, or at least inaccessible, and their culture – described so
vividly by Herodotus[177] – had no material influence on the Greeks
who had settled among them. The Greek hero Heracles was said
to have encountered a Libyan giant, Antaios, and wrestled with
him. A fine Athenian vase painting of little before 500 (*Fig. 199*)
renders Antaios in a manner in which Libyans are often shown in
Egyptian art; in sharp contrast with the sleek civilized Heracles.[178]

Some degree of 'native' influence can be seen in the worship of Zeus Ammon in Cyrene.[179] The cult derived from the famous oasis shrine of Amun, whose oracle came to share the reputation accorded to those of Dodona and Delphi in Greece. The head of Zeus wearing Amun's ram-horns appears on coins of Cyrene (*Fig. 198*). The shrine was at Siwa, in the Libyan desert.[180] One of the finest tombs there is probably fifth-century in date and may be the tomb of a Greek who took the name Si-Amun, 'man of Amun', since he is shown with his son in the tomb paintings in Egyptian pose but bearded and with the son's dress rendered in the Greek manner (*Fig. 200*).[181] Some other decorative features of the tomb seem Greek-inspired also. There is brief mention by Herodotus of another oasis in which some Samians were living in 525;[182] it is probably Khargeh Oasis. They had called it the Isle of the Blessed, and were probably veteran mercenaries who had settled down to a quiet life: surely one of the most unusual and appealing of the remote Greek communities in this period.

200 Tomb painting at Siwa; 5th c.

South Italy and Sicily

5

Italy, Sicily, and the West

Greek colonization on the shores of the western Mediterranean is well documented and forms an essential part of any history of the Greek world. It was with the western Greeks that the growing power of Rome first had to deal, and so to them in large part are due the continuity and transmission of Greek culture through Rome to the later western world.

The Greek cities in the west were prosperous, *nouveaux riches*; their temples were that little bit bigger than those at home, their art that little bit more ornate. Artists and philosophers could readily be tempted from Greece by commissions or lecture tours, and their work did not always suffer. And in more recent times these cities were more readily accessible to excavators, whose experience on other Italian sites had led them to appreciate sources of major architectural or sculptural work. In all this the archaeology of the earliest years of the colonies has generally come off second best, except where the early cemeteries gave promise of yielding Greek vases as handsome as those from the Etruscan graves.

The evidence in ancient historians for the foundation and early history of the colonies is well set out in other works, and this is no place for an account of their internal politics and wars. Here our main interest is in the physical history of the colonies in their earliest days, their relations both with native populations and rivals like the Phoenicians, and the characteristics of the arts which they derived from homeland Greece and then developed independently. It is in these matters that the archaeologist can hope to fill out the literary record, and for some problems – of relations with foreigners and even relative dates of foundations – his evidence may sometimes claim priority; remembering, of course, how much his chronology still depends on the ancient historians' dates for some colonial foundations.[1] Where exact dates are given in this chapter, it will be realized that they are derived from ancient writers. But first something must be said about the colonists – who they were, where they came from, and why they went where they did.

The Colonists

The assumption that all Greek colonial foundations were made purely to ease population or subsistence problems at home dies hard. These are the only reasons usually offered by ancient writers but archaeology, geography and commonsense combine to suggest that trade normally preceded the flag and that in the case of some of the earliest colonies trade rather than land was the dominant factor in choosing a site. Two chapters already in this book have been largely devoted to overseas trading enterprises by the Greeks, in the east and in Egypt, and it would be idle to pretend that considerations of trade did not provide some part of the motive in founding many colonies, and the major part in a few. Certainly, knowledge of possible sites for colonial development could only have been won from the reports of merchants who had already explored the shores of the western Mediterranean. There is evidence for their activity in the pre-colonial vases found in Etruria (at Veii), Campania (at Capua and Pontecagnano), and Sicily (Villasmundo).[2]

The earliest colonies in the west were founded by Euboeans, not on the nearest good farmland, but in a position which gave the most immediate opportunities for trade with Etruria, and they were supported by foundations safeguarding the passage to them through the Straits of Messina. They may even have done some preliminary exploration in South France and North Africa, as we shall see. As in the east, the commodities most sought after were metals – iron, copper, and (from remoter sources supplying Etruria) tin. And as in the east, the Greek states who initiated these trading settlements were the Euboean cities of Eretria and Chalcis, with the difference that here our evidence for their identity is literary as well as archaeological. Much later, Marseilles too was founded primarily as a port for trade with Gaul, on the tin route from the north; and once her routes were closed to her, new towns on the North Adriatic took her place.

For most of the colonies, however, the choice was more simply strategic and economic. First, to find a defensible position – steep acropolis, peninsula, or offshore island – the last being the sort of site which merchants dealing with the natives would already have sought out. Secondly, to see that they had at hand good cultivable land to support a growing community. There were not many such sites, and most of them were already occupied, so that the native population usually had to be dealt with, by diplomacy or force; and very soon Greek met Greek, and the interstate quarrels which form the pattern of early Greek history grew as lively and as vicious in the new foundations as they were at home, and could only be forgotten (and that only by some) in the face of a common foe – the Persians in the east, the Carthaginians in the west.

Of the cities which sent the colonies, those with an interest in trade, like the Euboeans, were prompted by the same motives which had led them to the markets of the Near East over a generation before. The others were those whose growth of population had outstripped their agricultural resources, and who were not prepared to meet the crisis by attacking their neighbours like the Spartans, or by a radical change in their home economy – an export drive – like the Athenians and the Chians. It was not only the large cities which had cause to dispatch part of their population to fend for themselves overseas, but it was generally they who had the resources and transport for mounting such an expedition, in which families from smaller towns would take part. But it was not always whole families who emigrated, nor was the move always voluntary. The Therans who went to Cyrenaica were men chosen by lot, one from each family; they went unwillingly and were stoned when they tried to return home.[3] Such parties, sometimes only a few dozen men, would find their wives from among the natives. Again, the Spartans sent to found Tarentum were illegitimate children, born in a time of war when the Spartans had sworn not to return until victorious, but had yielded to the complaints of their women and sent some youngsters home on compassionate leave. The children, grown up, came to resent their lack of rights, fomented revolt, and were packed off to found a colony.[4] The Therans were set on the move through a drought at home; the Chalcidians to Rhegium through famine, sending one tenth of their folk. Elsewhere too we read of a dissident party within a city choosing, or being obliged, to emigrate, like the Messenians who joined the Chalcidians at Rhegium.[5] A more tragic reason might be like that of the Phocaeans,[6] whose city was beleaguered by the Persians and who went to look for a new home. Once in these new homes, the colonists were politically independent of their mother city, and formed new city-states in their own right; but there were still ties of blood, religion, and, we may be sure, trade.[7]

The Chalcidians, Spartans and Therans emigrated on the advice of Delphi, and the oracle seems to have intervened effectively with such advice on many other occasions. Its priests could exploit their role as clearing-house of information in the Greek world, and use it to the political advantage of their friends.[8]

The colonizing cities are usually clearly defined in the historical record and from their institutions. The archaeological evidence for the earliest days of the colonies often reflects both their source and the identity of their new friends. First, however, we should remark on the ubiquity of Corinthian pottery. Corinth herself was only involved in the foundation of Syracuse in 733, but such was the popularity of her pottery that it was carried and used by many other states, as we have already observed in previous chapters. Indeed, of the colonizers, the Achaean cities had no other fine ware, and this may be true of the Megarians also. The pottery of the Euboeans, first to settle in the west, is recognized in their earliest colony, at Pithekoussai, and its style can be traced at

Cumae and in early Greek vases made for Etruria. But after the eighth century the Euboeans' active interest in the west dwindles, and their pottery can no longer be recognized there, although their colonies waxed strong. Rhodes was the first of the East Greeks to send a colony to the west, but East Greek pottery is found in many other of the early colonies. This is more an indication of trading interests than of cooperation in the settlements. Sixth-century Chian wine jars and the island's finer pottery can be recognized on many of the western Greek sites and in Etruria. So can Fikellura vases and there are many fine East Greek pots, not all perhaps Rhodian, on other sites from the mid seventh century on. There is also a host of plainer striped vases from unidentified East Greek centres, among them probably Phocaea, which were widely carried and often locally imitated, as in Gaul. The most important of these are the so-called Ionian cups.[9] Crete joined Rhodes in founding Gela, but there is little Cretan pottery in the west, and some earlier identifications of Cretan flasks have to be revised in favour of the Euboeans.[10] The western markets, Greek and Etruscan, were the proving grounds for the selling qualities of the more ambitious black-figure vases of the sixth century. Here the Athenian wares seem to have driven the Corinthian out of the competition, but there was always a small market for Sparta's finer cups. This trade in fine pottery tells us nothing of fresh settlement or even the identity of the traders, but the consumer demand had some interesting effects on production, as we shall see.

Before we turn to the individual cities we may briefly consider earlier Greek contacts in this part of the Mediterranean. There is evidence for a lively Cretan and Mycenaean interest in the Lipari islands and parts of Sicily – especially the south east – from about 1600 BC to the end of the Bronze Age. In the islands at least there seem to have been small trading establishments. In Italy itself a settlement was certainly established at Tarentum, not quite on the site of the later colony but at Scoglio del Tonno opposite. It flourished from about 1400 to 1200 BC, and from the style of the Mycenaean vases found there it seems likely that it was used as a trading post by Rhodians. Slighter Mycenaean finds have been made in Italy – notably on the island of Ischia, where the city of Pithekoussai was later to be founded, in Etruria and in Malta.[11] While echoes of Mycenaean civilization may be caught as far away as Spain or even Britain, there is no question of direct connections with the Aegean world. The memory of Greeks in Italy and Sicily survived in a most confused form in some myths, and especially in the stories of Odysseus' wanderings, but the break in contact after 1200 BC was almost complete, and the later Greek voyages to the west do not seem to have been conditioned or guided by the experience of their Mycenaean forebears as much as they were in the east, where the break was incomplete or of considerably shorter duration.

Greek Cities in Italy and Sicily

In this section the earliest finds in the principal colonies are discussed and their archaeological record followed down to the early fifth century. This is done in outline only, since their story soon becomes one with that of mainland Greece rather than an account of settlements on foreign soil. Indeed, to later historians, the cities of South Italy were known collectively as Great Greece, Magna Graecia, a term extended by some to include Sicily.

The strict chronological order of foundation is broken here, to keep together important groups of colonies or colonizers. We have, then:

Euboeans in central Italy	Pithekoussai, Cumae
Euboeans in eastern Sicily	Naxos, Leontini, Catane
Euboeans in the Straits	Zancle, Mylae, Rhegium
Dorians in Sicily	Syracuse, Megara Hyblaea
Rhodians and Cretans in Sicily	Gela
Achaeans in South Italy	Sybaris, Croton, Caulonia, Metapontum, Posidonia
Spartans and others in South Italy	Tarentum, Siris, Locri
Syracusan expansion	Helorus, Acrae, Casmenae, Camarina
Colonies in western Sicily	Selinus, Acragas, Himera
The latest foundations	Lipara, Elea

The earliest colonists in the west were the Euboeans, whom we have met as pioneers in the east also: on this texts and archaeology agree. For the foundation of their first colony we have only an archaeological date, but this cannot have been their first adventure in western waters. The pendent-semicircle cups which attested their presence at Al Mina (p. 41) have now been found at Veii in Etruria and Villasmundo in Sicily. Another early Euboean type, the 'chevron skyphos', appears in the pre-Greek graves of Cumae and again at Veii. These all probably indicate Euboean trading interest before any adjacent Euboean or other Greek colonies were established. They were only to be expected but they had eluded discovery for a long time.[12]

PITHEKOUSSAI (Ischia). There is an ancient tradition that Pithekoussai was founded by the Euboeans of Eretria and Chalcis before they settled at Cumae, on the mainland opposite, and this tradition has been vindicated by the recent excavations.[13] The town lay at the north of the island of Ischia, the acropolis being the promontory of Monte di Vico, the cemetery in the adjacent Valle San Montano, and beyond it an important early suburban area on the hill Mezzavia (Fig. 201). The acropolis has yet to be properly explored, but has already yielded pottery of the eighth century and architectural terracottas from a sixth-century temple. A native settlement at Castiglione farther to the east had received some Mycenaean pottery.[14] It is the cemetery of the Valle San Montano which has been fully excavated. The graves are at first inhumations, then cremation burials, covered by low stone tumuli. The earliest pottery probably takes us back to about 770,

201 The site of Pithekoussai (Ischia). The promontory is the acropolis (Monte Vico) with the cemetery in the valley (Valle di S. Montano) behind it and the Mezzavia ridge next inland

and the main phase is over soon after 700, but there is continued use into the sixth century. There is a fair quantity of Corinthian, but some Euboean too, notably the imitations of Corinthian of the type found in Al Mina, the Euboeans' eastern trading town (see p. 40, group 2: *Fig. 202*). Locally made vases are in a style which we should recognize as Euboean, and include an unusual Late Geometric scene of a shipwreck (*Fig. 203*), which may tell of an incident on the voyage west (there *are* sharks in the Mediterranean).[15] There is some Cretan and East Greek pottery in the early graves, and our earliest Greek potter's signature (*Fig. 204*).[16] A Rhodian cup from one of the early graves is inscribed with a challenge to Nestor's famous cup of which Homer sang (*Fig. 205*).[17] It reads: 'Nestor had a most drink-worthy cup, but whoever drinks of mine will straightway be smitten with desire of fair-crowned Aphrodite.' More interesting reflections of Euboea's interests at the other end of the Mediterranean are the Cilician seals,[18] the Egyptian faience and scarabs,[19] and a Syrian flask with a head modelled at the neck (*Fig. 206*),[20] which also appear in the eighth-century graves.

Two locally made vases are inscribed in Aramaic and Phoenician,[21] so it seems that easterners also made their way to this

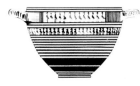

202 Cup (kotyle) of Corinthian type but Euboean manufacture, from Pithekoussai; late 8th c. (Ischia; H. 10 cm)

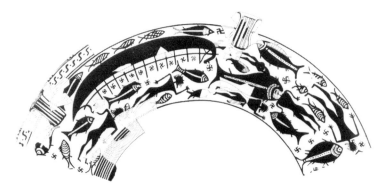

203 Shipwreck on a vase from Pithekoussai; late 8th c. (Ischia)

204 Crater fragment with part of a potter's signature – '… inos made me', from Pithekoussai; about 700 B C. (Ischia)

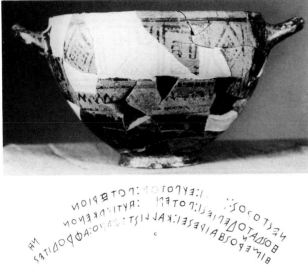

205 'Nestor's cup'; East Greek cup with incised verse inscription, from Pithekoussai; late 8th c. (Ischia; H. 10·3 cm)

206 Syrian clay flask from Pithekoussai; late 8th c. (Ischia; H. 11·7 cm)

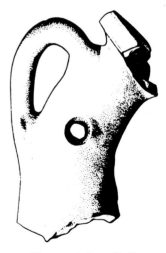

207 Clay mouthpiece of bellows for a furnace, from Pithekoussai; late 8th c. (Ischia; H. about 20 cm)

western Euboean outpost, which was at first probably much more like a trading post, such as Al Mina, than a colony or *apoikia* ('home from home').

Strabo says that the Eretrians and Chalcidians of Pithekoussai quarrelled, and the former left – an echo of the bitter rivalry which flared up in the eighth century between the mother-cities in Euboea. He adds that the settlers left the island after a volcanic eruption and earthquakes; and Castiglione at least, where some Geometric pottery has been found, seems to have been overwhelmed. An ancient reference to 'gold mines' in the island is questionable, and might simply refer to production of jewellery there.[22] It is absurd to suppose that Pithekoussai was settled purely for its agricultural advantages. The volcanic island has a soil good for nothing but vines and its present booming population is the result of the tourist trade: the Euboeans came neither to make wine nor to build hotels. Its interest in the metal trade is shown by early evidence of iron working on both Mezzavia and Monte di Vico itself, where slag, blooms and the mouthpieces of bellows were found (*Fig. 207*). The iron cannot have been mined on Ischia, and analysis suggests that it came from Elba.[23] There was soon need, however, to look for a more accommodating, less defensive site.

CUMAE lies on the mainland opposite Ischia, twelve miles west of Naples. There is a good acropolis, a marshy hinterland, and a safe beach rather than a sheltered harbour. It was primarily a foundation of the Chalcidians. To the north of the town lay the early cemetery, and much of this has been excavated.[24] A number of native pre-Greek graves can be identified, furnished with plain pottery and bronzes of Italian types. These also contained pottery evidence for visiting Euboeans even earlier than Pithekoussai,[25] as well as cups and Egyptian faience which must have come from Pithekoussai, and represent contact between the newly arrived Greeks and the natives before ever there was a Greek town at Cumae. The earliest pottery in the wholly Greek tombs is later than the earliest from Pithekoussai. It should probably be dated little before 725 BC, but unfortunately there is no plausible date for the foundation in any ancient author. The pottery is mainly Corinthian, but there are Euboean and local styles, probably derived from Pithekoussai. There is one fine Cycladic vase of the mid seventh century,[26] but on the whole there are few other imports to be recognized until the mass of Corinthian pottery, which is most common from about 600 and is then displaced by the arrival of the fine Athenian black-figure vases later in the sixth century. With these come a few Spartan. There is very little East Greek at all until the sixth century, and then mainly perfume flasks. As trade with Etruria grew, more and more Etruscan objects – pottery, bronzes, jewellery – arrived; but the artistic relations of the Euboean colonies with Etruria are best considered later in the chapter.

One find at Cumae, or alleged to be from Cumae, deserves special mention. It is a bronze cauldron with bulls-head attachments, now in Copenhagen[27] (*Fig. 42*). It is typical of the eastern bronzes which reached the Greek world before and after 700 BC (see pp. 65 ff.), and its appearance in Euboean Cumae underlines Euboea's part in the eastern trade; or it might be said to support an ancient tradition that Cumae (Kymai) is named after Aeolian Kyme in Asia Minor, which had ready access to Phrygia where the bulls-head cauldrons were known. In view of the flow of Syrian and Phoenician objects to Pithekoussai and Cumae, and to Etruria beyond, the former explanation for the cauldron is probably correct. There are also late eighth-century burials at Cumae in which the ash urn, a cauldron, is placed in a stone box, an unusual practice closely matched by near-contemporary burials at Eretria (West Gate).[28]

NAXOS. According to Thucydides the first Greek foundation in Sicily was made by the Chalcidians at Naxos in 734. The site was the first landfall in Sicily for ships rounding the 'toe' of Italy from the east. It was a headland site, just south of Taormina, made virtually a peninsula by the stream to its south, and it enjoyed the use of a small but fertile valley inland, which proved especially favourable to the vine. In recent excavations in the town, pottery from its earliest days has been found and a sixth-century fortification wall. There were clear signs that the Greek settlement displaced a native one on the same site.[29] There was some early production of pottery at Naxos, of Euboean type, and in the fifth century an elegantly appointed sanctuary of Aphrodite. The town was never of first importance in Sicily, but in its early years it served as a base for the foundation of two other colonies, at Leontini and Catane.

LEONTINI. Six years after the foundation of Naxos, the Chalcidians there set out to found another colony, at Leontini, with reinforcements from home. The city was occupied by native Sicels, whom they expelled: a circumstance attested by Thucydides and by the terminal date of the native cemetery.[30] It lay on the far side of the rich plain through which the River

208 Vase fragments from Leontinoi; about 700 BC. (Syracuse Mus.)

209 Bronze cauldron with rams' head attachments, from Leontinoi; about 550 BC. (Berlin; H. 21·5 cm)

Symaithos flows, but more than six miles from the sea, so it was primarily an agricultural community. Recent excavations have shown that the first settlement was on the hill of San Mauro, and that there was a fortified circuit built about the middle of the seventh century.[31] The earliest pottery found so far is Corinthian, but some Euboean types are represented also, as well as a local ware with figure decoration (*Fig. 208*). At about 600 or soon after, the circuit was enlarged to take in a second hill, Metapiccola, where foundations of a sixth-century temple have been exposed. No tombs earlier than the mid sixth century have been found so far. From old excavations in the cemetery comes a superb bronze bowl with rams-head attachments (*Fig. 209*).[32] There are traces of the native Sicel village below the Greek town on San Mauro, and there was another Sicel village on Metapiccola.

Not far from Leontini, nearer the coast, at Villasmundo, there has recently been found the first evidence for Euboean pre-colonial activity in the island – a pendent-semicircle skyphos.[33]

CATANE. Chalcidian control of the rich plain of the Symaithos was established by the foundation of Catane, on its north side, soon after the foundation of Leontini at the south. The settlers came from Naxos. Unlike Leontini, Catane was on the coast, and it had a good harbour. Eruptions of Etna and lava-flow have rendered the ancient town unrecognizable, but a pre-Greek native cemetery has been excavated, and more recently a notable collection of votive pottery has been recovered[34] from a sanctuary of Demeter on what must be the site of the ancient acropolis. None of it is earlier than about 600, but besides the expected Corinthian, Athenian, and 'Chalcidian' there is a lot of Chian pottery, some other East Greek wares, and good Spartan vases.

At the same time as the establishment of these sites on the east coast of Sicily the Euboeans took steps to see that they could control the approach to their earlier foundations at Pithekoussai

and Cumae. To effect this, Zancle and Rhegium were founded, on
either side of the straits between Italy and Sicily:

ZANCLE (later Messina) was founded perhaps very soon after
Naxos by settlers from Cumae (who had especial interest in free
passage through the straits) and from Chalcis. The very first
settlers are said to be 'pirates' from Cumae – something of a
reflection on the trading techniques of Greeks in the west. Zancle
lies just south of the narrowest point in the straits, but it is blessed
with a superb natural harbour whose sickle shape perhaps gave
the town its name. The earliest town seems to have been largely to
the south of the harbour, but finds are scattered and not very
informative. At the tip of the natural mole encircling the harbour
there seems to have been a sanctuary, and here the earliest pottery
has been found – Corinthian and imitations (? Euboean), of the
later eighth century. In the seventh and sixth centuries there is the
expected showing of Corinthian and Athenian wares, and a very
little East Greek.[35]

Zancle's strength lay in her position on the straits and in her
harbour. She had virtually no agricultural resources, and was
obliged to look for a dependency to supply her needs. This was
Mylae.

MYLAE (Milazzo). Twenty miles west of Zancle, on the north
coast of Sicily and facing the Lipari Islands, is a small coastal plain
behind a long rocky peninsula. Mylae was founded at the base of
this peninsula by settlers from Zancle, who evicted the natives in
occupation there. Recent excavations may tell us more of Mylae
than we can hope for from her mother city. The earliest datable
Greek pottery is of course Corinthian, and can be compared with
the earliest from Syracuse, so the foundations may be somewhat
earlier than that suggested by ancient sources (716 BC) and nearer
that of Zancle, as we might expect. From the later eighth and
seventh centuries a quantity of 'Cycladic' pottery is reported
(probably Euboean or of Euboean type). In the late seventh and
sixth centuries there is much more East Greek, including plain
striped wares and Chian wine jars. Here, and in other Euboean
colonial cemeteries, cremation was practised more freely than in
colonies from other states, and this seems to reflect the Euboean
homeland practice.[36]

RHEGIUM. The Chalcidians of Zancle invited the Messenians
from the Peloponnese to join them in the foundation of Rhegium,
and there was a party from Chalcis itself, sent after a famine. It lay
nearly ten miles south of Zancle, on the other side of the straits,
chosen (as was Zancle) for its strategic position controlling the
passage. The date of its foundation cannot have been long after
that of the city opposite. The ancient town lies beneath modern
Reggio, and our knowledge of it derives largely from chance finds
and sporadic excavation.[37] Of its earliest years almost nothing is
known beyond its general location south of the modern harbour.
One early vase of about 700 BC is like the Euboean and Cycladic

210 Vase from Canale; late 8th c.

imitations of Corinthian.[38] From the later seventh century on are some Corinthian vases, and in the sixth century a growing import of Athenian and East Greek, with some Spartan pieces and many 'Chalcidian', to which we shall return. The Greek pottery of Euboean type (*Fig. 210*) found in native villages to the east, near the later colony of Locri, may represent the spread of Euboean interests on this side of the straits, which was curtailed when Locri was founded.[39]

SYRACUSE (*Fig. 211*). The richest of the Greek cities in Sicily was Syracuse. It was founded by the Corinthians, only one year after the Euboeans settled in Naxos, in 734 according to Thucydides.[40] Naxos had the most opportune harbour for shipping from the east on this coast of Sicily, but Syracuse had the best. Similarity in place-names in Chalcis and Syracuse (such as the spring Arethusa) has led some to argue that the Euboeans were interested in Syracuse before the Corinthians. This might seem to be supported by the presence of eighth-century Euboean sherds in the native town of Castelluccio not far away inland, and some of the earliest pottery from Syracuse itself shows affinities with the wares of the Greek islands and Euboea. But we may also remember the tradition that Archias, the leader of the Corinthian settlers, picked up some Greeks en route, from Zephyrion at the toe of Italy.[41] The same tradition says they were Dorians, but archaeological evidence shows Euboeans near the Zephyrion promontory (by Locri, see above) at this time.

The deep bay at Syracuse was partly closed by the island Ortygia (Quail-island), which was nearly attached to the mainland at its northern edge. There was a native Sicel settlement on the island, which was replaced by the new Greek town. This long remained the heart of the colony – easily defensible, with harbours to north and south, and a good source of water, the spring Arethusa. A sanctuary of Athena there may have been one of the first to be built by the new settlers and has yielded some of the earliest pottery. Of the temple we know nothing until the earlier sixth century, when there is the evidence of elaborate clay revetments which adorned the brick and wood building. At the end of the century its altar was rebuilt in a more ornate form, with some Ionic decoration. The temple's fifth-century Doric form is still largely preserved in the fabric of the later cathedral.[42] Another and earlier Doric temple on Ortygia was for Apollo. It is of the mid sixth century, 25·6 m. by 55·3 m., with the long plan and deep porches seen elsewhere in Sicily, but the site has also now yielded material not only of the foundation period, but of the earlier native settlement where scraps of Greek pottery indicate a measure of pre-colonial contact.[43] A remarkable find of recent years has been the remains of an enormous (about 56 m. long) but unfinished Ionic temple of the later sixth century, clearly inspired by the colossal temples of Ionian Ephesus and Samos, which in many respects it resembled.[44]

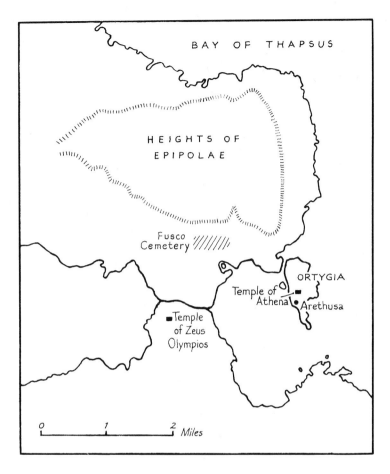

211 Sketch plan of
Syracuse

In the later sixth century the island Ortygia was linked to the
mainland by a causeway, but it is clear from the finds of pottery
that even in the early years of the colony the landward slopes
below the cliffs of the Epipolae heights were occupied. It was here
that the later market place (agora) stood. Farther south, and a little
inland from the great bay, stood the temple of Olympian Zeus. Its
seventh-century form again is known only from clay revetments.
In its Doric stone form it is very like the Apollo temple on
Ortygia, but some twenty-two feet (seven metres) longer and
possibly a little older.

The early cemeteries lay to the west and north of the landward
part of the city; the earliest (Fusco) being to the west. The use of
stone sarcophagi reflects homeland practice in Corinth. Almost
all the earliest Greek pottery (apart from the traces of early
Euboean interest) – from the area of the cemetery, from the
temples of Apollo and Athena, and from the town – is Corinthian,
and this of course remains the most popular ware here. Even the
sixth-century Athenian vases which won almost all other markets
are comparatively rare. As a result, perhaps, other Greek wares are

212 Vase from the Fusco cemetery, Syracuse; about 700 BC. (Syracuse Mus.; H. 50 cm)

better represented. East Greek vases arrive from about 700 on; some are recognizably Rhodian, and in the sixth century a few Chian and Fikellura are found. Two very early fragments are more curious than important – one, of the mid eighth century, is Cycladic; the other, little later, is one of the few Athenian pieces which travelled west so early.[45] Of the first half of the seventh century are some local vases (as *Fig. 212*) decorated, it seems, by an immigrant Argive painter who had a fairly eclectic taste.[46] Literary references to Argive interest or cult in Syracuse have sometimes puzzled historians.[47] Among the smaller finds we may pick out ivories[48] – fibulae, a relief, and a seal – which are very like those found in the Peloponnese, but are almost unknown otherwise in the western colonies; and Cycladic stone lamps.[49] The general archaeological picture shows a steady growth in prosperity through the seventh and sixth centuries, with ambitious temple-building programmes, sponsored by one of the longest surviving and prosperous of Greek aristocracies, the Gamoroi. In the fifth century the city was to become one of the great powers not merely in the west but in the whole Greek world.

MEGARA HYBLAEA. The only Megarian colony in Sicily was not easily established.[50] The first settlement was made on the east coast at Trotilon. The settlers were invited to move to Chalcidian Leontini, near by, but were later expelled and moved to the rocky peninsula of Thapsos. A late eighth-century burial there, in a reused native chamber tomb, may well be that of their leader, Lamis. The site gives its name to a class of pottery (e.g., *Fig. 213*) which is very common in Megara Hyblaea and has caused chronological problems in discussion about the foundation dates

213 A 'Thapsos cup' from Aetos, Ithaca; late 8th c. (Vathy, Aetos R 1; H. 13·5 cm)

of Megara Hyblaea and Syracuse (see below).[51] After a few months on Thapsos the Megarians were invited by the local Sicel king Hyblon to occupy a site on the coast which was inevitably dominated by the greater city of Syracuse some ten miles to the south. Thucydides says that Megara Hyblaea was founded six years after Syracuse. Archaeological arguments have been adduced to reverse this order,[52] but the Megarians' difficulties in settling down, and their final home in a poorish site so near to the

214 Vase fragment showing an unidentified myth scene with men pulling on a rope, from Megara Hyblaea; mid-7th c. (Syracuse Mus.)

215 Plan of the Archaic agora, Megara Hyblaea

magnificent harbour of Syracuse, perhaps speak more clearly than over-detailed arguments from few vases of rather dissimilar types, and recent finds at Syracuse have done much to redress the balance.

The city of Megara Hyblaea lay on a small plateau by the sea, where there was no natural harbour but an adequately sheltered anchorage. Recent French excavations have told us much more about the site's early history than the earlier sporadic exploration.[53] There was clearly no native site here when the Greeks first settled. The earliest pottery is Corinthian, but from about 650 East Greek and Etruscan vases appear, and in the sixth century Athenian and one or two Spartan. Some local vases of the mid seventh century are in a colourful style (*Fig. 214*) owing something to various Peloponnesian wares, including Argive, but distinct from the Fusco craters of Syracuse, and there seems to have been a flourishing school through much of the seventh century.[54] In the town, some early houses have been excavated, and there are traces of seventh- and sixth-century temples – one Doric with fine clay revetments, another a simpler structure with plain ashlar walls. In the same area are votive deposits going back to about 700 BC. The town was laid out in a regular plan, allowing clear space for an agora (*Fig. 215*), which can be distinguished in the second half of the seventh century.[55] The southern part of the later city is said not to have been occupied before 650, yet this is the part nearest to the anchorage, and the cemetery beyond the southern limits of the town seems to be the earliest, with pottery of near foundation date. The cemeteries of later date appear to have been particularly well supplied with tomb sculpture, including a kouros set in a small Doric shrine[56] with some elaborately carved mouldings, and an unusual product of a local school of about 550 (*Fig. 216*).[57] In 483 the city was destroyed by Syracuse, and there are no other finds until its reoccupation in the fourth century BC.

GELA. The last of the major Dorian foundations in Sicily was a joint effort by the Rhodians and Cretans. Thucydides dates it to 688. An old contention that ancient Gela lies at the modern port Licata has never been completely answered[58] but only the site at modern Gela has been properly explored.[59] The town here occupied a low hill by the sea just west of the mouth of the River Gelas on the south coast of the island, and commanded a rich coastal plain. A native settlement was displaced from the hill, but the early Greek town did not occupy the whole great area of the classical city. It may have been no more than a walled citadel with extra-mural sanctuaries to the east. The most notable early temple is that of Athena, which was decorated with a fine series of painted clay revetments. A smaller sanctuary, of Demeter, lay on the

216 Woman suckling twins, limestone group from the cemetery, Megara Hyblaea; about 550–525 BC. (Syracuse Mus.; H. 78 cm)

217 Crater, with griffins, from Gela; mid-7th c. (Gela Mus.; H. 13·5 cm)

other side of the river (Bitalemi) and was founded before the end of the seventh century.[60] Pottery has been recovered from the temple deposits and tombs. As well as the customary succession of Corinthian and Athenian vases, the East Greek wares – especially of Rhodes, with some of Chios – are quite common; and the joint-founder, Crete, is represented by a few early pieces.[61] There was a local school for figure-decorated pottery in the mid seventh century (*Fig. 217*),[62] comparable with those of Syracuse and Megara Hyblaea. The Rhodian character of the colony remains clear well into the sixth century, with numerous imports and great similarity in burial customs – inhumation in storage jars, etc. The period of Gela's greatest prosperity was at the end of the sixth century and the beginning of the fifth. It is marked by considerable building activity and a great variety of the finest bronzes, vases, and other imports from Greece.

Euboean and Corinthian colonies had established trading points close to Etruria, then commanded the Straits of Messina, and controlled the best farmland in east Sicily. The next series of colonies, sent by the Achaeans from the north-west Peloponnese, were founded in the 'instep' of Italy and on the west coast south of Cumae, in positions which could exploit overland routes between the Ionian and Tyrrhenian Seas, by-passing the Straits of Messina. These are Sybaris, Croton, Metapontum, and to the west, Posidonia (Paestum). In the same region Tarentum (Taranto) was founded by Sparta, Siris by Colophon (in Ionia), and Locri by Locris (in Central Greece).

SYBARIS was chosen for the immensely rich plain it commanded rather than for its convenient position on the west–east coastal route and its overland proximity to the shores of the

218 Phoenician bronze bowl from Francavilla; 8th c. (Reggio Mus.; Diam. 19·5 cm)

Tyrrhenian Sea. It was particularly noted for the wealth of its cornlands and the excellence of its wine. The foundation is dated in literary sources to about 720 BC. The city's size and wealth, as well as the extravagant tastes of its citizens, became proverbial (cf. our 'sybarite'). And no less famous was its utter destruction by Croton in 510 BC, when the waters of the river Crathis were diverted to lay waste the site. It was refounded in 443 by the Athenians as Thurii. The ancient city is almost inaccessible, nearly five metres below the water table, and beneath a heavy alluvial deposit. Although excavations have so far revealed nothing of its former glory, a serious attempt to recover something of its archaeological record is now being made. The record is scrappy, but includes material of the city's earliest days (Thapsos class pottery) and even some architectural features are emerging, including a possible shipyard.[63] A nearby Oenotrian site at Francavilla[64] shows strong Greek influence as soon as Sybaris is founded, and progressive hellenizing of the native settlement until it suffered the same fate as Sybaris. The variety and quality of the finds, including orientalia (*Fig. 218*)[65], reflect something of Sybaris' lost glory. Amendolara, near by, has a comparable record.[66]

Sybaris commanded routes to the coast on the west and to the towns of Scidrus (not located), Sirinus, and Laus, which sheltered refugees from the disaster of 510. It is said to have served as the main entrepôt for Milesian trade with the Etruscans, and when Sybaris fell Miletus declared public mourning.

CROTON was founded soon after Sybaris, about 710. It too commanded good farmland, not so extensive as its rival's, but it also had a small double harbour by the promontory on which the citadel stood, and the mouth of the river Aisaros was immediately adjacent. Recent excavations have shown that the early town was extensive, on both sides of the river, and pottery of its earliest days (Thapsos class, again) has been found.[67] Little is otherwise known of it archaeologically but an important extra-mural sanctuary of Hera Lacinia, which stood on another promontory some six miles to the south-west, has been excavated. The main structure is of the fifth century, but the earlier finds include a figurine of a goddess holding her breasts, of the later seventh century.[68]

Croton's territory lay mainly to the south-east. Its most important subsidiary foundation was at CAULONIA, which is better known from excavations, at least in the period of its greatest prosperity – the fifth century. Some fragments of early seventh-century pottery suggest an early foundation date, but after them hardly anything has been found earlier than some mid-sixth-century graves. The site embraced low hills beside a straight open beach with no real harbour.[69]

METAPONTUM is about thirty miles west of Tarentum. It had no harbour to speak of, but enjoyed good farmland and lay at the end of a route west to Posidonia.[70] The sanctuary area includes an archaic temple of Apollo Lykeios, a smaller one to Hera and two others. No structures are earlier than the late seventh century but there are votive figurines which perhaps go back to 700,[71] and cemeteries of this date and later have recently been found. Two miles to the north, a sanctuary of Hera was built on a low hill where there had been a native settlement. The Doric temple was built there about 500 BC. Fifteen of its columns still stand, known as the 'Knights' Tables' – Tavole Paladine. And in another nearby, native site at L'Incoronata, there are signs of substantial Greek interest in the area perhaps even before the foundation of Metapontum.[72]

POSIDONIA (Paestum). The foundation of Posidonia on the west coast of Italy, little over 50 m. south-east of Cumae, was the first challenge to the Euboean colonies' monopoly of trade with Etruria. The city may have been founded from Sybaris. There are good overland routes to the south, which can be traced through sites like that at Sala Consilina, where many sixth-century Greek finds have been made.

Two sites are involved, both partly excavated, of which the smaller, which seems to be the earlier, may be considered first. It lies near the mouth of the River Sele and comprises a sanctuary in which several temples and treasuries have been excavated.[73] For the earlier history of the site, some late seventh-century Corinthian pottery takes us back to near its foundation date. The main temple, to Argive Hera, was a Doric building of little before 500 BC. Some of its sculptural decoration (relief metopes) has been found (*Fig. 219*). Just north of it is a 'treasury', perhaps built by some other west Greek state to honour the goddess, from which there is a rich series of relief metopes with various mythological scenes. These date to the years around the middle of the sixth

219 Limestone metope from the Heraeum near Paestum, showing Heracles struggling with Apollo for the tripod; mid-6th c. (Paestum Mus.; H. 88·2 cm)

century. Other architectural sculpture must be attributed to other archaic buildings, not yet certainly identified.

The city site lay some eight miles to the south-east, on a low flat plateau quite near the sea.[74] There are traces of its sixth-century walls, and the earliest finds reported are of the end of the seventh century. But the town's greatest glory lies in its three great Doric temples which still stand so well preserved and have excited the imaginations of visitors and artists for so long. The temples lay to the west of the main north–south road in the town. To the south are the so-called Basilica, which is a temple to Hera (mid sixth century, *Fig. 220*) and another Temple of Hera (mid fifth century), and to the north the so-called Temple of Ceres (late sixth century) which is probably better identified as of the goddess Athena (*Fig. 229*). Beside the last are the remains of a smaller temple of the earlier sixth century. An exciting find of recent years, a little to the south of the Athena Temple, is a small stone chamber whose roof alone shows above ground level (*Fig. 221*). It is in the form of a tomb, with a central bench supporting spits, bronze jars full of honey along either wall and an Athenian painted vase in one corner; but no body. It stood in a small enclosure or precinct, and is very probably a cenotaph for a distinguished citizen or founder.[75] The building is dated by the vases in it to about 520 BC.

220 View of Posidonia (Paestum) with the Archaic temple of Hera; mid-6th c.

A distinctive feature of the rich cemeteries near by is the presence of slab tombs decorated with painting in Greek style on the inner faces. The earliest of these, the Tomb of the Diver (*Fig. 222*), is late Archaic and in a nearly pure Greek style, but it and its successors may have honoured native Lucanians, not Greeks.[76]

There are many native, perhaps Oenotrian, sites and cemeteries near by. In the twin-sites of Palinurus and Molpa on the promontory thirty-five miles south of Posidonia, Greeks and natives may have lived side by side after about 550 BC, to judge from finds in excavations around the walls and in tombs.[77]

221 Underground cenotaph (?) at Posidonia; late 6th c.

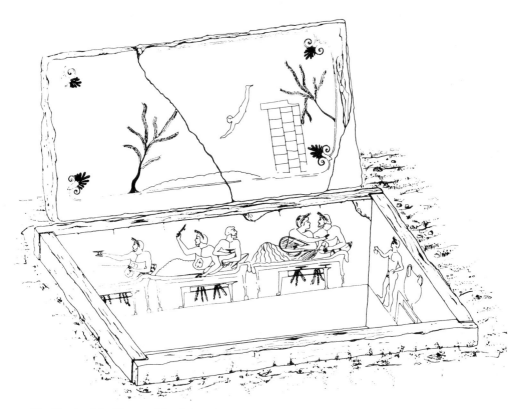

222 The Tomb of the Diver and detail from the painting on its wall; early 5th c. (Paestum Mus.)

TARENTUM (Greek TARAS). We have already had occasion to remark on the choice of settlers sent by Sparta to Tarentum (p. 163). Literary sources suggest a date for the settlement in the last decade of the eighth century, and the earliest tomb found in the town cemetery contains Corinthian vases which look of appropriate date. However, the native Iapygian site at Scoglio del Tonno, opposite the Greek town, seems to have been in intermittent touch with Greece from Mycenaean times down to the early years of the colony, and in the seventh century the native towns inland were receiving Greek vases. Closer to Tarentum, several small villages were occupied by Greeks. Of these we may mention Satyrium, just east of Tarentum, where Mycenaean pottery has also been found, and where the founders of Tarentum were said to have settled first, displacing the natives. Here there is clearer evidence for pre-colonial visits by Greeks.[78]

The Greek city of Tarentum lies beneath the modern Taranto, on a fine peninsula site which embraces a large lagoon (the Mare Piccolo).[79] Its port is the best in South Italy, and it commands good cornlands. Except for parts of a large sixth-century Doric temple, little is known of the early buildings, but the city's art and wealth are well attested by stray finds of votive offerings and the contents of tombs.[80] Its connections with its mother city are reflected in the fine Spartan vases found in sixth-century tombs. There is also a little East Greek and island pottery, including Chian, as well as the usual Corinthian and Athenian vases. The city's Spartan origin is revealed in many ways – cults, and the practice of burial within the walls, at least from the fifth century on. Tarentine chamber tombs, which begin in the Archaic period, are the most ornate of the early western Greek graves.[81]

SIRIS is supposed to have been founded by settlers from Colophon, in Ionia, who had been driven from their homes by the Lydians. This must have been just before 650 BC. It was then an isolated Ionian colony on a coast otherwise dominated by Dorian settlers. Yet it prospered for a while, and no doubt it shared the overland trade west to the coast of the Tyrrhenian Sea. There is hardly anything to show for the early town, except an early sixth-century loom weight inscribed (significantly in Ionic script) 'I belong to Isodike'.[82] About the middle of the century the town was destroyed by its non-Ionian neighbours Metapontum, Sybaris, and Croton. It was re-born in the foundation near by of HERACLEA (Policoro) by Tarentum in 433–432, a site occupied by Greeks even earlier than Siris, since its pottery goes back to the late eighth century. The Ionian city may have taken it over as a fortified outpost.[83]

LOCRI was founded from Locris in Central Greece in 673 (according to Eusebius). Nearby native Sicel villages (notably at Canale) had already been in close contact with Greeks, since several Greek vases have been found in them, some apparently made locally by Greek potters. There was a tradition that Dorian

Greeks in this area were picked up en route by the expedition which founded Syracuse (see p. 172), but to judge from the pottery in the native towns any Greeks in this area seem rather to have been islanders or Euboeans, who elsewhere too seem to have got on better with the Sicels than the Corinthians did. The vases are of the latest eighth and early seventh centuries. When Locri was settled the natives were ejected. We know most about the town and its temples in the fifth century, but temple building at the site of the famous Classical temple at Marasà can be traced back to the seventh century. The town has no natural harbour, but would have served as the last port of call in Italy on a voyage to Sicily.[84]

Locri established some colonies of her own, especially at Medma, Hipponium, and Metaurus, at the other ends of routes across the 'toe' of Italy to the Tyrrhenian Sea. The earliest finds at MEDMA, from tombs and votive deposits, take us back to near the beginning of the sixth century, so the foundation might even be seventh-century.[85] At METAURUS the graves certainly go back to the mid seventh century, and at HIPPONIUM there are now finds of the end of the century.[86] Graves in a Sicel town near by, at Torre Galli, contain Corinthian pottery of the late seventh century to the later sixth; and Greek contacts (and perhaps occupation) induced a change in funeral customs from inhumation to cremation.[87]

The seventh century saw the consolidation of the earliest Greek colonies in Sicily, and their expansion in the island with new foundations. Syracuse confirmed her control of the south-east by founding Helorus, Acrae, Casmenae, and Camarina. Megara Hyblaea struck farther west to Selinus. Other moves to the west were by Zancle at Himera, and by Gela at Acragas. With the foundation of Acragas in 580, the Greek colonizing of Sicily was virtually at an end.

Of the Syracusan towns HELORUS, half way to the southern tip of the island, was the earliest, and may have been settled by 700.[88] ACRAE lay in a strategic position inland, just in sight of Syracuse.[89] It had been an important Sicel hill town before the Greeks settled there in 663 (Thucydides' date). None of the pottery from the graves seems as early as the mid seventh century. Within the town there was a Doric temple of the later sixth century, and some other architectural pieces in an Ionic style which can be matched in the same period at Syracuse – notably decoration from an altar.[90]

A little farther inland, at Monte Casale, a fortified town was established. The earliest pottery is of the late seventh century and an early fortification wall, archaic houses, tombs, and a sanctuary have been uncovered.[91] This town is almost certainly the best of the candidates for CASMENAE (said to have been founded in 643). MORGANTINA, in central Sicily, was first settled by Greeks in the sixth century, and their walled acropolis stood for some years beside a native town which was eventually eclipsed, but it was not a formal colony though it is likely that the first Greeks here came from the east coast, perhaps Syracuse.[92] CAMARINA, the most westerly Syracusan town, lay on the coast less than twenty miles south-east of Gela. It was founded in 598, and tombs to the north-east together with votives from a temple in the town belong to its earliest years. In 552 the city joined the native Sicels in a revolt against Syracuse and was defeated and destroyed, but its survival as a town is proved by the many graves with pottery of the later sixth century.[93] It had no natural harbour, and the coast here and along much of South Sicily is marked by a succession of sandy cliffs and dunes.

SELINUS. The ruins of Selinus are the most impressive of any Greek city in Sicily (*Fig. 223*).[94] The site is not naturally a very good one, but it has a harbour and it commands good cultivable land. There was a native settlement near by, in an area occupied by one of the early Greek cemeteries. The walled acropolis lay on a low hill by the sea with the town spreading to the north of it. There is evidence for a regular planned town grid as early as the sixth century. Within the town are four large Doric temples. (The temples at Selinus defy ready identification by deities,[95] and are known by letters, for which two different series operate.) Temple C is of the mid sixth century (cf. *Fig. 230*), Temple D a little later, and Temples A and O of the mid fifth century. There are also traces of earlier temples going back to the end of the seventh century, and new excavations are beginning to reveal the plan of the Archaic city.

Outside the walls were other sanctuaries. Beyond a stream to the west lay that of Demeter Malophoros (Apple-bearer), who was worshipped by the same name in the mother city of Megara.[96]

Sketch plan of Selinus

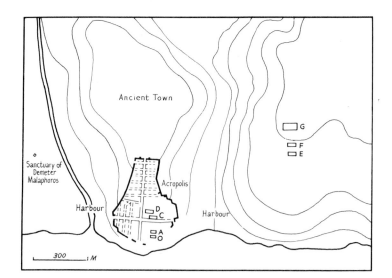

Her temple was a simple hall, but the precinct must have been one of the first to be laid out by the settlers. There was an associated cult of Zeus Meilichios, to whom simple stelae crowned by two carved human heads were dedicated.[97] These are odd objects (*Fig. 224*), and the inspiration for them may be native, or even Punic, but the inscriptions on them are Greek. To the north, another small archaic temple and altar have been discovered in recent years. East of the town lay three more Doric temples. Temple E(R) is of the fifth century, but both Temple F(S) and Temple G(T) (for Apollo) were begun in the last quarter of the sixth century. The last was a colossal building measuring 50·1 m. by 110·1 m., only exceeded in size by the slightly later Temple of Zeus at Acragas and the Ionic, earlier temples of East Greece.

No less impressive than the site itself are the finds of architecture, sculpture, and vases which it has yielded, and which represent the best of colonial Greek art in Sicily. For the early years of the colony our evidence comes from tombs and from the sanctuary of Demeter Malophoros. The dating of Corinthian pottery of the later seventh century has long relied on the earliest finds here and on Thucydides' date for the foundation, 627 BC. However, some Corinthian pottery from both the Demeter sanctuary and the acropolis should, on conventional dating, go back to the mid century, and this has suggested to some that the Eusebian foundation date of 650 is to be preferred. The pottery dating cannot easily be adjusted, since finds at other sites have confirmed it, and it is still not clear whether Thucydides' date is to be upheld.[98] The early finds seem too numerous now to be regarded as already old when they arrived at Selinus, but recent excavations north of the acropolis have shown that there was a native settlement being supplied with Greek pottery by 650, and it may be that the final Megarian foundation in 627 ousted earlier Greek infiltration in the area, probably from Gela. Most of the early pottery at Selinus is Corinthian, being replaced by Athenian in the second quarter of the sixth century, but there is also a fair amount of East Greek (Rhodian and some Chian) of the first half of the century, a little Spartan, and an unusual and large 'orientalizing' vase of the late seventh century painted in Sicily by an immigrant artist from one of the Greek islands.[99]

224 Limestone twin-head stelae, from Selinus; late 6th c. (Palermo Mus.; H. 18, 26 cm)

Selinus takes its name from the wild parsley (Greek *selinos*) which grew there, and which appeared as the device on the city's coinage.

ACRAGAS (Agrigento) was founded in 580 by Gela, and by the Rhodian settlers there, with reinforcements from home, rather than by the Cretans.[100] It lies less than forty miles west of Gela, and the area had certainly often been visited before the town was established. There may even have been settlement, since pottery of the latest seventh and early sixth century is reported from a cemetery between the town and the sea (Montelusa),[101] and there is a spring-house shrine of Persephone outside the walls (San

Biagio) which may also have been in use by Greeks before 580.[102] There may have been a disaster too, to judge from a late seventh-century mass burial,[103] and it is clear that a native Sican settlement had been displaced. The steep acropolis lies over two miles from the sea, but the town – which spreads on the terraced ground to the south – was also included within a circuit wall before the end of the sixth century. The whole area enclosed is about one and a half square miles, an extravagant piece of planning for a young colony.

The temples on the great terrace which lay within the south limit of the town are for the most part of the fifth century, but the greatest of them, to Zeus Olympios, was begun at the end of the sixth century. Its size rivalled that of the great Temple G(T) at Selinus, whose building had already started when the Acragas temple was laid out, nearly 3 m. wider. But the plan and construction are quite different, and a unique feature is the use of giant figures (Telamones) as structural supports on the outer screen walls. There were smaller temples of the later sixth century near the Temple of Zeus and the Temple of the Dioscuri, and one of the second half of the century, also on the south terrace (Villa Aurea). The Athena temple on the acropolis is of about 500 BC. Some archaic houses have also been excavated in the southern quarter of the town.

Apart from the inevitable succession of Corinthian and Athenian pottery in the sixth century, there is also a fair amount of pottery from Rhodes, mainly clay figurines and figure-vases. There is some archaeological evidence for the spread of Greek interests in the rich hinterland of Acragas in the sixth century. This is the time of the notorious tyrant Phalaris, and his brazen bull in which he roasted his opponents. But the zenith of the city's fortunes was not reached until the fifth century, when it wholly eclipsed its mother city Gela.

HIMERA. Expansion westward along the north coast of Sicily was left to the Chalcidian colonies of the straits, and of them Zancle had established a colony at Himera as early as 649 BC. It was an easily defensible site, though not over-richly endowed in natural resources – land or harbour.[104] But it might have proved a useful post for western trade, and it was to prove a challenge to the Phoenicians in the west of the island. It saw the defeat of the Carthaginians in 480, and was itself razed by them in 408. To recent excavation we owe knowledge of an important Archaic sanctuary and habitation area going back to near the foundation date. Earlier excavations had been mainly devoted to the temple by the river, built to commemorate the victory of 480.

LIPARA. The Lipari islands had been visited by Mycenaean Greeks, and must certainly have attracted Greek attention again as soon as the new colonies were founded. One early token of interest there is the faience *aryballos* (*Fig. 150*). In the same private collection as this vase and also, it was said, from Lipari, were four *ushabti* figures of Egyptian faience.[105] Their style is late and not closely datable, but it looks as though an Egyptian, or a Greek from Egypt, had intended his tomb to be properly furnished in the Egyptian manner. But when the Greeks came to live at Lipara, the acropolis had been unoccupied for some twenty years, as the finds show. A colony was established in the 570s, and then by Cnidians and Rhodians who, led by Pentathlos, had just failed to establish themselves in western Sicily at Lilybaeum, in the teeth of the Phoenicians. In recent excavations in the acropolis and cemeteries of Lipara, pottery from the earliest years of the colony has been reported – mainly Corinthian and East Greek.

ELEA (Hyele, Velia).[106] The last of the South Italian colonies was founded in about 535 by Phocaeans, whose unhappy wanderings after the destruction of their city by the Persians will be spoken of later. Posidonia is about twenty-five miles north of Elea, and the greater city seems to have favoured an enterprise which could hardly challenge her power. The small fortified hill site and a sanctuary have been explored, and has yielded pottery of its earliest days. The mouths of the rivers on either side of the town afforded two harbours.

Greeks and Natives in Sicily and Italy

The Greek tradition about the natives of Sicily was a simple one. They, the Sicels, had invaded the island from Italy some time in the eleventh century, and driven the Sicans whom they found there into the centre and south.[107] The archaeological story is rather different, for if there were any invasions they made little impression on a culture which in the main had more in common with the Greek Aegean than with Italy. The only Italian people in this area are represented by the 'Ausonians', who lived in the Lipari Islands and in Sicily at Milazzo-Mylae, perhaps, until the arrival of the Greeks in the west. In the disturbed years of the early Iron Age, the Sicels had gathered themselves for protection into large communities. One of the greatest was at Pantalica (just west of Syracuse), perhaps the ancient Hybla, seat of the king Hyblon with whom the Greeks had dealings. When the Greeks arrived, the Sicel culture had perhaps only just admitted painted pottery beside the plain incised wares. They had some skill in bronze working, and they buried their dead in rock-cut chamber tombs which honeycomb the hillsides near all Sicel towns. Almost all the sites chosen by the Greeks for their colonies had been occupied by Sicels, and in every instance the latter seem to have been ejected. Hyblon was friendly enough to the Megarians in showing them a home, but his capital did not long survive.[108] And when, in the seventh and sixth centuries, the colonies began expanding by making new foundations, these were always at the expense of Sicel communities.[109]

225 Sicel vase from Leontinoi; 7th c.

The impact of Greek ideas and culture was immediate. On many Sicel sites near the early colonies we find Greek vases, and often too vases which are native in shape but quite Greek in decoration (*Fig. 225*). Where these have figure decoration, it certainly looks as though they had been painted by Greeks especially for their Sicel neighbours.[110] The natives also learnt from the Greeks to make bronze and clay figurines, in which an interesting mixture of styles is revealed, and their bronze work in particular was stimulated and encouraged by the Greeks. They adopted a form of the Chalcidian alphabet. Whether we should also admit the possibility that Greek families lived in Sicel towns is another matter. A common pattern seems to have been the infiltration of Greek goods into a native site, possibly the establishment of a Greek quarter, followed by the establishment of a wholly Greek town either near by or at the expense of the native settlement. Once the colonies were well grounded the amount of Greek material need not attest Greek presence, though this is likely, but it can only be proved by the presence of purely Greek-style burials or a Greek sanctuary, as seems to have been true at, for instance, Grammichele, west of Leontini, and at Torre Galli, near Hipponium.[111]

At any rate it is clear that in most places the Greeks and Sicels got on well enough, even if only in the relationship of master and slave (there was a Sicel slave-woman in Homer's Ithaca). The natives weighed their new prosperity, brought by the Greeks, against the sites and land they had lost to them, and were generally satisfied – or at least had short memories. In the mid fifth century there was a nationalist Sicel movement, but by then the natives had been almost completely hellenized.

We might expect to find some native influence in the matter of religion or customs upon the newly-come Greeks, with whom there must surely have been intermarriage. It has been suggested that the siting of some of the extra-mural sanctuaries in Greek colonies was dictated by pre-existent native cult-places, and this is highly probable, but the goods were purely Greek and conceded nothing in attributes or function to native belief, though the character of votive offerings might in places be affected by local traditions.[112] An important concession to Sicel usage was the adoption by some cities of weights for their coinage which would suit both native and Greek standards.[113] Farther off we find a Sikelos and a Sikanos working in the potters' quarter in Athens in the later sixth century, but they do not have to be Sicilian slaves. In the west the Greeks had nothing to learn, much to teach.

In central Sicily, the Greeks at Gela and Acragas had to deal with the Sicans, who are less well-known archaeologically but who, in the literary record, seem to have been more belligerent than the Sicels. Several native sites in this area seem to have been destroyed or taken over in the course of the seventh and sixth centuries, notably Butera, in a dominant position overlooking the

226 Clay votive model of a temple, from Sabucina; 6th c. (Caltanisetta Mus.; H. 50 cm)

plain of Gela.[114] Its cemeteries attest increasing Greek influence through the seventh century, ended only by its overthrow at the hands of the Geloans. At Sabucina, farther inland in central Sicily, a native site was progressively hellenized becoming wholly Greek by the mid sixth century, but admitting as a votive a native clay model of a simple Greek temple (*Fig. 226*).[115]

In South Italy the story is much the same, but the archaeological character of the natives whom the Greeks met – Iapygians, Oenotrians, etc. – is less clearly defined.[116] Here too, though, Greek goods and ideas rapidly penetrated. Near Locri, as in Sicily, there were Greeks decorating vases for the natives in the years around 700 BC. Only in Apulia (the 'heel' above Tarentum) did the native tradition in vase shapes, allied to Greek geometric patterns, survive long as an independent and flourishing style. The routes across the 'instep' of South Italy are particularly rich in Greek finds – notably the sixth-century bronze vases of Spartan type – which attracted the attention of the native villagers before they could pass on to the Greek colonies on the west coast and from them perhaps to Etruria. At Torre Galli near Hipponium it looks as though there may have been Greeks living in the native village, and this probably happened far more often than the archaeological evidence may lead us to think. In the town by the sanctuary of Apollo Alaios, on the Crimissa promontory between Sybaris and Croton, there may have been another mixed community. The sanctuary was used by Greeks in the seventh century, and a Doric temple was built there, perhaps before the end of the sixth century.[117]

Farther north, at Cumae and Posidonia, the natives met by the Greeks belonged much more closely to the Apennine cultures of central Italy.[118] Here too Greek goods and influence penetrated quickly. Naples (Parthenope) had already been settled by Rhodians by 650, to judge from the reported finds;[119] and before the end of the sixth century there were other settlements at Puteoli (founded by refugee Samians in 531) and Pompeii, where there was a small Doric temple, and Greek pottery arriving by 550.[120] In Rome there is Euboean and Corinthian pottery within fifty years of the legendary date of its foundation by Romulus in 754–753; but in this area, and to the north in Etruria, the influence and arrival of the Greeks worked profound changes which are best considered separately, later in this chapter.

Western Greek Colonial Art

The main imports to the western colonies have been mentioned in the remarks on the individual cities, and need only be summarized here. From the beginning, Corinthian pottery was in great demand, although Euboean styles are naturally prominent in the earliest days of the Euboean colonies. By the mid sixth century, Athenian vases replaced the Corinthian; but this was a victory for the artists rather than the merchants, and the Corinthian colony Syracuse resisted the change in fashion for a while. East Greek vases travelled far, though in little quantity except to the Rhodian foundation at Gela, where the continued popularity of even plainer wares suggests continued support from home. Crete is represented in her own joint foundation at Gela. Spartan vases come in numbers to Spartan Tarentum, and there are a few on other sites. Ivories of the type found in Peloponnesian sanctuaries appear in Corinthian Syracuse[121] and Megara Hyblaea, and Corinth may have brought the more trivial Spartan vases which are found in Sicily. Etruscan pottery and other objects reached a few of the Greek cities, especially those in nearby Campania and Selinus, but no more than we would expect from such proximity and in such busy waters.[122] In other materials, there are fine stone lamps of the late seventh and early sixth centuries from the Greek islands in Selinus and Syracuse,[123] and some pieces of archaic marble statuary.[124] From the earlier seventh century the Sicilian colonies received Rhodian trinkets and perfume vases in faience. Later faience objects may be from Rhodes, Egypt (Naucratis), or Phoenicia. Of truly oriental imports there are Near Eastern seals[125] brought to their earliest colonies in the west by the Euboeans, and some decorated metal vases.

The earliest Greek settlements in the west had to be self-sufficient. Where they could, they made their own vases in styles familiar to them at home, and their architecture and other works of art copied forms which they remembered or their artists had brought with them. There was virtually no question of adapting

these Greek forms to native usage, although some concessions had to be made to the different materials available. Nevertheless, the more flourishing colonies came to develop individual styles and tastes independently of each other and of homeland Greece. New settlers from Greece included artists, and the flow of imports kept them in touch with Greek fashions. To this extent colonial art is a simple extension of Greek art, and it might have gone the way it did in any other part of the ancient world where there was no native art of a quality to invite imitation. Here I shall mention only those products of the Greek west which betray some originality of taste and an independence of the forms current in homeland Greece.

Most of the finely decorated pottery used by the western Greeks was imported, but there is some evidence for local schools also. Grave vases (craters as *Fig. 203*) at Pithekoussai are local products of Euboean artists,[126] and at Cumae in the earlier seventh century some local potters turned out extremely good copies of

227 Crater signed by Aristonothos – fight between a warship and an armed merchantman, from Caere; mid-7th c. (Rome, Conservatori Mus.; H. 36 cm)

Corinthian vases, imitating the pale clay by using a fine creamy
slip. In Sicily there was a little work for the natives, but about the
middle of the seventh century, before rather than after, there were
experiments in an outline 'orientalizing' style. At Syracuse the
inspiration seems Argive, but there are related styles at Gela and
Leontini, as well as a distinguished polychrome style at Megara
Hyblaea. The famous crater signed by Aristonothos, which
reached Caere in Etruria, may be of the same family (*Fig. 227*). It
shows a sea fight, and Odysseus with his companions blinding
Polyphemus (Cyclops).[127] In the later seventh century some fine
vases in the East Greek 'Wild Goat' style found in South Italy have
prompted the suggestion that they were made locally, by immigrant potter-painters.[128] The style is 'pure'. In the sixth century,
isolated imitations of black-figure do not deserve more than
passing mention, but there was one important workshop which
flourished through the second half of the century. This produced
the 'Chalcidian' vases (as *Fig. 228*), so named for the style of the
lettering in their inscriptions.[129] The painting on them betrays the
influence of Corinth, Athens, and East Greece a little; but the
artists were no mere copyists, and they produced a ware which at
its best rivals the best Athenian vases for finesse and composition,

or perhaps excels them in general decorative effect. The finds are almost evenly distributed between Etruria and Rhegium (the Chalcidian colony), with a few in other western Greek cities, and in Aegean Greece so far only at Smyrna. The quality is far above anything made by the Greeks in Etruria, and it is tempting to suppose that the first painters of the school learned their craft in Greece – perhaps in Chalcis, although there is little there or elsewhere in Euboea to suggest that it could be the nursery of such fine artists. It is likely that they worked in Rhegium itself. After them there is nothing worthy of note until immigrant Athenian painters established workshops for red-figure vases in South Italy in the mid fifth century.

In their architecture, the western Greeks – most of them Peloponnesian by origin – preferred the Doric order. In details their temples often show a considerable lag behind models in mainland Greece, but there were ambitious and original architects in the west also. Some of the most unusual features of western Doric are, however, to be attributed to the influence of Ionic decorative forms – the elaboration of the necking on some capitals, acroteria, balustrades on altars, whole columns at Posidonia (*Fig. 229*). It may be that the 'double-fronted' plans of the great temples at Syracuse and Selinus owe something to the Ionic earlier temples of Samos and Ephesus, and the unfinished Ionic temple at Syracuse was certainly inspired by them.[130] Most of the earlier and many of the later western buildings are especially distinguished by the painted clay revetments (*Fig. 230*) which encased or protected the wooden parts of their roof and gables.[131] The models for such revetments are Corinthian, but in Sicily the type was elaborated in a manner which is not met in Greece and which can be claimed as wholly Sicilian in its development, if not in its invention.

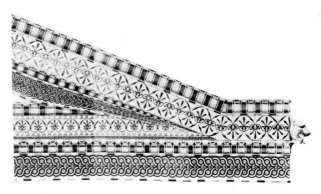

229 East, inner porch of the Athena temple, Posidonia (Paestum); late 6th c.

230 Clay revetment from Temple C, Selinus; about 550–525 BC.

The western Greeks had no fine marble for their sculpture, and had to use the coarser local stones, or turned more often to major works in clay. The few archaic marble statues found on Sicilian and South Italian sites were all imported ready made from the Peloponnese, Athens, and East Greece.[132] In Sicily there was an early school of about 600 BC making sculptures in the archaic Greek 'Dedalic' style and using soft limestone. The main achievements, though, were in architectural sculpture, and the metope-reliefs from the Heraeum by the Sele (Posidonia, as *Fig. 219*) and Selinus between them tell the story of western sculpture from the earlier sixth century on. Their style has much in common with Peloponnesian work, but the artists were generally slow to admit the rapid development which characterizes the sixth century in Greece itself, and were perhaps consciously archaizing. There is an occasional 'looseness' of style and touch of realism which also stamps their work as provincial, although none the worse for that.[133] There are some minor local schools working in a more primitive style, as that which produced the remarkable goddess suckling twins from Megara Hyblaea (*Fig. 216*). Perhaps a little earlier in the sixth century are the three figures from a small fountain-shrine just east of Acragas (at Montechiaro) – some of the very few examples of wooden statuary preserved from the archaic period (*Fig. 231*).[134]

231 Wooden statuette from Montechiaro; early 6th c. (Syracuse Mus. 47134; H. 16·7 cm)

For minor works in clay – figurines and other votives – it is again Corinthian models which we most often see copied, but soon distinctive local shops and types can be made out. Small clay altars with reliefs at their sides and sometimes painting (*Fig. 232*) represent a type developed wholly in the west and almost unknown in Greece itself. At Gela there was a vogue for clay coffins with Ionic architectural mouldings in relief.[135] In the later decades of the sixth century more East Greek influence is admitted, and there is some distinguished work especially from the South Italian sites, while at Tarentum there was an important

232 Clay altar (arula) of Sicilian type. On the front Heracles and Triton, in relief; on the side Circe and a transformed companion of Odysseus, painted; about 530 BC. (Paris, Louvre CA 5956; H. 34·8 cm)

school of coroplasts whose earliest work in a wholly individual style takes us back to the first half of the sixth century (*Fig. 233*).[136]

There was a limited production of bronzes in the west.[137] In the later sixth century there were workshops in South Italy, although the recent claims made for the Chalcidian cities seem somewhat exaggerated. Locri and Tarentum in particular seem to have been making fine bronze vases and mirrors with figure attachments, and there have been one or two good finds in Sicily. From Grumentum, near Metapontum, comes a bronze horseman (*Fig. 234*) – in the British Museum – which was certainly made somewhere in the west before 550 BC.[138] But the whole problem of the identification of local schools of bronze workers is complicated by the presence of imports, which are largely Peloponnesian, and by our ignorance of Sybaris, which is likely to have been an important artistic centre in its day.

We hear nothing of the names of artists in Sicily and South Italy. One who did work in the west is the sculptor Pythagoras who came from Samos soon after 500 BC.[139] The expensive offerings made in the Greek sanctuaries by the western tyrants and kings are the work of Greek craftsmen working at home. The sanctuary of Zeus at Olympia was the obvious place for dedications from the west. On the terrace of the Treasuries[140] – the small shrine-like buildings dedicated by the Greek states – half of the buildings

233 Clay figure from Tarentum; about 560 BC. (Oxford 1886.744; H. 15 cm)

234 Bronze horseman from Grumentum; mid-6th c. (London 1904.7–3.1; H. 25·2 cm – the feet restored)

were given by westerners: Gela, Metapontum, Sybaris, Selinus, Syracuse. Most were built in the sixth century, and the earliest of them, of Gela, is decorated with elaborate clay revetments in the Sicilian style. It might be worth considering whether the 'Megarian' treasury was not originally a dedication of the Sicilian Megara, adopted by the mother city after the colony's destruction. The colony was certainly far wealthier than homeland Megara at the time the treasury was built and decorated with sculpture and revetments in which scholars have detected Sicilian traits.

Coinage

235 Silver drachm of Zancle, showing its sickle-shaped harbour and a dolphin; about 510 BC. (London)

Some of the colonies began to mint their own silver coinage about the middle of the sixth century, and others soon followed suit. The silver could have been obtained from Spain – indeed two of the earliest cities to coin (Himera, Selinus) are well placed for the western trade – or from Greece. Greek coins were often overstruck in the colonial mints. The choice of weight-standard was determined by current usage and commercial convenience, but the sources of some of the standards in use are still far from clear, and for the dates of the coins there is generally little more to go on than their style.[141]

The Euboean colonies used a light standard[142] which could easily be related to other Greek standards and to those used in Etruria and, it seems, by the Sicels. The devices usually have some significance. For Himera ('day', daybreak) a cock; for Naxos (wine-growing) Dionysus' head and grapes; for Zancle a dolphin sporting in her sickle-shaped harbour (*Fig. 235*). Syracuse was late to coin (about 510), just as she was late to open her market to other than Corinthian vases. She chose the Attic standard, which could readily be adjusted to the native Sicel usage, as had Selinus for her coins bearing the canting device of a parsley leaf.

236 Silver stater of Metapontum showing an ear of barley in relief (obverse) and intaglio (reverse); about 550–530 BC. (Berlin)

The Achaean cities of South Italy began to mint on the Corinthian standard after the middle of the sixth century. They chose, or invented, an unusual type of coin on which the device which appears in relief on the front is repeated on the back reversed, in intaglio, and often simplified. This is not a style met in Greece proper; but in the west Rhegium, Zancle, and Tarentum also adopted it for some issues. Some fine examples are of Metapontum, with an ear of corn as device (*Fig. 236*); and there is an interesting sidelight on Sybaris' subjection to Croton after 510 in coins carrying the devices of both cities (Croton's tripod, Sybaris' bull). The same style of coin was minted at Posidonia, at first on a local standard.[143]

Greeks and Etruscans

The problem of the origins of the Etruscans is one which has vexed scholars for generations and is likely to do so for many years more. Fortunately it requires no detailed discussion here. The Greeks thought the Etruscans had arrived in Italy from western Asia Minor, and for their neighbours, the Romans, they had the tale of Rome's foundation after the escape from Troy of Aeneas and his family and their wanderings to the west (Virgil's story). Archaeologically the culture of Etruria seems mainly explicable in terms of local development, not without influence from the north, down to the eighth century and the later stages of the Villanovan culture in what were to be the main Etruscan cities. Problems to be resolved concern their language – not its script or decipherment but its associations, which do not seem Italian, and the sources of the rapid and fundamental cultural change.[144]

Before the end of the eighth century Etruscan culture was completely transformed by the intrusion of 'orientalizing' objects and techniques. To some this has seemed the moment at which immigrants from the east settled in Etruria, but the new 'orientalizing' features do not derive from any one eastern centre, and they share the same range and variety as the orientalizing features which Greece had accepted a little earlier and which we have already discussed in Chapter 3. Beside these new eastern forms we also observe a number of Greek Geometric ones. The source of these is easy to divine, since the earliest of the Greek colonies in the west had been deliberately planted in a position which was particularly favourable for trade with Etruria, at Pithekoussai and Cumae. Etruria admits both the eastern and the Greek at the same time, and it is worth considering whether she did not accept them from the same source. The Greeks at Pithekoussai and Cumae were Euboeans, the same folk who had opened up the east to the Greek world nearly a century before. The Etruscans were a rich but artistically immature and impoverished people, and they became ready and receptive customers for anything exotic that the Euboeans could bring them – to a small degree the forms of Greek Geometric art, and to a great the wonders of the east, gold, jewellery, and bronzes. These are years in which the Phoenicians too (see below) are plying western waters and direct eastern influence might be suspected and has been argued.[145] However, now that the presence of easterners in Greek Pithekoussai has been demonstrated[146] it might still be held that the Greeks were largely responsible, and that the different response of Greeks and Etruscans should be explained by their different traditions, and the cultural vacuum presented by the rich Etruscan cities.[147] That the new look in Etruria followed immediately on the foundation of the adjacent Greek colonies cannot be merely accidental.

If this is true, the orientalizing phase of Etruscan civilization is very largely due to trade with the Greeks. In effect they were exposed to the same new art forms and techniques of the eastern world as the Greeks had been. The difference in the reactions of the two peoples is a measure of the difference in their quality and originality. The Greeks chose, adapted, and assimilated until they produced a material culture which was wholly Greek, despite all the superficial inspiration which the east provided. The Etruscans accepted all they were offered, without discrimination. They copied – or paid Greeks and perhaps immigrant easterners to copy – with little understanding of the forms and subjects which served as models. They had their gold worked into extravagant pastiches of eastern jewellery, and gave the Greeks the metal they wanted in return for what was often hardly more than the bright beads with which merchants are usually supposed to dazzle natives. The result, with a further massive injection of Greek influence in the sixth century, was 'Etruscan art'; the showy blend of Greek, oriental, and barbarian taste which can still inspire or impress those who cannot come to terms with the more controlled achievements of Greek art.

The full measure of the effect of eastern art in Etruria cannot be taken here, but there are some things which may illustrate the part the Greeks played as middlemen. Near Eastern seals of the latest eighth century can be traced through Pithekoussai to Etruria.[148] Bronze cauldrons of eastern type with bull's-head or siren attachments can be traced through Cumae where there is a plainer cauldron of the same general type. Other orientalizing bronzes, cauldrons, and a bowl in Etruria (at Praeneste and Capena) are of an oriental workshop which seems to have been established at some time in Greece, probably in Crete (see p. 58 ff.).

We are more directly concerned, however, with (1) Greek imports to Etruria; (2) the evidence for Greeks working and living in Etruria; and (3) the influence of Greek rather than oriental models on Etruscan art.

1. We have already noticed the few types of vases which demonstrated pre-colonial trade. Once the Euboean colonies were founded both Euboean and Corinthian vases found their way to Etruria. The Corinthian vases continue to arrive through the seventh century together with a growing number of East Greek. The sixth century sees the liveliest trade, with the fine Athenian vases gradually winning the market from the Corinthian. But the Athenian vases were not carried by Athenians, nor the Corinthian necessarily by Corinthian ships. Merchants' marks scratched on the bases of vases may betray Ionian hands, and much of the carrying was probably done by Phocaeans, Chians, or others from the eastern Aegean.[149] In effect, not very much fine East Greek pottery was carried to Etruria – some Chian and Rhodian of the later seventh and sixth centuries – although figure-flasks were popular later. Of the other vases, we may note only the vogue for Spartan cups through the second and third quarters of the sixth century, for 'Chalcidian' vases (see p. 194) in its second half, and (carried for their contents) Chian wine-jars and Athenian oil-jars. The Greek potters were careful to observe Etruscan taste. Before the mid sixth century, both Corinthians and Athenians

237 Athenian amphora
('Tyrrhenian') by the
Timiades Painter, from
Vulci; about 550 BC.
(Boston 98.916; H.
39·4 cm)

238 Athenian amphora
made by Nikosthenes from
Etruria; about 530 BC.
(Castle Ashby; H. 30·9 cm)

239 Athenian kyathos,
satyrs in a vineyard, from
Etruria; about 520 BC.
(Castle Ashby; H. 13·2 cm)

catered for Etruscan delight in colourful story-telling on, respectively, their craters (wine-mixing bowls) and the so-called Tyrrhenian amphorae (*Fig. 237*).[150] The inscriptions labelling the figures on the latter did not always make sense, but the Etruscan buyer was not likely to realize that. After the mid sixth century, when the Athenian vases had won the market, the potter Nikosthenes started supplying vase-shapes (an *amphora* — *Fig. 238*; and dippers – *kyathoi*: as *Fig. 239*) familiar to the Etruscans in their plain native *bucchero*, but decorated with the usual Athenian figures, the amphorae being virtually monopolized by Caere.[151] This sort of ingenuity ensured a brisk market. It may be too that vases with particular scenes were picked out for this western market, for instance, those showing Aeneas rescuing Anchises from Troy – a theme with western relevance.

2. For evidence of Greeks actually working and living in Etruria there is even a literary record. One Demaratus, a Corinthian noble, emigrated about the middle of the seventh century at a time of political crisis at home, and settled in Etruria, at Tarquinii, where he married a local lady, sired the fifth king of Rome (Tarquinius Priscus) and carried on his prosperous business. With him he brought a painter and three clay-modellers, who introduced the new technique of clay statuary to Etruria.[152]

Greek work or influence is most readily shown by the pottery. There are geometric vases in Etruria of the late eighth and early seventh centuries whose shape and decoration are still Greek, although they are clearly not imported from Greece or necessarily from the Greek colonies. Important examples are standed craters

240 Amphora from Vulci; late 8th c. (Rome, Villa Giulia 75871; H. 47 cm)

241 Cup by the Swallow Painter from Vulci; about 600 BC. (Rome, Villa Giulia 65455; H. 24 cm)

from Vulci (*Fig. 240*)[153] and Bisenzio, which seem likely to be the work of Euboean artists working in Etruria. Other painted vases of non-Greek local shapes may also have been made by Greeks, but it becomes difficult to draw the line here. Etruscan painters must quickly have picked up the techniques and patterns, and for over a hundred years nearly all the vases painted in Etruria are probably the work of local artists, heavily influenced by contemporary, or slightly out-of-date Corinthian fashions, but adding some orientalizing decoration derived from imported metalwork. At the end of the seventh century an immigrant East Greek artist, the Swallow Painter,[154] seems to have set up shop in Vulci, producing Wild Goat vases in a style which makes few concessions to local taste (*Fig. 241*). A similar phenomenon has been suspected for these years in the Greek colonies of South Italy (see above). He has more distinguished successors.

After the middle of the sixth century, the Ionian 'diaspora' led many East Greek artists to look for new homes. Some came to Etruria and set up shop to supply a market whose taste for finely decorated pottery was already highly developed; and this too was no doubt the most active period of East Greek trade through Sybaris. Black-figure painters of the 'Clazomenian' school produced two series of vases in Etruria, which admit some local patterns as well as much influence from the popular Athenian styles. These are the so-called 'Northampton Group' amphorae of the 530s (*Fig. 242*), and the 'Campana *dinoi*' which are very closely related (*Fig. 243*).[155] The work of the same artists, or at least artists from the same schools, can be traced in East Greece, and in Egypt (see p. 137 f.), and was carried to Greek cities on the Black Sea. Of about this date is another group of vases, all of one shape certainly made at Caere: the 'Caeretan *hydriae*'[156] (as *Fig. 244*). Their painters (perhaps two masters) had a lively sense of humour and appreciation of how colour could be effectively employed in what

242 The Northampton amphora, from Etruria; about 540 BC. (Castle Ashby; H. 32·4 cm)

243 'Campana dinos' showing the return of Hephaestus to Olympus; about 520 BC. (Würzburg H 5352; H. 20·8 cm)

244 'Caeretan' hydria showing the Negro bodyguard of King Busiris – for the main scene see our *Fig. 186*; about 530–520 BC. (Vienna 4593; H. 45 cm)

245 Stone anchor inscribed with a dedication by Sostratos, from Gravisca; about 500 BC. (L. 1·15 cm)

246 Painted clay ('Campana') plaque from a tomb wall (Campana Tomb) at Caere showing a priest seated before a statue of a goddess and a snake; late 6th c. (Paris, Louvre; H. about 1·3 m)

was basically a black-and-white technique. The elements of their style are Ionian and Corinthian, but it is their individuality which is most impressive. They had no followers.

One or two Etruscan cities have a special place in this story. Caere must have been a partly Greek city. The Greeks called it Agylla and dedicated a treasury at Delphi.[157] Gravisca, port of the great Etruscan city of Tarquinii, also had a rich Greek quarter from the early sixth century on, including Greek temples.[158] The Archaic imported pottery includes an unusually high proportion of East Greek wares, and a bronze griffin from a cauldron of Samian type.[159] Another striking dedication is a stone anchor, given by Sostratos to 'Aiginetan Apollo' (Fig. 245). Herodotus knew of a successful Aiginetan trader in the west of this name, and the SO graffiti and dipinti found on many Athenian vases exported to Etruria have also been associated with him.[160]

Another field in which we may suspect the work of Greek artists is tomb-painting. Some of the paintings on the walls of Etruscan tombs seem in a wholly Greek style (Fig. 246), and the 'Caeretan' vase-painter may even have worked in this medium also. There is no comparative material from Greece itself, where chamber tombs of this type were not built, but we are offered points of comparison now with painting executed by East Greek artists in Phrygia and Lycia (Fig. 122) and with the new tomb at Posidonia (Fig. 222).

3. The influence of Greek artists and art on Etruscan products is quite easily recognized. The Euboean and Corinthian Geometric and early orientalizing styles which became familiar after the

founding of the first Greek colonies were slavishly copied by native artists, who were especially attracted by the simple 'metope pattern' which could be mass-produced with a multiple brush.[161]

All Corinthian styles were imitated in the 'Italo-Corinthian' vases, which can be traced at least down to the middle of the sixth century. Vase-shapes are copied, and all the elements of figure and abstract decoration, with one or two other patterns suggested by imported oriental bronzes and ivories. The mixture of patterns and disposition of the decoration is seldom quite as the Corinthian (*Fig. 247*). The animals are often caricatures of their models and behave in a non-Greek way, with dismembered bodies in their mouths.[162] Throughout the same period, Etruria developed her own plain black ware (*bucchero*) admitting Greek shapes and impressed or moulded decoration of Greek and oriental style.

As Athenian vases replaced Corinthian in the markets, so they were in turn copied in a comparatively jejune manner. One class, mis-called 'Pontic', admits more colour and variety (*Fig. 248*). It may have been founded by Greeks, but was later developed by Etruscan artists influenced by Athenian, Ionian, and the later Corinthian styles. And in the fifth century even red-figure was imitated, at first by painting the figures in red instead of leaving them reserved in the clay ground of the vase.[163]

In tomb painting the Etruscans soon followed the Greek lead (see above), often distorting proportions or misunderstanding subjects, but at times inspiring their work with a sense of lively movement or of grim other-worldliness.

In bronze work they developed several types – as of fibulae – which were introduced by the Greeks but did not become so

247 'Italo-Corinthian' alabastron; about 550 BC. (Oxford, Queens Loan 8; H. 17·5 cm)

248 'Pontic' amphora, with centaurs; about 530 BC. (Würzburg 778; H. 36·7 cm)

249 Ivory writing tablet inscribed with an abecedarium, from Marsiliana d'Albegna; about 700–650 BC. (Florence; 8·8 × 5·1 cm)

popular in Greece itself. Their metalwork was of a high quality, dependent in varying degrees on Greek models for vase shapes (though some are Phoenician or native) or plastic attachments, the latter generally inspired by Peloponnesian (often Spartan) bronzes.

Demaratus' companions were said to have introduced clay modelling to Etruria, and this was soon a craft in which the Etruscans approached the skill of the Greeks. It was one they practised more, for they did not have – or at least did not exploit – any sources of fine white marble for statuary such as the Greeks used. Finally we should remark that the Etruscans learned their alphabet from the Chalcidians, and that the earliest Etruscan A B C is inscribed on an ivory writing tablet which imitates an eastern form (*Fig. 249*).[164]

In return, the Etruscans had nothing to offer but raw materials.[165] Some vases reached the western colonial cities, and a few *bucchero* cups were carried as curios to Greece itself in the years around 600.[166] In the early period of colonizing a simple Etruscan vase reached Ischia,[167] and a belt was brought back home by an Eretrian.[168] Helmets of pre-colonial date reached Olympia and Delphi.[169] A bronze tripod of about 500 from the Vulci workshop was found on the Acropolis at Athens; there are bronze strainers at Olympia and Lindos (Rhodes) and a bronze attachment at Dodona. Olympia is perhaps the obvious place for us to look for Etruscan things, and Pausanias says that an Etruscan king was the first barbarian to make a dedication there.[170] There is part of a silver diadem of mid seventh century date from Olympia which seems certainly Etruscan, and scraps of bronze shields which might also be. The fibulae of types most popular in Italy are not necessarily imported dedications, or certainly not all of them.[171] Even in the fifth century the occasional fine object reached Greece from Etruria, casually and not by way of trade.

Despite this record of cultural dependence, the political relations between Greeks and Etruscans worsened after the mid sixth century. The Etruscans had acquired a considerable fleet, and in 540 joined the Carthaginians in driving the Phocaeans from the seas at Alalia. In 524 they attacked Cumae, but were defeated; and when they had to face the Latin alliance against them, they found Greeks in the ranks of their enemies. The Etruscan fleet dominated the waters north of the Messina Straits, and only the overland routes to Campania remained in Greek hands. Soon after 500, the flow of Greek goods to Etruria began to fall off, but by then the Greek-trained or Greek artists in Etruria could supply all needs, and at any rate the Greeks were soon to regain control of the seas.

Rome deserves more than a passing mention in our story. In its early culture it shares the history of the Villanovans, Etruscans and other Italic peoples, but these are years in which its identity as a state becomes established and the Republic is born. Like its Etruscan neighbours it received Greek pottery – Euboean and Corinthian – from the end of the eighth century and there is a continuing flow of Greek goods through the Archaic period. Excavations in Rome in recent years have enhanced the story, notably those by the later Forum Boarium (the S. Omobono area) where there is an important sequence of finds from the Late Geometric on.[172] Pliny tells us that Vulca was summoned from Veii in Etruria to make the clay Jupiter for Rome's Capitol, and a clay Heracles.[173] In the late Archaic temple at S. Omobono, recently excavated, a clay group of Heracles and Athena (*Fig. 250*) displays that subtle blend of Greek and Etruscan styles, devoted to

250 Clay group of Heracles and Athena at S. Omobono, Rome; about 500 BC. (Rome, Conservatori Mus.; restored H. with base about 1·65 m)

a Greek theme, which served as model for the art of the young Republic,[174] and in the fifth century it is Greek artists who decorate the temple of Ceres in the Circus Maximus.[175]

Greeks and Phoenicians

Ancient Greek historians believed that the Phoenicians had preceded the Greeks in trade and colonization in the western Mediterranean, and Thucydides says that they had been using promontories and islets off Sicily for trade with the natives until the arrival of the Greeks drove them to the western end of the island.[176] The archaeological evidence – indeed a simple glance on a map at the relative positions of the Greek and Phoenician towns – shows that this was not true. Indeed it is very difficult to demonstrate any pre-Greek trade with the natives of Sicily since the first foreign objects there are Greek, and in their train come some of the minor oriental trinkets which the Greeks used or distributed.

It has become clear in recent years that the Phoenicians had been interested in the western waters of the Mediterranean at least as early as the Greeks.[177] It had seemed that the Greeks set the pattern of establishing substantial trading communities, then colonies, whence their control of the prime sites in east and central Sicily, but even if the Phoenicians were not town-makers on quite the scale of the Greeks, it is evident now that they were manning trading posts on the coasts of southern Spain, north Africa, west Sicily and probably Sardinia, before the end of the eighth century. A major attraction for traders from the East Mediterranean was the supply of metal in the west, especially tin. For tin the main source was probably Britain, even in quite early times. Trade was not, of course, the only motive for colonization, but if the Phoenicians had been interested only in land, there seems little reason why they should have taken pains to try to elbow out the Greeks on the important routes, and ignored nearer tracts of good farmland like Cyrenaica.

The tin reached the Mediterranean in two ways: (a) overland through France, whence it could be supplied to the metalworking centres of Etruria. This route was the one the Greeks first tapped through the Euboean foundations at Pithekoussai and Cumae, safeguarded by their colonies on the Straits of Messina, and later pursued by colonies on the south of France. The other tin route (b) was by sea to the south of Spain, where there were other important mineral resources – notably silver – to be won. Once the trade routes via Etruria had been secured by the Greeks, well before the end of the eighth century, only the Spanish route was open, and this the Phoenicians secured by their foundations at Carthage and in the other areas just named.

It is likely that the Greeks too would have had an interest in the route to Spain, but were ousted by the Phoenicians. There are

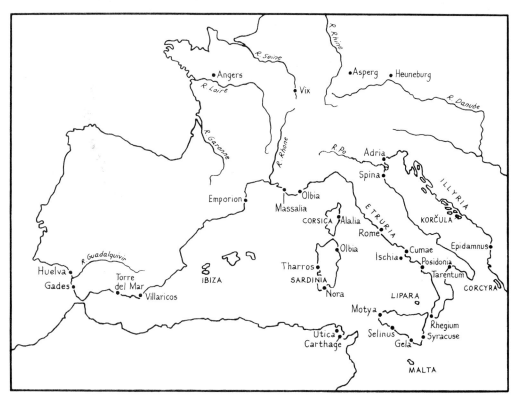

The Western Mediterranean and Europe

place-names in the Carthage area which have a Euboean ring – an island called Euboea, Naxian Islands, and Pithekoussai, the last two bearing names of the earliest Euboean colonies in Sicily and Italy respectively.[178] And there is a suggestion too in the Old Testament that Carthage lay once in the Ionian (Yavan) sphere. Excavation may one day explain these records. The earliest Phoenician settlement was supposed to be at Utica, just north-west of Carthage, but the finds there do not seem appreciably earlier. Carthage itself was razed to the ground by the Romans in 146, but it has left fairly rich pickings for the archaeologist. The earliest datable deposits there are caches of vases in the Tanit sanctuary – likely to be one of the earliest buildings. Many of the vases are Greek of the later eighth century – Corinthian, or imitations of Corinthian such as the Euboeans made.[179] At this early date such a deposit of Greek vases might suggest some direct Greek interest in this area, but it seems that the Phoenicians were ready carriers of Greek decorated pottery and it may be that Greeks could live with easterners in dominantly eastern settlements, just as easterners did beside Greeks at Pithekoussai (above, p. 166). Stray Greek vases from the Carthage cemeteries may be earlier yet, but the earliest Phoenician objects in Carthage can be dated only by their context with Greek things. So far it seems unlikely that the city was occupied until the second half of the eighth century – about the time of the earliest Greek foundations in Sicily and South Italy. It may be significant too that some of Carthage's own early vases are decorated with the multiple brush, a technique that could only have been picked up from the Greeks.[180]

In western Sicily the Phoenicians established cities at Motya, Solus, and Panormus (Palermo). Only Motya yields anything Phoenician or Greek obviously earlier than the seventh century.[181] During this century the Greek cities in Sicily expanded westward, with foundations at Himera and Selinus, on the borders of the Phoenicians' territory, but the latter enjoyed the cooperation of the native Elymians and retained their hold on this part of the island.

We should expect the other Phoenician foundations in the western Mediterranean to belong to this period also. On Malta a tomb was found to contain two Greek vases – Corinthian and Rhodian of the earlier seventh century – together with a Cypriot bronze lamp stand and Phoenician vases.[182] In Sardinia, at Nora, a Phoenician inscription on local stone may be our earliest evidence. Debate over its date and message has been lengthy but a recent translation suggests that it might indicate Phoenician colonization in Sardinia no later than the early eighth century.[183] The first vase from this area that we can date offers Euboean Geometric decoration on a local shape (*Fig. 251*).[184] The Ionians more than once thought of emigrating to Sardinia when they were under pressure from Persia, and it is by no means clear whether Greeks or Phoenicians had the upper hand there in the early sixth century. Olbia, in the north, may have been a Greek settlement, but nothing has been found there earlier than the fifth century. In the Balearics Ibiza was said to have been founded in 654, but again has yielded nothing datable earlier than about 600 BC, and the earliest

251 Geometric vase from Sulcis, off Sardinia; late 8th c. (Cagliari Mus.; H. 16·5 cm)

finds are many of them Greek.[185] The islands were supposed to have been colonized by the Rhodians at some time.

There is much more evidence now in the south of Spain for a substantial Phoenician presence in the eighth century,[186] including striking eastern finds such as the alabaster jars with cartouches naming ninth-century Egyptian kings, found at Sexsi near Almuñecar. But these were found with Greek pottery of around 700, which indicates the date of arrival.

Some Phoenician or Punic ivories from sites up the River Guadalquivir are seventh century, to judge from finds of the same class in Samos and from the fact that one of the figures on them wears a helmet of a Greek type which was not invented until about 700 (*Fig. 252*).[187] Bronze jugs of Phoenician shape from the same area are matched in Etruria, but are no earlier than the mid seventh century.[188] Phoenician gold jewellery from Aliseda may be as early.[189] But this, if ever, was the time of the 'grave Tyrian trader' driven west by the 'merry Grecian coasters, the young light-hearted Masters of the waves', to

> There, where down cloudy cliffs, through sheets of foam
> Shy traffickers, the dark Iberians come;
> And on the beach undid his corded bales

– though Arnold set the encounter of Tyrian and Greek in the Aegean.

The priority of Greek or Phoenician interest in south Spain remains undetermined. The balance of the evidence tends now rather in favour of the latter, but finds of Greek pottery in the Phoenician trading posts are regular, and indeed often provide the only secure dating evidence. Greek poets of these years knew of the Hesperides and the Atlantic. Kolaios the Samian, blown rather a long way off his course to Egypt in about 638 BC, passed through the Straits of Gibraltar (the 'pillars of Heracles' to the Greeks), visited Tartessos (in Cadiz Bay) and came away with such a load of silver that it would seem that the market was a new one – or at least long unvisited: 'inviolate' Herodotus calls it.[190] There were dedications, said to be of 'Tartessian bronze', at Olympia of an even earlier date (648).[191]

252 Ivory plaque from Bencarron (Carmona); 7th c. (New York, Hispanic Society D 513; 12·7 × 4·9 cm)

253 Handle from a Greek bronze oinochoe from the Granada area; about 600 BC. (New York, Hispanic Society R 4428; L. 20 cm)

It was the Phocaeans, according to Herodotus, who were the first Greeks to undertake long voyages and who came upon Tartessos in their long ships, and were encouraged there, even to come and settle, by the local king, Arganthios. The historian also claims for them exploration of the Adriatic and 'Tyrrhenia' (Etruria).[192] Such excavations as have been made in their home town have not been published and the Phocaeans are hard to identify archaeologically,[193] but an East Greek class of bronze oinochoai, possibly Phocaean, is found before and after about 600 in Spain (Fig. 253), France, South Germany and even Britain, Picenum (up the Adriatic), Etruria and South Italy.[194] At home too, on the borders of Ionia and Aeolis, they were users of pale grey *bucchero* pottery, and we shall find comparable ware well distributed in their colonizing area in France.

In the 540s the western Phocaeans were reinforced by their kinsfolk, who had been driven from their homes by the Persians and came to live at Alalia in Corsica, founded from Marseilles in about 565.[195] To judge from this colonizing at Marseilles in 600 and later in Corsica (and perhaps Sardinia), the Phocaeans were by then avoiding the North Africa route to the west. How many of the Greek finds in Spain were carried there by Greeks it is difficult to judge, but there are some substantial pieces apart from the pottery found in many coastal sites – a Corinthian helmet at Jerez, which had been made in the earlier seventh century (Fig. 254),[196] and another of the sixth century from the Huelva; a bronze griffin protome from an East Greek cauldron of the early sixth century,

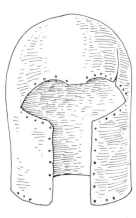

254 Greek bronze helmet from Jerez; first half of 7th c. (Jerez; H. 22·5 cm)

and other bronze vases.[197] In the other Phocaean towns on this coast, Hemeroskopeion and Mainake, nothing earlier than the fifth century has been found, and the location of the former at the Ifach peninsula is not completely certain.[198]

In 540 the Phocaeans provoked a naval battle with the Carthaginians and Etruscans, and although they were successful their losses were such that they had to abandon their colony at Alalia.[199] Thence they fled to a new home in Elea (see p. 189). The struggle for mastery of the western seas went on for some years. We hear of a victory for the Phocaeans from Marseilles, and of a treaty between Carthage and the Etruscans defining spheres of interest.[200] By 500 whatever Greek trade there had been with Tartessos was at an end, and we cannot take the far-spread finds of Archaic Greek pottery in Spain, Algeria and Morocco as evidence for Greek-inspired exploration.[201]

The clash between Greeks and Phoenicians had begun earlier in the sixth century. In the 570s Rhodians and Cnidians tried to establish a colony at Lilybaeum, a promontory overlooking the Phoenician town of Motya in west Sicily, but they were expelled and moved on to Lipara. Later the Phoenician and native towns became partly hellenized, admitting more Greek goods, and, at Segesta, Archaic temples in the Doric order were built in an enclosure over the ruins of a native settlement.[202] There seems to have been a clash with Selinus, but the city generally found it convenient to keep on good terms with its neighbours, Phoenician or native. Next comes the Phocaeans' naval battle at Alalia (540) and consequent Greek loss of Corsica to the Etruscans, and Sardinia to the Carthaginians. The direct western passage to Spain was closed. Then a Spartan, Dorieus, set out in 514 to found a colony in Libya, at Kinyps[203] on the coast between Cyrene and Carthage, but he was driven out by the Carthaginians and natives in little over two years. The scraps of Greek pottery at Sabratha and Leptis Magna do not indicate Greek settlement,[204] for at Carthage itself Greek objects were always arriving whatever the political climate. Dorieus moved on to west Sicily, where he founded another city at Heraclea (probably Trapani) by Mount Eryx, in Phoenician territory. Here again he was soon assailed by Phoenicians and natives, and succumbed. Some of his followers escaped, to settle at Heraclea Minoa between Selinus and Acragas.[205]

Cultural exchange between the Greeks and Phoenicians in the western Mediterranean appears to have been slight, despite the presence of Greek goods in so many Phoenician and Punic settlements. In Sicily the cities closest to the Phoenicians in the west, as Selinus, may have admitted some Phoenician practices, probably the result of a somewhat footloose population in early years.[206] Archaeologically we can observe in the rich series of Phoenician and Punic green jasper scarabs, which begins in the late Archaic period, several Greek subjects and some influence of

a

b

255 Green jasper scarabs from Tharros, Sardinia; early 5th c.: *a* – Heracles, with an Egyptian sceptre and cartouche in the field; *b* – a warrior with satyr-head shield in Greco-Cypriot dress (London, Walters nos. 395, 405; H. 1·7, 1·5 cm)

256 Gold rings from Utica showing a Greek satyr, and an eastern group of a god attacking a lion (Tunis, Bardo Mus.)

Greek style (*Fig. 255*)[207] – a return for what the Greeks at home had learnt of this craft earlier in the century. Some Greek finger-ring types too seem to have been adopted in Carthage and Utica (*Fig. 256*).[208] The disseminators of scarabs and amulets around the Mediterranean seem themselves to have been susceptible to trivia.

In the early fifth century, Gelon, tyrant of Gela, sought to revenge Dorieus's death and to open Africa to Greek trade. We know little of his early campaigns, but in 480 things came to a head. He had strengthened his position by obliging most of the inhabitants of Gela, Camarina, and Megara Hyblaea to move into Syracuse, which became his new capital. His rivals in Rhegium and Himera invited the Carthaginians to send a force to Sicily and overthrow him. Selinus, it seems, sided with its Phoenician neighbours. The force arrived under Hamilcar, encamped at Himera, and was utterly routed by Gelon's army. It was said that on the very same day that he liberated Sicily from the threat of Carthage, the Greek fleet finally repulsed the Persians at Salamis and the Greeks of east and west were saved from the barbarians. The battle in Sicily was commemorated by new temples – paid for from the Carthaginian indemnity – one of which was built at Himera. And Gelon struck a victory issue of coins generally recognized in a type (*Fig. 257*) which takes its place among the finest examples of Greek numismatic art.[209] At Delphi he and his brothers dedicated golden Victories and tripods 'having conquered the barbarians and extended the friendly hand of freedom to all Greeks'.[210]

Greeks in France and North Spain

An alternative route from the tin islands of Britain to that which led to the south of Spain lay overland across France. On the southern route the East Greek traders – mainly Phocaeans, it seems – had to face the competition of the Phoenicians, and not even their island bases on Corsica, Sardinia, and the Balearics were safe. As long as Etruria was friendly, though, they could push up a safe coastline to France and to the other tin route where the Phoenicians did not operate, at least in strength. In accordance with their practice elsewhere, they safeguarded their trade by founding colonies. But they may not have been the first Greeks to visit this coast.[211]

Clearly the most crucial point was at the mouth of the Rhône. Here, in native villages at Saint-Blaise and La Couronne, Greek pottery of the later seventh century has been found. The earliest datable pieces are Corinthian, but most of the pottery is East Greek, with some Athenian arriving after the middle of the sixth century, at Saint-Blaise. The Greek community here grew rapidly, and may have taken over the site eventually, although no ancient name is known for it. Nor is it clear which Greeks arrived there first in the seventh century.[212] There is some literary evi-

257 Silver tetradrachm of Syracuse; 480–479 BC (?)

dence for Rhodian colonization before the foundation of Marseilles, probably in this region and certainly farther along the coast at Rhode in North Spain. Unfortunately there is no archaeological evidence for the date of the foundation of Rhode.[213] The bronze vases which passed this way into South France and even Germany in the years around and before 600 are of the type we have already observed in Spain and thought to associate with Phocaeans.

The Phocaeans founded Massalia (Marseilles) just east of the mouth of the Rhône, in about 600 BC. The modern town has hampered excavation, but opportunities have been well taken, and the results – treated with caution – are most revealing. The Greek city lay on the hill to the north of the Old Harbour. Finds were made here and at Fort St Jean (which occupies the north side of the entrance to the harbour) early in this century; and demolitions during the last war gave the opportunity for excavations soon after it near the quayside of the Old Harbour just east of Fort St Jean.

The finds show that through the sixth century the town received a notable variety of imports from homeland Greece.[214] As well as the usual Corinthian, then Athenian, there are some Spartan, Etruscan, and 'Chalcidian' pieces. There is a good deal of East Greek pottery, as we would expect, though little of it is certainly Rhodian. There were fine Chian vases as well as wine jars from the island. The other wares are distinctive but not easily localized. There are striped vases of a type which became much copied locally; and there is pale grey *bucchero* pottery. This is a ware common in the northern states of East Greece and it is often recognized as Phocaean by import or example when it is found in the west. There is plenty at Marseilles, and it appears wherever there is any other Greek pottery on the French coast. Recent years have demonstrated clearly just how thorough the hellenization of South France was in the sixth century, and the variety of wares which are clearly of East Greek inspiration or origin.[215] Indications of Marseilles' prosperity in the later sixth century are her relatively prolific coinage and the fine marble treasury built by the city at Delphi.[216] The palm capitals of the columns in its porch are of a type met earlier at Phocaea.

A daughter foundation of Marseilles was at Emporion, modern Ampurias, in North Spain. It lies far beyond the overland tin route, and although it may have served to tap the metal resources of the Pyrenees, it is better regarded as a stage in Phocaean littoral exploration. A late Roman author, Avienus, wrote a poetical geography which seems in part based on an account of a journey from Marseilles, via Gibraltar, to Ireland and Britain. Details in it, notably its failure to mention Emporion, suggest that it may go back to an account of Phocaean voyages before the town was founded.[217] Emporion itself seems to have been established little if at all after Marseilles.[218] There is Corinthian and East Greek pottery from the beginning of the sixth century on, and eventually Athenian as well. The first settlement lay on an islet just offshore from a native town, but it seems that the Greeks had their cemetery on the mainland. Strabo says that when the Greek centre was established on the shore, it lay beside but distinct from the native town, but that they later combined.[219] Excavations in the town have shown Greeks living there in the last quarter of the sixth century, and have told much about the later history, but the details of topography in the early years of the Greek colony are still far from clear.

258 Vase fragment from Ensérune; 6th c.

The foundation of Marseilles was an important landmark in the history of the peoples of Gaul. Their culture was a branch of the Bronze Age 'Hallstatt' culture which obtained through much of central Europe, and for the west at least this was the first time that it was brought into close contact with the Greeks. There are some effects which the archaeologist can observe, other than simple imports. One is the production locally of vases painted freely with a multiple brush (*Fig. 258*, from Ensérune).[220] This could only have been learned from the Greeks, and began in the sixth century in the south of France and north of Spain. It may be, too, that the new type of bronze belt-hook (*Fig. 259*) which becomes popular in this same area at this time[221] owes something to the bronze belts which we have already seen in Phrygia and Ionia (*Figs. 100, 101*) and which may have been introduced to the west by the Phocaeans. Some examples of this western type found their way to Greece (Olympia, Corcyra).[222]

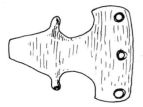

259 Bronze belt-hook from Cayla; 6th c. (Cayla, Taffanel Coll.)

The Roman historian Justinus says that 'from the Greeks the Gauls learned a more civilized way of life and abandoned their barbarous ways. They set to tilling their fields and walling their towns. They even got used to living by law rather than force of arms, to cultivating the vine and the olive. Their progress, in manners and wealth, was so brilliant that it seemed as though Gaul had become part of Greece, rather than that Greece had colonized Gaul.'[223]

260 Massalian wine amphora from Heuneburg; 5th c.

For the Greeks' introduction of the vine and even the olive to the south of France we may still be grateful. Marseilles soon became an active exporter of her own products, and although the occasional Chian and Athenian jar was imported in the sixth century, she was soon making her own pots for wine (*Fig. 260*) or oil, and conducting a lively trade with the natives. The first wine to be drunk in Burgundy was Greek wine from Marseilles.[224] With the wine jars went Greek pottery – mainly Athenian and East Greek of the second half of the sixth century. The greatest concentration of such finds is, of course, near the coast around Marseilles and the mouth of the Rhône, as at Arles, but there is much too from a number of sites in the Languedoc, to the north and south of Narbonne, notably Ensérune, where there must have been a Greek settlement.[225] To the east of Marseilles, and just west of Toulon, a new site (Mt Garou) gives a stratified picture of the archaeology of the region, with native Hallstatt settlement succeeded by a mixed level of the early sixth century containing Etruscan, Greek, and Phoenician pottery, and then Greek wares becoming dominant.[226] A similar pattern is emerging on sites inland, as at le Pègue.[227]

Inland, along the tin routes and to the richer Celtic 'Hallstatt' cities, the volume of Greek finds grows less, but more spectacular. There is one place, however, with enough Greek pottery to suggest that it played an important part in Marseilles' trade. This is the town at Mt Lassois overlooking the Seine, little over a hundred miles south-east of Paris. It lies at the crucial point where the river becomes no longer easily navigable and goods had to be unloaded for the journey south to the Saône, the Rhône, and Marseilles, or to the native cities to the east, or through the Swiss passes into North Italy. Some have held that it was by the last route that the Greek finds in central and eastern France arrived, but in the sixth century the Marseilles route is vouched for by the Massaliot pottery found at Mt Lassois, while strong Greek interest in North Italy and the Po valley comes only later.

261 Bronze crater from
Vix; about 530 B C.
(Châtillon-sur-Seine; H.
1·64 m)

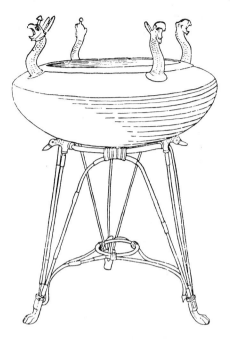

262 Bronze cauldron with tripod stand from near Mt Lassois (la Garenne); mid-6th c. (Châtillon-sur-Seine; H. 32 + 57 cm)

In 1953 the burial mound of a princess was excavated at Vix, the cemetery of Mt Lassois, and yielded finds whose artistic merit rivals their historical importance.[228] The offerings included the largest and finest Greek bronze crater (*Fig. 261*) yet known, its neck decorated in relief with warriors and chariots, its handles with gorgons, all its mouldings exquisitely cast and chased. It stood nearly 1·64 m. high with its lid, which was a dish with a superb statuette of a woman at its centre as handle. It had travelled in pieces, some of them lettered to facilitate its reassembly on arrival.[229] The crater is probably Spartan work, but besides there were three Etruscan bronze vases, two clay Athenian cups, one of the 520s which dates the burial to the end of the sixth century, as well as other bronzes, ornaments, and jewellery, including the gold diadem on the young woman's head.

Ninety years before the discovery of the Vix treasure, another tumulus two miles away had been excavated and found to contain a Greek bronze vessel of a very different type. It was a cauldron with four griffin protomes below its rim, complete with its tripod stand (*Fig. 262*).[230] Orientalizing cauldrons of this sort have already been discussed (p. 66). This is a late example of the first half of the sixth century, and it has been thought that it was made in the west, at Cumae; but it may well be from some other west Greek city, or even East Greece, like so many of the others. A griffin from another such cauldron was found in the Loire, near Angers.[231] This takes us far away to the west, to one of the other possible tin routes from the Channel and Brittany, which passed along the Loire to the Rhône. And these same cauldrons can be

263 Spartan bronze hydria from Grächwyl, Switzerland; about 600 BC. (Bernisches Histor. Mus. 11620; H. restored 64 cm)

264 Ivory sphinx with amber face, fastened to its backing by gilt nails, from Asperg; about 600 BC. (Stuttgart, Württemb. Landesmus.; H. 4·8 cm)

followed yet farther afield to Sweden, where one has been found near Stockholm, missing its griffins to be sure, but with clear signs of where they had been attached.[232]

Far to the east of Mt Lassois, in South Germany, the spread of Greek goods in the sixth century is marked by other East Greek bronze vases and a little Athenian pottery. A notable find is the Spartan bronze vase (Fig. 263), made about 600 BC, from Grächwyl in Switzerland.[233] At Asperg, near Stuttgart, is a Hallstatt burial of the early sixth century which recalls Mt Lassois in containing a tripod stand (as for Fig. 262) and Greek ivory sphinxes with amber faces, from Italy (Fig. 264).[234] And at Hochdorf, not far away, another Hallstatt grave, found in 1978, includes a bronze cauldron with three loop handles and lions on the shoulder, and other works said to be of Mediterranean, probably Italian and Etruscan, manufacture.[235] The most important site so far excavated in which Greek goods and influence can be recognized is the fortress town at Heuneburg, overlooking the Schwabian Danube, just south-west of Munich.[236] Here there is some Greek pottery of the later sixth century (cf. Fig. 260), but more remarkable is the possibility that the construction of its fortification walls in this period was inspired by – or even modelled on – Greek practice. Part of the circuit is built in the usual local style of rubble and timber, but there is a long stretch which is built of mudbrick on a stone socle (Fig. 265) with projecting rectangular bastions at regular intervals. Both plan and construction are quite foreign to central Europe at this time, quite

265 Mudbrick wall on a
stone socle at Heuneburg

familiar on archaic Greek sites. It is tempting to suppose that the
chieftains who so much prized Greek works of art were also
moved to invite Greek technical assistance.

About 500 B C events in central Europe took a turn which had a
profound influence on the Greek trade through Marseilles. For the
European archaeologist this is the transition between the cultures
of Hallstatt and La Tène. On the ground it is represented by the
abandonment of the Hallstatt fortress-towns, and a general shift
of the centre of wealth and power towards the east and north. The
town at Mt Lassois was abandoned. Marseilles lost her entrepôt
there, and trade down the Rhône came to a halt. At Marseilles the
transition is marked by a rapid falling off in imports of fine
pottery, which surely betokens a lapse in prosperity. Inland, the
imported bronzes and pottery are no longer Greek but Etruscan.
The new routes to the south led through the Alps and Switzerland
to North Italy. Within a single generation the western Greeks had
lost their routes through the Straits of Gibraltar, and through
France, but their cities were wealthy and well-established, strong
enough to resist Carthaginians and Etruscans, and already other
Greeks had moved up the Adriatic to meet the new routes into
North Italy. These we shall meet in the next chapter.

6

The North and the Black Sea

This chapter will take us from the Po Valley to the shores of the Black Sea. It is a vast range, in which the history of each area is closely involved with that of its neighbour, but for convenience the following scheme is adopted. First, the progress of the Greeks up the Adriatic to North Italy. Secondly, their colonizing along the Macedonian and the Thracian coast. Both these moves led them to contact with the natives of Illyria and Thrace, and this situation can be considered together with problems of earlier Greek relations with the north. Then there is the approach to the Black Sea, colonization on its shores, and relations with the Scythians; and we are brought full circle back to Asia Minor, the scene of the Greek migrations of the Early Iron Age which occupied us in Chapter 2.

Greeks in the Adriatic

The first Greek colony in the Adriatic[1] was on the island of CORCYRA (Corfu), and it was placed less with a view to further exploitation of the seas to the north, than as a port of call on the routes to the west. This is shown in part by the origins of the colonists: first the Eretrians, from Euboea, who with Chalcis had first sent colonies to Italy and Sicily; then, in 733, the Corinthians, who evicted the Eretrians and were at the same time on their way to found Syracuse in Sicily.[2]

The principal town on Corcyra faces the mainland and controls the narrow coastal straits. It is a fine peninsula site enclosing a good harbour. There is nothing to show as yet for Eretrian occupation, but the fortunes of the Corinthian settlement can be followed. There is little Corinthian pottery from the town's earliest years and from later in the seventh century,[3] but the most important finds are architectural, of the sixth century. These include the Temple of Artemis which gives us our first near-complete example of pedimental sculptures in Greek art.[4] This is of the early sixth century. Rather later is another Doric temple, not far away, in what is now the park of the Villa Monrepos,[5] and at the southern tip of the peninsula was a second sanctuary of

266 Part of the pediment of a temple on Corcyra, Dionysos at a feast; late 6th c. (Corfu Mus.; 2·73 × 1·3 m)

Artemis which has yielded some seventh-century clay votives showing the goddess with her lion.[6] A temple of Dionysos of late in the century is attested by a recent find of part of its pediment, showing the god with a boy favourite at a feast (*Fig. 266*).[7] The early cemetery lay to the north of the town, and is best known for two monuments of about 600 BC – one, a fine stone lion from a grave, the other the tomb of one Menecrates who was Corcyrean consul in a mainland Locrian town, and died at sea. This is a round stone structure a little over five yards across and nearly two yards high.[8]

Corcyra's early history shows that she was soon quite independent of her founder, Corinth, at times positively hostile, and in the seventh century the first Greek sea battle is recorded between these two states and in Corcyrean waters.[9] For all that, her art is always wholly in the Corinthian tradition.

Although at first Corcyra played her part largely on the routes to the west, she was naturally the first to explore further the coasts of the Adriatic itself, while Corinth concentrated on consolidating her position in the northern approaches to the Corinthian Gulf. The Euboeans had, it seems, already put settlements on the mainland opposite and at Oricum, far to the north on the borders of Illyria. Of these we have no more than stray references in ancient authors.

In 627 Corcyra and Corinth founded EPIDAMNUS (Roman Dyrrhachium, modern Durazzo) on the coast some 150 miles to the north. We do not know how the Illyrians reacted to this intrusion, and it seems to have taken a little while for trade to develop. Silver mines in Illyria may have been one of the attractions of the area for the Greeks.

Of the early town of Epidamnus we know nothing, but its foundation was followed shortly by another, this time by Corinth, at APOLLONIA on the coast to the south. The little

267 Limestone relief from Apollonia; about 500 BC. (H. 33 cm)

pottery which has so far been found there – both Corinthian and Rhodian – shows that Greeks were there by about 600 BC.[10] There is also a fine piece of later Archaic Greek relief sculpture, perhaps from an acropolis temple (*Fig. 267*).[11] The hill site of the ancient city is today separated from the coastline by five miles of lagoons and marshes.

The next major move up the Illyrian coast was again sponsored by the Corcyreans, who helped their East Greek friends, the Cnidians, to settle on 'Black Corcyra' (Korčula), an island in the Dalmatian archipelago. This apparently happened early in the sixth century, and the adjacent islands were also later settled by the Greeks. We know nothing archaeologically about the early towns, beyond an early sixth-century Corinthian vase from Korčula and another, later, from the island of Issa.[12]

On the other side of the Adriatic, Corinthian pottery appears on various sites in Apulia and Messapia on the far side of the 'heel' of Italy from the Greeks at Tarentum, but nothing to suggest settlement. There are even one or two seventh-century pieces from near Bari and Greek tombs near Brindisi.[13] The pottery may have come via Tarentum, and we may recall the tale of Phalanthus, who led the colonists to Tarentum, was expelled by his fellow citizens, and took refuge with the natives of Brentesion (Brindisi).[14]

At the head of the Adriatic a direct route from Greece was in use already by 600 and its effect can be seen on the 'Situla Art' bronzes of the eastern Alps and Este in the Po valley.[15] These offer a fascinating mixture of Greek and Etruscan styles adapted to serve the representation of local life. The influence persisted, and on a bronze of the early fifth century (*Fig. 268*) our rustic north Italian has climbed on to a couch for a feast, like any Greek.[16] But by this

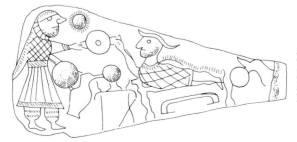

268 Bronze plaque in 'situla' style from Carceri, Este; early 5th c. (Este, Mus. Naz. Atestino 4845; L. 7·6 cm)

time there was another reason for Greek interest in this approach
to Europe, and it is better attested on the ground. The last chapter
has already indicated the importance of this area in the years after
the decline of the tin route through France and Marseilles. When
Herodotus says that it was the Phocaeans who first explored the
Adriatic,[17] it is tempting to associate this with their foundations at
Marseilles and their continued interest in the northern routes, but
there is little to support this archaeologically,[18] and there are only
a very few East Greek vases of the sixth century at all in the cities
of the Adriatic.[19]

The area from the Po south to Ancona was occupied by Enetians, Umbrians, and Picenes. They had already admitted some
orientalizing influences in their cultures by the sixth century, at
second hand via Etruria. During the sixth century, Etruscan
expansion to the south was being contained by the Greeks, and
they looked to the north-east. A group of Etruscan cities was
founded here with their centre at Felsina (Bologna). The attraction was probably twofold: excellent farmland, and the routes
from the north via Switzerland and the Alps.

A little Corinthian pottery was beginning to arrive in the new
Etruscan cities by the mid sixth century, and earlier still a slave
called Omrikos, presumably an Umbrian, was brought to
Corinth and named on a vase (which was then exported to Caere
in Etruria).[20] In the second half of the sixth century Felsina and
other sites begin to receive a quantity of Athenian vases, and in the
north of the Po delta the city of Adria was serving as an important
entrepôt for Greek trade with the Enetians.[21] As in the cities of
Etruria, so in Felsina and Adria there may have been Greeks, but
in one new city there were certainly Greeks living beside Etruscans, and in sufficient numbers for the town to be called Greek – at
least by the Greeks themselves – and it is far from clear whether it
was primarily an Etruscan or a Greek foundation. This is the city
of SPINA, on the southern arm of the Po delta, not far north of
Ravenna.[22] The low-lying waterlogged land of the delta is un-
promising archaeologically, but the cemeteries of Spina have
proved to be probably the greatest single source of fine Athenian
vases in the Greek world, or outside it. From the 1932 to 1935, and
again since 1954, drainage work has uncovered a great part of the
early cemetery of the city, with the groups of vases and other
offerings lying intact in the thick mud. The score of graves is by
now well over 4000, and the work continues. The earliest vases
are of about 520 BC, not quite as early as some from the other cities
we have mentioned. Nearly all the imported vases are Athenian,
and many are of the highest quality. There are inscriptions
scratched on the vases in both Greek and Etruscan.[23] A little of the
town itself can now be made out also. It seems to have been
something of an ancient Venice, with street-canals.

We have to think here of a Greek trading colony established in a
city newly founded by the Etruscans, or perhaps even a wholly

Greek foundation which admitted Etruscan families from the neighbouring cities. The Greeks, like the Etruscans, were attracted by the cornlands of the Po Valley and the routes from the north. The literary record says nothing about the origins of the Greeks in Spina. The imported fine pottery is nearly all Athenian, but it could hardly be anything else at this time. At least there is no South Italian pottery in the later years, so this is no extension of the activities of the earlier Greek colonies in the west. There is some indication, though, that Athenians were in fact taking a direct interest in Spina, at least later in the fifth century, for we find there white-ground *lekythoi*, a special type of funerary vase which was made for the cemeteries of Athens and for the Athenian community at Eretria in Euboea. A very few other examples have been found elsewhere, and we may suppose them to indicate the presence of Athenian families, since these vases never formed part of the general current of trade in decorated pottery. One reached Palestine; one Lycia; one or two South Russia; two were found in a tomb – no doubt of an Athenian – in Yugoslavia (Demir Kapija); and there are stray poor examples on a few Greek sites like Delos, as well as some imitations in South Italy. A few are reported at Spina, and this probably means Athenian families there.[24]

Greeks on the Macedonian and Thracian Coast

For the Greek colonies on the northern shores of the Aegean, our evidence is mainly literary. The earliest were planted in the eighth century by the Euboeans, whom we again meet as the first of the Greeks in a new colonizing area. But here, unlike Syria or Italy, the object was simply land, and there can have been little interest at first in trade. In this respect the move was an obvious one for the islanders, up past the Thessalians (with whom they enjoyed friendly relations) to the first available lands which were non-Greek, though partly hellenized, as we shall see. Chalcis was the most active colonizer here, and the promontory Chalcidice, projecting south into the Aegean like a grotesque three-fingered hand, takes its name from her. There were several Chalcidian colonies here, the most important of them Torone. Eretria's cities were for the most part on the western 'finger' of Chalcidice, notably at Mende and Scione. The Eretrians who were evicted from Corcyra by the Corinthians in 733 came to found Methone, on the western shore of the Gulf of Salonica. About the middle of the seventh century the island of Andros was helped by the Chalcidian cities to found new towns in the east of Chalcidice. The only intrusion into this area dominated by Euboeans and islanders was by Corinth, founding Potidaea about 600 BC.[25]

To the east the coastline was settled by other Greeks. Foremost were the Parians, who occupied the island of Thasos in the 680s and from it went on to found several cities on the mainland opposite, among them Neapolis (Kavalla) and Oisyme. They had some trouble with the native Thracians, and the Parian poet Archilochus sings of some of the encounters.[26] The other new-comers were East Greeks: Chians at Maroneia, Aeolians at Aenus (which lay at the end of an important overland route to the Black Sea), and Clazomenians at Abdera. The last was a short-lived venture, as the Greeks were soon expelled by the Thracians, but the city was reoccupied soon after the mid sixth century by other East Greeks from Teos, fleeing before the Persians.[27] The islanders of Samothrace also had mainland fortresses, including Mesembria, where there is East Greek pottery of about 600.[28]

269 Silver tetradrachm of North Greece, two nymphs with a wine jar; late 6th c. (London)

To the east again lay the Thracian Chersonese – a tongue of land flanking the Hellespont (Dardanelles). Two Greek colonies (Cardia, Limnae) facing west are the only Milesian foundations on this Thracian coast. The others were sited for their strategic positions on the straits, and can best be considered in the account of the Greeks' approach to the Black Sea, later in this chapter.

The physical attractions of the Thracian coastline can be considered briefly before we look at the scant archaeological record.[29] There are no good harbours and few reasonable anchorages. The cities are placed more with regard to defence, available land, and inland communications than with regard to the sea. The coastal plains are fertile though marshy, and until recent times have been malarial. The rich supplies of timber in Chalcidice and inland were much exploited in later days, and may have been an early attraction for the Greeks, whose homeland was rapidly becoming deforested and could not satisfy their demands for shipbuilding and architecture. The excellence of Thracian horses had been appreciated by the Greeks at an early date. The vine was introduced with notable success, especially at Torone, Mende, Maroneia, and – foremost – Thasos. The mineral resources of the region may not have been fully recognized by the earliest colonists. Gold and silver were mined around Mt Pangaeum, opposite Thasos. Here the Athenian tyrant Pisistratus owned mines to which he owed much of his wealth,[30] and he himself had to spend some years in the north while out of favour in Athens. Later on Histiaeus of Miletus was allowed by the Persian king to found the city of Myrcinus, on the Strymon, and enjoy the revenues from the silver mines and timber there.[31] Of the island of Thasos itself Herodotus says that part of it was turned upside down by the Phoenicians in their search for gold, but only recently have the Phoenicians and the mines been demonstrated.[32] The mines on the mainland were at first operated by the native Thracians, but were later owned by the Greeks. The resources of silver encouraged prolific coinage in many of the Greek cities, and we have already seen the way the East Greek states seem to have used silver from this area for their trade in the Ne   East and Egypt.

The cities most concerned with the wine trade chose Dionysiac subjects for the devices on their coins. Torone has simply a wine

270 Plate showing Bellerophon and Chimaera, perhaps Naxian, from Thasos; mid-7th c. (Thasos Mus. 2085; Diam. 28 cm)

jar, Mende an ass beside a vine. On Thasian coins appears a lively group of a satyr carrying off a nymph. On the early coins she puts up a token resistance, but later, in the fifth century, she goes quietly. On a unique coin in London which is from a yet unidentified city on this coast is the charming scene of two nymphs handling a wine jar (*Fig. 269*). To Abdera the Teans brought with them their civic device – a griffin – for their coins. Potidaea showed her patron Poseidon (who was also the patron of her mother-city Corinth) on a horse. Some Euboean colonies copy Euboean types, notably the cow with its head turned back, and the same device appears on some of the issues made by hellenized native princes. Thasos may have been one of the first northern cities to mint coins, but many others had their own issues too before the end of the sixth century.[33]

For the archaeology of the Greek cities themselves we know little enough of the early years. Abdera has yielded some East Greek pottery going back to the end of the seventh century,[34] and later Athenian, and a site near Amphipolis, perhaps the Thracian town Nine Roads, received much Greek pottery from as early a date.[35] Only Thasos has been dug at all systematically, by the French.[36] The city-site lay at the north-east of the island, at the point nearest the mainland, and has a fine acropolis as well as a harbour. It seems likely that it was founded from Paros by about 680 BC, in the time of the poet Archilochus's father. The inscribed memorial to one of the foundation heroes, Glaukos, set up about 600 BC, has been found in the agora there.[37] The earliest pottery is related to the Greek wares of the north-east Aegean and may indicate Thracian interest in the island before the arrival of the Parians.[38] Then there is a mass of pottery of the mid seventh to early sixth centuries brought north from the islands of the Cyclades.[39] A fine example is the plate showing Bellerophon on Pegasus fighting the chimaera (*Fig. 270*).[40] Paros, mother-city of Thasos, was using 'Melian' pottery at this time, and her taste is reflected in her colony. In the sixth century there is rather more East Greek pottery, especially Chian of the first half of the century, and it seems that Chian vase-painters worked on the island.[41] Athenian vases arrive from about 580, but Corinthian was always scarce in North Greece. In general the pottery reflects the island's contacts – with its founder Paros, with the East Greek states which had also founded cities on the Thracian coast, and with Athens, which had other concerns in the north at this time, as we shall see. Paros' sculptural record is also reflected on Thasos: from the colossal unfinished marble figure of a man carrying a ram, of about 600 BC, to the fine reliefs which flanked the city gates (*Fig. 271*) some hundred years later. An architectural oddity of about this time is the use of carved foreparts of winged horses as supporting members (*Fig. 272*) – a device met also in Chios.[42]

From the Thasian town of Neapolis, on the mainland opposite, the finds of pottery have been much the same: 'Melian', Chian, and Athenian, with a little Rhodian and Corinthian.[43] The earliest is of about 600, and there are comparable finds, perhaps not quite so early, from another site five miles to the west (Kalamitsa).[44] The most notable find at Neapolis, on a site largely hidden by modern Kavalla, has been parts of a fine Ionic temple.[45] This may take us a little outside our period, into the fifth century and after the passage of the Persian host through North Greece, but it is worth mentioning since its style is distinctive, and is echoed in the find of an Ionic capital near Salonica,[46] from what may be the ancient city of Aineia. From the Salonica area there are a few Corinthian vases, the earliest perhaps about 650 BC, but most of the Greek finds in this region which might be associated with the new colonizing movement from Euboea are not earlier than 600 BC. There is still very much to be learnt about these cities, from properly controlled excavations.

So far as our evidence goes, and it is not likely to be seriously misleading, the artistic centre of the northern Greek cities lay in Thasos and her cities on the mainland in the sixth century. Even there we can hardly speak of an independent colonial school of art, since all its products rely so heavily on fashions set in the Greek islands and Ionia. But in the years after the Persian Wars the most celebrated of the Greek painters was a Thasian, Polygnotus.

Illyrians, Macedonians, and Thracians

Excavations in what are now Albania, Yugoslavia, and Bulgaria have told us much about the northern neighbours of the Greeks in the Iron Age and supplemented the scant and often imaginative testimony of ancient writers. But there is still much to be under-

271 A gateway in the city wall of Thasos decorated with a relief showing a satyr; about 500 BC. (Total H. 2·54 m)

272 Marble protome of Pegasus, an architectural member from the Heraklion, Thasos; about 500 BC. (Thasos Mus. 4; H. 1·23 m)

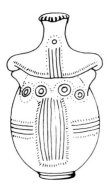

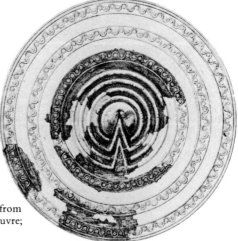

stood, and although the character of the civilization of these peoples is at times quite clear, its relationship to that of Greece itself, even in the simple matter of time, is not always so straightforward.[47]

Not the least difficulty is the problem of knowing where to draw the line between Greek and non-Greek in the Balkans in various periods. In the days before passports it was probably not of great importance. Illyrians and Thracians at least could be treated as thoroughgoing barbarians. The Macedonians were a borderline case, but the Macedonian royal family had to invoke a largely mythical family tree connecting themselves with the old royal family of Argos; and Alexander the Great was hard put to it in his attempt to justify his ambitions as champion of the Greeks against the barbarian east.

It was from the north that Dorian Greek tribes entered central and southern Greece during or after the troubles that marked the transition between the Bronze Age and Iron Age in the twelfth century. We should expect to find a clear archaeological record of their arrival, or of their former homes, but this either does not exist or, more likely, has not yet been properly recognized. Some pottery shapes and plain incised wares in Protogeometric Greece are thought to derive from the north (*Fig. 273*)[48] and it seems likely that the all-bronze corselet was re-introduced to Greece from the same direction.[49] A distinctive bronze shield type ('Herzsprung') with a wide distribution and imitation through Greece and into the Near East (*Fig. 274*), may also be of northern inspiration.[50] Its decoration of concentric rings interrupted by a notch reflects simpler construction with overlapping hides. While European (Hallstatt) chronology is still so uncertain, it is dangerous to draw far-reaching conclusions from similarities in finds in Greece and Europe. In later centuries too there are many things which con-

273 Incised, handmade clay vessels and figures from the Kerameikos, Athens, 10th–9th c. (Athens, Kerameikos Mus.)

274 Bronze 'Herzsprung' shield from Idalion, Cyprus; 8th c. (Paris, Louvre; Diam. 83 cm)

nect the cultures of Illyria and Macedonia with that of Greece, although their date and significance are not always readily understood.

Macedonia seems to have been part Greek in its culture in the early Iron Age, but there are some objects from this area which have seemed to many to point rather to close connections with the north – for example the so-called spectacle fibulae (*Fig. 275*). These are safety-pin brooches formed of wire and tight-rolled in an S-spiral. They are common in Macedonia, but found too in Greece, especially at Sparta. The spiral motif had long been known both in Central Europe and in the Aegean world, although in Greece it forms no part of the vase painter's repertoire of patterns in post-Bronze-Age times until well on in the eighth century. Fibulae seem to have been an Aegean invention, but the bronze type with spirals seems to have evolved in the north,[51] and then spread south, and in Greece they are imitated in ivory and bone in the seventh and sixth centuries.[52] For other objects, once thought northern, the process is reversed. The 'Illyrian' helmet is a type most popular in Illyria from the sixth century on, but demonstrably invented in Greece by about 700 BC, although its popularity there was soon eclipsed by other types.[53] Other bronzes in the north – like spiral beads – are in like case.[54] Painted pottery from Macedonia (*Fig. 276*) is in a Geometric style which recalls Greek work of the eighth century but is far closer to the wares of Phrygia in Asia Minor, both in this period and, for all we can as yet tell, earlier.[55] This broaches problems of the sources of the Phrygians, and of references to Phrygians in the Macedonia–Thrace area. This 'bridge' across from Europe to Asia saw so much passage and mingling of peoples that the archaeological record of the area is one of the most difficult to understand.[56]

Illyria is hardly simpler. Here again there is a distinctive fibula-type, apparently of the eighth to seventh centuries, which is met too in North Greece, and of which one example reached Chios (*Fig. 277*).[57] This again might easily be a barbarian product modelled on a Greek type which had less success at home. It was through Illyria, perhaps, that the Greeks received their supplies of Baltic amber in the eighth century and later: some to the south, along the coast into the Peloponnese, some via Macedonia and the Greek colonies into East Greece and the islands. This is the route by which the Hyperboreans were said to have sent their mysterious presents (perhaps amber) wrapped in straw to Delos.[58] There are plenty of amber beads in East Greece, but in general the Greeks were not greatly impressed by the material, and they seldom carved it with the care which we see lavished on it in Italy.[59]

The Greeks who arrived on the doorsteps of these barbarian or semi-barbarian neighbours had mixed receptions. They had little to do with the Illyrians, being more interested in the coastwise trade up the Adriatic.[60] A few Greek objects of the sixth century made their way up the valleys from the coast, and there was

275 Bronze spectacle fibula; 8th–7th c. (Oxford 1885.732; L. 15·5 cm)

276 Vases from Pateli and Boubousti, Macedonia; 8th c.

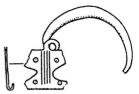

277 Illyrian bronze fibula from Emporio, Chios; late 7th c. (Chios Mus.; W. 5·4 cm)

278 Incised amber plaque pendants from Novi Pazar; 6th c. (Belgrade 678/I, 679/I; H. 6·3, 4·8 cm)

brisker trade as time passed.[61] A Late Archaic tomb at Novi Pazar is well stocked with fine Greek bronze vases, with goldwork, and with carved ambers, some perhaps of local workmanship, some Greek, possibly from South Italy, like the plaques in *Fig. 278*.[62] From Jerezine there is an unusual stone relief (*Fig. 279*) which looks as though it owed something, at several removes, to Archaic Greek art.[63]

Farther south, near Lake Ochrid in Macedonia, and at a point which may have been as readily accessible from the Greek cities on the Adriatic as from those on the Macedonian coast, we come across rich finds of Greek *objets d'art* which rival and indeed closely match those from the great tomb at Vix in France which we

279 Incised limestone slab from Jerezine; 6th c. (H. 49 cm)

discussed in the last chapter. At Trebenište Greek goods are already arriving in the seventh century, but in the second half of the sixth century there appear in native graves a series of superb Greek bronze vases (*Fig. 280*), most of them clearly from the same school or workshop which produced the great crater at Vix.[64] With them came a little Greek painted pottery and some Athenian and East Greek figurines, but the other tomb furniture betrays non-Greek funeral practice, although it may be that some of the objects, like gold masks, had been made by Greeks especially for customers in this region. Other native towns here, and in Thrace to the east, have yielded equally rich hoards of Greek metal-work, but of later date: Duvanlij, north of Plovdiv in Bulgaria, is one of them.[65] The earliest Greek finds here are of the first half of the fifth century and include Athenian pottery, East Greek figurines and a Chian wine jar.[66] At Pesnopoj are more vases, a helmet, and a clay coffin with relief decoration of Greek type: all apparently sixth-century.[67] To the west again there is a later grave at Demir Kapija, the first natural fortress up the River Vardar, which deserves a mention. It contained late fifth-century Athenian pottery, such as has been found in other graves there, but including two white-

280 Bronze crater with bulls in relief on the neck, from Trebenishte; late 6th c. (Belgrade; H. 68 cm)

237

281 Thracian woman (attacking Orpheus) with tattooed arms and neck, on an Athenian cup by the Pistoxenos Painter, from the Acropolis, Athens; about 460 B C. (Athens N M, Acr. 439)

282 Athenian youths in Thracian dress, on a cup by the Brygos Painter; about 480 B C. (Basel, Cahn Coll. 644)

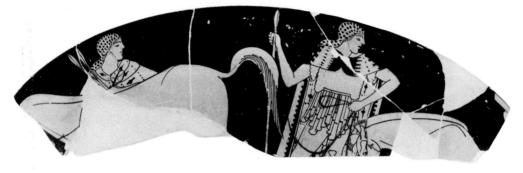

ground *lekythoi* of the type we have already had cause to comment on at Spina.[68] Here again they may indicate the presence of an Athenian family.

The Thracians[69] had proved the most hostile to the new Greek colonies, for all their readiness to let their mines to Greeks and buy Greek goods in later years. The Greeks thought little enough of them except as fighters, and brought many of them back home as slaves. Thracian nurses seem to have been in some demand. We can recognize them on Athenian vases from the tattoo marks[70] shown on their arms, their legs, and their necks. *Fig. 281* shows a fifth-century picture of a Thracian woman (attacking Orpheus). In the later sixth century Thracian horsemen were familiar figures in Athens, introduced by Pisistratus whose interests in the north we have noted, and their riding gear – the thick patterned cloak (*zeira*) and foxskin cap (*alopekis*) grew fashionable (*Fig. 282*).[71]

The Black Sea and its Approaches

To the Greeks the Black Sea was at first the 'Inhospitable Sea'; then, when they had made it theirs, the 'Hospitable' Euxine.[72] The earliest Greek foundations in the approaches to the Black Sea were not necessarily placed with an eye to further exploration of its shores, but they inevitably led to it. The approach itself is through the Propontis, which is like a broad vestibule with long narrow passages at each end – to the Aegean through the Hellespont (Dardanelles), and to the Black Sea past Byzantium (Constantinople) through the Bosporus. Winds and currents made access to the Black Sea difficult, though by no means impossible for early ships, and passage through the narrow straits would be largely controlled by the cities founded along them.[73]

Our evidence for Greek colonization here, and on the shores of the Black Sea itself, is unfortunately not of the quality of that available in Italy and Sicily, although most of the actual foundations were made at later dates than those in the west. The literary record gives us names, but seldom any dates which can be greatly relied upon. The archaeological evidence is sadly incomplete: best perhaps for the cities in South Russia; but we still lack much of the sort of evidence for Greek expansion and influence which is readily forthcoming from the many excavated sites in Italy and Sicily. Our most important sources are the Russian excavations of late in the last century and early in this, and the excavations of the

The Black Sea

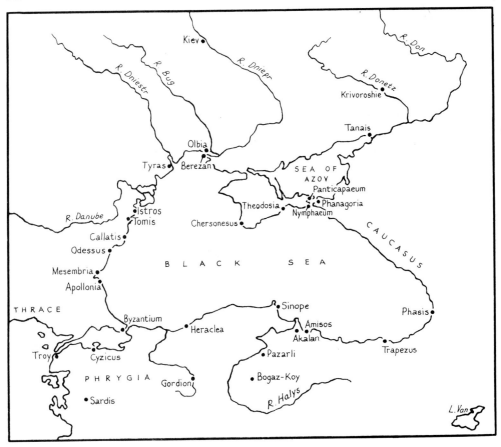

last twenty-five years in Russia, Rumania, and to a lesser degree Turkey.

In the circumstances it seems the best course to summarize briefly what we know of the pattern of Greek colonization in this quarter, and reserve for a separate section an account of the better-explored Greek cities.[74]

A growing number of scholars are today supporting the view that the Black Sea was being visited and its shores even being settled by Greeks in the eighth century BC, and they are undeterred by the many excavations which have so far produced no evidence for it.[75] The earliest material from the Propontis is said to be of the earlier seventh century; from the Black Sea cities there is nothing earlier than the latest seventh century. Literary evidence, not of the highest quality, puts the foundations of Sinope and Trapezus (Sinope's daughter-city) on the south shore of the Black Sea, and of Cyzicus in the Propontis, in the mid eighth century.[76] In Herodotus' day there were stories hereabouts of a warlock. Aristeas, who, in the earlier seventh century, had visited the northern shores of the Black Sea;[77] and there are indications too in ancient writers that something at least was known of the Black Sea by the end of the eighth century.[78] The story of the voyage of the Argonauts, in particular, implies some knowledge of these parts, although the geographical detail of this region may well have been added to the story at quite a late date. This does not of course imply that Greeks were living there by 700 BC, but there seems to be no particularly good reason for doubting that occasional voyages were being made into the Black Sea by East Greek sailors and merchants by that time, and it is not a historical point of the greatest moment. It is not until after 700 that we have any evidence for very active interst by East Greeks in any overseas trade or settlement in any other quarter.

An argument which has been used in favour of the early foundations of Sinope and Trapezus is that they were staging points in a 'North-east Passage' bringing oriental bronzes from the Urartu-Armenia region into the Greek world.[79] In other words that this is another source of the 'orientalizing' influences in Greece, to be added to those we have discussed in Chapter 3. This is always possible, but the hypothesis is an unnecessary one. An overland route to Phrygia for these bronzes is now shown to have existed from the finds at Gordion. And the sort of orientalizing objects which it is assumed could have been passed by this route have their effect more in mainland Greece and Crete than in Miletus or other parts of Greek Asia Minor.

Sinope and Trapezus were said to have been founded by the Milesians, and it is the Milesians whom we shall find the first to exploit other parts of these remote shores. The motive for their move along the south coast of the Black Sea may have been in part a search for land, but they seem to have travelled far for it, and the extent of their colonization – if wholly occasioned by land-hunger

– argues either a prodigious rise in the birthrate or a series of disastrous crop-failures. Even if these colonies did not necessarily serve to pass oriental bronzes to the Aegean, they would certainly have been well placed to encourage trade in metals with the rich mining areas of northern Asia Minor, Armenia, and the Caucasus.[80] There does, however, seem to be some connection between Caucasian and some Geometric Greek metal-work, and some Caucasian bronzes reached Samos (above, p. 65).

In the Propontis the Milesians founded Parion just east of the inner end of the Hellespont. In this they were joined by other Ionians: Erythraeans, and Parians who perhaps at about this time had occupied Thasos. Cyzicus, on the south shore of the Propontis, was founded by Milesians alone as an agricultural community. In the Hellespont itself they had Abydos as well as several smaller towns. They had been allowed to settle at Abydos by the Lydian king Gyges; this must have happened before the middle of the seventh century, and it is likely that some of the other Milesian foundations in the Propontis belong about now. The story about Abydos is interesting.[81] We should not, perhaps look for Greek settlement on the margins of the Phrygian empire until that empire fell before the Cimmerians in the early seventh century, and was succeeded by the Lydians, who could at times be friendly to the Greeks, or at least to some of them. We have seen already how the Aeolian Greeks had established themselves on the mainland opposite Lesbos and to the north as far as Troy, which was resettled before 700 BC. This coast was already theirs by the early seventh century, and they were later to press farther into the Hellespont, to the strong-point Sestos on the Thracian Chersonese. When the Milesians arrived, they had to move farther to the east, along routes which may or may not have been familiar to them already. One other important Ionian venture in the Hellespont which may be of this date was the Phocaean settlement of Lampsacus, invited there, it was said, by the native king to share his land in return for help rendered by the Phocaean king. The same story has it that the natives became jealous, but the Greeks asserted their claim to the site by force of arms.[82] The Samians came to Perinthus in about 600 and to other sites on the less hospitable northern shores of the Propontis.

This accounts for most of the important East Greek colonies on the Propontis, but they were not the only Greeks there. Megara, the town in central Greece just north of Corinth, which had already sent a colony to Sicily in the eighth century, also had an interest in this quarter. High dates are given for the Megarian colonies in the north-east, but it is generally agreed that their object was land rather than trade, and they were certainly slow to occupy any sites of strategic or commercial importance such as Byzantium. Their cities were at the remoter Bosporus end of the Propontis, and this alone might suggest that they had been forestalled by the East Greeks on the nearer sites. They settled

Astacus and Calchedon on the Asian coast of the Propontis, Selymbria on the north coast, and eventually the commanding site of Byzantium (Constantinople) at the inner end of the Bosporus. Even there, it seems, their first interest was in land, but they can hardly have overlooked its strategic value; 660 was a date given for its foundation, but nothing has been found there earlier than the end of the seventh century, and it certainly does not seem really necessary to believe in any Megarian colonization in this area as early as 700.

The general pattern of colonization along the Thracian and Asia Minor coasts would not lead us to expect that the Greek colonization of the Propontis began until the seventh century. The archaeological evidence is meagre in the extreme, and the earliest that can be offered is pottery of the first half of the seventh century at Dascylium, inland from Cyzicus, and Corinthian of little before 600 from Byzantium. It has been suggested that the story of Lydian Gyges letting the Milesians settle at Abydos really means that he put a Greek mercenary post there. Dascylium is named after Gyges' father, and it could be that the early pottery there betokens some similar Lydian venture rather than a wholly Greek colony. If so, it cannot be used as evidence for the date of foundations on the coast.[83]

This need not necessarily deter us from believing in quite high dates for the earliest colonies on the Black Sea itself – Milesian Sinope and Trapezus. They must have been placed for trade as much as for land, and the same motive had prompted the relatively remote siting of the first colonies in Italy by the Euboeans. Ancient authors implied dates before the middle of the eighth century for the two Milesian cities. Sinope at least was supposed to have been re-founded after the Cimmerian invasion and occupation (see p. 91), so its first occupation by Greeks should on this reckoning be near 700. Nothing has been found there, as yet, earlier than about 600. There is hardly anything Greek any earlier from other Black Sea sites, so it may perhaps be wiser not to believe in actual Greek settlements on its shores any earlier than the Greek settlements on the Propontis. And it may well be that all the Black Sea cities are to be put later than the first of the Propontis cities.

The Milesians ringed the Black Sea with their colonies. To mention only the better known or better explored, they added Amisos to Sinope and Trapezus on the south coast. In the farthest east there was Phasis, which gave immediate access to the mineral and agricultural wealth of the Caucasus. On the west were Apollonia and Odessus, Tomis and Istros near the mouth of the Danube, Tyras at the mouth of the Dniestr, Olbia and an island city (Berezan) at the mouth of the Dniepr-Bug. In the Crimea and approaches to the Sea of Azov are Panticapaeum and its daughter-cities. Nearby Phanagoria was founded by Teans in about 540, and we read that the Phocaeans were associated with the Milesians in some of their foundations. From the archaeological evidence, it would seem that the Chians were also well received in the cities founded by their allies the Milesians.[84] At least, Chian pottery is found in many of them throughout the first half of the sixth century (and even a little later), especially at Olbia, Berezan and Istros. What is more, at Olbia and Panticapaeum the only traces of early Ionic architecture are in a style which is most readily associated with the Chian school.[85]

The Megarians were far less venturesome in the Black Sea. They did not stray far from their colonies by the Bosporus, and did not indeed attempt any colonization until some time on in the sixth century. To the east was Heraclea, and to the north Mesembria and Callatis (founded from Heraclea). In the fifth century, they ventured across to the southern tip of the Crimea and founded Chersonesus, where the vine was grown with some success.

The overall character of the archaeological evidence from these Greek cities is fairly simple. Their siting and architectural history will be considered in a moment. The pottery from them should reflect the origins of their citizens and their most regular visitors. We do not know anything much of the pottery of either Miletus or Megara. There is plenty of East Greek pottery of what we conventionally call 'Rhodian' type, and this was probably carried and used by the Milesians, some of it perhaps made by them. The quantity of Chian pottery in the Milesian cities has already been mentioned. It is worth noting too that many of the early wine jars found on the Black Sea are Chian. The predominant wares in the second half of the sixth century are still East Greek, and wherever there is evidence for Greeks at all, there Fikellura, Clazomenian (or related black-figure), and the plainer vases are found. There is little Corinthian, inevitably, from the earliest days,[86] and towards the end of the sixth century the Athenian vases become more common.[87] They had begun to arrive by about 600 and appear in the second quarter of the century on many of the sites, just as soon as they became popular in East Greece itself. At the end of this chapter we shall have something to say about Athenian activities in the Hellespont and approaches to the Black Sea. Unexpected imports are one Eretrian vase at Olbia, of about 550 BC,[88] and three Boeotian vases alleged (perhaps rightly) to be from Olbia and Berezan.[89]

The Megarian colonies are so late that we would hardly expect them to be receiving fine vases made elsewhere than at Athens. The Megarian cities are the least well-explored in their earlier levels, so we are denied the opportunity to test this.

In view of what has been said already about the possible date of the Greek foundations in the Black Sea area, it is interesting to observe that most of the earliest datable Greek finds are not from the colonies themselves, but sometimes from places far inland and not on Greek sites.[90] Thus, there are East Greek vases of the later

283 Neck of an East Greek vase from Boltishka, 150 miles SE of Kiev; late 7th c. (Leningrad DN 1863,2/1)

284 Neck of an East Greek vase in the form of a ram's head, from Krivoroshie; late 7th c.

seventh century from Nemirov, 200 miles up the Bug; from Trachtemirov (a bird bowl) on the Dnieper barely 50 miles from Kiev (and sites to the south (*Fig. 283*) and east where Archaic Greek goods remained welcome);[91] from near Panticapacum; and from Krivoroshie,[92] between the Rivers Donets and Don, 250 miles from the sea. From the last is the top of an East Greek vase in the shape of a ram's head (*Fig. 284*) and there is a slightly later one with a bull's head from yet farther off. These finds, at least those from sites which were never Greek, may well indicate pre-colonization exploration, although not necessarily trade or the presence of Greeks.

The material attractions of this region are easily listed. The good agricultural land on parts of the shores of the Propontis, and on the north and west shores of the Black Sea, guaranteed an adequate supply of corn for the new Greek cities, and in places provided a rich source for trade with the corn-starved areas of the Aegean.[93] Here and there the Greeks were able to introduce the vine, and there were good supplies of fine timber for ships and building on the south shores of the Black Sea, as in Thrace. In its waters and rivers were plenty of fish, and there was a growing trade in dried or pickled tunny and other fish from the north and west shores. A notable feature of the excavations at Tyritake was the discovery of twenty-four reservoirs for fish pickling, with the bones and scales of 'Kerch herring' on their floors.[94] Of the River Dniepr (Borysthenes) Herodotus writes:[95]

It provides the finest and most abundant pastures, by far the richest supply of the best sorts of fish, and the most excellent water for drinking – clear and bright, whereas that of other rivers in the vicinity is turbid; no better crops grow anywhere than along its banks, and where grain is not sown the grass is the most luxuriant in the world. An unlimited supply of salt is formed by natural processes at the mouth of the river, which also produces a very large spineless fish, good for pickling and known locally as *antakaios*, and a number of other most remarkable things.

The search for metals had probably inspired the foundations along the southern shores of the Black Sea and in the east, where the resources of the Caucasus and of Armenia might be tapped. The Chalybes were the traditional iron producers for the Greek world,[96] and they were generally thought to live in northern Asia Minor, supplying their raw material to the Greeks through Amisos, on the coast. There was gold at Phasis, and remoter sources might also have been exploited.

Of relations with the natives on these shores we hear little. Troubles with the Thracians we have already mentioned, as also the relationship between the East Greeks and Phrygia and Lydia, whose empires spread far along the south coast of the Black Sea. In speaking of the archaeology of the Greek cities in the next section, there will be occasion to remark indications of contact with barbarian neighbours, who generally had to be displaced or 'pursuaded' from a site before the Greeks settled, but a feature of several sites on the west coast is the proximity of tumulus burials commonly identified, although perhaps not always rightly, as of interested Thracian nobles. In some of these burials the bodies are contracted, which is not a Greek practice in this period.[97] There are also a very few contracted burials in the Greek cemeteries, perhaps of foreign residents. The most absorbing archaeological record of relations with the natives concerns the Greeks and the Scythians, but this deserves separate treatment later in this chapter. Other natives on the Black Sea coast, like those discussed by Herodotus, are related in varying degrees to the Thracians, Scythians, or Cimmerians. The Tauri in the Crimea were said by Herodotus[98] to sacrifice 'all shipwrecked sailors and such Greeks as they happen to capture upon their coasts'. The people west of the Black Sea shared in the European Hallstatt culture, but they are archaeologically undistinguished, and it is very rarely that their coarse plain pottery or bronzes have been recognized on the Greek sites.

The Greek Cities

There are a few cities in the Propontis which may be briefly considered before we go on to the foundations on the Black Sea. The latter will be taken clockwise, around the coast. The Hellespont and Thracian Chersonese are discussed at the end of this chapter.

CYZICUS[99] stood on a large island just off the south shore of the Propontis. It faced the mainland across a narrow strait, now bridged by a broad low spit of sand. Later building effectively seals, or has destroyed, any substantial evidence for the earliest city here, but pottery of the early seventh century has been reported.[100] There is evidence too for interesting archaic sculpture and architecture – a capital, and reliefs including a frieze with chariots. A recent find is part of a cylindrical basis with dancing

285 Electrum staters of Cyzicus showing a lion-demon holding a tunny fish, and Heracles with a tunny in the field; late 6th c. (London, von Aulock Coll.)

women carved on it in relief.[101] These works fall within the period when this coast owed allegiance to the Persian king. The city had access to gold mines on the mainland, which she exploited from the later sixth century for a notable issue of electrum coins (*Fig. 285*).[102] The coins always show a tunny fish, which suggests another source of the city's wealth.

Inland from Cyzicus, some twenty miles away and on the far side of Lake Manyas, lies the site of DASCYLIUM. This became the seat of the Persian governor in later days, but excavations there have yielded pottery of the seventh century – some, it seems, of the first half of the century.[103] It has been thought that this indicates an early date too for Greek foundations on the coast, but the town's Lydian name may imply that the first Greeks there had other business, perhaps as mercenaries installed by Lydia. From DORYLAEUM (modern Eski-Shehir) yet farther inland is an Ionian stela of the usual type, of about 520, but with relief decoration (*Fig. 286*).[104] We cannot say whether it was for a Greek, Phrygian, or Persian. Other 'Greco-Persian' stelae from this general area show that combination of styles we have observed in an earlier chapter.[105]

On the north coast of the Propontis Samian PERINTHUS has yielded an inscribed gravestone of Samian type.[106] Nearer the Bosporus and on the south coast is CALCHEDON. In a tomb there of the second half of the sixth century most of the pottery was Corinthian, as we might expect in a Megarian town.[107] There is also from near by a strange gravestone[108] of about 550 BC, showing what might be a death-room scene and carrying an inscription in Ionic (not Megarian) lettering, and a small marble 'kore'. These stray finds of sculpture tell us little or nothing of the towns, since they are generally accidental finds, or from later buildings into which they had been set. Properly excavated evidence is still lacking.

It is little better with what was to become the greatest of the Propontis cities, BYZANTIUM. The ancient acropolis here lies at the east end of the city of Constantinople, behind Agia Sophia, overlooking the Golden Horn and the Bosporus. It has been little explored, but trenches in the Great Court of the Seraglio Palace yielded some Corinthian pottery of the later years of the seventh century.[109] Here again there might be good hope of more precise evidence from digging.

Within the Black sea we turn first to those cities within the borders of modern Bulgaria.

Milesian APOLLONIA, by modern Sozopol, is the first of the important Greek cities on this coast. There is a peninsula with an offshore island (St Kiriak) just north of it, which may have been the centre of the earliest town. The earliest finds, however, were recovered from Sozopol bay. Most of these are East Greek vases going back to about 600 BC, with a little later Corinthian and

286 Grave stele from Dorylaeum showing an Artemis or Anatolian goddess of animals; it had a palmette top, as other Greek Archaic stelae; about 520 BC. (Istanbul Mus. 526; H. 73 cm)

Athenian.[110] There are several interesting pieces of sculpture, the earliest a male figure of East Greek style of the third quarter of the sixth century (*Fig. 287*), and a late Archaic two-sided stela.[111] Later on the famous sculptor Calamis made for the city a colossal Apollo, which figures in its coins. There seems to have been no native settlement preceding the Greeks here. As well as its fisheries the city had ready access to good farmland and timber.

Megarian MESEMBRIA, at modern Nesebur, was a later foundation. It is a good peninsula site, of the sort so often chosen by Greek settlers, with an excellent anchorage to the south. It had first been occupied by native Thracians, and of the earliest Greeks there we hear only of sixth-century pottery. Its later archaeological history is better known.[112]

ODESSUS, to the north again, is at the modern Varna. The site is on high ground overlooking the north side of a bay which is comparatively well sheltered for shipping. It was said to have been founded little before 560, and the earliest datable vase from the town is a Corinthian cup of these years.[113] But so far the finds have been extremely slight.

287 Marble dressed kouros from Apollonia; about 540 BC. (Burgas Nat. Mus.; H. 90 cm)

The Danube formed a natural barrier between the north and the Balkans and also a natural channel for the passage of goods and peoples. It runs towards the Black Sea from the west along the present Bulgaria–Rumania border, but little over fifty miles from the coast it turns north for about a hundred miles, parallel to the coast, before turning again to enter the sea through a broad marshy delta. A rectangle of land is thus cut off, by the river to north and west, by the sea to the east, by a range of hills (now the Bulgarian frontier) to the south. This is the fertile Dobrudja, whose plains must have been as much an attraction to the Greeks who first came there as the riches carried by the Danube. Indeed they may well have been the greater attraction. The best positions from which to enjoy both lay not at the marshy delta but any-where to the south, where there was ready access inland to the main stream of the river.

Probably the most convenient position is at TOMIS, the Roman poet Ovid's place of exile and modern port of Costanza, where there was a good headland protecting a south-facing harbour. The modern town effectively covers the ancient, but recent finds there include a number of Chian wine jars of the first half of the fifth century, so it may well be that Tomis is to be numbered with the other Milesian foundations of the sixth century along this coast.[114]

The first Greek colony in this area lay at ISTROS (Histria, *Fig. 288*), half-way between Tomis and the Danube delta. Excavations have gone on since 1914, and the most recent work by Rumanian archaeologists shows that here we may expect perhaps the best picture we are likely to find of one of the early Black Sea colonies.[115] Today the site lies at the edge of saline, partly marshy ground, and seawards the approach is blocked by mud-banks

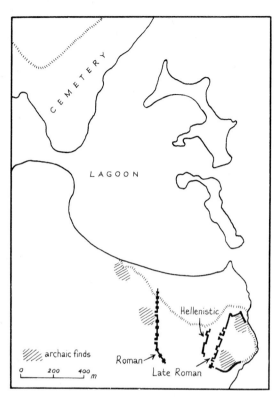

288 Sketch plan of Istros

deposited by the outflow of the Danube since antiquity. It is difficult to determine where the coastline ran in the seventh century BC, but it seems likely that the site, a low hill, lay at the end of a peninsula, although it has also been thought that it was an island. The tip was the part walled off as the acropolis of the classical city, and there is sixth-century pottery here in the neighbourhood of a later temple. But the best sequence of early levels is on the northern edge of the peninsula, nearly half a mile from its end, where it seems that there could have been a good sheltered anchorage. A wall and a destruction level are associated by the excavators with the Scythian raids of about 500. There are only a very few scraps of native pottery in the earliest levels, so the site may well not have been occupied before the Greeks arrived. The earliest houses here were little more than 'wattle-and-daub' shacks, but there are also, from the acropolis, pieces of an Ionic temple, no later than the early fifth century. A cemetery lay to the north, now on the other side of a lagoon. The tombs are covered by small tumuli, and contain mainly Greek vases – the earliest are Attic of about 530 BC. At the centre of each tumulus is the pyre, but near by, sometimes outside the tumulus, horses, men, and women are also found buried, unburnt.[116] These were not normal Greek burials, and are thought to be of native (Thracian) notables who chose burial here, near the Greek city which had brought

289 Crater fragment from Smyrna, signed by Istrokles; about 650 BC. (Izmir Mus.)

them new prosperity; but contemporary tombs of the Greek city have yet to be found. A Scythian mirror in one of the tombs reminds us how near the Scythians were by now. We are near in time to the Persian expedition against the Scythians which carried Darius far beyond the Danube.

Istros has yielded a great deal of early pottery – the earliest being East Greek of the later seventh century, little after the date for the foundation suggested by Eusebius. There is circumstantial evidence for early knowledge of the Danube in the vase-fragment from Smyrna, of the mid seventh century, which bears the name Istrokles (*Fig. 289*) – surely derived from the name of the river.[117] The sixth-century pottery is rich and varied. There are plenty of the 'Rhodian' vases, both figured and plain, but other East Greek wares are also well represented: Chian of the first half of the century (one piece no later than about 600) and Chian wine jars throughout it; much Fikellura and a very little Clazomenian, mainly of the second half of the century. This reflects pretty well the tastes of the East Greek world and the main pottery-producing centres, without saying very much about the particular interests of any one state. Less expected is a clay relief *pithos* (storage jar) of the later sixth century, probably from an East Greek city or from one of the islands.[118] Of other wares there are Athenian vases of the second quarter of the sixth century, if not earlier, as there are in East Greece, but there is very little Corinthian indeed. Locally the Greeks made plain wares, some of them resembling East Greek *bucchero*.[119]

There is evidence too for the early penetration of Greeks and Greek goods in this area. Less than fifteen miles west of Istros, a native town has been explored at Tariverde, and a number of Greek vases found, beside the local wares. Most are Athenian or East Greek, and the earliest are of the second quarter of the sixth century. Farther to the north west, at Barbosi, near where the Danube turns into its delta, late sixth-century Athenian vases have been reported.[120] In the fifth century there is a stronger flow, and

Athenian vases are found in several places along the Danube and its tributaries, as well as two fine bronze vases – one from a site near the Danube some 150 miles from the sea, another from the Carpathians about 400 miles from the sea.

TYRAS may be the site standing on a headland overlooking the southern waters of the estuary of the River Dniestr, and partly occupied by the Akerman fortress (modern Belgorod-Dnestrovsky). Although early pottery has been reported here, none has been published. It was well placed to enjoy the cornlands of the Dniestr's broad valleys. Others take this for Ophioussa, and look for Tyras higher up the river, near where two inscriptions naming the town have been found; but the Akerman site was obviously an important one in classical and Hellenistic times, and has yielded many Tyras coins. It must have been the earliest of the settlements on or near the Dniestr, and so is probably Tyras, since the same name is used for the river.[121]

OLBIA (Borysthenes) was the northernmost of the early colonies, and the richest. It lay on the right bank of the broad estuary of the River Bug as it flows into the broader estuary of the Dniepr. There was another early Greek town here which has no known ancient name, but is best discussed before Olbia, since some have thought it was the place which the Greeks first settled. It is on Berezan island which lies outside the estuary, nearer the open sea.[122] It is not clear whether it was an island in antiquity, and it may be that this is another peninsula site, chosen more for its defensibility than any good anchorage. It now seems, though, that there had been a native settlement here before the Greeks arrived; one to which the Greeks, or at least Greek wares, were admitted. The site has no architectural distinction, and most of the finds are from the cemetery, where an unusual crematorium-pit has been recognized.[123] The earliest pottery is of the late seventh century. From then on the town is well supplied with East Greek vases – 'Rhodian', Chian, Fikellura, Clazomenian, and other black-figure; plus Corinthian, Athenian after 570, and perhaps Boeotian vases.[124] The presence of a Chian storage jar of a type with a wide mouth (Fig. 290)[125] which could hardly have been used for the carriage of wine or oil, rather suggests the presence of a Chian family here soon after 600. There are minor objects of faience, as on East Greek sites, and one of the more charming finds is a clay lamp of the late sixth century inscribed 'I am the lamp of –, and I shine for gods and men alike'.[126] A remarkable recent find has been a private letter of about 500, written on lead, complaining about an attempt to claim a slave and deprivation of some commercial agency.[127] It was thought that the town did not survive long into the fifth century, and that its population had been absorbed by Olbia, but recent work has shown fifth-century and later settlement. Its main commercial value had probably been as a fishing station.[128]

There are other villages on the Bug–Dniepr estuary, before we

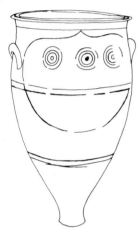

290 Chian storage jar from Berezan; 6th c. (Leningrad inv. B 454; H. 52·5 cm)

reach Olbia, which attracted Greek goods in the sixth and fifth centuries, and perhaps attracted Greek families too. Two are at Victorovka and Dneprovskoe (near Olbia);[129] the tombs at Gute Maritzyn will be described at the end of the next section.

OLBIA itself occupies a site shaped like an isosceles triangle, nearly a mile long and a half-mile across its base.[130] The base at the north and the long west side are limited by ravines, the east side by the waters of the Bug, here four miles across. The archaic town occupied all but the northern sector of this area, the acropolis being at the south. Later the whole triangle was occupied by the town, and fortified, with the acropolis located more centrally. Ships could be drawn up along the river bank towards the north of the site. Part of a good archaic house has been excavated in the area of the later acropolis, and it has been claimed that a proper 'grid' town plan was laid out by the end of the sixth century. There is evidence for earlier town planning of this sort in East Greece, at Smyrna. There is an elaborate architectural moulding of the later sixth century, which is close to contemporary fashions in Chios,[131] and Herodotus[132] speaks of a house which the Scythian prince Skyles had built for himself in the Greek city 'set about with marble sphinxes and griffins'. This and other stories reflect the town's good relations with the Scythians and its general prosperity. The earliest pottery closely matches that at Berezan already described, but is on the whole richer, and there is a greater variety of other objects: elaborate alabaster dishes, scraps of archaic sculpture, bronzes, and a painted clay coffin similar to the more elaborate types made in East Greece.[133] A sanctuary area north of the agora was established in the sixth century, and a temple to Apollo Delphinios built in the early fifth. There is more than a hint of the influence of Scythian taste on local products. This must have been one of the important centres for the production of the many Greco-Scythian works of art which we shall discuss in the next section. A good illustration of this is the find of a mould for casting an animal head of a type found on many of these Greco-Scythian objects.[134] The earliest coins of Olbia may have been made early in the fifth century.[135] They are of an unusual form: cast in bronze, not struck. Some are big discs with a gorgon's head and eagle with dolphin (*Fig. 291*); others are actually in the shape of dolphins.

CERCINITIS (crab-city) is not certainly located, but most Russian scholars identify it at a site (Eupatoria) about half way along the west coast of the Crimea in a rather exposed south-facing position. The old harbour may be represented by what is now a salt lake. The earliest finds are of the end of the sixth century.[136]

CHERSONESUS was founded by the Megarians from Heraclea at a point near the southern tip of the Crimea. This tip is, as it were, pulled round to the west, and the Greek city lay facing north. The site served long as a quarry for building stone for

291 Bronze coin of Olbia; gorgoneion; eagle with dolphin; early 5th c. (Oxford)

292 East Greek vase from Panticapaeum; early 6th c. (H. 21 cm)

nearby Sevastopol. The earliest published finds, of the later fifth century, go back to the city's earliest days, but still beyond the limits we have set. The few late sixth-century Greek finds might indicate Greek visits rather than an earlier, non-Megarian foundation.[137]

THEODOSIA, towards the eastern end of the Crimea, had been founded by Milesians. It stood on the sheltered northern side of a steep headland. The earliest find – an Athenian vase painted about 570[138] – was from the old excavations, but work began again on the site in 1949.

At its east the Crimea stretches out a broad peninsula towards a headland (Taman) projecting from the coast north of the Caucasus. The straits between form a sort of second Bosporus – known as the Cimmerian Bosporus – an approach to the Sea of Azov, which the Greeks knew as Lake Maeotis. At its furthermost recess the Greek city of Tanais was later to stand, at the mouth of the Don, but we have seen already how Greek goods passed this way in the very earliest days of Black Sea colonization. The most important of the early towns lay on either side of the Cimmerian Bosporus, and in the fifth century were to form the nucleus of a Bosporan Kingdom. On the western, Crimean, shore are Panticapaeum (Kerch), Myrmekion, Tyritake, and Nymphaeum; on the east are Phanagoria and Hermonassa. These are all certainly early foundations, although not all are mentioned as such by ancient authors. The Milesians were the most active in this area, but we hear of other Ionians, notably the Teans who founded

Phanagoria after they had been driven from their homes by the Persians. Panticapaeum in particular has been a rich source of classical and later Greek antiquities, but no small part of the interest attaching to these Greek cities is the close proximity of some of the richest Scythian tombs, which were in part furnished with Greek jewellery, vases, and other objects.

The acropolis of PANTICAPAEUM[139] became known as Mount Mithradates. It stands behind the modern town of Kerch, beside the sea. In antiquity it may have stood out more as a headland and enjoyed the use of a better harbour. The earliest Greek pottery may be of the last years of the seventh century, but recent reports speak of a pre-Greek town there with a Greek trading quarter in the seventh century. One of the arrivals of the early sixth century is an East Greek vase (*Fig. 292*) on which is painted a wine jar of the sort which was already being regularly supplied to the Greeks on the Black Sea.[140] The early pottery is very much as that at Olbia and Berezan. There are scraps of what seems to have been an Ionic temple of about 500, with column bases carved in a manner best matched in the island of Chios.[141] A gravestone carved with volutes and palmettes (*Fig. 293*) is in a provincial style rather far removed from the elegant stelae of East Greece.[142]

MYRMEKION was to the north of Panticapaeum,[143] looking across the bay, down the straits to the south. It has been the scene recently of joint Russian and Polish excavations. There is not much sixth-century pottery here, but what there is goes back to the first half of the century, and it seems likely that this was a post established quite soon by the settlers at Panticapaeum.

Some seven miles south of Panticapaeum is TYRITAKE, which has also been shown by recent excavations to be an early foundation.[144] There was an earlier 'Cimmerian' town here, but Greek houses of the second half of the sixth century are now reported. The pottery follows the by now familiar pattern. The earliest, in a strange orientalizing style which is not easily placed,[145] may not be much later than 600 BC in date, but most of the vases are no earlier than 550 BC. We have already noted its importance for the fish trade.

South again, some four miles, is NYMPHAEUM,[146] which seems to have been settled at about the same time as Tyritake and presumably represents part of the same movement of expansion by the Milesians of Panticapaeum. Excavations since the last war came upon an early sanctuary of Demeter by the harbour with Athenian vases of about 560 among the offerings, and temples of Aphrodite and the Cabeiri on the acropolis. Archaic kilns and a locally produced ware with simple linear decoration have been found.[147] A pre-Greek settlement is said to have been identified. Just outside the straits CIMMERICUM was settled by about 500 beside a Cimmerian town.[148]

PHANAGORIA[149] lay on the other side of the straits, at the recess of the deep bay. The site is low lying and undistinguished. From

293 Limestone grave stele from Panticapaeum; 6th c. (Kerch; H. 88 cm)

the literary evidence (see above) the foundation date should be about 540. The earliest pottery and figurines, East Greek in type, are very little later. KEPOI, to the north-east, may have been founded a little earlier.[150]

HERMONASSA[151] is nearer the modern town of Taman. Here, and on the other minor sites near by whose cemeteries have been partially explored, the earliest finds are pre-550.

The Greeks' hold on the eastern side of the straits seems to have been established roughly a generation after their first foundations on the Crimean shore, and it may never have been so firm. Not far to the east were some of the richest Scythian tombs. Near the famous group known as the Seven Brothers is a sixth-century native town described by the Russian archaeologists as most like a Greek citadel.

Of the remoter cities, TANAIS at the mouth of the Don was founded after the period which we have set out to discuss. But we have seen that more than one Greek vase had passed up the Don to the hinterland in the earliest day of colonizing. Recent underwater exploration in the Taganrog Straits just west of Tanais has come upon East Greek pottery of the end of the seventh century, and this might represent a pre-colonial trading post, as early as any colony in the Black Sea and far more remote.[152] PHASIS, in Colchis, on the extreme eastern shore of the Black Sea, was founded to give immediate access to the Caucasus and its mineral wealth. The earliest Greek finds in the area may be local coins of the early fifth century showing the Milesian lion and a Minotaur,[153] but the coast may have been visited and settled in the second half of the sixth century. This is suggested by the recent finds at Vani, a site on the Rioni over sixty miles from the sea, which has yielded superb Greek and Scythian works of the fifth and fourth centuries, but includes Attic pottery of around 500 and works which are late Archaic Greek in style, like the silver aryballos, *Fig. 294*.[154] This was the logical step beyond the colonies which had already been founded along the southern shore of the Black Sea, to which we may now turn.

294 Silver aryballos from Vani; about 500 BC. (Tiflis Mus.; H. 9·2 cm)

Of HERACLEA, the nearest to the Bosporus, and a Megarian foundation, we know almost nothing,[155] although the city soon became rich, and sponsored other colonies at Callatis (between Odessus and Tomis) and in the Crimea (Chersonesus).

Sinope and Trapezus were the important Milesian foundations, and we have already had something to say about the early dates attributed to them.

SINOPE, modern Sinop, occupies a peninsula site which commands a superb sheltered harbour to the south-east. Exploration of the city has been made virtually impossible by later building, and only in recent years has part of the cemetery, on the mainland, been explored.[156] The pottery from the graves is largely East Greek, but there is a little Corinthian too, which can be dated to little after 600 BC. It seems likely that the earliest graves have yet to be found, but the scraps recovered from the town site are no earlier. Of equal interest is the quantity of Phrygian pottery which has been found, and which attests the close relations with the peoples of the interior (see also below, under Amisos). The city's main prosperity must have been derived from her trade. In part this would have been due to her possession of the only good harbour between the Bosporus and Trapezus, in part to her position at the end of a comparatively easy overland route from Mesopotamia.[157] But she also had access to the mines and timber of the interior, and in later days was the major exporter of 'miltos', a mineral dye much valued by the Greeks.

TRAPEZUS (Trebizond) lay some 250 miles beyond Sinope, which was itself over 300 miles from the Bosporus. The city occupied a good acropolis site, but we know nothing of its early history from either excavation or casual finds. The city's importance for trade both with the Caucasus and with the area once occupied by the kingdom of Urartu, to the south-east, cannot be overestimated, though it may easily be dated too high.

AMISOS (Samsun) lies between Sinope and Trapezus, but much nearer the former. It is generally considered a later foundation, but in fact the little Greek pottery from the town is hardly any later than the earliest found so far at Sinope – after 600 BC.[158] It was perhaps better placed for trade inland, along the rivers, and we have already remarked that it was traditionally through Amisos that the 'steel-men', Chalybes, supplied the Greeks. The finds here, and near by, reflect these relations with the interior. It will be remembered that the 'natives' here were the heirs to the old Phrygian empire, and this is the nearest point on the coast to the old Hittite and Phrygian city at Boğaz-köy. About ten miles inland from Amisos, at Ak Alan, East Greek pottery of little after 600 has been found beside local Phrygian painted vases.[159] At the same site (Fig. 295), and at Pazarli, farther inland, appear the painted clay revetments which owe so much to East Greek inspiration, and which we have already mentioned in Chapter 3 (Fig. 103).[160]

295 Clay revetment from a building at Ak Alan, with a rampant lion and part of a spout; late 6th c. (Oxford 1944.89; H. 24·2 cm)

296 Archers in a version of Scythian dress (one named Kimerios), participants in the Calydonian Boar Hunt on the Athenian François Vase, from Chiusi; about 570 BC. (Florence 4209)

297 Archer in Scythian dress on an Athenian vase by Exekias, from Orvieto; about 540 BC. (Philadelphia Univ. Mus. 4873)

Greeks and Scythians

The Scythians of the South Russian steppes were originally nomad tribes who had come to settle in the plains and by the rivers. From the new Greek cities they were to acquire a taste for 'civilized' life and the trappings of urban civilization – wine and works of art. Not that the Scythians themselves were by any means uncivilized, as we shall see. But to the Greeks they must have seemed much as Red Indians do to the modern (or by now rather oldfashioned) schoolboy: a remote race of dusky warriors who wore long trousers and funny hats, were phenomenal bowmen and horsemen, and scalped their enemies. Their country was said to be one of darkness and intense cold, and the only Scythians most Greeks saw were either slaves or those enrolled in the Athenian police in the fifth century, although one Scythian (Anacharsis) was numbered by the Greeks with the Seven Sages. Their dress, which came to be standard uniform for archers, orientals, and Amazons in Greek art, may have been somewhat more familiar (*Figs. 296, 297*).[161]

It was generally held in antiquity that it was the arrival of the Scythians from the east that displaced the Cimmerians[162] and set them on their many destructive raids into Asia Minor. We have already met the Cimmerians here, attacking Greek cities in the seventh century, and compassing the fall of the Phrygian empire.

The Scythians were thought to come from the east, and there is certainly much Persian in their culture and names. Of more immediate interest to us are their fortunes in the Near East, for what they learned there formed an important part of their heritage when they came to their South Russian homes, and this may affect our opinions about the influence of Greek art in Scythia. But first we should say something about what is known of the Scythians themselves, their tombs and their art, in the early period which is our concern in this book. Their customs and way of life are described in a full and picturesque manner by Herodotus,[163] and we can learn something more of them from the contents of their graves. But most of these material remains date from the fifth century BC and later, and only a few of their tombs belong to the earlier period. These are, at all periods, their most impressive remains. There was generally a wooden tomb building, with an inner chamber to house the body. In the richer burials wives, servants, and horses were buried beside their master, who is fully dressed and armed. Over all a high earth tumulus was raised.

Scythian art too is best known from examples of the later period when Greek influence was already strong, sometimes paramount. Its native characteristics are fairly easily defined – an 'animal style' of decoration, with the bodies of the animals contorted into graceful curvilinear patterns. Extra limbs or heads of other creatures may grow from the bodies, to enrich the complexity of the compositions. We meet the style most often in plaques – often in openwork – of gold and bronze, which decorated furniture, equipment (especially harness), and dress. On larger objects, we can detect a desire to cover the whole available field, either by an almost endless development from the main central pattern or by the repetition of single motifs. There is a great deal here which looks back to the art of Persia, and Luristan in particular, and which looks forward to Celtic art, but there is much too which is not entirely foreign to Greek art. In East Greece, in particular in Ephesus (*Fig. 298*), we find objects decorated in an 'animal style' which is very close to Scythian work.[164] These are of the latest seventh and sixth centuries. They might be imports, and at any rate it would be wrong to think that the Scythians learned anything of this style from the Greeks. Rather, they were both drawing on older oriental traditions: the Greeks on that which developed in the town-civilizations of Mesopotamia; the Scythians on that which was evolved by the nomads of the European–Asian plains. The style is at its best on objects for which it was first adopted – like horses' harness or the traditional Scythian bow case.

298 Ivory figure of a boar from Ephesus; 6th c. (Istanbul Mus.; W. 4·5 cm)

257

299 Figures from a gold sheath in Melgunov's barrow; early 6th c. (Leningrad; H. about 4 cm)

In the eighth and seventh centuries, Scythian princes had invaded Asia Minor and the kingdom of Urartu, attacked the Medes and Babylonians, and even pressed far into Palestine. Of these years we find a few superb examples of the mixed eastern and animal style art, especially from Ziwiye (near Saqqiz) in the kingdom of the Mannai, beyond Urartu.[165] In a very similar style are the earliest finds in the Scythian tombs of South Russia, which must belong to the last years of the seventh century, when the Scythians were already being pressed north and out of the lands they had won from the Medes and Assyrians. Thus the most sophisticated products of Scythian art in the period before any very close contact with the Greeks are profoundly affected by Near Eastern fashions. In two or three of the great tombs (notably Melgunov's, far north of Olbia, and others some 400 miles away near the Kelermes in the Kuban) there is fine relief goldwork – on hilts, sheaths, etc. – which displays the developed animal style beside purely Assyrian motifs and figures (*Fig. 299*).[166] The artists were most skilful imitators of Assyrian forms, yet they could enter fully into the spirit of the animal style. The best examples of this work were found as long ago as 1763 by General Melgunov, who took them to St Petersburg for the Empress Catherine II to admire.

It is at the end of the seventh century that the Greeks too reach the north shores of the Black Sea. With one of the earliest Greek vases to reach Russia, in the tomb at Krivoroshie (see p. 244), we find an example of the oriental goldwork which has just been mentioned.[167] And in Melgunov's barrow, beside the Scytho–Assyrian objects, is a gold plaque with a monkey and birds in relief (*Fig. 300*) which may be an early intimation of Greco-Scythian work.[168] Greek art of this period is also 'orientalizing', but already much that was borrowed from the east has been changed and adapted beyond recognition. Still, it is not always easy to be sure whether some of the 'orientalizing' objects found in South Russia are Greek or genuinely oriental; for

300 Gold plaque from Melgunov's barrow; 6th c. (Leningrad; H. 2·6 cm)

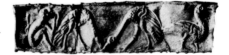

example, the fine ivory lions' heads from near Smêla (*Fig. 301*).[169] The fact that their eyes are inlaid with amber suggests that they were made either in South Russia or Greece; their style, that they were made by a Greek or an easterner.

In the sixth century we begin to find the clearest indications of the impact of Greek art on the Scythians. This is conveyed in part by imported objects, in part by the work of Greeks, Ionians, on objects or in styles calculated to attract the Scythians. Their work was probably done actually in the Greek cities of the Black Sea coast. We must, however, remember that this was no ordinary barbarian market that they were serving, but one already used to most accomplished works of decorative art in a quite different style, and one well acquainted with the best work of certain more formal Near Eastern schools.

In general we find the Scythians readily accepting Greek products of hitherto unfamiliar forms, for instance the Ionian bronze mirrors with volute handles, decorative bronze vases, and to a lesser degree painted pottery. The Scythian fashion of sewing metal plaques on to clothing was matched in East Greece, and we find East Greek motifs, some subtly acknowledging the native animal style, in the small gold plaques which have been found in many Scythian tombs (*Fig. 302*).[170] Bracelets with animal-head terminals had become familiar to the Greeks from Near Eastern models, but some of their finest pieces seem to have been made for the Scythian (and even the Persian) market, and they set the standard for native work.

We have already mentioned the finds of Greek pottery of the later seventh century far from the Black Sea shores where the Greeks were founding their first colonies. They suggest the early interest shown by the Scythians in their new neighbours, but it is just possible that some of the Greek vases and settlers had arrived even before the Scythian princes from the south had established themselves near the great rivers of South Russia. Throughout the sixth century there are occasional finds of Greek pottery in Scythian towns far up the Dniepr, south of Kiev. The Scythians were not greatly impressed by Greek painted vases until the fifth, and particularly the fourth century, when the Athenian potters were producing lines especially designed for the Black Sea market. By far the greater part of our evidence for Greek goods penetrating Scythia, or the existence of Greco-Scythian art, belongs to the years after the end of the sixth century B C. For the first hundred years or so, the new colonies prospered and enjoyed a lively trade with Greeks at home from the produce of their own agriculture and fishery, or from what they obtained from native farmers, but we cannot pretend that there is much evidence for very close intercourse between the peoples. It seems almost that they were brought closer together by their shared antagonism to the growing strength of the Persians, although the Scythians themselves should have found much in common with them, and

301 Ivory head of a lion with amber eyes, from Vasilkov near Smela; 6th c.

302 Gold plaques – sphinx, winged lion – from the Seven Brothers Barrow and Nymphaeum; 6th c. (Leningrad; L. 2·6, 4·1 cm)

259

303 Gilt silver mirror from
Kelermes; mid-6th c.
(Leningrad; Diam. 17 cm)

for the latter part of the sixth century the Greek cities of Ionia,
who had sent the colonies, lay within the bounds of the Persian
empire.

A few Greek bronzes were already being sold in Scythia in the
archaic period. From various important Scythian sites south of the
Dniepr and some 200 miles north of Olbia, well on the way to
Kiev, we find pieces of a large bronze crater[171] very similar in
appearance, if not origin, to those found in Illyria and at Vix, and a
bronze mirror with, it seems, a Scythian handle.[172] Late archaic are
two more bronze mirrors with figure supports – both of women,
one naked, one clothed[173] – from sites nearer the Greek cities at the
mouth of the Dniepr.

As with the earlier, orientalizing objects, so with the Greco-
Scythian, it is in relief goldwork that we find the most interesting
products for the Scythian market. From the Kelermes tombs,
where some of the best Assyrianizing pieces were found, there is a
superb gilt mirror, with its back decorated in an almost wholly
Greek manner (*Fig. 303*).[174] Completely Greek – Ionian, we might
say, of the mid sixth century – are the Mistress of the Animals,
lions, sphinxes, rams, goat, fox, eagle, griffin, and lion tearing a
bull. The subjects are orientalizing, some of them; the treatment is
Greek. But beside them we see a bear, a small crouching animal
stylized in a Scythian manner, and an extraordinary scene of two

304 Gilt silver rhyton (horn-shaped pourer) from Kelermes; late 6th
c. (Leningrad; Diam. 6·5 cm)

hairy men grappling with a griffin. The last must be Arimasps –
who, the Greeks thought, lived in the frozen north and stole the
gold the griffins guarded: an appropriate scene for a Greek to
choose, and one which again appeared often on the Athenian vases
of the fourth century which were sold in some numbers in Greek
cities on the north coast of the Black Sea. Also from Kelermes, and
by the same artist, was a gilt silver rhyton of Scythian shape[175]
decorated with a winged goddess holding two griffins, and
various other figures (*Fig. 304*), including a centaur and a hero
fighting a lion. A gold diadem (*Fig. 305*) with a griffin's head
projecting at the front imitates jewellery of the type being made in
the Greek islands at this time.[176]

Yet more remarkable, yet more remote, are the finds made near
Vettersfelde in North Germany, little over fifty miles from Berlin,[177] a hoard comprising much of the equipment of a single
warrior, and so possibly from his tomb. The equipment is

305 Gold diadem from Kelermes; 6th c.
(Leningrad; H. 1·8 cm)

306 Gold fish from Vettersfelde; late 6th c. (Berlin misc. 7839; L. 41 cm)

Scythian. There are gold decorative pieces from harness or armour. One is in the form of a fish (*Fig. 306*), the tips of its tail stylized into rams' heads and its body covered with small figures in relief – an eagle, lions with a stag and boar, fish, and a Triton merman. Another piece is in the form of five joined discs, four of them decorated with small animals in relief. There is gold work from a sheath and dagger, and one gold earring with other minor ornaments. The style of the figure and animal decoration on the larger pieces is wholly Ionian, and hardly any later than the end of the sixth century. But the form of the objects is quite un-Greek, and we may be dealing with one of the most distant and early burials of a Scythian chief who was equipped with the finest gold work from the Ionian cities of the Black Sea coast. That it is originally from a burial, and not a hoard of gold captured from a Scythian (though it does include some less than martial jewellery), may be suggested by the other less exotic Scythian finds of about this date in Central Europe, which bear witness to their damaging raids and expansion to the north-west.

307 Gold stag from Kul Oba; late 6th c. (Leningrad; L. 31·5 cm)

308 Gold stag from Kostromskaya; 6th-5th c. (Leningrad; L. 31·7 cm)

Slightly later than the Vettersfelde finds is the gold stag from a Scythian tomb at Kul Oba, in the Crimea (*Fig. 307*).[178] The animal

is not wholly Scythian, but a Greek essay in the animal style, and its body is covered with small relief animals in a wholly Greek manner. We may contrast the more natural 'animal style' treatment of the same motif (*Fig. 308*).[179] But with the Kul Oba stag and other gold work from Scythian tombs in Crimea and Kuban, we are beginning to meet the fully classical Greco-Scythian art of the fifth century which we cannot discuss in detail here.

To these earlier years of the fifth century belongs a remarkable tomb at Gute Maritzyn, near the Bug/Dniepr estuary between Olbia and Berezan. It and others near it well illustrate the way Greek and Scythian peoples and customs had already intermingled. The tombs are of Scythian type: wooden chambers in low tumuli. One was unusually well preserved,[180] and its contents are worth detailing (*Fig. 309*). At either end of the body – of a man – stood a Chian Greek wine jar. Thirst was further served by a fine black Athenian cup, a Greek bronze dipper, and a strainer, the last carrying elaborate incised patterns. The man was a warrior. He had an iron sword, two spears with iron heads, three knives (two bronze, one iron); to one side of him lay his corselet with iron scales sewn on to it, to the other his stock of arrows. From the last, 377 bronze arrowheads were counted, all of the socketed type which the Scythians introduced to the Greeks. From other early graves came more Chian wine jars, Athenian black-figure pottery of about 500 BC and just after, and a mirror with the figure of a woman incised on the handle by a Greek artist. This was not a Greek town, but we would be hard put to it to say from the finds whether it is Greeks or Scythians who are buried there. A study of

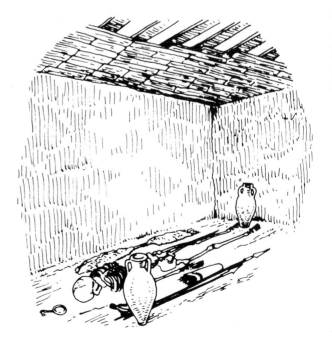

309 Sketch of a tomb at Gute Maritzyn; early 5th c.

the skulls suggested that some from the cemetery were certainly Greek. It is easy to see how later the terms Hellenoskyth or Mixellene were coined.

These apparently mixed communities, and the remarkable monuments of Greek work for the Scythians, are more eloquent testimony to the relations between the two peoples – the colonists and the natives – than the finds of objects imported from other parts of the Greek world. They show that the wealth of the Scythians and of the Black Sea trade attracted some of the finest Ionian artists to the northern colonies, where they adapted their natural style to the tastes and styles of the Scythians. We have noticed elsewhere – in Egypt, in the west, in Greece itself – the effect of the 'diaspora' of Ionian artists in the troubled years of the sixth century when their home cities were attacked or subjugated by the Lydians and Persians. The development of Greco-Scythian art was perhaps the strangest issue of the same movement.

Athenians, Persians, and the Hellespont

We have seen little enough of Athens taking any active interest in overseas foundations, although her pottery was carried so far by other Greeks and was appreciated so much by the barbarian neighbours of the Greek colonies. But in the sixth century Athens made a deliberate bid to secure a footing on, and indeed control of the Hellespont, surely to secure 'strongpoints on an artery of growing commercial importance to her'.[181]

Sigeum, on the southern side of the entrance to the Hellespont, had been occupied by Aeolians from Lesbos. About 600, Athens seized the town and became involved in a protracted conflict with the Lesbians. Among these was the poet Alcaeus who sang, unashamed, of the time he threw away his shield and ran, to fight another day.[182] The Corinthian tyrant, Periander, was called in as arbitrator, and he awarded the town to the Athenians. They seem to have lost it some time later, since the Athenian tyrant Pisistratus had to reoccupy it. In 510 his family took refuge there, but now it stood on the borders of the new Persian empire.[183]

Earlier in Pisistratus' career Athens had also gained control of the northern shores of the Hellespont.[184] Herodotus tells the picturesque story of how a deputation of Thracians (Dolonci) had come to Delphi for advice in their struggles with neighbours. They were told to invite as their leader the first man who offered them the shelter of his home after they left the sanctuary. They had to travel as far as Athens before they met the hospitable Miltiades. He was a rich man, perhaps a rival of Pisistratus, who was no doubt happy to see him go. The Dolonci lived in the Thracian Chersonese, the tongue of land on the north side of the Hellespont. Miltiades and the Athenian settlers he took with him occupied the whole area and built a wall across the narrowest point – just east of Gallipoli. We do not know on what terms his new settlements dealt with the Milesian and Lesbian colonies. The Lesbians probably suffered as they had in Sigeum. In the Thracian Chersonese Miltiades established a minor dynasty, which spent much of its energy fighting the Phocaean town Lampsacus, which faced it across the Hellespont. Miltiades himself was once captured, but freed when the Lydian king Croesus threatened the Lampsacenians. In about 516, the younger Miltiades was sent out from Athens, put down a revolt, married a Thracian princess, and occupied the islands of Lemnos (see p. 85) and Imbros in about 500.[185]

310 Fragment of a clay bowl (lekane) from Elaeus; mid-6th c. (Oxford, author's Coll.; L. 7 cm)

There is some archaeological evidence for this period of Athenian interest in the Hellespont. On the Thracian Chersonese there is little enough to show for the earlier colonies founded by the East Greeks, and the only early find is a Corinthian vase of about 630 from Koila, a city nearly half way along the north coast which only much later became at all important.

The most interesting site for us is that of Elaeus, which admitted Athenian settlement by about 550. This stands on the broad promontory to the east of the small bay at the very mouth of the Hellespont. Excavations there were occasioned by the military operations in Gallipoli in the First World War, and the French continued to explore the area in later years.[186] The new Turkish war memorial is now standing on the site, which is regularly visited, though seldom recognized, by Hellenic cruises. Most of the finds have come from graves to the east, although there is plenty of early pottery to be picked up on the town site. The earliest pottery, Corinthian and East Greek, takes the history of the site back to the 620s. Athenian vases only become at all common from about 550 on, but there is one group of vases from Elaeus which directly reflects the Athenian occupation. So far as we can judge, they were made around the middle of the sixth century or later, and were decorated quite simply with stripes and silhouette birds (*Fig. 310*). The type is Athenian, but this particular group is not found in Athens. Its distribution is significant – Elaeus and the Troad (including Troy and Sigeum), with isolated pieces in Black Sea cities. It was probably produced in an Athenian pottery established at Elaeus or Sigeum.[187] There are also crude, local imitations of Athenian and Corinthian decorated vases.

311 Silver tetradrachm of the Thracian Chersonese (not inscribed); about 500 B.C. (Berlin)

Coins can tell us a little too. Miltiades issued some labelled Cher(sonese), which combine an Athenian device with the Milesian lion (*Fig. 311*) – perhaps a reference to the Milesian cities in the Chersonese.[188]

On the other side of the Hellespont the archaeological record is less informative. Troy was resettled by Aeolian Greeks before 700. From Sigeum there is a gravestone on which the epitaph was engraved once in Ionian letters, and again, somewhat expanded, in Athenian letters.[189] The circumstances which led to the double inscription are not readily divined. The stone itself may well belong to a characteristically Athenian type of grave monument.

312 Silver obol of Athenian type. Obverse, head of Athena. Reverse, ear of corn, owl and inscribed Hip [pias?]; late 6th c. (Paris)

Epigraphists date the inscriptions about the middle of the century. Pisistratus' son Hippias may have minted coins at Sigeum – of Athenian types but with his name upon them (*Fig. 312*).[190] The late sixth-century temple at Assos, down the coast, may have something to do with Athenian influence in this area since it is the only Doric temple of this period in East Greece and its sculpture, with Heracles scenes, recalls the Athenian Acropolis pediments.[191] Lampsacus was the other big city on this side of the Hellespont – a Phocaean colony, hostile to the Athenians, and later a Persian base. Of the early town nothing is known, but there is in the writer's possession an East Greek cup of about the middle of the sixth century said to be from a grave there (*Fig. 313*).

By the end of the sixth century the Persians were at the gates, and like the other leaders of the East Greek states, Miltiades acknowledged the suzerainty of the Great King. In about 513 the Persian Darius mounted an expedition against Scythia, and Miltiades, with other East Greek leaders, went with him. Herodotus says that Miltiades tried to persuade his fellow Greeks to destroy Darius' bridge over the Danube while his army was beyond it, but that they saw too clearly how precarious their own positions would be at home without Darius' protection.[192] In 490 Miltiades met Darius' army again, on the battlefield of Marathon, but now he led his fellow Athenians against the Persian king.

The Persian occupation of the Greek cities of the Thracian coast is no part of our story. When Xerxes, Darius' son, led his army this way against Greece in 480 he bridged the Hellespont and watched the Greek grain ships going by to Aegina and the Peloponnese.[193] His 'fighters drank the rivers dry' as they moved through Thrace into Greece, to Thermopylae, to defeat at Salamis and, in the next year, Plataea. Three centuries before, the Greeks had coveted the wealth and knowledge of the east. Now their own strength and skills stood as challenge to the greatest empire the east had seen.

313 East Greek cup from Lampsacus; about 550 BC. (Oxford, author's Coll.; H. 5 cm)

Notes

ABBREVIATIONS

(other than the self-explanatory)

AA	Archäologischer Anzeiger		CRAI	Comptes Rendus de l'Académie des
AAA	Athens Annals of Archaeology			Inscriptions et Belles Lettres
ADelt	Archaiologikon Deltion		CVA	Corpus Vasorum Antiquorum
AE	Archaiologike Ephemeris		Desborough, GDA	Desborough, V. R. d'A., The Greek
AJA	American Journal of Archaeology			Dark Ages (1972)
Åkerström, GSI	Åkerström, Å., Der Geometrische Stil		Dunbabin	Dunbabin, T. J., The Western Greeks
	in Italien (1943)			(1948)
Akurgal, Birth	Akurgal, E., The Birth of Greek Art		JdI	Jahrbuch des deutschen archäologischen
	(1968)			Instituts
AM	Athenische Mitteilungen		Jeffery, AG	Jeffery, L. H., Archaic Greece (1977)
AntK	Antike Kunst		Jeffery, LSAG	Jeffery, L. H., Local Scripts of Archaic
ARepts	Archaeological Reports			Greece (1961)
Artamonov	Artamonov, M., Treasures from the		JHS	Journal of Hellenic Studies
	Scythian Tombs (1970)		JNES	Journal of Near Eastern Studies
ASMG	Atti e Memorie della Società Magna		Kraay	Kraay, C. M. Archaic and Classical
	Grecia			Greek Coins (1977)
ASSO	Archeologia nella Sicilia Sud-orientale		Kraay-Hirmer	Kraay, C. M. and Hirmer, M., Greek
	(edd. Pelagatti, P. and Voza, G.;			Coins (1966)
	Centre J. Bérard, 1973)		Kurtz-Boardman	Kurtz, D. C. and Boardman, J., Greek
Austin	Austin, M. M., Greece and Egypt in the			Burial Customs (1971)
	Archaic Age (1970)		Langlotz-Hirmer	Langlotz, E. and Hirmer, M., The Art
BABesch	Bulletin Antieke Beschaving			of Magna Graecia (1965)
BASOR	Bulletin of the American Schools of		MEFRA	Mélanges d'Archéologie et d'Histoire de
	Oriental Research			l'École Française de Rome, Antiquité
BCH	Bulletin de Correspondance Hellénique		Meiggs-Lewis	Meiggs, R. and Lewis, D. M., A
BdA	Bollettino d'Arte			Selection of Greek Historical Inscriptions
Beazley, ABV	Beazley, J. D., Attic Black-Figure			(1975)
	Vase-Painters (1956)		Minns	Minns, E., Scythians and Greeks (1913)
Beazley, ARV²	Beazley, J. D., Attic Red-Figure Vase-		Morel	Morel, J.-P., 'L'Expansion phocéenne
	Painters (1963)			en occident: dix années de recherches
BICS	Bulletin of the Institute of Classical			(1966-1975)' in BCH 99 (1975) 853ff.
	Studies, London			(there is a briefer version in RA 1975,
Boardman, ABFH	Boardman, J., Athenian Black Figure			142ff.)
	Vases (1974)		NSc	Notizie degli Scavi
Boardman, ARFH	Boardman, J., Athenian Red Figure		PAE	Praktika tes archaiologikes Etaireias
	Vases: Archaic Period (1975)		PdP	Parola del Passato
Boardman, CCO	Boardman, J., The Cretan Collection in		PEQ	Palestine Exploration Quarterly
	Oxford (1961)		RA	Revue Archéologique
Boardman, GSAP	Boardman, J., Greek Sculpture: Archaic		RM	Römische Mitteilungen
	Period (1978)		Robertson, HGA	Robertson, M., A History of Greek Art
BSA	Annual of the British School at Athens			(1975)
CAH	Cambridge Ancient History (2³.2, 1975;		SE	Studi Etruschi
	3², forthcoming)		Simon-Hirmer	Simon, E. and Hirmer, M. and A.,
Coldstream, GG	Coldstream, J. N., Geometric Greece			Die Griechischen Vasen (1976)
	(1977)		Snodgrass, EGAW	Snodgrass, A. M., Early Greek
Coldstream, GGP	Coldstream, J. N., Greek Geometric			Armour and Weapons (1964)
	Pottery (1968)			
Cook, GPP	Cook, R. M., Greek Painted Pottery			
	(1972)			

1 The Nature of the Evidence

General Bibliography

Standard works for consultation in this book are, for pottery – Cook, GPP; for inscriptions – Jeffery, LSAG; for art history in general – Robertson, HGA. More detailed handbooks on vases and sculpture are Boardman, ABFH, ARFH, GSAP.

The historical background in the seventh to sixth centuries is best surveyed in Burn, A. R., The Lyric Age of Greece (1960) and Jeffery, AG, where it is treated regionally. The forthcoming new editions of CAH 3 and 4 are relevant and see CAH 2³.2 chs. 36, 38, 39b.

Up-to-date bibliographies and brief accounts of Greek cities including colonies will be found in The Princeton Encyclopedia of Classical Sites (1976).

For criteria of identification of sources and dates down to 700 see Desborough, GDA; Snodgrass, A. M., The Dark Age of Greece (1971); Coldstream, GGP and GG; Cook, GPP ch. 11 with bibl. 356–8; adding J. Ducat, BCH 86 (1962) 165ff. on colonies and dates.

1 H. Payne, Protokorinthische Vasenmalerei (1933, 1974); Necrocorinthia (1931) chs. 1–4. Other regional styles are best studied through Cook.

2 Payne, op. cit. last n. Some drastic down-dating of Corinthian has been proposed (cf. E. Walter-Karydi, Samos 6. 1 (1973) 96–8, with references) but not generally accepted.

3 On Athenian vases and chronology see Boardman, *ABFH* 193ff.
4 A shrewd study of the problems by Cook, *JdI* 74 (1959) 114ff. and his *GPP* ch. 13. The Corinthian pottery trade, C. Roebuck, *Hesperia* 41 (1972) 116ff.
5 Chian – cf. J. Anderson, *BSA* 49 (1954) 168ff. (our *Fig. 1* = *BSA* 53/4 (1958/9) 16). 'SOS' – A. W. Johnston and R. Jones, *BSA* 73 (1978) 103ff. (our *Fig. 2* = no. 2).
6 Price inscriptions – D. A. Amyx, *Hesperia* 27 (1958) 287ff.; T. B. L. Webster, *Potter and Patron in Classical Athens* (1972) 273–9.
7 On the identification of carriers from graffiti on vases, Johnston, *Greece and Rome* 1974, 138ff.
8 J. D. Beazley, *BSA* 40 (1939/40) 83f.
9 C. G. Starr, *The Economic and Social Growth of Early Greece* (1977) ch. 3 and 90ff. (slaves).
10 C. M. Kraay, *JHS* 84 (1964) 76ff.; Starr, op. cit., 108ff.
11 *Works and Days* 618ff. and 650–3.
12 Passages of historical value are remarked in D. L. Page, *Sappho and Alcaeus* (1955); C. M. Bowra, *Greek Lyric Poetry* (1961).
13 Solon, *Eleg.* fr. 23 (West).
14 R. Carpenter, *Beyond the Pillars of Hercules* (1966) chs. 3, 7.

2 The Background

General Bibliography

See the General Bibliography for ch. 1, and Roebuck, C., *Ionian Trade and Colonization* (1959).

For recent work in Asia Minor reports by J. M. Cook and D. Blackman in *ARepts* 1959/60, 27ff.; 1964/5, 32ff.; 1970/1, 33ff. and annually by M. Mellink in *AJA* 59 (1955) on.

1 In general on Greek Bronze Age contacts overseas see *CAH* 2³. 2, 181ff.; 207ff., 350ff.; V. Desborough, *The Last Mycenaeans* (1964) chs. 8–10.
2 N. K. Sandars, *The Sea Peoples* (1978).
3 Kurtz – Boardman, chs. 1–4 and 9.
4 On these 'migrations' J. M. Cook, *CAH* 2³. 2 ch. 38 and *The Greeks in Ionia and the East* (1962) chs. 1, 2; E. Akurgal, *AJA* 66 (1962) 369ff. M. Sakellariou, *Le Migration grecque en Ionie* (1958) for literary evidence.
5 Mycenaean finds on this coast, Desborough, op. cit. (n. 1) 158ff. and GDA 365–7, site index; H. G. Buchholz, *AA* 1974, 361ff. and forthcoming; M. Mellink, *AJA* 80 (1976) 270. R. Hope Simpson and J. Lazenby, *BSA* 68 (1973) 174ff. Y. Boysal, *Anadolu* 15 (1971) 63ff. C. Mee, *Anat. Stud.* 28 (1978) 121ff. In the following notes only post-Mycenaean finds are remarked.
6 Desborough, *GDA* ch. 10.
7 Ibid., 180f.; Hope Simpson and Lazenby, op. cit.
8 Coldstream, *GG* 258.
9 J. M. Cook, *CAH* 2³. 2 790–5.
10 Hdt. 1. 146.
11 *Iliad* 2. 867f.
12 Desborough, *GDA* 179f., 183f.; the Dark Age pottery is heavily dependent on Attic types and the Ionian foundation, by Neleus, was said to have come straight from Athens – Hdt. 9. 97; Paus. 7. 2. J. M. Cook, *Gnomon* 1967, 213. Coldstream, *GG* 260f. G. Kleiner, *Die Ruinen von Milet* (1968).
13 Vitruvius 4. 1. 3–5; Jeffery, *AG* 208f.; G. Kleiner *et al.*, *Panionion und Melie* (1967).
14 L. B. Holland, *Hesperia* 13 (1944) 137f.; R. A. Bridges, *Hesperia* 43 (1974) 264ff. (Mycenaean).
15 *ARepts* 1969/70, 40.
16 J. M. Cook, *AE* 1953–4. 2, 149ff.
17 J. M. Cook, *BSA* 53/4 (1958/9) 1ff. for the main account of the site (15, fig. 3 = our *Fig.* 4). More recent work reported in Akurgal, *Ancient Civilizations and Ruins of Turkey* (1973) 119ff. Desborough, *GDA* 183f.
18 Hdt. 1. 149f.
19 R. V. Nicholls, *BSA* 53/4 (1958/9) 35ff.
20 Ibid., 15.
21 Akurgal, op. cit., 116–8; *Türk. Ark. Derg.* 7 (1957) 39.

22 Desborough, *GDA* 223; Coldstream, *GG* 252–7; H. Walter, *Heraion von Samos* (1965). On the town, R. Tölle-Kastenbein, *AM* 90 (1975) 189ff. Reports appear in *AM* 55 (1930) on.
23 Boardman, *Greek Emporio* (1967) – xiv, fig. 3 = our *Fig.* 5.
24 W. Lamb, *BSA* 35 (1934/5) 138ff.
25 Boardman, *BSA* 49 (1954) 123ff.
26 G. L. Huxley, *The Early Ionians* (1966) for a good account of the league. Jeffery, *AG* ch. 13. J. M. Cook, *Proc. Cambs. Phil. Soc.* 7 (1961) 9ff.
27 Hdt. 1. 147.
28 *Iliad* 9. 129f.
29 Coldstream, *GG* 262f.; Lamb, *BSA* 31 (1930/1) 146ff.; 32 (1931/2) 41ff.
30 Boardman, *Greek Emporio* (1967) 135.
31 *AJA* 68 (1964) 164.

3 The Eastern Adventure

General Bibliography

GREEKS AND THE EAST

Barnett, R. D. in *The Aegean and the Near East* (Studies H. Goldman, 1956) 212ff.
Coldstream, *GGP* 383ff.; *CAH* 3². 3, ch. 36a (T. F. R. G. Braun).
Cook, J. M., *Greeks in Ionia and the East* (1962)
Dunbabin, T. J., *The Greeks and their Eastern Neighbours* (1957)
Herrmann, H. V., 'Hellas' in *Reallexikon der Assyriologie* (1975) – imports to Greece listed.
Poulsen, F., *Der Orient und die frühgriechische Kunst* (1912)
Riis, P. J., *Sukas* i (1970) ch. 7.

NEAR EASTERN HISTORY AND ART

CAH 3². 1 and 3². 2.
Reports on archaeology in Western Asia Minor: see General Bibl. for ch. 1.
Akurgal, E., *Phrygische Kunst* (1955); *Die Kunst Anatoliens* (1960); *Birth of Greek Art* (1968) – reviewed *CR* 20 (1970) 379f.; *Urartäische und altiranische Kunstzentren* (1968); *Ancient Civilizations and Ruins of Turkey* (1973)
Frankfort, H., *Art and Architecture of the Ancient Orient* (1954)
Hanfmann, G. M. A., *Sardis und Lydien* (1960)
Harden, D. B., *The Phoenicians* (1962)
Moorey, P. R. S., *Biblical Lands* (1975)
Moscati, S., *The World of the Phoenicians* (1968)
Olmstead, A. T., *History of Assyria* (1923); *History of the Persian Empire* (1948)
Orthmann, W. (ed.), *Der alte Orient* (1975, Propyläen Kunstgeschichte)
Porada. E., *Art of Ancient Iran* (1965)
Pritchard, J. B. (ed.), *Ancient Near Eastern Texts* (1955)
Wiseman, D. J., *Chronicles of the Chaldaean Kings* (1956)
Young, R. S. (Phrygian) and Hanfmann, G. M. A. (Lydian) in Schefold, K., *Die Griechen und ihre Nachbarn* (P. K. G. 1967) 277ff., 282ff.

1 F. J. Stubbings, *Myc. Pottery from the Levant* (1951); V. Desborough, *The Last Mycenaeans* (1964) 207ff.; *CAH* 2³. 2, 181ff, 338–42; V. Hankey, *Levant* 6 (1974) 131ff.
2 N. K. Sandars, *The Sea Peoples* (1978).
3 *CAH* 2³. 2, 354–6, 678–81.
4 Ibid., 363–6, 679f.; 3². 2, ch. 36.
5 G. E. Bean, *Turkey's Southern Shore* (1968) part 2; A. Erzen, *AA* 1973, 388ff.; C. Brixhe, *Le Dialecte grec de Pamphylie* (1976) 147ff.
6 Boardman, *CCO* ch. 5; Coldstream, *Praktika I. Kypr. Synedr.* (1972) 1, 15–22.
7 Desborough, *Kret. Chron.* 1972, 245ff.
8 V. Karageorghis, *BCH* 94 (1970) 35–44; in *Antichitá Cretesi* 2, 168ff.
9 *ARepts* 1976/7 12f., fig 27; M. Sznycer, forthcoming.
10 H. W. Catling, *Cypriot Bronzework in the Myc. World* (1964) ch. 8, esp. 198f. (194, no. 6 = our *Fig.* 7; 207, no. 35 = our *Fig.* 8). As well as Crete they are found in

Samos and Thera (8th cent. grave: *ARepts* 1974/5, 23, fig. 43).

11 Boardman, *CCO* 132–4 (fig. 49b = our *Fig. 9*; *BSA* 38, (1937/8) pl. 34). Kato Syme – *PAE* 1973, pl. 188a (= our *Fig. 10*; more complete in *ARepts* 1977/8, 64, fig. 112); 1974, pl. 168a.

12 *Archaeology* 25 (1972) 16–19; M. R. Popham and H. Sackett, *Lefkandi* 1 (1979/80).

13 H. V. Herrmann, *JdI* 81 (1966) 131ff.; *Hesperia* 37 (1968) 77–116; R. A. Higgins, *BSA* 64 (1969) 143–54 on early jewellery in Greece.

14 J. Muhly, *Berytus* 19 (1970) 19ff. for a survey of early Greek knowledge and views on the Phoenicians. On their ships, L. Basch, *JHS* 97 (1977) 1ff.

15 Karageorghis, *Kition* (1976); *Salamis in Cyprus* (1969); *CAH* 3². 1, ch. 12. The argument that there was a positive heroic or Homeric element in the manner and furnishing of these tombs is, I think, exaggerated (Coldstream, op. cit., n. 6).

16 R. R. Dyer, *PdP* 20 (1965) 115ff. A D. Trendall and T. B. L. Webster, *Illustrations of Greek Drama* (1971) III. 5. 6, for a fourth-century scene of Darius' Asia being coaxed from safety to defeat.

17 L. Woolley, *JHS* 58 (1938) 1ff., 133ff.; 68 (1948) 148; and *A Forgotten Kingdom* (1953) ch. 10.

18 C. M. Robertson, *JHS* 60 (1940) 2ff. and for fifth century pottery J. D. Beazley, *JHS* 59 (1939) 1ff. Identifications of groups 1–4, Boardman, *BSA* 52 (1957) 1ff.

19 Popham and Sackett, *Excs. at Lefkandi* 1964–66 (1968) 23ff.; *Lefkandi* 1 (our *Figs. 11, 12, 13* = pls. 37. 16, 36. 2, 265a); *AAA* 3 (1970) 314ff. (Eretria).

20 Boardman, *Anat. Stud.* 9 (1959) 163–9 (no. 20 = our *Fig. 14*).

21 Ibid., 166f. and cf. elaborate examples, *BCH* 97 (1973) 667, fig. 103; *Cesnola Atlas* 3, pl. 146. 1081, and many more recently from excavations and observed in collections. Clay analysis does not so far support their attribution to Cyprus, however.

22 *Byblos* 2 (1954–8) 225, 939.

23 *CAH* 3². 1, ch. 18 (Boardman).

24 *CAH* 3². 1, ch. 18; S. C. Bakhuizen, *Chalcis in Euboea* (1976) and *World Archaeology* 9 (1977) 220ff.; Desborough in *Tribute to an Antiquary* (Essays, Marc Fitch) 25ff. On the importance of hoplites and their armour see Snodgrass, *JHS* 85 (1965) 110ff.; P. Cartledge, *JHS* 97 (1977) 11ff; J. Salmon, ibid., 84ff.

25 *Lefkandi* 1, pls. 12, 13a (= our *Fig. 15*).

26 J. du Plat Taylor, *Iraq* 21 (1959) 62–92. On the dating of Al Mina pottery see Coldstream, *GGP* 310–6. E. Gjerstad's attempt to upset this, in *ActaArch.* 45 (1974) 107ff., is not acceptable, and J. P. Descoeudres' in *Eretria* 6 (1978) 7ff., little better.

27 Coldstream, *GGP* 349–51. For a summary of Geometric and Archaic finds in Cyprus, Gjerstad, *Swedish Cypr. Exped.* 4.2 (1948) 274ff. and *Greek Geometric and Archaic Pottery found in Cyprus* (1977). For Cypriot chronology in this period, J. Birmingham, *AJA* 67 (1963) 59ff.

28 Coldstream, *GGP* 302–21; Riis, *Sukas* 1 (1970) 142–64. One of the earliest (second half of ninth century) imports is a pyxis (Argive ?) from Tambourit, near Sidon: P. Courbin, *Berytus* 25 (1977) 147ff.

29 Ras el Basit – P. Courbin, *RA* 1974, 1ff.; *Ann. Arch. Arabes Syr.* 22 (1972) 45ff.; 23 (1973) 25ff.; 25 (1975) 59ff.; *Archéologia* 116 (1978) 48ff.; Riis, *Sukas* 1 (1970); the pottery in G. Ploug, *Sukas* 2 (1973). On routes inland H. Seyrig, *Syria* 47 (1970) 296f.

30 For the distribution of these see now H. G. Buchholz, *Methymna* (1975) 90–2. Add from Khaldé near Beirut, *IX. Congr. Int. Arch. Class.* (1971) 194f.; Pritchard, *Sarepta* (1975) fig. 26.14 (Lebanon coast); Ras el Basit (above, n. 29); and cf. Coldstream, *GG* 94, and below, ch. 5, n. 12.

31 For rare Phoenician clay figure-decorated vases see E. Stern, *PEQ* 1978, 11ff.

32 For the text with the raid in the 730s see H. W. Saggs, *Iraq* 25 (1963) 76ff. Yamani are further discussed by T. F. R. G. Braun in *CAH* 3².3, ch. 36, to whom I am indebted for these references. A similar word was used

for 'Greeks' from Persia to India – C. Töttössy, *Acta Arch.* 3 (1955) 301ff.

33 Barnett, *Liverpool Annals* 26 (1939/40) 98ff.

34 Coldstream, *GGP* 320f.

35 K. R. Maxwell-Hyslop, *Iraq* 36 (1974) 139ff.

36 Berossus *FGH* 680 F7c (ch. 29); Abydenus *FGH* 685 F5 (ch. 6).

37 Boardman, *JHS* 85 (1965) 5–15. J. D. Bing, *JNES* 30 (1971) 99ff., suggests that there was a formal colony from Lindos in Rhodes at Tarsus at this time. At the best there may have been a trading concession but there was memory of earlier Rhodian interest here and along the coast to the west.

38 D. D. Luckenbill, *Annals of Sennacherib* (1924) 73. 60.

39 See n. 18, above.

40 A. W. Johnston and R. Jones, *BSA* 73 (1978) 103ff.

41 *JHS* 60 (1940) 19, fig. 8 1–n.

42 Coldstream, *GGP* 298–301; Boardman, *Greek Emporio* (1967) 132–4. Our *Fig. 16* = Oxford *CVA* 2, IID pl. 1.6.

43 Boardman, op. cit., 142. Our *Fig. 17* = Munich *CVA* 6, pl. 272.

44 Classes (d)–(e) have been recently discussed in Boardman and Hayes, *Tocra* 2 (1966) 111ff.

45 'Ad' sherds in Cambridge. Cf. *BSA* 52 (1957) 6; I. Strøm, *Acta Arch.* 33 (1962) 267ff.

46 A. Furtwängler, *Aegina* Fig. 339, pls. 108. 35–7, 112. 9–11, 118. 58; cf. 111. 2–3, 117. 12 (below, n. 232).

47 Above, n. 37; Hanfmann, *Tarsus* 3 (1963).

48 C. Clairmont, *Berytus* 11 (1955) 85ff.; cf. 12 (1956/7) 1ff. for Classical black vases.

49 Above, n. 37.

50 Snodgrass, *EGAW* 31; Barnett, *RDAC* (1977), 157ff., suggests a heroic occasion.

51 Snodgrass, *EGAW* 14.

52 Woolley, *Carchemish* 2 (1921) pl. 24; *Olympia Bericht* 5 (1956) 46–50.

53 J. Naveh, *Israel Expl. J.* 12 (1962) 89ff.; *Archaeology* 15 (1962) 108ff.; Austin, 53.

54 Above, n. 29.

55 S. Weinberg, *Proc. Israel Acad. Sc. & Hum.* 4.5 (1969) 88ff.; and see above n. 48.

56 D. L. Page, *Sappho and Alcaeus* (1955) 223ff.; cf. *BASOR* 164 (1961) 19f. for the campaign.

57 E. F. Weidner in *Mél. Dussaud* 2 (1939) 932ff.; F. Wetzel et al., *Das Babylon der Spätzeit* (1957) pl. 47.

58 *JHS* 66 (1946) 125 and Oxford 1954. 306 (dots and crescents).

59 Above, n. 48.

60 Woolley, *A forgotten Kingdom* (1953) 176, fig. 26.

61 Kraay, 148f., 301–5.

62 E. F. Schmidt, *Persepolis* 2 (1957) 110ff.; M. Price and N. Waggoner, *Archaic Greek Silver Coinage* (1975) 16.

63 Cf. O. Eissfeldt et al., *Elements orientaux dans la religion grecque ancienne* (1960); P. Walcot, *Hesiod and the Near East* (1966); M. L. West, *Early Greek Philosophy and the Orient* (1971); G. S. Kirk, *The Nature of Greek Myths* (1974) ch. 11.

64 *Epinomis* 987d.

65 *Od.* 17. 383–5.

66 Akurgal, *Späthethitische Bildkunst* (1949) and *Birth* chs. 3, 4. W. Orthmann, *Untersuchungen zur späthethitischen Kunst* (1971). Recent articles on dating – D. Ussishkin, *Anat. Stud.* 19 (1969) 121ff. and *BASOR* 181 (1966) 155ff.; Mellink, *Anatolia* 14 (1970) 15ff. and in *Anat. Studies.* H. Güterbock (ed. K. Bittel, 1974) 201ff. Names and dates – J. D. Hawkins, *Iraq* 36 (1974) 67ff.

67 Akurgal, *Anatolia* 4 (1959) 77ff. and *Urart. u. altiran. Kunstz.* (1968); R. Ghirshman, *Iranica Antiqua* 3 (1963) 60ff.; M. N. van Loon, *Urartian Art* (1966); H. V. Herrmann, *JdI* 81 (1966) 79ff., for relevance to Greece; B. B. Piotrowski, *Urartu* (1969).

68 Akurgal, *Birth* ch. 1.

69 I. Winter, *Iraq* 38 (1976) 1ff. and *Met. Mus. J.* 11 (1976) 25ff., for two important studies on Phoenician and Syrian ivories. Also the *Nimrud Ivories* series, especially 3 (1974; M. Mallowan and G. Herrmann).

70 V. Karageorghis and J. des Gagniers, *La céramique Chypriote de style figuré* (1974–5).

71 Karageorghis, *Kition* (1976); Gjerstad, *Swedish Cypr.*

Exp. 4.2 (1948) and *Opusc. Arch.* 4 (1946) 1–18 (metal bowls).

72 Barnett (*JHS* 68 (1948) 1) aptly quotes Philostratos (*Vita Apoll.* 5, 20) on the travelling masons and ivory-workers of the old days who made statues of the gods in the temple sanctuaries.

73 Boardman, *BSA* 62 (1967) 57–70 (pl. 11.2 = our *Fig. 23*) and in *Dädalische Kunst* (Hamburg Mus., 1970) 15f. Belt and quiver, J. K. Brock, *Fortetsa* (1957) nos. 1568–9 (= our *Fig. 24*). A. Lebessi, *BSA* 70 (1975) 169–76, sees continuity into the 7th cent. 'Daedalic', but the rings she publishes belong with the eighth century group. On later jewellery faces are smaller, hair is layered and there are no cloisons. She also denies the need for immigrant craftsmen but techniques such as these cannot be learned by observation, nor are the new forms in any degree essentially Greek. On eastern comparanda for the gold Porada, *Artibus Asiae* 32 (1970) 98f.

74 R. A. Higgins, *BSA* 64 (1969) 145–9; D. L. Carroll, *AJA* 74 (1970) 37ff. (earrings).

75 Below, n. 152.

76 E. Kunze, *Kretische Bronzereliefs* (1931) – our *Fig. 27* = nos. 1, 6; F. Canciani, *Bronzi orientali e orientalizzanti a Creta* (1970); Boardman, *CCO* ch. 3, 138f. and in *Däd. Kunst* (above, n. 73) 16–18.

77 Kunze, op. cit., no. 74, pl. 49 (= our *Fig. 26*).

78 Herrmann, *Die Kessel der orientalisierenden Zeit* (1966) 177–80, and below, n. 120. Vol. ii of this work (1979) deals with the lion and griffin protomes and rod tripods. It is not further referred to here.

79 Above, n. 76.

80 *JdI* 81 (1966) 81, fig. 2.

81 Boardman, *CCO* 80–4, pl. 28, frontispiece.

82 R. Hampe, *Kret. Löwenschale des 7ten Jdts v. Chr.* (1969).

83 Boardman in *Däd. Kunst* (above, n. 73) 19 with notes 24–6. Our *Fig. 29* = Hampe, op. cit., pls. 13b–15.

84 Boardman, op. cit., 18–23.

85 A good summary in B. Freyer-Schauenburg, *Elfenbeine aus dem samischen Heraion* (1966) 117–26. Smyrna – Akurgal, *Kunst Anatoliens* (1961) figs. 140–2. Ephesus – ibid., figs. 150–2. Crete – Kunze, *AM* 60/61 (1935/6) 218ff. and Boardman, *CCO* 151, n. 4. Rhodes – C. Blinkenberg, *Lindos* 1 (1931) no. 1582. Thasos – *BCH* 86 (1962) 95ff. (for our *Fig. 32*). Athens – *JHS* 68 (1948) 5, fig. 3. On the relevant eastern types see above, n. 69; our *Fig. 33* = *Sendschirli* 5 (1943) figs. 64–5.

86 Barnett, *Cat. Nimrud Ivories* (1957) 165 and *JHS* 68 (1948) 1, n. 4; Boardman, *JHS* 85 (1965) 13; Moscati, *World of the Phoenicians* (1968) 20 (in seventh century Tyre).

87 Kunze, *AM* 55 (1930) 147ff.; Akurgal, *Birth of Greek Art* (1968) pls. 49, 65a–d; F. Schweitzer, *Greek Geom. Art* (1969) pls. 146–8. M. Weber, *AM* 89 (1974) 27f., shows that they were supports or handles, like their eastern counterparts, and not independent figures. Our *Fig. 35* = Barnett, *Cat. Nimrud Ivories* pl. 74. S 210.

88 R. M. Dawkins (ed.), *Artemis Orthia* (1929) ch. 8; E.-L. Marangou, *Lakonische Elfenbein- und Bein-schnitzereien* (1969). Boardman, *BSA* 68 (1973) 4f. on dating and *JHS* 88 (1968) 9–12 on relationship to East Greek.

89 T. J. Dunbabin (ed.), *Perachora* 2 (1962) pt. 2.

90 Boardman, *Island Gems* (1963) 150f.; *JHS* 88 (1968) 9f. (Samos).

91 Boardman, *Island Gems* (1963) 145–55.

92 *Perachora* 2, 433ff.; Boardman, *Greek Emporio* (1967) 211; Boardman and Hayes, *Tocra* 1 (1966) 163; 2 (1973) 89, for references and dating.

93 Boardman, *Island Gems* (1963) 154f. and above, n. 88. *JHS* 68 (1948) pl. 6c, d; the closest parallel is Phrygian.

94 D. G. Hogarth, *Excavations at Ephesus* (1908) pls. 21–6; P. Jacobsthal, *JHS* 71 (1951) pls. 34–6; Akurgal, *Kunst Anatoliens* (1961) figs. 154–61, 165–73; G. M. A. Richter, *Korai* (1968) figs. 257–62. Compare the lyre-fitting in Berlin, *Jb. Berl. Mus.* 7 (1965) 125ff.; Boardman, *GSAP* fig. 53.

95 Boardman, *Greek Emporio* (1967) pl. 96. 596.

96 Akurgal, *Kunst Anatoliens* (1961) figs. 140–2.

97 *Perachora* 2, pl. 173. A 9; Boardman, *GSAP* fig. 51.

98 *ADelt* 22 (1967) Chr. 364, pl. 272. I am indebted to Professor Dontas for permission to illustrate this.

99 P. Amandry, *Syria* 24 (1944/5) pls. 10–11; F. Salviat,

BCH 86 (1962) 105; Boardman, op. cit., fig. 52. K. Schefold, *AA* 1970, 574ff., proposing an improbably early date.

100 Detailed references in the following notes, but there are also important survey essays: Amandry, *Ét. d'Arch. Class.* 1 (1955/6) 3ff.; *Syria* 35 (1958) 73ff.

101 Herrmann, *JdI* 81 (1966) 79ff.; Amandry, op. cit. and *Gnomon* 1969, 798f.; R. S. Young, *JNES* 26 (1967) 145–54; R. V. Nicholls, *ARepts* 1970/1 74f.; Barnett in *Vorderasiatische Archäologie* (Studien ... Moortgat, 1964) 21ff.

102 J. Bouzek, *Památky arch.* 65 (1974) 278–341 and in *European Community in Later Prehistory* (Studies ... Hawkes, 1971) 77–104; *IX. Congr. Int. Arch. Class.* (1971) 89ff. And cf. U. Jantzen, *Samos* 8 (1972) 80ff. (pl. 81 = our *Fig. 40*); Herrmann, *JdI* 83 (1968) 31ff. For the Persian role see now Muscarella, *J. Anc. N. East Soc. Col. Univ.* 9 (1977) 31ff.

103 The fullest study in Herrmann, *Kessel* (see n. 78). Cyprus, with sirens and griffins: Karageorghis, *Salamis* 3 (1973) 97ff. (our *Fig. 47*). Also O. Muscarella in *Art and Technology* (M.I.T., 1970) 109–28; M. Weber, *AM* 89 (1974) 27ff.; H. Kyrieleis, *Marburger Winckelmann-Programm* 1966, 1ff.

104 Amandry in *Aegean and the Near East* (Studies ... Goldman, 1956) 239ff. (our *Fig. 42* = pl. 28, 44 = pl. 29. 2) and *Syria* 35 (1958) 73ff.; U. Liepmann, *JdI* 83 (1968) 39ff.; Muscarella, *Met. Mus. J.* 1 (1968) 7ff.; Herrmann, *Kessel* 114ff. (our *Fig. 43* = pl. 55); *Samos* 8, 76ff. H. Kyrieleis, *AM* 92 (1977) 71ff., points out the distinguishing features of the Greek protomes.

105 Herrmann, *Kessel* 131ff.

106 Herrmann, *Kessel* 153ff. *Fouilles de Delphes* 5 (1969) 95ff. *Samos* 8, 63. There are important reviews of this volume, often cited in later notes, by Herrmann in *Gnomon* 1975, 392ff., by Muscarella in *AJA* 77 (1973) 236f. Cf. *ADelt* 20 (1965) Chr. pl. 503 (Macedonia).

107 Herrmann, *Kessel* 1–17. A clay copy (?) Athenian Agora 8 (1962) pl. 23. 402.

108 Herrmann, *Kessel*, and see n. 103.

109 Jantzen, *Griechische Greifenkessel* (1955) for the Samos series; and *AM* 73 (1958) 26ff.; 83 (1968) pl. 113. 4, 5 (mould); *AA* 1966, 123ff. *BCH* 96 (1972) 7–11 for an example attached to a rod tripod. *Klio* 52 (1970) 149ff. (Miletus). Cf. a stone example from Asia Minor, *Münzen und Medaillen Auktion* 40 (1969) no. 162 and the Samothrace 'throne', Boardman, *GSAP* fig. 264.

110 H. Luschey, *Die Phiale* (1939); F. Poulsen, *Der Orient* (1912) ch. 3 (figs. 12, 13 = our *Fig. 48*); *Olympia* 4, pl. 52; *Fouilles de Delphes* 5 (1969) pl. 18; A. de Ridder, *Bronzes de l'Acropole* (1896) no. 218; Kunze, *Kret. Bronzerel.* (1931) 159; *Perachora* 1, 148ff.; *AM* 83 (1968) pl. 117 (Samos); Boardman, *Greek Emporio* (1967) 158; Boardman and Hayes, *Tocra* 1 (1966) 158. For the famous series from Nimrud see now Barnett, *Riv. Stud. Fenici* 2 (1974) 11ff. (p. 15 for their kin in Greece). Phoenician – W. Culican, *Syria* 47 (1970) 65ff. Cypriot – Gjerstad, *Opusc. Arch.* 4 (1946) 1ff. Nicholls, see n. 101. An inscribed Carian phiale of Persian type, H. Jucker and M. Meier, *Mus. Helv.* 35 (1978) 104ff.

111 Luschey, op. cit.; *Perachora* 2, 80; Boardman, *Rept. Dept. Ant. Cyprus* 1968, 14f.

112 Luschey, *AA* 1938, 760ff.; Beazley, *ARV* 17, no. 18.

113 Dunbabin, *BSA* 46 (1951) 61ff.

114 K. Tuchelt, *Tiergefässe in Kopf- und Protomen-gestalt (Ist. Forsch. 22*, 1962).

115 Young, *AJA* 62 (1966) 139, pl. (= our *Fig. 51*); *Samos* 8, 74; *AM* 83 (1968) pl. 121.

116 H. Hoffmann, *Attic red-figured rhyta* (1962) and *AntK* 4 (1961) 21ff.

117 Boardman, *Greek Emporio* (1967) 224.

118 Boardman, *JHS* 85 (1965) 13f.

119 *Olympia Bericht* 5 (1956) 81–4; *ADelt* 17 (1961–2) Chr. 115, 129, 130; *Ist. Mitt.* 18 (1968) 149ff. (Miletus).

120 Herrmann, *Kessel* pl. 76; K. Kubler, *Kerameikos* 6.2, 396ff., pls. 123–5.

121 *Samos* 8, 56–8, 70ff. (pl. 51 = our *Fig. 54*); J. Börker-Klähn, *Baghdad. Mitt.* 6 (1973) 4ff.; Babylonian bronzes *JdI* 94 (1979) 32ff. Cf also Kyrieleis, *AA* 1969, 166ff. for an eastern bronze in London from Samos.

122 *Samos* 8, 43ff.
123 Boardman, *CCO* 118–20. U. Naumann, *Submin. u. Protogeom. Bronzeplastik auf Kreta* (1976) raises the date of some comparable pieces, perhaps rightly.
124 *Samos* 8, 58–62 (pl. 53 = our *Fig.* 55); *RA* 1933, 147 (Eretria); *Ist. Mitt.* 7 (1957) 126ff. (Miletus); Barnett, op. cit. (n. 101) 21ff.
125 *Samos* 8, 64f. for imported Syrian examples. H. A. Potratz, *Pferdetrensen des alten Orient* (1966).
126 *Baghad. Mitt.* 6 (1973) 51ff., pls. 25. 2, 26.
127 Herrmann, *JdI* 83 (1968) 1ff., and other bronzes of Luristan type. *Samos* 8, 74f.; cf. Boardman, *BSA* 57 (1962) 30. P. R. S. Moorey, *Iran* 12 (1974) 190ff.
128 On the technique, *Proc. Preh. Soc.* 37 (1971) 167ff. Late Bronze Age Cypriot ivory: Karageorghis, *Kition* (1976) pl. 35, and many later ivories, as from Nimrud, as well as on Greek ivories as at Sparta. Submyc. fibula, *JdI* 77 (1962) 87, fig. 5. 9 and cf. *BCH* 94 (1970) 1029, fig. 300 (Vitsa Zagoriou); K. de Vries, *AJA* 75 (1971) 99; Jacobsthal, *Greek Pins* (1956) 209ff. Dr Moorey tells me of N.W. Persian evidence for the technique on metalwork, but not closely datable.
129 Boardman, *CCO* 46–8. Many recently found examples from Kato Syme, e.g. *ARepts* 1972/3, 30; 1974/5, 28; A. Lebessi, *PAE* 1972, pls. 191–4; 1973, pls. 189, 192; 1974, pl. 167; *Expedition* 18 (1976) 2ff.
130 Snodgrass, *EGAW* 194f.
131 *Hesperia* 37 (1968) pl. 33; *BCH* 92 (1968) 737f.; Boardman, *Greek Gems and Finger Rings* (1970) 108–10.
132 Boardman, *Island Gems* (1963); op. cit. (n. 143) last n., 111ff.
133 *Perachora* 2, 461ff. Early arrivals at Eleusis, Isis grave, *AE* 1898, pl. 6; Lefkandi, *Archaeology* 25 (1972) 19; *Lefkandi* 1, PLS. 233e, 235c–e.
134 J. Boardman and G. Buchner, *JdI* 81 (1966) 1ff. (our *Fig.* 57 = nos. 5, 14, 23); Boardman, *Intaglios and Rings* (1975) 112; *Lefkandi* 1, pl. 67u.
135 Boardman, *Archaic Greek Gems* (1968) 20–2.
136 *Olympia* 4, 187; *AA* 1965, 825ff. (Samos); *BCH* 71/2 (1947/8) 240ff., fig. 39 (Delos); cf. Boardman, *Island Gems* (1963) 111.
137 Boardman, *Archaic Greek Gems* (1968) chs. 1, 2; op. cit., n. 131, ch. 4.
138 Boardman, *AntK* 10 (1967) 3ff.; op. cit. (n. 131) 154–7.
139 C. Blinkenberg, *Lindiaka* 2 (1926) 5ff.; Amandry, *Syria* 35 (1968) 96ff.; S. Stucchi, *Boll. d'Arte* 44 (1959) 158ff. R. A. Stucky, *Engraved Tridacna Shells* (*Dédalo* 19; São Paulo 1974) – the fullest study (our *Fig.* 58 = no. 68). Add – Bozra – *Arch. in the Levant* (Essays K. Kenyon, 1978) 167, fig. 4a; O. Rubensohn, *Das Delion von Paros* (1962) 76; Etruria – *AJA* 65 (1961) 385. Cf. R. Amiran and Y. Aharoni, *Ancient Arad* (1967) 24, fig. 17 (bowl). For related palettes – C. Bennett, *Antiquity* 41 (1967) 197ff.; Culican, *PEQ* 1970, 65ff.
140 Boardman, *Greek Emporio* (1967) 243 and references.
141 *Perachora* 2, 525f.; found on various Greek sites and apparently not from Sicilian beds, being rare in the west in this period.
142 E. J. Peltenburg, *Levant* 1 (1969) 73ff. (our *Fig.* 59 = IA. 24); adding *AM* 83 (1968) 301 (Samos); *Xanthos* 4, no. 149; Rhodes 11051 (from Koukia).
143 H. Walter, *AM* 74 (1959) Beil. 115–17; ibid., 70ff. for the type in ivory and stone and Freyer-Schauenburg, op. cit. (n. 85) 98–103; See also n. 82, and Stucky, *Berytus* 20 (1971) 11ff; R. M. Boehmer, *Die Kleinfunde von Boğazköy* (1972) 211f. *BCH* 96 (1972) 12f. for a bronze variant from Kyme.
144 C. Davaras, *Die Statue aus Astritsi* (1972) 12, 28; Boardman, *GSAP* fig. 15. Our *Fig.* 61 = *Fortetsa* no. 1568.
145 Boardman, *GSAP* 14, figs. 31, 32.
146 Ibid., 25f., figs. 74–8; F. W. Hamdorf, *AM* 89 (1974) 47ff.; E. Paribeni, *ASMG* 9/10 (1968/9) 61ff.; Selinus; Moorey, *Levant* 5 (1973) 89f. for some eastern parallels, and in Cyprus, *AA* 1978, 218.
147 G. Schmidt, *Samos* 7 (1968) esp. 117f., favouring a Cypriot origin for several types previously regarded as Greek imitations. Our *Fig.* 63 = Richter, *Kouroi* no. 27.
148 B. Lewe, *Studien zur archaischen kyprischen Plastik* (1975) 25–30.
149 *Samos* 11 (1974) no. 76.
150 Boardman, *GSAP* 69f., figs. 82–4.
151 Gold was available in Greece from Bronze Age sites and tombs as well as the ground. Silver may have been refined in Argos again by 900: P. Courbin, *Études arch.* (1963) 98ff.; and little later in Attica, Coldstream, *GG* 70f.
152 D. Ohly, *Griechische Goldbleche* (1953) (our *Figs.* 65, 66 = A11, A20); Higgins, *BSA* 64 (1969) 147, 152f.; *AAA* 5 (1972) 170ff. (Kynosarges, *BCH* 97 (1973) 266f.); *AntK* 12 (1969) pl. 36. 4 (Eretria); *AJA* 74 (1970) 37ff. (earring pendants). Related material from Skyros (*BCH* 99 (1975) 365ff.) may derive from Euboean studios; cf. the orientalizing band, C. Bérard, *Eretria* 3 (1970) 36ff. For impressed gold plaques from Rhodes see now R. Laffineur, *L'Orfèvrerie Rhodienne* (1978).
153 *Lefkandi* 1, pls. 171, 231d.
154 C. Kardara, *AJA* 65 (1961) 62–4.
155 Higgins, *Greek and Roman Jewellery* (1961) ch. 11; E. Karydi, *AA* 1964, 266ff.
156 D. B. Harden, *Arch. J.* 125 (1969) 46ff.; Freyer-Schauenburg, *Anadolu* 17 (1973) 141ff. (finds at Pitane; 166ff., origins, etc.). Phoenician glass head-amulets, published as from an eighth century context in Athens (*Hesperia* Suppl. 8 (1949) 427ff. and often cited, are now seen to be fourth century or later (E. Haevernick in *Festschrift von Lücken* (1968) 647ff.).
157 Boardman, *Greek Emporio* (1967) 202.
158 *Artemis Orthia* (1929) ch. 9. Many have been found in recent British excavations at the Menelaion. Cf. Boehmer, op. cit. (n. 143) 164 (our *Fig.* 69 = no. 1707). K. Emre, *Anatolian Lead Figurines and their Moulds* (1971).
159 H. Möbius, *AA* 1941, 1ff. and in *Festschrift W. Eilers* (1967) 449ff.; *Studia Varia* (1967) 14ff. Add *EADélos* 18, pl. 101. 893.
160 P. J. Riis, *Berytus* 9 (1949) 69ff. and *Mél. Univ. St. Joseph* 37 (1961) 193ff.; W. Albright, *Mél. Dussaud* 1 (1939) 107ff.
161 Dunbabin, *Greeks and their Eastern Neighbours* (1957) 37; Boardman, *GSAP* figs. 23, 24, cf. 26, 27 (= our *Figs.* 72, 73, 74).
162 J. Schäfer, *Studien zu den geiechischen Reliefpithoi* (1957); M. E. Caskey, *AJA* 80 (1976) 19ff.
163 Early examples: Crete – *BSA* 57 (1962) 31f.; 68 (1973) pl. 28. 112. Cf. Eretria – *ARepts* 1970/1, 7, fig. 7; Ischia – Boardman, *Greek Gems and Finger Rings* (1970) 113, fig. 166; Nimrud – *JHS* 68 (1948) pl. 8g.
164 Boardman, *CCO* 108ff.
165 Boardman, *GSAP* 13ff. and see nn. 155, 162.
166 E.g., Boardman, *Greek Emporio* (1967) 186ff.; *Samos* 7 (1968).
167 *Artemis Orthia* (1929) pls. 47–62 (our *Fig.* 75 = pl. 61.1; *Fig.* 76 = Barnett in Eissfeldt, op. cit. (n. 63) pl. 1b); Boardman, *Archaic Greek Gems* (1968) 38, 43. *AM* 76 (1961) Beil. 22 (Samos); *PAE* 1965, pl. 227a (Thera). And see below, n. 180.
168 Coldstream, *GG* 68.
169 Coldstream in *Praktika I. Diethn. Kypr. Synedr.* 1 (1972) 15ff.; J. K. Brock, *Fortetsa* (1957) 190f., 217f.; *AAA* 4 (1971) 384ff.
170 Coldstream, *BICS* 16 (1969) 1ff., who argues for Phoenician settlement at Ialysos.
171 V. Karageorghis and L. Kahil, *AntK* 10 (1967) 133ff.
172 H. G. Buchholz, *JdI* 83 (1968) 58ff.
173 A. L. Oppenheimer, *JNES* 8 (1949) 172ff.; J. V. Canby, *Iraq* 33 (1971) 31ff.; J. Nick-Zissen, *AA* 1966, 576f.
174 J. L. Benson, *Horse, Man and Bird* (1970) for arguments in favour of Bronze Age inspiration. G. Ahlberg, *Fighting on Land and Sea in Greek Geometric Art* (1971) for eastern inspiration of fighting scenes.
175 H. Sackett, *BSA* 71 (1976) 123ff. (for the Knossos vase). For the subject – *ADelt* 22 (1967) Chr. pl. 87. 2 and *Münzen und Medaillen Auktion* 22 (1961) pl. 67. 204 (other gold bands). Cf. our *Fig.* 65; Schweitzer, op. cit. (n. 87) pls. 69–71; *CVA* Louvre 17, pls. 6. 1, 9. 5 (Boeotian) and the Idaean Cave Hunt Shield (*Fig.* 27b). Coldstream compares the relief scene on a Cypriot bronze stand (Catling, op. cit. (n. 10) 208, pl. 35), and a Late Cypriot cylinder.
176 H. Payne, *Necrocorinthia* (1931) ch. 7; H. Gabelmann,

Studien zum frühgr. Löwenbild (1965); Akurgal in *IX. Congr. Int. Class. Arch.* (1971) 5 ff, for a survey of lion and other animal figure borrowings. Muscarella, *Met. Mus. J.* 5 (1972), for possible Persian inspiration.

177 A. Dessenne, *Le Sphinx* (1957); F. Matz, *JdI* 65/66 (1950/1) 91ff.; H. Walter, *Antike und Abendland* 9 (1959) 63ff.; Boardman, *BSA* 56 (1961) 80 (helmets); N. Verdelis, *BCH* 75 (1951) 1ff.

178 I. Flagge, *Untersuchungen zur Bedeutung des Greifen* (1975); N. B. Reed, *Hesperia* 45 (1976) 365ff.

179 Dunbabin in *Studies ... D. M. Robinson* 2 (1953) 1164ff.; Boardman, *Island Gems* (1963) 55f. For our *Figs. 79, 80* see Dunbabin, *Greeks and their Eastern Neighbours* pl. 15.

180 Boardman, *Archaic Greek Gems* (1968) 37ff. It has nothing to do with Humbaba (ibid., nn. 49, 58f. and above, n. 167) as often alleged, but there are other bearded, horned eastern demons: Culican, *JNES* 35 (1976) 21ff. Our *Fig. 81* – cf. R. Moorey, *Iraq* 27 (1965) 35. *Fig. 82* = Payne, *Necrocorinthia* 80, fig. 23a.

181 K. Shepard, *The Fish-tailed Monster* (1940).

182 E. Spartz, *Das Wappenbild des Herrn und der Herrin* (1962).

183 P. Kahane, *AntK* 16 (1973) 114ff.; *BICS* 18 (1971) pl. 1b, c (= our *Fig. 83*); Boardman in Popham and Sackett, *Lefkandi* 1; Thasos – *BCH* 86 (1962) 100 (our *Fig. 84*), but not recognized. Aegina gold band, *BM Cat. Jewellery* pl. 14. 1218.

184 J. Carter, *BSA* 67 (1972) 25ff.; K. Fittschen, *Untersuch. zum Beginn der Sagendarstellungen* (1969); K. Schefold, *Myth and Legend in Early Greek Art* (1966).

185 G. Ahlberg, *Opusc. Athen.* 7 (1967) 177ff.; Boardman, *JHS* 86 (1966) 4f. (our *Fig. 85*); *AJA* 73 (1969) pl. 127. 1.

186 Schefold, op. cit., pl. 5a. On another leg of the vessel he carries an animal, recalling Herakles' role as saviour of flocks.

187 *BCH* 45 (1921) 384, fig. 45. Cf. Schweitzer, op. cit. (n. 87) pl. 181 (Carchemish).

188 E. g. Schweitzer, op. cit., pl. 77; cf. Boardman, *Intaglios and Rings* (1975) no. 210.

189 Boardman, *Island Gems* (1963) 69.

190 F. Hölscher, *Die Bedeutung archaischer Tierkampfbilder* (1972); Boardman, *Archaic Greek Gems* (1968) ch. 12 and *GSAP* 154f., figs. 190–2, cf. 203.

191 Barnett, *Syria* 34 (1957) 243ff.

192 C. Watzinger in *Genethliakon W. Schmid* (1929) 141ff.

193 Payne, *Necrocorinthia* (1931) ch. 10.

194 Jacobsthal, *Greek Pins* (1956) 185ff.

195 G. M. A. Richter, *Furniture of the Greeks, Etruscans and Romans* (1966). The folding stool, *diphros okladias*, is of eastern or Egyptian origin and appears in Greek art about 600.

196 Boardman, *Antiq. J.* 39 (1959) 212ff.; B. Wesenberg, *Kapitelle und Basen* (1971); P. Betancourt, *The Aeolic Style in Architecture* (1977).

197 Chian elements – Boardman, op. cit., 193ff.; *Greek Emporio* (1967) 76.

198 B. Fehr, *Orientalische und gr. Gelage* (1971); J. M. Dentzer, *RA* 1971, 215ff. Ashurbanipal, as Sardanapalos, later enjoyed a reputation with the Greeks for soft living. Our *Fig. 90* = Payne, *Necrocorinthia* pl. 27.

199 L. H. Jeffery, *LSAG* part 1 (our *Fig. 91* = 68f., pl. 1. 1), *AG* 25f. and *CAH* 3². 1, ch. 20; Coldstream, *GG* ch. 11. J. Naveh, *AJA* 77 (1973) 1ff., argues an earlier date for the adoption; also A. Demsky, *Tel Aviv* 4 (1977) 22f. Relevant essays in *PdP* 31 (1976).

200 Hdt. 5, 88; L. H. Jeffery and A. M. Davies, *Kadmos* 9 (1970) 118ff.; R. Willetts, *Civilization of Ancient Crete* (1977) 186f.; cf. G. P. & R. B. Edwards, *Kadmos* 13 (1974) 48ff.

201 Boardman, *ABFH* 12; *ARFH* 9f.

202 *BSA* 57 (1962) 126f.

203 C. W. Blegen, *Troy* 4 (1958) 255ff.; Coldstream, *GGP* 376f.; J. M. Cook, *The Troad* (1973) 101.

204 The site at Buruncuk: E. Boehlau and K. Schefold, *Larisa am Hermos* 1–3 (1940–2). Cf. J. M. Cook, *BSA* 53/4 (1958/9) 20; 63 (1968) 33f.

205 *AJA* 67 (1963) 189f.

206 K. Lehmann, *Samothrace, a Guide* (1975).

207 Cook, *The Troad* (1973) 246f.

208 Ibid., 360–3.

209 Gem – *Annuario* 15/16 (1942) 78, figs. 126–7. Ibid., for the Hephaistia cemetery. Protogeometric? – *JdI* 15 (1900) 52, fig. 110. J. A. S. Evans, *Class. Phil.* 58 (1963) 168ff. on Miltiades.

210 Hdt. 6. 137–40.

211 W. Brandenstein, *Die tyrrhen. Stele von Lemnos* (1934). M. Gras, in *Mélanges ... J. Heurgnon* (1976) 341ff., suggests that the stories of Etruscan pirates in the Aegean in the sixth century, based on Lemnos, should perhaps be taken literally and might account for the distribution of some sixth century Etruscan finds in the Aegean world. The idea is attractive but not yet verifiable.

212 Boardman, *Greek Emporio* (1967) 254f.

213 G. L. Huxley, *Early Ionians* (1966) 83f.

214 Ibid., 38.

215 H. Metzger, *Xanthos* 4 (1972) 188f.; *AJA* 80 (1976) 275.

216 For the site see reports in *Annuario* 39/40 (1961/2) and following. *ARepts* 1970/1, 46f. On the early pottery, Coldstream, *GG* 97.

217 P. Devambez and E. Haspels, *Le Sanctuaire de Sinuri* 2 (1959) pls. 23–4.

218 Y. Boysal, *Anadolu* 11 (1967) 63ff. (Turgut-Lagina); C. Ozgünel, *Belleten* 40 (1976) 3ff. (Dirmil); cf. *AA* 1977, 8ff. I cannot believe the 'Carian' inscription painted on a Late Geometric East Greek vase, in *Zur gr. Kunst* (Festschrift H. Bloesch, 1973) 74ff. Our *Fig. 93* = Charles Ede, 20. ix. 1976, nos. 34, 35.

219 Pollux 9. 83; Aristotle fr. 611, 37, Rose; Hdt. 1. 14. Cf. Huxley, *Gr. Rom. Byz. Stud.* 2 (1959) 83ff. on Midas and Greeks.

220 Mita and Sargon – J. N. Postgate, *Iraq* 35 (1973) 21ff.

221 In general on Phrygia see *CAH* 2². 2 (1975) ch. 30 (Barnett); 3². 2, ch. 34a (Mellink). Gordion excavations summarized – Young, *Proc. Amer. Phil. Soc.* 107 (1963) 348ff.; *Gordion, Guide to excavation and museum* (1975). J. Birmingham, *Anat. Stud.* 11 (1961) 185ff. on routes in Anatolia and distribution of objects in the Greek world.

222 *AJA* 64 (1960) pl. 60. 25c; Snodgrass, *EGAW* 26f.; *Dark Ages and Nomads* (ed., M. Mellink, 1964) pl. 20. 2.

223 Akurgal, *Phrygische Kunst* (1955; reviewed by Mellink, *AJA* 61 (1957) 392–5 – our *Fig. 94* = pl. 14a); *VIII. Congr. Int. Arch. Class.* (1965) 467ff. (cf. Amandry, ibid., 486f.); *Anatolia* 4 (1959) 115ff. (chronology); M. Riemschneider in *Gr. Vasen* (Rostock, 1969) 495ff. (handle rotelles); G. K. Sams, *Anat. Stud.* 24 (1974) 169ff., on the Syrian origin of Phrygian animal drawing.

224 Coldstream, *GGP* 378f.; *AJA* 63 (1959) pl. 65. 1.

225 Muscarella, *Phrygian Fibulae from Gordion* (1967: our *Fig. 95* = pl. 9. 47–8) and cf. *JNES* 26 (1967) 82ff., 30 (1971) 49ff.; *Samos* 8, 48f.; Boehmer, op. cit. (n. 143) 46ff.

226 Muscarella, op. cit., pl. 16. 83–4.

227 *Münzen und Medaillen List* 263 (1966) nos. 35, 36; *Ashmolean Visitors Rept.* 1970, pl. 12. 8. (= our *Fig. 96*).

228 Young, op. cit. (n. 221) 362–4; *Hesperia* 38 (1969) 252ff.; M. Lejeune, *Kadmos* 9 (1970) 51ff.; Muscarella, op. cit., 62f.; *CAH* 3². 2, ch. 34b (O. Masson).

229 *AJA* 62 (1958) 139, pl.

230 C. F. C. Hawkes and M. Smith, *Antiq. J.* 37 (1957) 171ff.; Boardman, *Greek Emporio* (1967) 224; Muscarella, op. cit., 60. *AM* 83 (1968) 260, fig. 10 (Samos, clay). Our *Fig. 97* = G. & A. Körte, *Gordion* (1904) 70.

231 Akurgal, *Phryg. Kunst* (1955) ch. 4; Birmingham, op. cit. (n. 221) 187ff.; Boardman, op. cit., last n., 129f.; *Samos* 8, 54f.; A. K. Knudsen, *Berytus* 15 (1964) 59ff. (Lydian clay copy); Young, *AJA* 62 (1958) pl. 25. 21, and op. cit. (n. 221) 361 (our *Fig. 98*); *AA* 1974, 64. Our *Fig. 99* = Boardman, *GSAP* fig. 88.

232 Boardman, *Anatolia* 6 (1961) 179ff., *Greek Emporio* (1967) 214ff. (fig. 140 = our *Fig. 101*) and *Anat. Stud.* 16 (1966) 193f. (= our *Fig. 102*; a comparable example was recently on the London market). *Ist. Mitt.* 13/14 (1963/4) pl. 31. 2–4 (Didyma); *Samos* 8, 49ff.; Boehmer, op. cit. (n. 143) 72f.; possibly, A. Furtwängler, *Aegina* pl. 117. 12. Cf. Barnett, *Anat. Stud.* 22 (1972) 173 (Urartian). Our *Fig. 100* = *AJA* 61 (1957) 327, pl. 92, fig. 23.

233 Assyrians and Mita, Mellink in *CAH* 3². 2, ch. 34a and in *Bossert Gedenkschrift* (1965) 317ff. Above, n. 219.
234 Cimmerian attacks well summarized in A. R. Burn, *Lyric Age of Greece* (1960) 100–6.
235 Snodgrass. *EGAW* 148ff.
236 Above, n. 231.
237 Akurgal, *Phryg. Kunst* (1955) 39f., 49f.; K. Bittel, *VIII. Congr. Int. Arch. Class.* (1965) pl. 118. 1–3 (Boğazköy).
238 Akurgal, op. cit., ch. 3; Å. Åkerström, *Die architektonischen Terrakotten Kleinasiens* (1966) 216ff.
239 E. Haspels, *Phrygie* 3 (1951) pls. 7–9 (Midas City; some late seventh century).
240 A. M. Mansel, *Anatolia* 3 (1958) pl. 1.
241 Haspels, op. cit., pl. 47.
242 *ARepts* 1959/60, 35.
243 Mellink (forthcoming); Boardman, *Greek Emporio* (1967) 26f., 203f., and cf. the gold diadem from Kelermes, our *Fig. 305*.
244 Boardman, *Antiq. J.* 39 (1959) 195f.; E. Langlotz, *Studien zur nordostgr. Kunst* (1975) 163; Akurgal, *Phryg. Kunst* (1955) pl. 44.
245 K. Bittel, *Antike Plastik* 2 (1963) 7ff.; Akurgal, *Kunst Anatoliens* (1961) figs. 55–60. Our *Fig. 107*=Boardman, *GSAP* fig. 87.
246 Langlotz, loc. cit.
247 Barnett in *Aegean and the Near East* 218f.
248 Hanfmann, *VIII. Congr. Int. Arch. Class.* (1965) 491ff. Her name on a Lydian vase, M. R. Gusmani, *Kadmos* 8 (1969) 158ff.
249 Annual reports on Sardis in *BASOR*, and Mellink annually in *AJA* 64 (1960) and following. Hanfmann, *Sardis und Lydien* (1960); *Letters from Sardis* (1972), with bibl.; *Sardis* 1 (1975, with J. C. Waldbaum); *From Croesus to Constantine* (1975). *CAH* 3². 2, ch. 34a (Mellink). Desborough, *GDA* 184.
250 Hipponax fr. 42 (West); Hdt. 1, 93; Hanfmann, *BASOR* 170 (1963) 52ff., 177 (1965) 27ff.; K. Schefold (ed.), *Die Griechen und ihre Nachbarn* (1967) 283.
251 Strabo 590.
252 Hdt. 1. 7–25.
253 Hdt. 1. 26–7.
254 L. H. Jeffery, *BCH* 51 (1956) 157ff.; Meiggs-Lewis, no. 8.
255 For the excavations, fortifications and sack of Old Smyrna see J. M. Cook and R. V. Nicholls, *BSA* 53/4 (1958/9) 1–137, and the same volume for finds of Corinthian and Attic pottery. For East Greek finds of the sixth century, *BSA* 60 (1965) 114ff. and 69 (1974) 55ff. Recent excavations, Akurgal, *Ancient Civilization and Ruins of Turkey* (1973) 119ff.
256 Above, n. 249.
257 D. L. Page, *Sappho and Alcaeus* (1955) 87ff. (fr. 96); 82ff. (fr. 16).
258 Akurgal, *Birth* 211 for pictures. Our *Fig. 111* = Akurgal, *Kunst Anatoliens* 15. Terpander and Lydian feasts, Pindar, fr. 125, Snell.
259 Summarized in Boardman, *AA* 1976, 284–6. Our *Fig. 112* = Beazley, *ARV* 588, 73; Boardman, *ARFH* fig. 334.
260 Gusmani, *Lydisches Wörterbuch* (1964); *CAH* 3². 2. ch. 34b (O. Masson).
261 C. H. Greenewalt, *Calif. Stud. Class. Arch.* 1 (1968) 139ff.; 3 (1970) 55ff.; 5 (1972) 113ff.; W. Schiering, *Berliner Museen* 18 (1968) 2ff. Aeolian styles – E. Walter-Karydi, *AntK* Beiheft 7 (1970). A number of apparently related vases which have reached the European market in recent years are probably modern.
262 *AJA* 74 (1970) pl. 43. 12 and cf. 80 (1976) 273 (in Pisidia), and *Anadolu* 18 (1974) 63ff., far to the north, south of Dascylium.
263 Greenewalt, *Cal. Stud. Class. Arch.* 1 (1968) 148 and refs.; cf. also *AA* 1968, 159f.; 1969, 341 (our *Fig. 114*); J. D. Beazley, *Paralipomena* (1971) 113 (q. v. for our *Fig. 116*; and there are other Attic). Our *Fig. 115* = Munich *CVA* 6, pl. 303. 1.
264 *JHS* 68 (1948) 23, fig. 20; Akurgal, *Kunst Anatoliens* pl. 7 a, b; *Iliad* 4, 141f. for Lydian (Maionian) and Carian ivory-workers (women).
265 Hanfmann, *RA* 1976, 35ff.
266 *BCH* 3 (1879) pls. 4, 5; Higgins, *Greek and Roman*

Jewellery (1961) 110. New finds of Lydian work in precious metal, A. Greifenhagen, *AntK* 6 (1963) 13ff.
267 Hdt. 1. 14, 25.
268 Page, *Sappho and Alcaeus* (1955) 226ff. (fr. D 11).
269 Hdt. 1. 50–4.
270 Hdt. 1. 92; *BM Cat. Sculpture* 1. 1 (1928) 38f.
271 Hdt. 1. 30–3, 74–5.
272 Xenophon, *Hell.* 3. 1. 7.; *Kyrop.* 7. 1. 45; *BSA* 53/4 (1958/9) 20, n. 47.
273 Aelian, *VH* 3. 26; Polyainos 6. 50.
274 Boardman, *GSAP* fig. 107.
275 Hdt. 6. 125.
276 Hdt. 1. 69–70; 3. 48.
277 E. S. G. Robinson, *Num. Chron.* 16 (1956) 1ff.; Kraay-Hirmer, 354; Kraay, 20ff., (and *Gnomon* 1978, 211ff.) against a recently proposed early date for the Ephesus finds: L. Weidauer, *Typos* 1 (1975). C. Starr, *Economic and Social Growth of Early Greece* (1977) 108ff.
278 Jacobsthal, *JHS* 71 (1951) 85ff.; Robinson, ibid., 156ff. on the coins.
279 Hanfmann and Waldbaum in *Near eastern Archaeology in the 20th. cent.* (Essays ... N. Glueck, 1970) 310ff.; Hanfmann, *Letters from Sardis* (1972) 228–37, 249. R. M. Cook, *Historia* 7 (1958) 257ff.
280 Kraay and Weidauer, opp. citt. (n. 277); *Ashmolean Visitors Rept.* 1968, 44; M. Thompson, *Museum Notes* 12 (1966) 1ff.
281 Hdt. 1. 94. Our *Fig. 118* = Kraay, 23, pl. 3. 55.
282 Hdt. 1. 76–86, 162–70.
283 Boardman, *Antiq. J.* 39 (1959) 200–2.
284 Hdt. 1. 171.
285 A good account of Samos in Jeffery, *AG* 214ff.
286 Hdt. 1. 135.
287 Hdt. 3. 129–37 (Demokedes).
288 C. Nylander, *Ionians in Pasargadae* (1970) 14f.; W. Hinz, *JNES* 9 (1950) 1–7 (text).
289 Pliny, *NH* 34. 68.
290 Nylander, op. cit. 91–102; D. Stronach, *Iran* 2 (1964) 22ff. and 9 (1971) 155ff. (rosette), *Pasargadae* 1 (1978) 24ff. (our *Fig. 119* = pl. 22); W. Kleiss, *AA* 1971, 157ff.; cf. Åkerström, op. cit. (n. 238) 52ff.
291 Nylander, op. cit. 103–10, 139–42 (rosettes), 53–6 (chisel); and *AJA* 69 (1965) 49ff. (masonry techniques); Stronach, *Pasargadae* 1, 99f. (chisel).
292 Nylander, op. cit. (n. 288) notes 72, 211, 379; Stronach, *Pasargadae* 1, 21f. At Persepolis, R. Nicholls and M. Roaf, *Iran* 15 (1977) 149f.
293 *AJA* 76 (1972) 183; Hanfmann, *From Croesus to Constantine* (1975) 11; Nylander, *Proc. 2 Symp. Arch. Res. Iran* (1974).
294 Nylander, op. cit. (n. 288) 121–38; A. Farkas, *Achaemenid Sculpture* (1974). Our *Fig. 120* = *Pasargadae* 1, pl. 82c, d.
295 Frankfort, *Art and Arch. of the Ancient Orient* (1954) 215–25.
296 Richter, *AJA* 50 (1946) 15–30. For the panel see Roaf and Boardman, *JHS* 100 (1980).
297 Above, n. 62.
298 E. g., *Mem. Del. Perse* 1 (1900) 79; *Mem. Miss. Iran* 30 (1947) 75, 80.
299 Hdt. 1. 171; 5. 26.
300 Akurgal, *Gr. Reliefs des VI Jdts. aus Lykien* (1941); *Xanthos* 1 (1958) 37ff., 2 (1963) 49ff. Robertson, *HGA* 200f. In general on Xanthos, Metzger and Demargne in *RE* s. v. 'Xanthos'.
301 Mellink annual reports on Excavations at Elmali in *AJA* 74 (1970) and following; *Mél. Mansel* (1974) 537ff.; *RA* 1976, 21ff. Our *Fig. 122* = *AJA* 77 (1973) pls. 43–4.
302 *Xanthos* 4, 192ff. Cf. J. Mellaart, *Belleten* 19 (1955) 115ff. on Iron Age pottery, including Greek, in southern Anatolia.
303 Beazley, *Some Attic Vases in the Cyprus Museum* (1948) 33; *Attic Black-figure Vase-painters* (1956) 441; Gjerstad, op. cit. (n. 27; 1977) nos. 490, 492–4.
304 Ionic revolt: Jeffery, *AG* 219ff.
305 F. G. Maier, *Chiron* 2 (1972) 24ff., and *Alt-Paphos* 1 (1977).
306 Hdt. 6. 101, 119; F. Grosso, *Riv. Fil.* 36 (1958) 350ff.; *Anth. Pal.* 7, 259.

307 Strabo 517–8, 634; Plut., *Mor.* 557b.
308 Hdt. 6. 20.
309 Hdt. 6. 9, 32.
310 *Olympia Bericht* 7 (1961) 129ff.; Herrmann, *Olympia* (1972) pl. 32b. The helmet is of Assyrian type.
311 G. Goossens, *Nouvelle Clio* 1/2 (1949/50) 34f.
312 A. Rehm, *Didyma* 2 (1958) 6f., no. 7; Jeffery, *LSAG* 334.
313 Jantzen, *Gr. Greifenkessel* (1955) no. 142.
314 Schmidt, *Persepolis* 2, pls. 38–9.
315 Ibid., pl. 31. 1.
316 Athenaeus 514f; Pliny, *NH* 33. 51.
317 O. Broneer, *Univ. Cal. Publ.* 1 (1929) 305ff.; D. B. Thompson in *Aegean and the Near East* 281ff.; A. W. Lawrence, *JHS* 71 (1951) 111ff.; H. von Gall in *Festschrift F. Brommer* (1977) 119ff.
318 Boardman, *Iran* 8 (1970) 19ff. Our *Fig. 126* = no. 6.
319 Akurgal, *Iranica Antiqua* 6 (1966) 147ff.; J. Borchhardt, *Ist. Mitt.* 18 (1968) 161ff. (our *Fig. 127* = 192ff., no. 2); P. Bernard, *RA* 1969, 17ff.; Metzger, *Ant. Class.* 40 (1971) 505ff.; H. Möbius, *AA* 1971, 442ff.
320 Boardman, *Greek Gems and Finger Rings* (1970) ch. 6; *Intaglios and Rings* (1975) 29ff.
321 Kraay-Hirmer, fig. 618.
322 Above, n. 116. On the choice of Attic pottery for export to the Persian empire in the fifth century see K. de Vries, *AJA* 81 (1977) 544ff.
323 An Athenian mission had in fact offered submission ('earth and water') to the Persians at Sardis in 507, but were disgraced when they returned: Hdt. 5. 73; cf. L. L. Orlin in *Michigan Oriental Studies . . . George C. Cameron* (1976) 255ff.

4 The Greeks in Egypt

General Bibliography

Austin, for a good general study; *CAH* 3². 1, ch. 13; 3². 2, chs. 35, 36a (Braun).
Bernard, A., *Le Delta Égyptien d'après les textes grecs* (1970)
Cook, R. M., *JHS* 57 (1937) on Greek finds in Egypt.
Drioton, E. and Vandier, J., *L'Égypte* (1952–69)
Gardiner, A., *Egypt of the Pharaohs* (1961) chs. 12, 13
Kienitz, F. K., *Die politische Geschichte Ägyptens* (1953)
Lloyd, A. B., *Herodotus Book II, an Introduction* (1975); and *Herodotus Book II, Commentaries 1–98* (1976)

1 *CAH* 2³. 2, 182f.; Lloyd, *Introduction* ch. 1.
2 N. K. Sandars, *The Sea Peoples* (1978).
3 References in Austin, 50f. A useful earlier survey in J. Pendlebury, *Aegyptiaca* (1930) and cf. B. Porter and R. Moss, *Topographical Bibliography* 7 (1951) 401ff. R. Brown, *Provisional Cat. of and Commentary on Eg. and Egyptianising Artefacts* (Diss., 1975).
4 V. Webb, *Levant* 4 (1972) 150 ff., and *Archaic Greek Faience* (1978). A glazed pot may be identified in Athens in the second quarter of the seventh century: E. Brann, *Athenian Agora* 8 (1962) 58, no. 287 (where too the suggestion that a metal one is depicted on a late Geometric Theran vase).
5 S. Bosticco, *PdP* 12 (1957) 218, no. 102; Coldstream, *GGP* 316, *GG* 229; H. Hencken, *Tarquinia, Villanovans and Etruscans* (1968) 366f.
6 *Perachora* 1, pl. 46.
7 *AJA* 43 (1939) 437f., fig. 24; and cf. a Horus from the Athens Acropolis, Pendlebury, op. cit. (n. 3) pl. 4. 159; and a statuette from Tegea, *BCH* 45 (1921) 358f., fig. 18. 57. The situla from Pherae in Thessaly (Pendlebury, op. cit. (n. 3) pl. 3. 227) may be of much later date, R. V. Nicholls informs me.
8 G. Roeder, *Ägyptische Bronzefiguren* (1956) 320, 322; *Clara Rhodos* 6/7 (1932/3) 345 and pl. 13 (XI. 19); cf. C. Blinkenberg, *Lindos* 1 (1931) no. 800 (situla).
9 *Ist. Mitt.* 7 (1957) pl. 40. 2. (The piece compared in *Fig. 130* is Roeder, op. cit., pl. 57e.)
10 Boardman, *Greek Emporio* (1967) 227.
11 Boardman, *CCO* 152. Culican studies Phoenician versions in *Rev. de la Univ. Complutense* 25 (1976) 83ff.

12 *Archaeology* 25 (1972) 18; *Lefkandi* 1, pls. 187 (33. 15), 243a–c.
13 *AM* 60/61 (1935–6) pl. 84A. 8; *BSA* 57 (1962) 30f. (Hathor plaque, possibly earlier; cf. *Rept. Dept. Ant. Cypr.* 1977, 83f., pl. 18).
14 D. Levi, *Annuario* 10–12 (1927–9) 240, 461, pl. 19; *Hesperia* 14 (1945) pl. 25; Boardman, *CCO* 62 and *BSA* 57 (1962) 33f.
15 *Samos* 8, 5ff. (our *Fig. 133* = pl. 15. 2, 3); *AM* 68 (1953) 127ff., 74 (1959) 35ff., 83 (1968) 292f.; *AA* 1964, 81f., 228ff.; 1965, 439; B. Freyer-Schauenburg, *Elfenbeine aus dem samischen Heraion* (1966) 111ff.
16 On Herodotus in Egypt, T. S. Brown, *Amer. J. Phil.* 86 (1965) 60ff.; Lloyd, *Introduction* ch. 2.
17 Hdt. 2. 152–4; Austin, ch. 2; Lloyd, *Introduction* 14ff.
18 Diodorus 1. 67.
19 Gardiner, *Egypt of the Pharaohs* 353; Lloyd, *Introduction* 14ff.
20 Hdt. 2. 159.
21 Woolley, *Carchemish* 2 (1921) 123ff., House D.
22 Hdt. 2. 159; Lloyd, *J. Eg. Arch* 58 (1972) 268ff. and *Introduction* 32ff.
23 Hdt. 2. 161.
24 Gardiner, *Egypt of the Pharaohs* 359f.
25 A. Bernand and O. Masson, *Rev. Ét. Gr.* 70 (1957) 1ff.; Meiggs-Lewis, no. 7.
26 A. Rowe, *Ann. du Service* 38 (1938) 157ff.; Austin, 57; S. Pernigotti, *Stud. Class. e Or.* 17 (1968) 251ff.
27 Kienitz, op. cit., 43f.; J. H. Breasted, *Anc. Records of Egypt* 4 (1906) 506–8; Austin, 19f.
28 Hdt. 2. 163, 169; Gardiner, op. cit., 361f.
29 Ibid., 362.
30 Hdt. 2. 181, 154; Austin, 20f.
31 Hdt. 2. 178–9.
32 Strabo 801, 792.
33 W. M. F. Petrie, *Naukratis* i (1886); A. E. Gardner, *Naukratis* 2 (1888); D. G. Hogarth, *BSA* 5 (1898–9) 26ff., *JHS* 25 (1905) 105ff. General accounts – Austin, 22ff.; F. W. von Bissing, *Bull. Soc. Roy. Arch. Alex.* 39 (1951) 33ff., on the towns and buildings; R. M. Cook, *JHS* 57 (1937) 227ff. A. Bernand, *La Delta ég. d'après les textes grecs* 2 (1970) 575ff.
34 E. Gjerstad, *Acta Arch.* 30 (1959) 147ff.; Austin, 59f.
35 *Naukratis* 2, 11ff., 33ff.
36 C. Roebuck, *Class. Phil.* 45 (1950) 241f.
37 H. Hoffmann, *AJA* 57 (1953) 189ff.
38 *Naukratis* 1, 11ff.; *BM Cat. Sculpture* 1.1, 171ff.
39 A. Fairbanks, *Cat. Boston Vases* (1928) pl. 37. 340; H. Payne, *Necrocorinthia* (1931) 340 (the provenience is not wholly assured).
40 Op. cit. (n. 33).
41 Most of the pottery is in London but there are rich collections also in Cambridge, Oxford and Boston, as well as smaller ones in other museums. An attempt is being made to reassemble the evidence. The early publication was very summary and selective but there is useful illustration by E. M. Price in *JHS* 44 (1924) 180ff. The categories given above are defined by Cook, *GPP* and I confine myself to citing specific pieces or studies. Many East Greek fragments are assigned by E. Walter-Karydi in *Samos* 6.1 (1973) not altogether reliably. Clay analysis of samples is being undertaken and may offer some answers in time.
42 R. M. Cook, *BSA* 44 (1949) 154ff. on distribution; Boardman, *Greek Emporio* (1967) 119ff., 156ff. for main categories. Our *Fig. 139* = *Naukratis* 2, pl. 6.
43 This is argued by the writer in *BSA* 51 (1956) 55ff. Versions of the polychrome style are now known in the Aegean world, at Pitane, but not of the finest polychrome of Naucratis. Clay analysis suggests that, if there were Chian potters at Naucratis, they imported their clay from home – a practice attested in later periods of ceramic history and suggested in antiquity: Egyptian clay is unsuitable for fine-walled hard-fired wares. Our *Fig. 140* = Price, op. cit., pl. 6. 11, 15.
44 On the inscriptions, R. M. Cook and A. G. Woodhead in *BSA* 47 (1952) 159ff.; Boardman, *BSA* 51 (1956) 56ff.; Austin, 61f.
45 Also well represented elsewhere in Cyrenaica, Boardman and Hayes, *Tocra* 1 (1966) 57ff., 2 (1973) 24ff.

46 Boardman, *Greek Emporio* (1967) 168.
47 'Little Master' cups: E. Kunze, *AM* 59 (1934) 81ff.; *Samos* 6.1, pls. 49–53, 57, *passim*.
48 H. Prinz, *Funde aus Naukratis* (1906) 83.
49 V. Grace, *Hesperia* 40 (1971) 68f., 79f.
50 The standard treatment remains that by R. M. Cook in *BSA* 34 (1933–4) 1ff.
51 In *Samos* 6. 1 they are assigned to various centres. Clay analysis by the French at Dijon suggests Miletus as the source and this seems quite plausible.
52 R. M. Cook, *BSA* 47 (1952) 123ff. and *CVA* British Museum 8, 14ff.
53 Austin, 63f.; on the Cyrene heresy, E. A. Lane, *BSA* 34 (1933–4) 182ff.
54 J. D. Beazley and H. Payne, *JHS* 49 (1929) 253ff. Our *Fig. 142* is a crater fragment, probably by the Nessos Painter; *CVA* Toronto 1 (forthcoming).
55 Richter, *Kouroi* (1970) nos. 28, 59–61, 81–5 (84 = our *Fig. 143*).
56 See above, p. 74.
57 *Naukratis* 1, pl. 19; *BSA* 5 (1898–9) pl. 14; *JHS* 25 (1905) 127ff.
58 This production is studied in detail and with full illustration by V. Webb, *Archaic Greek Faience* (1978).
59 Ibid., pls. 1–11; our *Fig. 146* = no. 1.
60 Ibid., pls. 12–16.
61 Ibid., pls. 19–21.
62 Ibid., pl. 19. 845.
63 Ibid., pl. 19. 840.
64 Ibid., pl. 18. 763–779 (our *Fig. 150* = no. 766).
65 Boardman, *Archaic Greek Gems* (1968) 161.
66 *Naukratis* 1, 37, pl. 38 below.
67 Webb, op. cit., pl. 22.
68 *Naukratis* 1, 15.
69 See above, ch. 3, n. 139.
70 *Naukratis* 1, 41.
71 Ibid.
72 Austin, 35f.
73 W. M. F. Petrie, *Tanis* 2 (1888) pl. 36. 5.
74 O. Masson, *Rev. dePhil.* 36 (1962) 46ff.
75 J. G. Milne, *J. Eg. Arch.* 25 (1939) 177ff.; C. Roebuck, *Class. Phil.* 45 (1950) 236ff.; Austin, 37ff.; Lloyd, *Introduction* 30f.; H. Sutherland, *Amer. J. Phil.* 64 (1943) 143ff.
76 von Bissing, op. cit. (n. 33) 33ff. On Naukratis as an asylum town, D. van Berchem, *Mus. Helv.* 17 (1960) 26ff.
77 *BSA* 47 (1952) 161f.; 51 (1956) 59.
78 *Naukratis* 2, 65, pl. 7. 1, 21. 778; Hoffmann, op. cit. (n. 37); Boardman, *Antiquaries Journal* 39 (1959) 203f.
79 *Naukratis* 1, 55, pl. 33. 218; Hdt. 3. 4.
80 *JHS* 25 (1905) 116, no. 6.
81 *Naukratis* 2, 66, pl. 21. 798.
82 Hdt. 2. 134–5 (Rhodopis); Strabo 808 (Rhodopis = Doricha); D. L. Page, *Sappho and Alcaeus* (1955) 45ff. (Doricha); Jeffery, *LSAG* 102 (Rhodopis at Delphi); Ath. 596b, c (Rhodopis *not* Doricha).
83 Hdt. 2. 135; *BSA* 5 (1898–9) 56, no. 108.
84 Solon fr. 28 (West); Plutarch, *Solon* 26.
85 Strabo 37.
86 Petrie, *Tanis* 2 (1888); R. M. Cook, *JHS* 57 (1937) 229ff., *CVA* British Museum 8, 57ff.; Austin, 20, 56; Weinberg, op. cit. (ch. 3, n. 55) 15ff.
87 Hdt. 2. 30.
88 Cook, op. cit. (n. 86).
89 For situlae – *CVA British Museum* 8, 29ff.; our *Fig. 154* = pl. 1. 1; *Fig. 155* = pl. 2. 2. Clay analysis suggests, however, that the clay used may have been brought over from Rhodes. Samian jars, above, n. 49. Lesbian jar – Miss Grace refers me to London UC 19247.
90 I am indebted to Dr E. Oren for information about this site and photographs. The Greek Magdolos, Hdt. 2. 159; Jeremiah 44. 1.
91 Hdt. 2. 154. The pottery finds are not comprehensively published; see Austin, 2–20, 56f. Our *Fig. 157* = *Berytus* 11 (1955) pl. 22. 8 (*not* Naucratite). Also A. Swiderek, *Eos* 51 (1961) 55ff.
92 *J. Eg. Arch.* 56 (1970) pl. 10; *ARepts* 1970/1, 76. O. Masson, G. T. Martin and R. V. Nicholls, *Carian Inscriptions from North Saqqara and Buhen* (1979) no. 3.

93 Jeffery, *LSAG* 355, 358, no. 50; O. Masson, *Rev. d'Eg.* 29 (1977) 53ff.
94 K. Parlasca in *Wandlungen* (Fest. Homann-Wedeking, 1975) 57ff.
95 Ibid. pl. 10 d–f.
96 Masson, Martin and Nicholls, op. cit. (n. 92) 64ff.
97 See above, n. 92.
98 Parlasca, op. cit. (n. 94) pl. 10b, c.
99 C. C. Edgar, *Cat. Cairo Greek Sculpture* (1903) pl. 1. 27431.
100 Boardman, *Island Gems* (1963) 52, no. 185.
101 Jeffery, *LSAG* 355, 358, no. 49.
102 Jeffery, *LSAG* 314; Strabo 813; A. and E. Bernand, *Les inscriptions du Colosse de Memnon* (1960).
103 Boardman, *JHS* 78 (1958) 4ff. Clay analysis reveals a marked difference from that of the name vase of the Northampton Group, but overall similarity to that of Clazomenian black figure.
104 H. W. Parke, *The Oracles of Zeus* (1967) ch. 9; H. M. Schenke, *Das Altertum* 9 (1963) 72f.
105 A. Fakhry, *Siwa Oasis* (1944) 167.
106 Private, Switzerland.
107 *CVA* Oxford 2, IID pl. 4. 17.
108 Boston 21. 2286 (Beazley *ARV²* 772f., 1669; L. Kahil, *Rev. Arch.* 1972, 283). Paris CA 3825 (Beazley, *Paralipomena* 416; Kahil, op. cit., 271ff.).
109 O. Masson and J. Yoyotte, *Obj. phar. à ins. carienne* (1956); Masson, *Bull. Soc. Fr. Ég.* 56 (1969) 25ff. On Carian mercenaries, Austin, 17f.
110 Gjerstad, *Swed. Cypr. Exped.* 4. 2, 240ff.; Masson, *Inscr. Chypriotes* (1961) 353ff.
111 Hdt. 2. 41.
112 Hdt. 3. 1, 4, 11, 13, 25–6.
113 von Bissing, *Zeitschr. Deutsch. Morgenl. Gesellsch.* 84 (1930) 226ff., pl. 1; *Führer durch das Berliner äg. Museum* (1961) pl. 56.
114 J. M. Cook, *Gnomon* 1962, 823.
115 Hdt. 2. 180–2; 3. 47 (Sparta).
116 These are the subject of a forthcoming study by Andrée Gorton.
117 *Clara Rhodos* 6/7 (1932/3) 288; Jeffery, *LSAG* 348.
118 H. E. Angermeier, *Das Alabastron* (1936); K. Schauenburg, *JdI* 87 (1972) 259, with references. Our *Fig. 168* = *CVA* Oxford 2, IID pl. 1. 27.
119 P. Bruneau, *BCH* 86 (1962) 193ff.; S. Morenz in *Fest. Schweitzer* (1954) 87ff.; on Aesop and the east I. Trencsényi-Waldapfel, *Untersuch. zur Religionsgesch.* (1966) 181ff.
120 J. J. Coulton, *Greek Architects at Work* (1977) ch. 2.
121 Boardman, *GSAP* (1978) 162.
122 Boardman, *Antiquaries Journal* 39 (1959) 212ff.; Coulton, loc. cit.
123 *Annuario* 10/12 (1927/9) 187, 451; Boardman, op. cit., 211f.
124 B. Wesenberg, *Kapitelle und Basen* (1971) 43ff.
125 Boardman, *GSAP* 18ff.; B. S. Ridgway, *Archaic Style* (1977) ch. 2; K. Levin, *AJA* 63 (1964) 13ff.
126 E. Iversen, *Mitt. Inst. Kairo* 15 (1957) 134ff. An extreme study of Egyptian canons in Archaic kouroi by E. Guralnik in *Computers and Humanities* 10 (1976) 153ff. Our *Fig. 172* = Boardman, *GSAP* fig. 107.
127 Diodorus 1, 98, 5–9; Iversen, *J. Eg. Arch.* 54 (1968) 215ff.
128 Boardman, *GSAP* fig. 269; *Expl. Arch. Délos* 24 (1959).
129 K. Tuchelt, *Die arch. Sk. aus Didyma* (1970); Boardman, *GSAP* figs. 94–5.
130 Hdt. 2. 170.
131 N. Breitenstein, *Cat. Terracottas Danish Nat. Mus.* (1941) pl. 11. Cf. *Liverpool Annals* 10 (1924) pl. 23 (Sanam); the ivory find on the Athens Acropolis, *JHS* 68 (1948) 5, fig. 3; stone fragments on Samos, *AA* 1965, 845–8.
132 On the Spartan mirrors, T. Karagiorgha, *ADelt* 20 (1965) 96ff. Egyptian – Roeder, op. cit. (n. 8) 319f. and ivory counterparts found in Samos, Freyer-Schauenburg, op. cit. (n. 15) 111f.
133 W. L. Brown, *The Etruscan Lion* (1960) 119 and cf. 71f., 112. H. Gabelmann, *Stud. zum frühgr. Löwenbild* (1965) 69ff.
134 Gabelmann, op. cit., 84ff.; Boardman, *GSAP* fig. 270.

135 V. Webb, op. cit. (n. 58). A late Archaic relief faience vase with a very Greek subject, *BABesch* 46 (1971) 100ff.
136 See also V. Wilson, *Levant* 7 (1975) 77ff.
137 C. Blinkenberg, *Lindos* 1 (1931) 559ff. Our *Fig. 180* = Boardman and Hayes, *Tocra* 1, pl. 100. 48.
138 C. Blinkenberg, op. cit., nos. 1793–5 (our *Fig. 181* = no. 1795).
139 G. M. A. Richter, *Furniture of the Greeks, Etr. and Rom.* (1966) 17. Our *Fig. 182* = Boardman, *GSAP* 165, fig. 253.
140 Boardman, *GSAP* 165, fig. 253.
141 G. Mylonas, *Protoattike Amphoreus* (1957) 105, fig. 57d.
142 *Samos* 6. 1, pl. 46; Simon-Hirmer, pl. 35.
143 Above, n. 103.
144 B. A. Sparkes, *BABesch* 51 (1976) 47ff.
145 Boardman, 165, *ABFH* fig. 186.
146 Ibid. fig. 95.
147 Simon-Hirmer, pl. XV.
148 cf. F. Matz, *AA* 1921, 11ff.; W. Wrede, *AA* 1923/4, 11ff.; J. M. Hemelrijk, *Caeretan Hydriae* (forthcoming).
149 M. A. Littauer, *AJA* 72 (1968) 150ff.; our *Fig. 187* = Boardman, *ABFH* fig. 206.
150 M. T. Derchain-Urtel, *Stud. Altäg. Kultur* 1 (1974) 89ff. (I am indebted to Jody Maxmin for this reference.) Our *Fig. 188* = Boardman *ABFH* fig. 65.
151 A. Furtwängler and K. Reichhold, *Gr. Vasenmalerei* pl. 3; Boardman, *ABFH* fig. 46. 8; B. Freyer-Schauenburg in *Wandlungen* (Fest. Homann-Wedeking, 1975) 76ff.
152 *Arch. Rel. Wiss.* 12 (1909) 195; E. Haspels, *Attic Black-figured Lekythoi* (1936) 67f.; Beazley, *ABV* 470, 103.
153 F. M. Snowden, *Blacks in Antiquity* (1970). Our *Fig. 191* = Beazley, *ABV* 614.
154 W. C. McDermott, *The Ape in Antiquity* (1938).
155 K. Schauenburg, *BonnerJb.* 155/6 (1955/6) 59ff.; 162 (1962) 98ff. Our *Fig. 192* = *BSA* 60 (1965) 123f.
156 Boardman, *JHS* 78 (1958) 1ff. Our *Fig. 193* = Boardman, *ABFH* fig. 99.
157 S. Karouzou, *Amasis Painter* (1956) pl. 11 (our *Fig. 194*); Beazley, *ABV* 155, 64. Cf. above, n. 118.
158 Beazley, *ARV²* 267ff.; Boardman, *ARFH* fig. 208 (our *Fig. 195*).
159 Hdt. 4. 150–8.
160 Boardman, *BSA* 61 (1967) 149ff.
161 Hdt. 4. 186.
162 Hdt. 4. 159–67, 200–5.
163 R. G. Goodchild, *Cyrene and Apollonia* (1970) for a good general account. F. Chamoux, *Cyrène sous la monarchie des Battiades* (1953); H. Büsing in *Thiasos* (ed. T. Lorenz, 1978) 51ff. on the heroon of the founder.
164 D. White, *Expedition* 17. 4 (1975) 28ff.; *AJA* 79 (1975) 33ff.
165 J. Cassels, *BSR* 23 (1955) 1ff.; Kurtz-Boardman, 324–6.
166 E. Paribeni, *Cat. delle Sc. di Cirene* (1959); J. G. Pedley and D. White, *AJA* 75 (1971) 39ff.
167 *AM* 52 (1927) 53; Coldstream, *GGP* 214, n. 4.
168 *Africa Italiana* 4 (1931) pl. 3. 12 (cf. *BSA* 51 (1956) 61). The new excavations at the sanctuary of Demeter are the most rewarding source of early pottery.
169 *BSA* 63 (1968) 41 ff., and from the sanctuary of Demeter.
170 See above, ch. 3, n. 139.
171 Kraay-Hirmer, 38of.; Kraay, 296ff.
172 Hdt. 4. 169; Theophrastus, *Hist. Plant* 6. 3; Pliny, *N.H.* 22. 23; H. Schafer, *Rhein. Mus.* 95 (1952) 159ff.
173 M. Vickers and A. Bazama, *Libya Antiqua* 8 (1971) 149ff.
174 Boardman, *BSA* 61 (1967) 149ff.
175 Boardman and Hayes, *Tocra* 1 (1966), 2 (1973) and pp. 3–5 in the latter for a brief analysis of the pottery.
176 Boardman in *Libya in History* (ed. F. F. Gadallah, 1968) 89ff.
177 Hdt. 4. 168–99.
178 Simon-Hirmer, pls. 104–5; Chamoux, op. cit. (n. 163) pl. 1. 1–2.
179 H. W. Parke, *Oracles of Zeus* (1967) 202ff.
180 A. Fakhry, *Ann. du Service* 40 (1940) 779ff. and *Siwa Oasis* (1944); Parke, op. cit.
181 Fakhry, *Ann. du Service* 40 (1940) 793ff.; *Siwa Oasis* (1944) 140.
182 Hdt. 3. 26.

5 Italy, Sicily, and the West

General Bibliography

Dunbabin (a basic work, though dated, equally reliable on literature and archaeology); Morel (for recent work); *CAH* 3².3, ch. 38 (A. J. Graham); *ASSO*; Åkerström, *GSI*; Langlotz-Hirmer (art).
Bérard, J., *La Colonisation grecque* (1957; 1941 edition with bibliography of sites supplemented by Dunabin in *BSR* 18 (1950) 104ff.)
Nenci, G. and Vallet, G. (edd.), *Bibliografia Topografica* 1 (1977) – ; a new bibliography replacing Bérard's.
Bérard, J. *L'Expansion et la Colonisation grecque* (1960), useful summary of text evidence.
Brea, B., *Sicily before the Greeks* (1957)
Guido, M., *Sicily* (1967) and *South Italy* (1972); guides.
Kirsten, E., *Süditalienkunde* 1 (1975); detailed guide.
Richter, G. M. A., *Ancient Italy* (1955); art.
Popoli e Civiltá dell'Italia antica 1–3 (1974); review by Ridgway, *JRS* 66 (1976) 212ff.
Trendall, A. D. reports on S. Italy and Sicily – *ARepts* 1966/7, 29ff.; 1969/70, 32ff.; 1972/3, 33ff.
Ridgway, D., reports on central Italy and Etruria – *ARepts* 1967/8, 29ff.; 1973/4, 42ff.
Fredericksen, M., report on S. Italy and Sicily – *ARepts* 1976/7, 43ff.
Important periodicals with relevant material and reports are *NSc*, *Kokalos*, *ASMG*, *Convegni di Studi sulla M.G.*, and the French Centre Bérard in Naples is an important forum for discussion and publications. I have been economical in references to Greek colonies. The text evidence can be found in Dunbabin and Bérard and fuller accounts of the sites in Kirsten and the *Princeton Encyclopedia*. For western Greek temple architecture consult W. B. Dinsmoor, *Architecture of Ancient Greece* (1950); G. Gruben, *Die Tempel der Griechen* (1976)

1 G. Vallet and F. Villard, *BCH* 76 (1952) 289ff.; T. J. Dunbabin, *AE* 1953/4. 2, 247ff.; J. Ducat, *BCH* 86 (1962) 165ff.; Coldstream, *GGP* 322ff.
2 See below, nn. 12, 33.
3 Hdt. 4. 153, 156.
4 Strabo 278.
5 Strabo 257.
6 Hdt. 1. 163ff.
7 A. J. Graham, *Colony and Mother-city in Ancient Greece* (1964).
8 W. G. Forrest, *Historia* 6 (1957) 160ff. on Delphi and colonization, and in *CAH* 3². 2, ch. 39d (W. G. Forrest).
9 Boardman and Hayes, *Tocra* 1 (1966) 111ff. for a recent account.
10 Coldstream, *GGP* 195.
11 W. Taylour, *Myc Pottery in Italy* (1958); Desborough, *The Last Mycenaeans* (1964) ch. 9; *CAH* 2².2, 184f., 356; F. Biancofiore, *La Civ. Mic. nell'Italia merid.* (1967); E. Sjoqust, *Sicily and the Greeks* (1973) ch. 1. References in *ARepts* 1976/7, 64.
12 D. Ridgway and O. Dickinson, *BSA* 68 (1973) 191f.; Ridgway, *SE* 35 (1968) 311ff. and in *Greeks, Celts and Romans* (ed. C. F. C. Hawkes, 1973) 5ff., an important study; Coldstream, *GG* 223f. Cf. *ARepts* 1976/7, 44 (Capua), 56 (near Metapontum), 66f. (Sicily).
13 Ridgway, op. cit.; G. Buchner (the excavator), *Expedition* 8 (1966) 4ff.; in *Metropoli e Colonie di Magna Grecia* (Atti III Convegno, stud. M.G., 1964); *Dialoghi di Arch.* 3 (1969) 8 5ff.; *ARepts* 1970/1, 63ff.; *Cahiers J. Bérard* 2 (1975) 59ff. Coldstream, *GG* 225ff.
14 Ridgway, *Celts* (see n. 12), 24.
15 *RM* 60/61 (1953/4) 37ff.; *Opusc. Rom.* 4 (1962) 165ff. On Ischian vases Coldstream, *GG* 229f. and *BICS* 15 (1968) 86ff. Problems of distinguishing local from imported, Ridgway, *Papers in Italian Arch.* 1 (1978) 121ff.
16 *ARepts* 1970/1, 67; Jeffery, *AG* 64.
17 Jeffery, *LSAG* 235f.; H. Metzger, *Rev. Ét. Anc.* 67 (1965) 301ff.; Meiggs-Lewis, no. 1.
18 Boardman and Buchner, *JdI* 81 (1966) 1ff. There are several subsequent finds.

19 S. Bosticco, *PdP* 54 (1957) 215ff.; F. de Salvia, *Cahiers J. Bérard* 2 (1975) 87ff.
20 Ridgway, *Atti VIII Conv. Naz. Stud. Etr.* (1974) pl. 63a, and *Celts* (see n. 12) 14, fig. 2b.
21 *ARepts* 1976/7, 44; Buchner, *PdP* 33 (1978) 130ff.
22 Strabo 247. Buchner in *Cahiers J. Bérard* 2 (1975) 59ff. (revised in *The Italian Iron Age* (edd. D. and F. Ridgway, 1979) attributes much of the early jewellery in Cumae and Etruria to Euboean studios; an extreme view countered by F. W. von Hase, *Hamburger Beitr. Arch.* 5 (1975) 99ff.
23 Ridgway, *Celts* (see n. 12) 17ff. (our *Fig. 207* = fig. 4); op. cit. (n. 20) 289f.; Buchner, op. cit., last n. Answering R. M. Cook, *Historia* 11 (1962) 113f.; A. J. Graham, *JHS* 91 (1971) 43ff. On metal working J. Klein, *Expedition* 14 (1972) 34ff. and S. C. Bakhuizen, *Chalcis in Euboea* (1976) and *World Archaeology* 9 (1977) 220ff., who suggests that the Euboeans introduced an advanced iron technology to Italy.
24 The tombs were published in *Mon. Ant.* 13 (1903) 201ff., 22 (1913) 9ff. On recent work see W. Johannowsky, *Dialoghi di Arch.* 1 (1967) 159ff., 3 (1969) 31ff. and in *Cahiers J. Bérard* 2 (1975) 98ff.; Buchner in *I Campi Flegrei* (Convegno Lincei 33, 1977) 131ff.
25 See above, n. 12
26 *Mon. Ant.* 22 (1913) pl. 32. 1, 33.
27 P. Amandry, *Ét. d'arch. class.* 1 (1955/6) pl. 7.
28 C. A. Livadie in *Cahiers J. Bérard* 2 (1975) 53ff.; C. Bérard, *Eretria* 3 (1970); Buchner in *The Italian Iron Age* (see n. 22).
29 *ARepts* 1976/7, 68f.; P. Pelagatti, *BdA* 1956, 326ff.; 1964, 149ff.; 1972, 211ff. On the Chalcidian-Naxian role N. M. Kontoleon in *Europa* (Fest. E. Grumach, 1967) 180ff.
30 Thuc. 6. 2.
31 G. Rizza, *BdA* 1957, 63ff., including pottery in an unusual local seventh-century style; *Chron. di Arch.* 1 (1962) 1ff. On the Sicels at Leontinoi, *ARepts* 1976/7, 70; E. Sjoquist, *Sicily and the Greeks* (1973) 21ff.
32 *RM* 15 (1900) 87, fig. 30; H. Winnefeld, *Bronzebecken aus Leontini* (1899); cf. *Quad. Imerese* 1 (1972) 88, n. 84.
33 *ARepts* 1976/7, 66f. cf. G. Voza in *ASSO* 57ff.
34 G. Rizza, *BdA* 1960, 247ff.
35 G. Vallet, *Rhégion et Zancle* (1958).
36 B. Brea and M. Cavalier, *Il Castello di Lipari* (1958) pl. 21, and *Mylai* (1959); *Meligunis-Lipara* 2 (1965), sixth-century tombs.
37 Vallet, op. cit.
38 Ibid., pl. 5. 1.
39 At Canale. *Mon. Ant.* 31 (1926) 211ff.; Åkerström, *GSI* 37ff. (our *Fig. 210* = pl. 10. 5); Coldstream, *GG* 237f.
40 Dunbabin, 48ff.
41 Strabo 270. On Corinth and western colonising C. Roebuck, *Hesperia* 41 (1972) 111ff.; M.-P. Loicq-Berger, *Syracuse* (1967).
42 Dunbabin, 50–2, 60; *Mon. Ant.* 25 (1918) 353ff. for early finds.
43 Early finds – *ARepts* 1976/7, 64f.; *ASSO* 76ff.
44 Pelagatti, *Dialoghi di Arch.* 3 (1969) 141ff.; G. V. Gentili, *Palladio* 1967, 61ff.; *ASSO* 74ff.
45 Attic, Coldstream, *GGP* 78, no. 33; Cycladic, *BCH* 76 (1952) 332, fig. 7. Cf. Åkerström, *GSI* 35.
46 P. Arias, *BCH* 60 (1936) 144ff.; Vallet-Villard, *MEFRA* 68 (1956) 23. And cf. *SE* 42 (1974) pl. 87 (from Incoronata).
47 Cf. Dunbabin, 56, 93f.; R. van Compernolle, *Kokalos* 12 (1966) 75ff.
48 *Mon. Ant.* 25 (1918) 589ff., figs. 181, 195, 199; E. -L. Marangou, *Lak. Elfenbein-Schnitzereien* (1969) 199f.
49 *ASSO* 91, no. 310 and references. On the type, Beazley, *JHS* 60 (1940) 22ff.
50 Thuc. 6. 4.
51 For the Thapsos Class see Coldstream *GGP* 102–4 (our *Fig. 213* = pl. 20c). It appears to be Corinthian but of unusual technique, range of decoration and distribution. I had wondered whether it might in fact be Megarian (*Gnomon* 1970, 496; cf. Cook, *GPP* 24) but clay analysis has not been encouraging (Boardman and Schweizer, *BSA* 68 (1973) 278–80, and N. Bosana-Kourou, *Stele* (Eis mnemen N. Kontoleontos, 1978)

318ff.).
52 Vallet-Villard, *BCH* 76 (1952) 289ff.; Coldstream, *GGP* 324f.
53 Annual reports in *MEFRA. Megara Hyblaea* 2 (1964), the pottery; *ASSO* 161ff.
54 *MEFRA* 78 (1966) 281f.; *Megara Hyblaea* 2 (1964) 137ff.; *ASSO* pls. 53–4. Archaic kilns, Villard, *CRAI* 1952, 120f.; *Kokalos* 10/11 (1964/5) 603ff. (our *Fig. 214* = fig. 7).
55 Implications of the agora, Vallet, *BdA* 1967, 33ff.; Vallet-Villard, *MEFRA* 81 (1969) 7ff.; R. Martin, *L'Urbanisme* (1976) 309ff.; Vallet-Villard-Auberson, *Megara Hyblaea* 1 (1976), the site.
56 Richter, *Kouroi* no. 134 for the doctor Sombrotidas.
57 *NSc* 1954, 389ff., Langlotz-Hirmer, pl. 17.
58 Argued by G. Navarra, *Città sicane, sicule e greche nella zona di Gela* (1964) (cf. Boardman, *Class. Rev.* 1966, 213–5) and *RM* 82 (1975) 2ff.; cf. G. Uggeri, *RM* 75 (1968) 54ff.
59 P. Griffo, *Gela* (1973); *Mon. Ant.* 46 (1963) 1ff, archaic deposit.
60 P. Orlandini, *Kokalos* 12 (1966) 8ff.; 13 (1967) 177ff.; *Riv. Ist. Arch.* 15 (1968) 20ff.
61 Cf. *Mon. Ant.* 17 (1906) figs. 155, 404?, 406, 410, 412?, pl. 5 centre; *NSc* 1960, 100, fig. 17.
62 *Arch. Class.* 5 (1953) 244ff. (our *Fig. 217* = pl. 109. 1).
63 F. Rainey, *AJA* 73 (1969) 261ff. on the location. Summary of results, P. G. Guzzo, *PdP* 28 (1973) 278ff.; *ARepts* 1976/7, 58. Annual reports in *ASMG* and see *NSc* 1970, Suppl. 3.
64 P. Zancani, annually, in *ASMG. ARepts* 1976/7, 59; Coldstream, *GG* 238f.
65 *ASMG* 11/12 (1970/1) 9ff.; Lyre-Player seal, *ASMG* 15–17 (1974–6) pls. 22–3, but its inscription is imaginary.
66 J. de la Genière, reports in *NSc* 1971, 439ff.; 1975, 483ff.; and cf. *MEFRA* 85 (1973) 7ff.
67 *ARepts* 1976/7, 60f.; P. G. Guzzo, *Prospettiva* 11 (1977) 33ff.
68 *NSc* 1911, Suppl. 77ff., figurine, fig. 99.
69 *Mon. Ant.* 23 (1914) 686ff. G. Schmiedt and R. Chevalier, 'Caulonia e Metaponto' in *L'Universo* 3 (1959).
70 *ARepts* 1972/3, 37f.; 1976/7, 53f.; *BdA* 1975, 26ff. (Archaic temple); *Convegni M. G.* 13 (1974.)
71 *NSc* 1940, 94ff. (*AJA* 37 (1941) 472.)
72 *ARepts* 1972/3, 38; 1976/7, 55f. D. Adamesteanu in *Neue Forsch, in gr. Heiligtümern* (1976, ed. U. Jantzen) 151ff.; *ASMG* 15–17 (1974–6) 177ff. (mid-eighth-century Corinthian).
73 P. Z. Montuoro and U. Z. Bianco, *Heraion alla foce del Sele* 1–2 (1951–4).
74 P. Sestieri, *Arch. Class.* 4 (1952) 77ff. on origins and natives. M. Guarducci in *Gli Arch. Italiani in onore di A. Maiuri* (1966) 201ff. on foundation.
75 B. Neutsch, *Tes nymphas emi hiaron* (1957); U. Kron, *JdI* 86 (1971) 117ff.; Kurtz-Boardman, 299.
76 M. Napoli, *La Tomba del Tuffatore* (1970).
77 R. Naumann and B. Neutsch, *Palinuro* 1–2 (1958, 1960).
78 F. Lo Porto, *BdA* 1964, 67ff.; Coldstream, *GG* 239.
79 Dunbabin 87ff.; *X Convegno di Studi sulla M. G.* (1974); *ARepts* 1976/7, 51.
80 The pottery, F. Lo Porto, *Annuario* 37/8 (1959/60) 7ff.
81 Kurtz-Boardman, 313; *ASMG* 8 (1967) 31ff.
82 Jeffery, *LSAG* 286.
83 Neutsch, *Herakleia-Studien* (1967); A. Adamesteanu, *Siris-Heraclea* (1967); *ARepts* 1976/7, 57f. LAGARIA, a site between Siris and Sybaris with a myth-historical foundation story, has pottery of the seventh century: T. de Santis, *La Scoperta di Lagaria* (1964).
84 *XVI Convegno di Studi sulla M. G.*; *ARepts* 1976/7, 62; *VII Congr. Int. Arch. Class.* (1961) 109ff.
85 Dunbabin, 163.
86 *ARepts* 1976/7, 61f.; A. de Franciscis, *ASMG* 3 (1960) 21ff.
87 Dunbabin, 165–7; *Mon. Ant.* 31 (1926) 5ff.; J. de la Genière, *MEFRA* 76 (1964) 7ff.
88 *ASSO* 117ff.; *ARepts* 1976/7, 67.
89 B. Brea, *Akrai* (1956); *ASSO* 127f.

90 Brea, op. cit., pl. 25.
91 A. di Vita, *VII Congr. Int. Arch. Class.* 2 (1961) 69ff.; *ASSO* 129ff.
92 Reports in *AJA* 61–68 (1959–64) and 74 (1970) 354ff.; E. Sjoquist, *Kokalos* 8 (1962) 52ff., *Sicily and the Greeks* (1973) 28ff.
93 P. Pelagatti, *BdA* 1962, 251ff. and *Sicilia Arch.* 1974–6; *ASSO* 133ff.; *ARepts* 1976/7, 71.
94 Dunbabin, 301ff.; M. Santangelo, *Selinunte* (1961); *ARepts* 1976/7, 73f.; J. de la Genière, *Kokalos* 21 (1975) 68ff., the acropolis.
95 The deities, V. Tusa, *Kokalos* 13 (1967) 186ff.
96 *Mon. Ant.* 32 (1927) 6ff.
97 Ibid., pls. 27–9; Dunbabin, 174f.; Jeffery, *LSAG* 270f.; A. M. Bisi, *Stud. Mat. Stor. Rel.* 36 (1965) 99ff.
98 Dating problems, Vallet-Villard, *BCH* 58 (1958) 16ff.; J. Ducat, *BCH* 86 (1962) 165ff.; J. de la Genière, *Kokalos* 21 (1975) 102ff.; *ARepts* 1976/7, 74.
99 *Mon. Ant.* 32 (1927) pls. 79, 80; Jeffery, *LSAG* 270, n. 3.
100 Dunbabin, 350ff.; P. Griffo, *Agrigento* (1962); *ARepts* 1976/7, 72; E. de Miro, *Kokalos* 8 (1962) 122ff.
101 Dunbabin, 307.
102 Ibid., 307f.
103 Kurtz-Boardman, 257; *Fasti Arch.* 1 (1946) 722.
104 Dunbabin, 300f.; A. Adriani et al., *Himera* 1–2 (1970, 1976); *Quad. Imerese* 1 (1972).
105 James Stevenson Coll., sold at Sotheby's, 13 June 1944, lots 128–47, found on the edge of the crater of the volcano. Aryballos – our *Fig. 150*; ushabtis – Oxford 1944. 41–4.
106 Essays in *PdP* 21 (1966) and 25 (1970), especially 108ff. (Villard). J. P. Morel in *Simposio de Colonizaciones* (Barcelona, 1974) 139ff., suggesting a possible earlier Phocaean (?) interest in the site (but cf. *ARepts* 1976/7, 48); *BCH* 99 (1975) 858–61.
107 B. Brea, *Sicily before the Greeks* (1957); Dunbabin, ch. 5; E. Manni, *REA* 71 (1969) 5ff.; Sjoquist, op. cit.; E. de Miro, *BdA* 1975, 123ff.
108 Dunbabin, 36ff.; 9; *ASSO* 53f.
109 RAGUSA (Hybla Heraia) between Camarina and Casmenae, offers a native town with an adjacent Greek settlement growing and succeeding it in the sixth century: Dunbabin, 107f., A. di Vita, *BdA* 1959, 293ff.
110 Åkerström, *GSI* 20–3 (our *Fig. 225* = pl. 3. 3). Good examples are local vases with Greek Geometric decoration derived from Euboean at Sabucina: *Arch. Class.* 17 (1965) pls. 53–4, 58; *BdA* 1975, 123ff., figs. 8, 9.
111 Dunbabin, 122–5: Sjoquist, op. cit., 23ff.
112 Dunbabin, 177ff.
113 Kraay, 230f.
114 D. Adamesteanu, *Mon. Ant.* 44 (1958) 205ff.; *NSc* 1958, 350ff.; *Kokalos* 4 (1958) 40ff. Some have thought this the ancient Omphake, but Pausanias (8. 46. 3) says Omphake was sacked by the tyrant of Gela. On Greek penetration here also P. Orlandini, *Kokalos* 8 (1962) 69ff.
115 Ibid., 103ff.; Sjoquist, op. cit., 70ff.
116 J. de la Genière, *MEFRA* 82 (1970) 621ff. and *RA* 1978, 257ff. on relations with natives; *Popoli anellenici in Basilicata* (1971, exhibition); F. Lo Porto, *Mon. Ant.* 38 ser. misc. 1. 3 (1973) on Lucania.
117 P. Orsi, *Templum Apollinis Alaei* (1933), esp. figs. 81, 91; Dunbabin, 159, 175f.
118 D. H. Trump, *Central and Southern Italy before Rome* (1966). Penetration in Campania from the later eighth century on, *ARepts* 1976/7, 46f.
119 S. de Cara, *Rend. Acc. Arch. Nap.* 1974, 37ff.
120 Puteoli – A. de Franciscis, *Rend Acc. Arch. Nap.* 1972, 109ff. Pompeii – *RE* s.v., 2018f.
121 Above, n. 48.
122 Below, n. 165.
123 Above, n. 49.
124 Richter, *Kouroi* 92f., 129, nos. 134, 181–9.
125 Above, n. 18.
126 Above, n. 15.
127 B. Schweitzer, *RM* 62 (1955) 78ff.; Simon-Hirmer, pls. 18, 19.
128 References in *ARepts* 1972/3, 38; 1976/7, 58; *Convegno* 13 (1974) pls. 95–7.
129 A. Rumpf, *Chalkidische Vasen* (1927): R. M. Cook, *GPP*

158; Boardman, *BSA* 68 (1973) 27f., analyses; *BSA* 60 (1965) 125f. (Smyrna).
130 Dunbabin, 280ff., 295ff. Our *Fig. 229* = F. Krauss, *Die Tempel von Paestum* (1959) fig. 45.
131 Dunbabin, 268ff. Our *Fig. 230* = *Mon. Ant.* 35 (1933) pl. 25.
132 Above, n. 124.
133 Western sculpture: Robertson, *HGA* 115ff.; Langlotz-Hirmer, 30ff.; B. S. Ridgway, *Archaic Style* (1977) 238ff.; R. Ross Holloway, *Influences and Styles.... Sicily and Magna Graecia* (1975).
134 Richter, *Korai* (1968) figs. 109–12.
135 Altars –P. Orlandini, *RM* 66 (1959) 97ff. A fine painted and relief example, P. Devambez, *Mon. Piot* 58 (1972) 1ff. (our *Fig. 232*). Gela coffins – Kurtz-Boardman, 312.
136 R. A. Higgins, *Greek Terracottas* (1967) 54f.; Richter, *Kouroi* no. 62 (our *Fig. 233*).
137 U. Jantzen, *Bronzewerkstätten in Grossgriechenland und Sizilien* (1937).
138 London 1904. 7–3. 1; W. Lamb, *Greek and Roman Bronzes* (1929) pl. 39b.
139 Robertson, *HGA* 647; Richter, *Sculpture and Sculptors of the Greeks* (1970) 156ff.
140 H. V. Herrmann, *Olympia* (1972) 97ff.
141 Western coinage, Kraay-Hirmer, 279ff.; Kraay, 161ff.
142 A late eighth-century 'weight' on the Euboean standard is reported from Ischia. Buchner, *Cahiers J. Bérard* 2, 81f.
143 An optimistic view of the historical significance of the distribution of standards in the early west, L. Breglia, *Le antiche rotte del Mediterraneo* (1956), reviewed by Kraay, *Num. Chron.* 1957, 289ff.
144 On Etruscan origins, M. Pallottino, *The Etruscans* (1974) ch. 2 and *SE* 29 (1961) 3ff.; L. Banti, *Etruscan Cities and their cultures* (1973); H. Hencken, *Tarquinia and Etruscan Origins* (1968); D. Strong, *The Early Etruscans* (1968); H. H. Scullard in *Studies V. Ehrenberg* (1966) 225ff. on the Greek tradition.
145 As by von Hase (*Hamburger Beitr. Arch.* 5 (1975) 99ff. and cf. *AA* 1974, 85ff.) studying the sensitive area of goldsmithing, with technique novel to both Greeks and Etruscans but which the latter were perhaps the quicker to learn and better able to afford. See also above, n. 22 and I. Strøm, *Problems concerning the Origins and Development of the Etruscan orientalising style* (1971). On later associations with the east M. Renard in *Hommages A. Grenier* 3 (1962) 1299ff.; A. Hus, *Rech. Statuaire en pierre* (1961).
146 Above, n. 21.
147 And cf. R. Maxwell-Hyslop, *Iraq* 18 (1956) 150ff.
148 Above, n. 18.
149 A. W. Johnston, *Greece and Rome* 21 (1974) 138ff.
150 Payne, *Necrocorinthia* (1931) ch. 8; Boardman, *ABFH* 36f. (our *Fig. 237* = fig. 56).
151 Boardman, *ABFH* 64. For the bucchero models of the amphorae, M. Verzár, *Antike Kunst* 16 (1973) 45ff. Kyathoi, M. Eisman, *AJA* 77 (1975) 71ff.; *Archaeology* 28 (1975) 78ff.; *J. Paul Getty Mus. J.* 1 (1974) 43ff.; the kyathoi are not exclusively either Nikosthenic or export models. M. A. Tiberios, *AE* 1976, 44ff., finds a possible connection between Nikosthenes and the earlier 'Tyrrhenian' studio. Our *Fig. 238–9* = *CVA* Castle Ashby nos. 17, 34.
152 A. Blakeway, *JRS* 45 (1935) 129ff.; Pliny, *N. H.* 35. 152; Livy 1. 34; Dionys. Hal. 3. 46.
153 F. Canciani, *Dialoghi di Arch.* 8 (1974/5) 79ff.; E. La Rocca, *MEFRA* 90 (1978) 465ff.
154 A. Giuliano, *JdI* 78 (1963) 183ff. (our *Fig. 241*); *AA* 1967, 7ff.; *Prospettiva* 3 (1975) 4ff.; W. Schiering, *RA* 1974, 3ff.
155 R. M. Cook and J. M. Hemelrijk, *Jb. BerlinerMus.* 5 (1963) 107ff.; Villard, *Mon. Piot* 43 (1949) 33ff. (dinoi); *CVA* Castle Ashby pls. A, 1–3 (Northampton name vase = our *Fig. 242*); *CVA* Würzburg i. 35f. (our *Fig. 243*.)
156 Hemelrijk, *de Caeretaanse Hydriae* (1956) and *Caeretan Hydriae* (forthcoming).
157 Strabo 220.
158 M. Torelli, *NSc* 1970; 1971, 195ff.; *PdP* 26 (1971) 44ff.; *ARepts* 1973/4, 49–51; Morel, *BCH* 99 (1975) 862f.;

PdP 32 (1977) 398ff. for the sanctuaries.
159 PdP 32 (1977) 410.
160 Hdt. 4. 152; ARepts 1973/4, 50; Torelli, PdP 26 (1971) 56ff, the find; A. W. Johnston, PdP 27 (1972) 416ff. (dipinti and graffiti); P. A. Gianfrotta, PdP 30 (1975) 311 (anchor); F. D. Harvey, PdP 31 (1976) 206ff. (S. as trader).
161 Åkerström, GSI 51ff.
162 J. G. Szilagyi, Etrusk-Korinthosi Vázafestészet (1975); Arch. Class. 20 (1968) 1ff.
163 P. Ducati, Pontische Vasen (1932) – our Fig. 248 = pl. 12; C. M. Stibbe (forthcoming); L. Hannestad, The Paris Painter (1974) and Followers of the Paris Painter (1976); Beazley, Etruscan Vase Painting (1947); added-red Praxias Group, see also Szilagyi, Arch. Polona 14 (1973) 95ff.
164 Jeffery, LSAG 236f.; J. A. Bundgaard, Analecta Rom. Inst. Danici 3 (1965) 12ff.
165 Villard in Hommages A. Grenier 3 (1962) 1625ff.
166 M. Gras in Mél. J. Heurgnon (1976) 344ff.
167 Ridgway in Celts (see n. 12) 14, fig. 2c.
168 J. Close-Brooks, BICS 14 (1967) 22ff.
169 K. Kilian, in Ét. Delphiques (BCH Suppl. 4, 1976) 429ff., helmets.
170 Paus. 6. 19. 2.
171 G. Karo, AE 1937, 316ff.; E. Kunze, Studies D. M. Robinson 1 (1951) 736ff.
172 A survey of this work in ARepts 1973/4, 45–7. E. la Rocca, Dialoghi di Arch. 8 (1974/5) 86ff. and in Civiltà del Lazio primitivo (1976) 367ff., pls. 21–3 (and cf. finds at Decima, 18 km. south of Rome, ibid., pl 23; Lavinium, ibid., 291ff., pl. 78; and Satricum, ibid., 323ff., pl. 87). For S. Omobono see now PdP 32 (1977) 9ff., 382ff., and ibid., 375ff. on other Greek finds in Latium. Cf. also D. van Berchem and E. Gjerstad in Mél. Piganiol 2 (1966) 739ff., 791ff.; E. Paribeni, Bull. Comm. Arch. Rom. 76 (1956–8) 3 ff., 77 (1959/60) 109ff. for imported Greek pottery.
173 N. H. 35. 157. On Etruscan artists in Rome M. Cristofani, Prospettiva 9 (1977) 2ff.
174 A. S. Mura, PdP 32 (1977) 62ff. for a fully illustrated summary.
175 Pliny, N. H. 35. 154.
176 Thuc. 6. 2. 6.
177 On Phoenician colonization important articles by W. Culican in Abr-Nahrain 1 (1959/60) 36ff.; Levant 2 (1970) 28ff.; and C. R. Whittaker,, Proc. Camb. Phil. Soc. 200 (1974) 58ff. L'Espansione fenicia nel Med. (= Studi Semitici 38 (1971)). J. M. Blazquez, Tartessos y los origines de la Colonizacion fenicia en occidente (1975). On the importance of metals in the west, J. Jully, Opusc. Rom. 6 (1968) 27ff.
178 H. Treidler, Historia 8 (1959) 257ff.
179 P. Demargne, RA 1951, 44ff.; Coldstream, GGP 386f.; P. Cintas, Manuel (next n.) 1, pls. 10–11; Culican, Abr-Nahrain 1 (1959/60) 47f. Survey of imported Greek pottery by E. Boucher Colozier, Cahiers de Byrsa 3 (1953) 11ff.
180 On early Carthage, P. Cintas, Céramique punique (1950); Manuel d'arch. punique 1–2 (1970, 1976); B. H. Warmington, Carthage (1969) and above, n. 177. A. M. Bisi, La ceramica punica (1970).
181 Coldstream, NSc 1970, 580–2; B. Isserlin and J. du Plat Taylor, eds., Motya 1 (1974), esp. 83f. Seventh-century pottery, e.g., Mozia 7 (1972) pls. 41–2, 57; 8 (1973) pls. 9, 38. E. Manni in Mél. Piganiol 2 (1966) 699ff.
182 Dunbabin, BSR 21 (1953) 39f.; and cf. BMQ 27 (1964) pl. 39e, an imitation of Protocorinthian.
183 F. M. Cross, Bull. Amer. School Or. Res 208 (1972) 13ff.; B. Peckham, Orientalia 41 (1972) 457ff.
184 G. Pesce, Sardegna punica (1961) 70, fig. 116.
185 A. Garcia y Bellido, Hispania Graeca 2 (1948) pl. 74. 2; G. Trias de Arribas, Cerámicas griegas de la peninsula Ibérica (1967–8) pls. 146–7.
186 Whittaker, op. cit. (n. 177), 59ff.; Blazquez, op. cit. (n. 177) pl. 113; Morel, 885ff.; Culican, Levant 2 (1970) 28ff. (alabaster); H. G. Niemeyer, Mitt. Deutsch. Or. Gesell. 104 (1972) 5ff. Toscanos and Torre del Mar are the important sites. Reports in Madrider Mitt. (Greek finds – 3 (1962) pl. 14c; 9 (1968) pl. 23a; 13 (1972) pl. 24; AA 1964, 487, Attic sherd, c. 700).

187 Whittaker, op. cit. (n. 177) 61; B. Freyer-Schauenburg, op. cit. (ch. 4, n. 15) 104ff. and Madrider Mitt. 7 (1966) 89ff.
188 Tartessus y sus Problemas (V Symp. int. preh. penins., 1969) 163ff.; A. Garcia y Bellido, Archiv. Esp. 37 (1964) 50ff.; Culican, Syria 45 (1968) 275ff.
189 Culican, PEQ 1958, 97ff.
190 Hdt. 4. 152.
191 Paus. 6. 19.
192 Hdt. 1. 163. R. Carpenter, Beyond the Pillars of Hercules (1966) ch. 2, with the suggested association of the name Arganthonios with argentum, and the possibility that the Charybdis of the Odyssey shows knowledge of Atlantic tides.
193 Akurgal, Anatolia 1 (1956) 3ff. and in Princeton Encyclopedia; Morel, 855–7. Arguments that the Phocaeans were the dominant cultural influence in the western Mediterranean have been developed by E. Langlotz, Die kulturelle und künstlerische Hellenisierung... Phokaia (1966) – see Morel.
194 B. B. Shefton, forthcoming. They are generally called Rhodian. Some have been identified hitherto as Etruscan. An archaic Phocaean coin from Spain, A. E. Furtwängler, AM 92 (1977) 61ff. Their trade in precious metals, P. Ebner, PdP 21 (1966) 111ff. Our Fig. 253 = Garcia y Bellido, op. cit. (n. 185) pl. 21.
195 The important sixth-century finds are discussed by Morel, 861. J. and L. Jehasse, La nécropole préromaine d'Aléria (1973). On the significance of the battle, J. Jehasse, Rev. Ét. Anc. 64 (1962) 241ff.
196 Snodgrass, EGAW 24f., C8.
197 For Greek finds in Spain see works cited by Morel, whose article is fundamental for evidence about Phocaeans in the west, and Garcia y Bellido, op. cit. (n. 185) – pl. 20. 2, the griffin protome. For the pottery, Trias de Arribas, op. cit. (n. 185). And cf. Madrider Mitt. 6 (1965) pls. 31–6 (vase handle, Malaga); X Congr. Nac. de Arq. (1969) 440ff. (crater fr.); Trabajos de Prehistoria 34 (1977) 371ff. (satyr figurine); Blazquez, op. cit. (n. 177) pl. 67a (Protoattic vase from Cadiz); M. del Amo, Huelva Arq. 2 (1976) 41. fig. 9. 9 (mid-eighth-century Geometric).
198 Morel, 886f.
199 It was not, as it seems, completely deserted. See above, n. 195.
200 On Etruscan-Punic relations J. M. Turfa, AJA 81 (1977) 368ff.; E. Colozier, MEFRA 65 (1953) 63ff.
201 Villard, Bull. Arch. Maroc 4 (1960) 1ff.; Whittaker, op. cit. (n. 177) 67–9.
202 V. Tusa, VIII Congr. Int. Arch. Class. (1961) 31ff. Segesta and Hellenism – J. de la Genière, MEFRA 90 (1978) 33ff.
203 Kinyps has been identified about 20 km. east of Leptis from air photographs. On Greco-Punic relations in the sixth century, F. P. Rizzo, Kokalos 16 (1970) 139ff.
204 Ill. London News 1952 March 29, 538 (Sabratha); T. H. Carter. AJA 69 (1965) 123ff. (Leptis); D. E. L. Haynes, The Antiquities of Tripolitania (1955).
205 For Dorieus – Hdt. 5. 41–66; Dunbabin, 348–52, 362–4; A. S. Graf von Stauffenberg, Historia 9 (1960) 212ff. Herakleia by Mount Eryx is not identified. At Herakleia Minoa a cemetery of the later sixth century has been found.
206 V. Tusa, Kokalos 10/11 (1964/5) 589ff.
207 Boardman, Greek Gems and Finger Rings (1970) 153f.; Intaglios and Rings (1975) 35f.; RA 1971, 196ff.
208 Boardman, Antike Kunst 10 (1967) 3ff. Examples at Utica and Carthage, as Arch. Viva 1. 2 (1969) 74f., 130–5 (for our Fig. 256); Karthago 2 (1951) 54; Bull. Arch. 1924, 157.
209 The identification of the Demarateia is in dispute: see Kraay-Hirmer, 388; Kraay, 205f.
210 Dunbabin, ch. 14. Gelon's thank-offering to Delphi, Meiggs-Lewis, no. 28. Simonides fr. 106, Diehl.
211 Late Geometric pottery, allegedly from the south of France, is generally now discounted, but some of it looks Euboean and there is nothing surprising in early exploration of this coast by Euboeans. A. Blakeway, BSA 33 (1932/3) pl. 33. 85–7; F. Benoit, Provence historique 6 (1956) 3ff.; Villard, La cér. grecque de Marseille

(1960) 75f.; Coldstream, *GGP* 388 (Melian ?).

212 H. Rolland, *Fouilles de Saint-Blaise* (1951); Morel, *PdP* 25 (1970) 383ff. and Morel, 868.

213 Strabo 654. Morel, 868. Hind, op. cit. (n. 217) 48.

214 Villard, op. cit.; H. Gallet de Santerre, *REA* 64 (1962) 378ff. The tin route – Villard, op. cit., 143ff.; J. V. S. Megaw, *Antiquity* 40 (1966) 38ff.; P. Amandry, *Hommage... J. Carcopino* (1977) 13ff.

215 Morel, 882f., for the rich literature. Villard, *PdP* 25 (1970) 108ff.; J. Jully, *Archiv. Esp.* 48 (1975) 22ff. on Phoenician in N. Spain and S. W. France, and *L'Ant. Class.* 46 (1977) 5ff., on Greek vases from tombs in this area. On Celts and the Mediterranean world, C. F. C. Hawkes, *VIII Congr. Intr. Arch. Class.* (1965) 61ff.

216 E. Langlotz, *Stud, zur nordostgr. Kunst* (1975) 45ff.; Morel, 876, n. 84.

217 J. Hind suggests that Avienus refers to Emporion as Pyrene, *Riv. Stor. dell 'Ant.* 2 (1972) 39ff.

218 E. Ripoll, *Ampurias* (1973); Morel, 876.

219 Strabo 159f.

220 *RA* 1948. 1, 459 (our *Fig. 258*); Jully, op. cit. (n. 215, 1975) 63ff. Cf. S. Nordström, *La cér. peinte ibérique de la prov. d'Alicante* (1969; 1973).

221 M. Louis and O. & J. Taffenel, *Le prem. âge du fer Languedocien* 2 (1958) 63; *XI Congr. Nac. de Arq.* (1970) 494ff.

222 *Olympia* 4, pl. 66. 1151; *ADelt* 19 (1964) Chr. pl. 365.·3 (Corfu).

223 Justinus 43, 41–2. A rather dated survey by F. Benoit, *Rech. sur l'hellenisation du Midi de la Gaule* (1965) and in *Hommages A. Grenier* 1 (1962) 274ff.; and Villard op. cit., 125ff. *Actes du Colloque sur les influences helléniques en Gaule* (Dijon, 1958).

224 Our *Fig. 260* = *Germania* 49 (1971) pl. 5, with 41ff.; Benoit, op. cit. (1965) 167ff.

225 J. Jannoray, *Ensérune* (1955); Gallet de Santerre, *Archaeology* 15 (1962) 163ff.

226 Cf. *Gallia* 18 (1960) 308ff.

227 J. J. Hatt, *VII Congr. Int. Arch. Class.* 3 (1961) 177ff.; C. Lagrand and J. P. Thalmann, *Les Habitats protohist. du Pegue* (1973).

228 R. Joffroy, *Trésor de Vix* (1954); E. Gjodesen, *AJA* (1963) 333ff., argues an earlier date and Corinthian origin for the crater. Other finds, Joffroy, *L'Oppidum de Vix* (1960) 120ff.

229 Jeffery, *LSAG* 191f., 375.

230 *Ét. d'arch. class.* 1 (1955/6) pl. 1; Joffroy, *Mon. Piot* 51 (1960) 1ff. – one of the griffins is a replacement in a provincial style, resembling the piece from Angers (next n.).

231 Ibid., 14.

232 Ibid., 16f.

233 H. A. Cahn in *Colloque, Dijon* (n. 223) 21ff.; H. Jucker, in *Zur gr. Kunst* (Fest. H. Bloesch, 1973) 42ff.

234 Just north of Stuttgart. H. Zürn and H. V. Herrmann, *Germania* 44 (1966) 74ff. and *Hallstattforsch. in Nordwürtt.* 16 (1970) 25ff.

235 J. Biel, *Denkmalpflege in Baden-Württemberg* 7 (1978) 168ff.

236 W. Dehn, *Germania* 32 (1954) 22ff.; W. Kimmig and E. Gersbach, *Germania* 49 (1971) 21ff.; *Colloque, Dijon* (n. 223) 55ff.; *AA* 1964, 467ff. Greek pottery at Marienburg (Würzburg) – *Germania* 41 (1963) 103ff.; *Antike Welt* 1975. 1, 51, fig. 11. I am indebted (through the kindness of B. B. Shefton) to the Inst. für Vor- und Fruh-geschichte, Tübingen for the hitherto unpublished photograph in *Fig. 265*.

6 The North and the Black Sea

General Bibliography

Minns and Artamonov (Scythians and Greeks, and their art); *CAH* 3², ch. 37 (A. J. Graham), ch. 33a (T. Sulimirski). Belin de Ballu, E., *L'Histoire des colonies grecques du littoral nord de la mer noire* (1965). A descriptive bibliography.

RE Suppl. 9 (1962) s.v. 'Pontos Euxeinos' (C. M. Danoff). Sulimirski, T., *Bull. Inst. Arch. London* 11 (1973) 1ff. Survey of recent work on colonization and the early Iron Age in S. Russia.

Brashinsky, I. B., *Eirene* 7 (1968) 81ff. Survey of recent excavations on the Black Sea coast.

Reports on recent discoveries in *ARepts* 1962/3, 34ff. (Boardman), 1971/2, 48ff. (K. S. Gorbunova).

Rostovtseff, M., *Iranians and Greeks in South Russia* (1922). idem, *Skythien und der Bosporus* 1 (1931).

1 R. L. Beaumont, *JHS* 56 (1936) 159ff. on Greeks and Greek finds in the Adriatic. G. Vallet, *MEFRA* 62 (1950) 33ff. L. Braccesi, *Grecità adriatica* (1971), reviewed *Gnomon* 1973, 308f.

2 Plut., *Gr. Q.* 11. C. Rodenwaldt et al., *Korkyra* 2 (1939) 168ff.

3 *ADelt* 19 (1964) Chr. pl. 366; 20 (1965) Chr. pls. 442–3; 21 (1966) Chr. pls. 331–2; V. G. Kallipolitis, *Kernos* (Fest. V. G. Bakalakis, 1972) pl. 20, Euboean imitations of Protocorinthian. Coldstream, *GG* 185.

4 Boardman, *GSAP* 153, fig. 187.

5 F. P. Johnson and W. B. Dinsmoor, *AJA* 40 (1936) 46ff.

6 Rodenwaldt, op. cit. (n. 2) 154, 172.

7 Boardman, *GSAP* fig. 207a; A. Choremis, *AAA* 7 (1974) 183ff.

8 Boardman, *GSAP* fig. 266; Kurtz-Boardman, 239, 245, fig. 54, pl. 65; Jeffery, *LSAG* 232, 285.

9 Thuc. 1. 13, cf. 1. 25.

10 C. Praschniker, *ÖJh* 21/2 (1922) Beibl. 23ff.; Payne, *Necrocorinthia* (1931) 186.

11 M. Gjødesen, *Acta Arch.* 15 (1944) 183ff.; *Albania* 5 (1935) pl. 15.

12 P. Lizičar, *Crna Korkira* (1951) pl. 5. Issa, Payne, loc. cit.

13 F. G. Lo Porto, *ASMG* 5 (1964) 111ff.; *NSc* 1962, 130 (Gioia del Colle).

14 Strabo 282.

15 O. H. Frey, *Die Entstehung der Situlenkunst* (1969). And Greek art, Boardman, *Eur. Community in Later Prehistory* (Studies, C. F. C. Hawkes, 1971) 123ff.

16 Frey, op. cit., pl. 67. 18.

17 Hdt. 1. 163.

18 The oinochoai in Picenum, above, p. 214.

19 J. P. Morel, *BCH* 99 (1975) 857f.

20 Payne, op. cit., 122; cf. *PdP* 32 (1977) 406–8 for an Ombrikos, dedicator at Gravisca of a late sixth-century Attic vase.

21 Pottery, *BdA* 49 (1964) 289ff. G. Fogolari and B. M. Scarfi, *Adria antica* (1970). G. Colonna, *Riv. Stor. Ant.* 4 (1974) 1ff.

22 *Spina e l'Etruria Padana* (Suppl. to *SE* 25, 1959). N. Alfieri et al., *Spina* (1958). J. D. Beazley, *SE* 25 (1959) 47ff. *ARepts* 1967/8, 46f., L. Laurenzi, *Hommages A. Grenier* (1962) 961ff. (origins; M. Pallottino, ibid., 1207ff. on Etruscans in N. Italy).

23 Alfieri, op. cit., 16; G. Colonna, *Riv. Stor. Ant.* 4 (1974) 3; P. Uggeri, *SE* 46 (1978) 288ff.

24 D. C. Kurtz, *Athenian White Lekythoi* (1975) 59, 141–3.

25 Bérard, *L'Expansion* 66–8, 94.

26 J. Pouilloux in *Entretiens Fond. Hardt* 10 (1964) 3ff.

27 Bérard, op. cit., 92–5; Hdt. 1. 168.

28 Hdt. 7. 108; *BCH* 96 (1972) 750, fig. 373.

29 S. Casson, *Macedonia, Thrace and Illyria* (1926) 33ff. Macedonia, *CAH* 3², ch. 40 (N. G. L. Hammond).

30 Hdt. 1. 64; *Ath. Pol.* 15. 1–2.

31 Hdt. 5. 11, 23.

32 Hdt. 6. 47. *BCH* 88 (1964) 280ff.

33 Kraay-Hirmer, 330ff.; Kraay, 138ff.

34 *BCH* 91 (1967) 724, fig. 6, 729, figs. 15–16; *ADelt* 20 (1965) Chr. pls. 540, 558.

35 *ADelt* 20 (1965) Chr. 444, pls. 512–14.

36 *Guide de ·Thasos* (École Fr., 1968) for a full account. Annual reports in *BCH*. A. J. Graham, *BSA* 73 (1978) 61ff.

37 *Guide de Thasos* 12, fig. 3, 198.

38 P. Bernard, *BCH* 88 (1964) 77ff.

39 *Guide de Thasos* 155ff.

40 *BCH* 84 (1960) 347ff.

41 L. Ghali-Kahil, *Ét. Thas.* 7 (1960) 35. Cf. the crater from Neapolis, *VIII Int. Congr. Arch. Class.* (1965) pl. 53. 1; D. Lazaridis, *Kavalla Museum Guide* (1969) pl. 36.

42 *Guide de Thasos* 58–65, (= our *Fig. 271*), 109–11, 118f.
(= our *Fig. 272*); Boardman, *GSAP* figs. 69, 223. C.
Picard, *Ét. Thas.* 8 (1962), gateways.

43 On Neapolis, G. Bakalakis, *AE* 1936, 1ff. and reports in
PAE 1937–8; *ADelt* 1960–7. D. Lazaridis, op. cit., 13ff.
and *VIII Congr. Int. Arch. Class.* (1963) 293ff.

44 *PAE* 1935, 40; 1936, 74f.

45 Bakalakis, op. cit., 8ff.

46 Ibid., 17 n. 1, figs. 25, 26.

47 Casson, op. cit. (n. 29).

48 J. Bouzek, *Opusc. Ath.* 9 (1969) 41ff.; in Athens graves,
H. Müller-Karpe, *JdI* 77 (1962) 96ff.; Desborough,
GDA 142f.

49 Snodgrass, in *Eur. Comm.* (see n. 15) 31ff.

50 H. Borchhardt, *Kriegswesen* 1 (1977) E 42. For an eastern origin H. Hencken, *AJA* 54 (1950) 295ff.; B. Gräs-
lund, *Acta Arch.* 38 (1967) 59ff. Cf. Snodgrass, *Early
Greek Armour and Weapons* (1964) 55f., 210f. (our *Fig.
274* = pl. 24).

51 J. Alexander, *Atti VI Congr. preist. protoh.* 6f. and *AJA*
69 (1965) 7ff.

52 References in *Perachora* 2, 433ff.; Boardman and Hayes
Tocra 1, 163.

53 E. Kunze, *Ol. Bericht* 6 (1958) 125ff.; Snodgrass, op.
cit., 18ff.

54 On Macedonian bronzes and the Greek world, Bouzek,
Greco-Mac. Bronzes (1973) and *Památky Arch.* 65 (1974)
278ff.

55 Akurgal, *Phrygische Kunst* (1955) 26–8, pls. A, B (our
Fig. 276).

56 N. G. L. Hammond, *History of Macedonia* 1 (1972) 407ff.

57 Boardman, *Greek Emporio* (1967) 211, no. 240 and refs.

58 Hdt. 4. 33.

59 D. Strong, *BM Cat. of the Carved Amber* (1966); Boardman, op. cit., 238; C. W. Beck, *Archaeology* 23 (1970)
7ff.

60 Beaumont, *JHS* 56 (1936) 184, suggested that the
Corinthians were interested in Illyrian iris for their
perfumed oil. Cf. Pliny, *N.H.* 13. 2, 21. 40.

61 J. Alexander, *Antiquity* 36 (1962) 123ff.; L. B. Popović,
Archaic Greek Culture in the Balkans (1975).

62 D. M.-Zisi and L. B. Popović, *Novi Pazar* (1969) and
Iliri i Grci (1959) pl. 10.

63 *Wiss. Mitt. Bosn. Herz.* 3 (1895) pl. 12.

64 B. Filow, *Die archaische Nekropole von Trebenischte*
(1927) – our *Fig. 280* = no. 63; P. Jacobsthal, *Greek Pins*
(1956) 201ff.; L. B. Popović, *Katalog ... Trebeništa*
(1956).

65 Filow, *Die Grabhügelnekropole bei Duvanlij* (1934);
Hoddinott, op. cit. (n. 69) 58ff.

66 Filow, op. cit., 57, 92, pls. 12, 13 (Attic; also *JdI* 45
(1930) 317, pl. 11); fig. 104 (Chian); fig. 113 (figurine).

67 *Godišnik na muzei, Plovdiv* 3 (1954) 265ff. In general on
Greek finds in Thrace see J. G. Szilagyi, *VIII Int. Congr.
Arch. Class.* (1965) 386ff. (Hungary); C. M. Danov,
Altthrakien (1976) 56ff.; P. Alexandrescu, *Thraco-Dacia*
(II Congr. Int. Thrac., 1976) 117ff. (pottery). A. Fol and
I. Marazov, *Thrace and Thracians* (1977); *CAH* 3².2, ch.
33b (V. Mihailov).

68 *Starinar* 9/10 (1958/9) 281ff.; *RA* 1973, 39ff.

69 R. F. Hoddinott, *Bulgaria in Antiquity* (1975).

70 Cf. R. Lullies, *AA* 1957, 382ff.; M. Schmidt, *Zur gr.
Kunst* (Fest. H. Bloesch, 1973) 103; Boardman, *ARFH*
fig. 277; B. Fellmann, *JdI* 93 (1978) 1ff. Our *Fig. 281* =
Beazley, *ARV* 860, no. 2.

71 J. G. P. Best, *Thracian Peltasts* (1969); H. Cahn, *RA*
1973, 13–15. (our *Fig. 282* = fig. 15).

72 Strabo 298; W. S. Allen, *Class. Quarterly* 1947, 86ff. on
the eastern origin of the 'first' name, meaning 'of dark
colour'.

73 R. Carpenter, *AJA* 57 (1948) 1ff.; A. J. Graham, *BICS* 5
(1958) 25ff.

74 Literary sources, Bérard, *L'Expansion* 95ff.

75 Graham, *JHS* 91 (1971) 39ff.

76 R. Drews, *JHS* 96 (1976) 18ff. argues early dates and
Greek interest in north Anatolian iron.

77 Hdt. 4. 13–16; J. D. P. Bolton, *Aristeas of Proconessus*
(1962).

78 Hesiod, fr. 241 (Merkelbach/West), *Theogony* 339; *Iliad*
2, 851–7; perhaps Eumelos: cf. Drews, op. cit., 19–21.

79 R. D. Barnett, in *The Aegean and the Near East* (Studies
H. Goldman, 1956) 228ff.

80 Drews, op. cit., 26ff.

81 Strabo 590.

82 Bérard, *L'Expansion* 99.

83 Contra, Graham, op. cit. (n. 75) 41f.

84 R. M. Cook, *BSA* 44 (1949) 160f.

85 *ARepts* 1962/3, 45. Cf. I. P. Pichikyan, *Vestnik* 1975. 1,
117ff.

86 C. Roebuck, *Ionian Trade and Colonization* (1959) 125;
S. P. Boriskovskaya, *Wiss. Zeit. Rostock* 16 (1967) 425ff.

87 S. Dimitriu and P. Alexandrescu, *RA* 1973, 23ff., cf.
195ff.

88 *ARepts* 1962/3, 42f. (cf. 56).

89 A. D. Ure, *Met. Mus. Stud.* 4 (1932) 34.

90 N. A. Onaiko, *Sov. Arch.* 1960. 2, 25ff. and *Antichnii
Import* (1966) (our *Fig. 283* = no. 1), summarized by
Alexandrescu in *RA* 1975, 63ff.

91 Last note (1966) for these finds and maps showing
distribution of Greek goods in this area through the
Archaic period.

92 *ARepts* 1962/3, 40f., figs 17 (= our *Fig. 284*), 18.

93 The importance of this trade before the end of the sixth
century has been questioned: T. S. Noonan, *Amer. J.
Phil.* 94 (1973) 231ff., against Roebuck, *Class. Phil.* 48
(1953) 9ff.

94 *Mat. Res.* 4 (1941); cf. *Fasti Archeologici* 4, no. 134.

95 Hdt. 4. 53.

96 Strabo 549, 551.

97 Kurtz-Boardman, 317–20.

98 Hdt. 4. 103.

99 F. W. Hasluck, *Cyzicus* (1916); *ARepts* 1959/60, 34;
E. Akurgal in *Princeton Enc.* s.v.

100 Akurgal, *Ancient Ruins of Turkey* (1973) 47.

101 Boardman, *GSAP* figs. 220–1, cf. fig. 178.

102 Kraay-Hirmer, 368f., figs. 698ff.

103 Akurgal, *Anatolia* 1 (1956) 20ff. and op. cit. (n. 100).
ARepts 1959/60, 34f.

104 E. Berger, *Das Basler Arztrelief* (1970) 39, fig. 39;
Kurtz-Boardman, pl. 50.

105 See above, ch. 3, n. 319.

106 Jeffery, *LSAG* 365. Other finds, cf. *Ann. Arch. Mus.
Istanbul* 13/14 (1966) 228f.

107 P. Jacobsthal, *Greek Pins* (1956) 32f.

108 Boardman, *GSAP* fig. 248; Jeffery, *LSAG* 366 and
BSA 50 (1955) 81ff.; Berger, op. cit., 103, fig. 124.

109 *Anatolia* 1 (1956) pl. 10.

110 Hoddinott, op. cit. (n. 69) 33ff.; *Bull. Inst. Arch. Bulg.*
18 (1952) 93ff.; 23 (1960) 239ff.; Gorov, *Mus. arch.
Bourgas* (1967). G. A. Short, *Liverpool Annals* 24 (1937)
141ff. on the siting of colonies on this coast.

111 Richter, *Kouroi* (1970) no. 124c, figs. 620–3; Berger, op.
cit. (n. 104) 56, fig. 57; *Bull. Inst. Arch. Bulg.* 32 (1970)
274f.

112 Hoddinott, op. cit. (n. 69) 41ff.; L. Ognenova, *BCH* 84
(1960) 221ff.

113 Hoddinott, op. cit. (n. 69) 49ff.; *Bull. Inst. Arch. Bulg.*
12 (1938) 188f.; 30 (1967) 157ff.

114 Cf. D. M. Pippidi, *I Greci nel Basso Danubio* (1971) 38.

115 Histria. *Monografie Arheologică* 1 (1954), 2 (1964), 4
(1978) – the Archaic and Classical pottery; D. M. Pippidi, *BCH* 82 (1958) 335ff. and op. cit. last n.; *ARepts*
1962/3, 35ff. Regular articles and reports in *Dacia* and
Materiale şi Cercetari Arh. Alexandrescu, *Studii Clasice* 4
(1962) 49ff. (foundation date).

116 *Dacia* 3 (1959) 143ff.; *Histria* 2 (1964) 133ff.

117 Jeffery, *BSA* 59 (1964) 45, pl. 5a.

118 *Stud. şi Cerc. de Ist. veche* 9 (1958) 275ff.

119 Alexandrescu, *Dacia* 16 (1972) 113ff.

120 *ARepts* 1952/3, 39 with refs.

121 *Eph. Dacoromana* 2 (1924) 378ff.; *Dacia* 3/4 (1927–32)
557ff.; Brashinsky, 82f.

122 *ARepts* 1952/3, 42; 1971/2, 49; *Mat. Res.* 50 (1956)
223ff.; Brashinsky, 86f.

123 Minns, 415f.

124 V. M. Skydnova, *Sov. Arch.* 1957. 4, 128ff.; 1960. 2,
153ff.; *Mat. Res.* 50 (1956) 211ff.; I. V. Fabricius, *Arch.
Karta* 1 (1951); L. V. Kopeikina, *Wiss. Zeit. Rostock* 19
(1970) 559ff.

125 *Sov. Arch.* 1960. 2, fig. 14; cf. Boardman, *Greek*

Emporio pl. 44x.
126 *AA* 1910, 227f.
127 *ARepts* 1971/2, 49f.; J. Chadwick, *Proc. Camb. Phil. Soc.* 1973, 35ff.
128 V. V. Lapin, *Kratkie Soob. Inst.* 11 (1961) 43ff.
129 *Mat. Res.* 50 (1956) 245ff.
130 Minns, 453ff. and *JHS* 65 (1945) 109ff., *Mat. Res.* 50 (1956) for important articles. E. Belin de Ballu, *Olbia* (1972) reviewed by Brashinsky, *Gnomon* 1977, 617ff., by Hind, *JHS* 94 (1974) 251f. A. Wasowicz, *Olbia Pontique et son Territoire* (1975); *ARepts* 1962/3, 42–4; Brashinsky, 87ff.
131 *ARepts* 1962/3, 45.
132 Hdt. 4. 78–80.
133 *AA* 1913, 199ff. Belin de Ballu, *Olbia* pls. 52–4 (sculpture), 64–5 (alabaster), 68–9 (bronze).
134 Cited by Minns, *JHS* 65 (1945) 111.
135 Belin de Ballu, op. cit. 62f.
136 *ARepts* 1962/3, 44. M. A. Nalivkina in *Antichnya Gorod* (1963) 55ff.
137 *Mat. Res.* 34 (1953); *Trudi Ermit.* 13 (1972) 17ff.
138 J. D. Beazley, *Development of Attic Black Figure* (1951) pl. 13. 3 (*ABV* 81, 7).
139 *Mat. Res.* 56 (1957), 103 (1962); *ARepts* 1962/3, 45–7; 1971/2, 53f.; Brashinsky, 97f. On its origins, T. S. Noonan, *AJA* 77 (1973) 77ff.
140 *ARepts* 1962/3, 46, fig. 26.
141 Ibid., 45, fig. 24.
142 C. Watzinger in *Genethliakon W. Schmid* (1929) 150, fig. 8.
143 *Mat. Res.* 25 (1952) 223ff.; 85 (1958); K. Michalowski, *Myrmeki* 1 (1958); W. F. Gaidukevich, *Mirmeki* 2 (1959); Michalowski, *VII Congr. Int. Arch. Class.* 2 (1961) 67ff.
144 *Mat. Res.* 25 (1952) 15ff., 227ff.; 85 (1958) 149ff.
145 *Mat. Res.* 25 (1952) 227, fig. 1. 2–8.
146 *Mat. Res.* 69 (1959) 5ff.; Chudyak, *Is Istorii Nympheya* (1962); *ARepts* 1962/3, 47f.; Brashinsky, 100f.
147 B. M. Skydnova, *Archeologiya* 10 (1958) 100ff.
148 *Mat. Res.* 85 (1958) 219ff.
149 *Mat. Res.* 19 (1951) 189ff.; 57 (1956); *ARepts* 1971/2, 56f.
150 Brashinsky, 105.
151 *Mat. Res.* 69 (1959) 154ff.; *Kratkie Soob. Inst.* 83 (1961) 53ff.; Brashinsky, 107f.
152 V. D. Blavatsky, *Archaeology* 16 (1963) 93f.; Brashinsky, 117.
153 D. M. Lang, *Num. Chron.* 1957, 138f.
154 *RA* 1971, 259ff.; O. Lordkipanidze, *Vani* 1 (1972) figs. 67 (Attic), 210 (aryballos) and *Kultyra Drevnei Kolchidi* (1972) with English summary; *BCH* 98 (1974) 897ff. on Greek finds in Georgia. See above, p. 64, on earlier Caucasian bronzes in East Greece.
155 J. M. Burstein, *Outpost of Hellenism: The Emergence of Heraclea on the Black Sea* (1976).
156 Y. Boysal, *AA* 1959, 8ff.; *ARepts* 1959/60, 34; 1952/3, 51. Cf. G. L. Huxley, *Greek Rom. Byz. Stud.* 3 (1960) 17ff., perhaps the Syrie of *Od.* 15, 403.
157 Hdt. 1. 72, 2. 34.
158 R. M. Cook, *JHS* 66 (1946) 82, n. 138.
159 *Ist. Mitt.* 26 (1976) pls. 6–9.
160 Å. Åkerström, *Die Arch. Terrakotten Kleinasiens* (1966) 121ff., 161ff., 191ff.
161 S. Vos, *Scythian Archers in Archaic Attic vase painting* (1963). Our *Figs.* 296–7 = Beazley, *ABV* 76, no. 1; 145, no. 16.
162 On Cimmerians in the north see T. Sulimirski, *Bull.*
163 Hdt. 4. 1–144. Herodotus on Scythia discussed by H. Kothe in *Klio* 51 (1969) 15ff. General works on Scythia and its art: Minns, Rostovtseff and Artamonov; T. Talbot Rice, *The Scythians* (1957); K. Schefold, *Euras. Septent. Ant.* 12 (1938) 1ff.; T. Sulimirski, *Artibus Asiae* 17 (1954) 282ff., a bibliography of recent studies in *Bull. Inst. Arch. London* 10 (1971) 99ff. and *CAH* 3².2, ch. 33a; *From the lands of the Scythians* (Exhib., New York, Los Angeles, 1975). On Greek and Scythian art, Boardman, *Pre-Classical* (1967) ch. 6; P. Amandry, *AA* 1965, 891ff.
164 D. G. Hogarth, *Ephesus* (1908) pl. 26. 3, cf. 22.2 and from Sardis, *AJA* 70 (1966) pl. 41. 13. Amandry, *JNES* 24 (1965) 149ff. on the Perso-Scythian origin of the 'folded animal' motif in Greece.
165 E. Porada, *The Art of Ancient Iran* (1965) ch. 10.
166 Minns, 171f.; Artamonov, fig. 3, pls. 1–3, cf. 6–8.
167 *Bull. Inst. Arch. Bulg.* 22 (1959) 58, fig. 2.
168 M. Ebert, *Reallex. Vorgesch.* 8, pl. 39.3; Artamonov, fig. 6.
169 Minns, 193, fig. 85 top r.; G. A. Bobrinsky, *Kurgany . . . Smely* (1887) frontispiece. And cf. the incised ivory plaques in Würzburg, *AM* 41 (1916) pls. 2, 3.
170 Artamonov, figs. 35, 49, 50 etc., pls. 94–113.
171 Minns, 375, fig. 278; Artamonov, pl. 67.
172 Minns, 191, fig. 83. 351, 266; Greco-Scythian mirrors, H. Hoffmann, *AJA* 69 (1965) 65f.
173 Minns, 376f., figs. 279–81; Artamonov, pls. 68–9.
174 M. Maximova in *Gr. Städte* (edd. J. Irmschev and D. B. Schelov, 1961) 35ff.; Artamonov, pls. 29–33.
175 Maximova, op. cit., 50ff. and *Sov. Arch.* 25 (1956) 215ff.; *BABesch* 41 (1966) 7ff.; Artamonov, pl. 20.
176 *AA* 1905, 59, fig. 4; *AA* 1965, 908, 911; Artamonov, pls. 25–6.
177 A. Furtwängler, *Der Goldfund von Vettersfelde* (1883); Minns, 236ff.; A. Greifenhagen, *Schmuckarbeiten in Edelmetall*, Berlin 1 (1970) 61ff., pls. 39–44. Scyths in central Europe, M. Dušek, *Praeh. Zeitschrift* 42 (1964) 49ff.
178 Minns, 203, fig. 98; Talbot Rice, op. cit., pl. 24; *From the lands* (n. 163) pl. 15.
179 Minns, 226, fig. 129; Talbot Rice, loc. cit.; Artamonov, pls. 62–4; *From the lands* (n. 163) pl. 3.
180 M. Ebert, *Praeh. Zeitschrift* 5 (1913) 1ff.
181 C. G. Starr, *Economic and Social Growth of Early Greece* (1977) 176.
182 Fr. Z105 (Lobel/Page); D. L. Page, *Sappho and Alcaeus* (1955) 152ff.
183 Jeffery, *AG* 89f., 238f.
184 Hdt. 6. 34–7.
185 Hdt. 6. 39–41, 140.
186 *BCH* 39 (1915) 135ff.; *CRAI* 1915, 268ff.; 1916, 40ff.; 1921, 130ff.
187 Boardman, *ABFH* 183; *CVA* Heidelberg 4, pl. 163. 3, 4; J. M. Cook, *The Troad* (1973) 121. The pottery from Elaeus in Paris will be published by A. Waiblinger: *CRAI* 1978, 843ff. Cf., at Olbia, *AA* 1913, 203, fig. 48.
188 Kraay-Hirmer, 334 (cf. fig. 432).
189 Jeffery, *LSAG* 72, 366f.; G. M. A. Richter, *Archaic Gravestones of Attica* (1961) 165ff.
190 E. Babelon in *Corolla Numismatica* (Essays Barclay V. Head, 1906) 1ff.; Kraay, *Num. Chron.* 1977, 196.
191 Boardman, *GSAP* 160, fig. 216.
192 Hdt. 4. 136–7.
193 Hdt. 7. 147.

Acknowledgements

The author and publishers are indebted to the museums, collectors and institutions named in the captions for photographs and permission to use them. The following other sources of photographs are also acknowledged:

Aphrodisias Expedition, *113*; Archaeological Exploration of Gordion, *95, 98*; Foto Marburg, *134*; French School, Athens, *32, 39, 270, 272*; German Institute, Athens, *34, 40, 41, 43, 54, 55, 91, 124, 133*; German Institute, Cairo, *160*; German Institute, Rome, *205*; Hirmer Verlag, *99, 183, 185, 198, 216, 220, 227, 235, 236, 285, 311*. N. Coldstream, *6, 213*; A. Frantz, *172*; L. H. Jeffery, *167*; M. Lowe, *36, 298*; M. R. Popham, *11, 12, 13, 15, 67, 131*; D. Stronach, *119*; P. G. Themelis, *83*; R. L. Wilkins, *126, 242, 310, 313*.

Author's photographs: *23, 52, 68, 85, 173, 180, 196, 197, 221, 255, 256, 271*.

Several scholars have been most generous with advice or helpful in procuring photographs:

E. Akurgal, T. G. F. Braun, H. A. Cahn, A. Choremis, N. Coldstream, R. M. Cook, G. Dontas, C. Ede, K. Erim, H. V. Herrmann, A. W. Johnston, V. Karageorghis, C. M. Kraay, M. Lazarov, M. Maximova†, D. Mitten, P. R. Moorey, R. V. Nicholls, E. Oren, M. R. Popham, M. Roaf, B. B. Shefton, V. Tatton-Brown (née Wilson), G. Vallet, M. Vickers, K. de Vries.

The drawings are by Marion Cox.

Index